A First Course in Linguistics

to Joy and Eric Simpson

< **A First Course in Linguistics** >

J.M.Y.SIMPSON

Edinburgh *at the University Press*

©J.M.Y. Simpson 1979
Edinburgh University Press
22 George Square, Edinburgh

ISBN 0 85224 319 7 (hardback)
        0 85224 376 6 (paperback)

Printed in Great Britain by
R. & R. Clark Ltd., Edinburgh

Preface

This is an introductory textbook for those with no knowledge of linguistics. It was designed as background for students receiving specialised courses of lectures; but it may equally well be used by the interested reader working alone.

The principal aim is of course to outline something of contemporary linguistics; yet I envisage other objectives. For example, I am concerned to impart awareness of the diverse phenomena found in natural languages: students of linguistics must not remain content with a knowledge limited to the patterns of the more commonly taught European tongues (and regrettably even this is denied to many educated in English-speaking countries). Secondly, I hope my readers will be stimulated to examine with new ears and eyes those languages they already know. Furthermore, since various schools of linguistics exist, it must be made clear that there is no 'correct' approach and that questions concerning the nature of linguistic theories and their comparison arise, even though they cannot be dealt with in this book. Above all, those being introduced to linguistics will, I trust, be encouraged to read primary texts, aided by an appreciation of a wider perspective in which to view them.

A first textbook cannot survey all the activities that have been or are being carried out by linguists (nor would that be desirable) and only a restricted number of topics is handled in the present volume; my selection has been governed by the need to expound not only that which I consider most important but also that which has gained general fame (or notoriety), though to some extent these categories coincide. Underlying the presentation is a conviction that knowledge of a subject's historical development is crucial to an appreciation of its contemporary state. Indeed it may not always be possible to apply the word 'outmoded' to a linguistic approach save in a purely chronological sense.

I may not agree with every linguistic viewpoint I describe, yet while I have had no qualms about inventing my own illustrations and examples, I trust that I have explained the arguments of others without distortion. Suggestions for further reading, including much primary literature, follow the text of the present chapters. And suggestions are also given for reading in areas of linguistics not covered in this book, for it is unfortunately possible to encounter advanced students (and scholars of other disciplines) who suffer from linguistic tunnel-vision and imagine that one particular linguistic school or other is the only valid approach: I am concerned to dispel such ignorance. Since not everyone is conversant with the still indispensable technical terms of traditional grammar, a glossary of these is given.

A linguist of all people will not deny the truth of Donne's famous metaphor 'No man is an Iland', least of all one who undertakes a book like this. Many people have contributed wittingly or unwittingly to the present volume, and it is they who should be thanked for all that is good in it.

My debts in matters linguistic cannot be repaid to the late C.T. Carr, my beloved mentor in Germanic letters and philology; to Edward Ullendorff, whose kindness not only enabled me to behold the Aladdin's Cave of Semitic philology, but introduced me to the works of de Saussure, Trubetzkoy, Sapir and Bloomfield; and to my teachers (later colleagues) in the University of Edinburgh, particularly to David Abercrombie, whose lucidity of thought and independence from mere fashion are matched by brilliant teaching and generous encouragement of his students.

Complete drafts of earlier elephantine versions of this book were read by David Abercrombie, Geoffrey Leech and R.H. Robins, all of whom made many detailed observations, and sections of various lengths were scrutinised and commented on by Jacques Durand, John Fox, Thomas MacCaffrey, M.K.C. MacMahon, M.L. Samuels, Peter Swinbank and W.S.-Y. Wang. These kind friends saved me from lapses into incomprehensibility, from errors and from idiocies, and must not be blamed for any blunders that I may have introduced despite their help, or for any particular points of view I express. Encouragement to write, and to continue, was entertainingly given by various people, particularly Sheila MacCrindle and above all Peggy Drinkwater. John Fox undertook the chore of compiling an index. Cecily Smith deserves the utmost praise for typing imperturbably and accurately innumerable drafts from typescripts and manuscrips of my own, all illegibly palimpsestuous. And my students over the years, as every teacher will empathise, have contributed to my own understanding to an extent that would astonish them if they but knew. To everyone I have mentioned I am humbly grateful.

J.M.Y. Simpson
Glasgow, November 1978

Contents

vii

Contents

Contents

Transcriptional Conventions

Asterisks are prefixed to unrecorded forms (including both conjectural reconstructions and impossibilities).

Square brackets enclose phonetic or partly allophonic transcriptions and slant lines phonemic transcriptions (see Chapter 8).

Examples from languages written in the Roman alphabet are given in their usual orthography followed by a more or less phonemic transcription in phonetic symbols. (For an explanation of these see the list of *Phonetic Symbols* opposite.) Occasional examples are given only in orthography, and these may read as though written in phonetic symbols (except that Latin *c* = /k/ and *qu* = /kw/).

Ancient Greek appears in a transliteration which may be read as our phonetic symbols. Sanskrit appears in the conventional transliteration which may be read as our phonetic symbols, except that *ñ* = /ɲ/, *n* = /ŋ/, *y* = /j/ and long vowels are marked by a bar, e.g. *ā* = /ɑ:/. Other languages normally written in non-Roman scripts are quoted here only in phonetic symbols.

The use of other symbols is explained in the course of the text.

Linguistic examples drawn from English are not generally prefixed by the word 'English'.

Phonetic Symbols

a   unrounded open front vowel, as in RP *hat*; primary CV symbol.

ɑ   unrounded open back vowel, as in RP *balm*; primary CV symbol.

ɒ   rounded open back vowel, as in RP *pot*; secondary CV symbol.

b   voiced bilabial plosive, as in *bee*.

ɓ   voiced bilabial implosive, as in Hausa ɓauna, 'buffalo'.

β   voiced bilabial fricative, as in Spanish *saber*, 'to know'.

c   voiceless palatal plosive, as in Hungarian *tyuk*, 'chicken'.

ç   voiceless palatal fricative, as in German *ich*, 'I' and some pronunciations of *hue*.

ɕ   voiceless alveolo-palatal fricative, as in Polish, *środa*, 'Wednesday'.

ɔ   rounded half-open back vowel, as in RP *caught*; primary CV symbol.

d   voiced alveolar plosive, as in *day*.

ɖ   voiced retroflex plosive, as in Hindi ɖəs, 'ten'; Swedish *mord*, 'murder'.

ð   voiced dental fricative, as in *those*.

e   unrounded half-close front vowel, as in French *thé*, 'tea'; Sc. English *day*; primary CV symbol.

ɘ   unrounded half-close central vowel, as in second syllable of some Sc. English pronunciations of *after*; not official CV symbol.

ə   unrounded half-open central vowel, as in first syllable of RP *about*; 'float' symbol (sometimes called *shewa* /ʃə'wɑ/).

ɛ   unrounded half-open front vowel, as in *get*; primary CV symbol.

ɜ   unrounded half-open central vowel, as in RP *earth*; not official CV symbol.

ɞ   rounded half-open central vowel, as in some RP pronunciations of *world*; Amharic wɜr, 'month'; Swedish *föra*, 'to lead'; not official CV symbol.

f   voiceless labio-dental fricative, as in *far*.

ɟ   voiced palatal plosive as in Hungarian *egy*, 'one'.

g   voiced velar plosive, as in *gun*.

ɢ   voiced uvular plosive, as in Persian tʃoɴɢɑ:'zi: 'when the judge'.

h   represents a series of voiceless vowels, as in *heel, hill, ham, whom*.

ħ   voiceless pharyngal fricative, as in Arabic ħamala, 'carried'.

ɦ   represents a series of breathy-voiced vowels, as in Czech *hlas*, 'voice', and in some RP pronunciations of e.g. *behave*.

ɥ   voiced lip-rounded labial-palatal approximant, as in French *huit*.

i   unrounded close front vowel, as in *see*; primary CV symbol.

ɪ   unrounded close front vowel, as in *fill*; 'float' symbol.

ɨ   unrounded close central vowel, as in Amharic giβ, 'goal'; Russian sin, 'son'; CV symbol.

xi

j	voiced palatal approximant, as in *yes*.
k	voiceless velar plosive, as in *cow*.
l	voiced alveolar lateral, as in *law*.
ɬ	voiceless alveolar fricative lateral, as in Welsh *llan*, 'church'.
m	voiced bilabial nasal, as in *mow*.
ɯ	unrounded close back vowel, as in Scots Gaelic *aon*, 'one'; Rumanian *gît*, 'neck'; Vietnamese *cứ*, 'advance'; secondary C V symbol.
n	voiced alveolar nasal, as in *now*.
ɲ	voiced palatal nasal, as in Italian *segno*, 'sign'.
ŋ	voiced velar nasal, as in *sing*.
ɳ	voiced retroflex nasal, as in Swedish *korn*, 'grain'; Malayalam eɳɳʌ, 'oil'.
N	voiced uvular nasal, as in Eskimo aNut, 'male person'.
o	rounded half-close back vowel, as in Sc. English *rope*; French *peau*, 'skin'; German *Not*, 'need'; primary C V symbol.
ɵ	rounded half-close central vowel, as in Swedish *upp*, 'up', not official C V symbol.
ø	rounded half-close front vowel, as in German *Söhne*, 'sons'; French *deux*, 'two'; secondary C V symbol.
œ	rounded half-open front vowel, as in German *Götter*, 'gods'; French *peur*, 'fear'; secondary C V symbol.
ω	rounded closish back vowel, as in General American and R P *pull*; 'float' symbol.
ɸ	voiceless bilabial fricative, as in Japanese ɸɯkɯ, 'to blow'.
p	voiceless bilabial plosive, as in *paw*.
q	voiceless uvular plosive as in Arabic (not Egyptian) qalb, 'heart'.
r	voiced alveolar trill as in Spanish *red*, 'net'; Italian *burro*, 'butter'.
ɾ	voiced alveolar tap, as in Spanish *pero*, 'but'; South African English *bread*; some Sc. English pronunciations of *red*, *for*; sometimes in R P *over-eat*.
ɽ	voiced retroflex flap, as in Hindi gaɽi, 'cart'.
ř	voiced alveolar fricative-trill, as in Czech *řeka*, 'river'.
ɹ	voiced post-alveolar fricative, as in some Sc. English *bread*; as approximant symbol, as in R P *red*.
ɻ	voiced retroflex approximant, as in Amer. English *string*.
R	voiced uvular trill, as in French cabaret singer's pronunciation of *rouge*, 'red'.
ʁ	voiced uvular fricative, as in Persian beʁɑːˈzi, 'to the judge', Parisian French *rouge*.
s	voiceless alveolar fricative, as in *see*.
ʃ	voiceless palato-alveolar fricative, as in *she*.
ʂ	voiceless retroflex fricative, as in Swedish *kors*, 'cross'.
t	voiceless alveolar plosive, as in *tea*.
ʈ	voiceless retroflex plosive, as in Hindi aʈa 'flour'; Swedish *fart*, 'speed'.
t'	alveolar ejective, as in Amharic ajɨt 'rat'.
u	rounded close back vowel, as in *fool*: primary C V symbol.
ʉ	rounded close central vowel, as in Norwegian *hus*, 'house'; Amharic wʉl, 'agreement'; some Sc. English *look*.

v   voiced labio-dental fricative, as in *vow*.
ʌ   unrounded half-open back vowel, as in *but*; secondary c v symbol.
w   voiced lip-rounded labial-velar approximant, as in *wail*.
ʍ   voiceless lip-rounded velarised bilabial fricative, as in Sc. English *whale*.
x   voiceless velar fricative, as in Sc. English *loch*; German *Buch*, 'book'.
χ   voiceless uvular fricative, as in French *prêtre*, 'priest'.
y   rounded close front vowel, as in French *pur*, 'pure'; German *für*, 'for'; secondary c v symbol.
ʎ   voiced palatal lateral, as in Italian *figlio*, 'son'.
ɣ   voiced velar fricative, as in Scots Gaelic *dhomh*, 'to me'; Spanish *luego*, 'place'.
z   voiced alveolar fricative, as in *zoo*.
ź   voiced alveolo-palatal fricative, as in Polish *źle*, 'badly'.
ʒ   voiced palato-alveolar fricative, as in *leisure*.
ʐ   voiced retroflex fricative, as in Pekingese Chinese ˊʐən, 'man'.
ɤ   unrounded half-close back vowel, as in Vietnamese *oˑ*, 'remain'.
θ   voiceless dental fricative, as in *thigh*.
ʔ   glottal stop, as in German *geöffnet*, 'opened'; Arabic alʔamiːr, 'the prince'.

ṇ, ṭ, etc. are consonants with dental (not alveolar) articulation.
n̡, t̡, etc. are palatised consonants.
s̴, ł, etc. are velarised consonants.
a̦, e̦, etc. are vowel sounds closer than those of the cardinal vowel symbols.
ḁ, n̥, etc. are voiceless vowels or consonants.
'   marks stress where necessary and is written before the stressed syllable, as in English in'spɛkt or *in'spect*.
ˌ   is written where necessary under a syllabic consonant or vowel, as in some English 'bʌtn̩, R P 'stɑrtəs.
^   marks a silent stress.
:   long vowel or consonant.
.   half-long vowel or consonant.

For the explanation of technical terms, see Chapter 7.

Terms Used in Traditional Grammar

accidence : the study of the various word-endings used in declensions and conjugations.

active : see voice.

adjective : a word such as *good, turbulent, gustatory*; often defined as a word which modifies or describes a noun. Closed subsets of adjectives include *interrogative* adjectives: in English *which* and *what* (e.g. *Which bird killed Cock Robin?*); *demonstrative* adjectives: *this, these*, etc. (e.g. *This chair is uncomfortable*); *possessive* adjectives: *my, your*, etc. (e.g. *Your tiny hand is frozen*); and the *relative* adjective *which* (e.g. *The Dean resigned, which action was very welcome*).

adverb : a word such as *often, almost, peremptorily*; often defined as a word which modifies or describes a verb, adjective or preposition.

article : in English there are two: the definite article *the* and the indefinite article *a* or *an*.

aspect : see *tense*.

case : a factor in the variant forms of a noun, pronoun or adjective in a declension.

clause : a group of words containing a verb but nevertheless not forming a sentence, e.g. *because he was too honest*.

complement : e.g. in *His grandmother was elected president* and *His grandmother was in full possession of her faculties*, the terms *president* and *in full possession of her faculties* are the complements of *was elected* and *was* respectively; often defined as the word or phrase used to complete the meaning of another word or phrase.

conjugation : the set of all the variant forms of an individual verb, expressing differences of number, person, tense, mood and voice, e.g. in Latin *amo* 'I love', *amabimini* 'you (pl.) will be loved', *amaverimus* 'we shall have loved'. The total number of such forms in Latin is about 100.

conjunction : a word such as *and, but, when, unless*; often defined as a word which links other words, phrases or sentences.

declension : the set of all the variant forms of an individual noun, pronoun or adjective, e.g. in Latin :

> *glis* : 'a dormouse'. *glires* : 'dormice'.
> *nominative case*, usually denotes the subject of a sentence.
> *glis* : 'oh dormouse!'. *glires* : 'oh dormice'.
> *vocative case*, used when addressing someone or something.
> *glirem* : 'a dormouse'. *glires* : 'dormice'.
> *accusative case*, often denotes the object of a sentence.

xiv

gliris : 'of a dormouse'. *glirium* : 'of dormice'.

    genitive case, usually denotes the possessor of something.

gliri : 'to a dormouse'. *gliribus* : 'to dormice'.

    dative case, often denotes the recipient in a transaction.

glire : 'by a dormouse'. *gliribus* : 'by dormice'.

ablative case, often denotes an instrument of an action.

There are five main declensional patterns in Latin; not one of these has a distinctive ending for every case. Almost every case carries a wider range of uses than indicated above.

gender : a factor in the declension of adjectives; e.g. Latin *magnus honor* 'great honour' is *masculine*; *magna arbor* 'large tree' is *feminine*; *magnum cor* 'big heart' is *neuter*. Since this declensional variation is dependent on the noun which the adjective modifies, gender is posited as a feature of nouns; therefore *honor* is said to be masculine, *arbor* feminine, and *cor* neuter. Pronouns may show the gender of nouns which they 'replace', so *hic*, *haec* and *hoc* may respectively replace *honor*, *arbor* and *cor*. A similar situation is seen in English *he*, *she* and *it*.

gerund : in English certain words ending in *-ing*, e.g. in *Drinking tea makes one ill*; it functions as a noun in being the subject of *makes* but also as a verb in taking the object *tea*.

interjection : a word such as *oh*, *ouch*, *wow*; often defined as an exclamatory word which indicates emotion.

intransitive : see *verb*.

mood : a factor in the conjugation of a verb, e.g. in Latin *amare* 'to love' is *infinitive* mood; *amat* 'he is loving' is *indicative* mood; *amet* is *subjunctive* mood appearing automatically after certain conjunctions or by itself meaning 'let him love!'; *ama* is *imperative* mood, giving the command 'love!'

noun : a word such as *hatter*, *hare*, *tea-pot*, *erudition*, *recitation*, *Alice*, *Mafeking*; often defined as the name of a person, animal, place or thing.

number : a factor in declensions or conjugations, e.g. in Latin the *singular* number very often indicates 'one' (e.g. *glis* 'a dormouse'; *dormiebat* 'it was sleeping') and the *plural* number very often indicates 'more than one' (e.g. *glires* 'dormice'; *dormiebant* 'they were sleeping').

object : e.g. in *Kenneth ate the bun* and *Kenneth gave his sister the bun* the words *the bun* represent the object (or *direct* object), often defined as the word or phrase designating the person or thing to which an action is directed; *his sister* is sometimes called the *indirect* object, defined as the recipient or beneficiary of an action.

participle : e.g. *smiling* in *The duke was smiling* and *The smiling duke spoke* (a *present participle active*) or *lost* in *The purse has been lost* and *The lost purse has turned up* (a *past participle passive*); often defined as a verbal form which has adjectival characteristics.

passive : see *voice*.

person : a factor in verbal conjugations and in pronouns. The *first* person is defined as referring to the speaker, e.g. Latin *nato* 'I am swimming',

xv

ego 'I'; the *second* person as referring to the hearer, e.g. *natas* 'You are swimming', *tu* 'you (sg.)'; and the *third* person as referring to the person spoken about, e.g. *natat* 'he is swimming', *ille* 'that man' or 'he'.

phrase : e.g. *the facts, under the bed, my old English manservant*; may be defined as a sequence of words which forms some sort of a coherent group but does not contain a verb.

predicate : everything (apart from any words in the vocative case) in a sentence which is not the subject; e.g. *was late, skidded, contained the lecturer and his wife, was found abandoned* are all predicates of those sentences which have *The taxi* as subject; it may be defined as what we say about the subject, or as the word or group of words that affirms or negates a property, condition or action of the subject of the sentence.

preposition : a word such as *above, under, to, with, from*; defined as a word placed in front of a noun or pronoun to show its relation to other words in the sentence.

pronoun : e.g. personal pronouns *I, you, he, she, it, we, they*; *interrogative* pronouns *who*? (e.g. *Who killed Cock Robin*?), *what*?; *demonstrative* pronouns *this, that* (e.g. *That was not my wife*); *relative* pronouns *who, which* (e.g. *Sheila, who paints landscapes, also sings exquisitely*); *possessive* pronouns *mine, yours*, etc., e.g. *That armchair is mine*; often defined as a word used to replace a noun.

sentence : a sequence of words such as *Babylon the great is fallen*; often defined as a group of words which makes complete sense, sometimes with the condition that it must contain a verb. Actually to define *sentence* in a way which does not beg questions or which is not immediately circular is extraordinarily difficult, perhaps impossible.

subject : e.g. the words *The taxi* in *The taxi was late, The taxi skidded, The taxi contained the lecturer and his wife, The taxi was found abandoned*; defined as the person or thing which is spoken about, or the agent performing the action (if the verb is active), or the person or thing on whom the action is performed (if the verb is passive).

syntax : the study of how words are put together in phrases, clauses and sentences.

tense : is a factor in conjugations which refers to the time of the action described relative to the moment of description. Latin has six tenses, namely *present rideo* 'I am laughing', *imperfect ridebam* 'I was laughing' or 'I used to laugh'; *future ridebo* 'I shall laugh'; *perfect risi* 'I have laughed' or 'I laughed'; *pluperfect riseram* 'I had laughed'; *future perfect risero* 'I shall have laughed'. The first three convey an *imperfect aspect* since they do not indicate the *end* of the action denoted by the verb, the last two express a *perfect* aspect since the end of the action is clearly indicated; the form *risi* is therefore ambiguous, as the English translation shows. The systems of tense and aspect vary greatly from language to language.

transitive : see *verb*.

verb : a word such as *is, seems, laughs, smokes, makes*; often defined as a type of word which expresses an action, process, state, condition or mode of existence. *Transitive* verbs are followed by a direct object (e.g. *loves* in *David loves cheese*); *intransitive* are not (e.g. *snores* in *Matilda snores loudly*).

verbal noun : sometimes applied to e.g. *poisoning* in *The poisoning of the Principal remained an unsolved mystery*. It is 'more of a noun' than the gerund, since preceded by *the* and followed by *of*.

voice : a factor in conjugations, e.g. in Latin *mordeo* 'I am biting' is *active* voice, *mordeor* 'I am being bitten' is *passive* voice; it may be defined as the category which expresses whether the subject of the verb is the agent of the action (active) or whether it is the target of the action (passive).

1. Introduction

To define in one sentence an area of study so that one explains something of its nature may be impossible: what could be a short, *informative* definition of mathematics, chemistry or philosophy? Linguistics is such a subject. We can only offer a definition and then enlarge upon it; the remainder of this book is an expansion of the statement that linguistics is the study of human language according to certain principles developed during this century.[1]

Linguistics is sometimes defined as the 'scientific study' of language, but there is no point in using 'science' or 'scientific' in this context without a clear idea of what these words mean. We omit from this book all discussion of whether linguistics, or any area within it, may be regarded as a science; such a discussion requires some knowledge of linguistics and an agreed definition of 'science', for opinions vary about the meaning of this tricky word. Admittedly, in Chapter 6 we quote the defining characteristics of a science, as understood by one distinguished linguist; but not everyone would agree with his views.

An area of study passes through historical stages. During each stage most practitioners are in general agreement about the object of the study, about the general aims of it and the methods employed, and about the problems that remain to be solved. Each period may of course have its share of 'non-conformists'.[2]

Any period is, according to its own standards, just as 'reasonable' as any later one, and it may interpret phenomena equally well. In .he Ptolemaic ('sun revolves round earth') view of the universe, the rising of the sun may be predicted as precisely as in the Copernican ('earth revolves round sun'). In the absence of a telescope, how could we choose between these theories? Indeed, for limited purposes, an earlier and simpler view may be retained without disadvantage: it does no harm to regard electricity as 'something flowing from positive to negative' when we are wiring a circuit or fitting plugs. Moreover, no theory can be shown to be 'true' even though it is of immense practical utility and interprets many phenomena; it may always be superseded by another that interprets more. For example, Newton's system of physics (in the light of which the great technological developments of the nineteenth

1

century were made) was succeeded by Einstein's. Therefore the history of a study is not, emphatically not, a tale of continual additions to a pile of 'true facts'. Instead it tells of a succession of increasingly 'powerful' theories, each of which interprets more phenomena than its predecessor.

Successive stages of a study may take different things into account. The study of the stars once considered their alleged influence on human beings; modern astronomers now study radio-stars, the existence of which was unknown to the ancients. So both the type of evidence admitted and even the objects of study may change; neither must be taken for granted. A point of view is of prime importance: it determines both the object of study and the evidence. There are therefore no facts without some kind of prior theory – hence there are no objective facts. [3]

The study of language is no exception; it has passed through various stages, and no linguistic theory including any held at present can be said to be 'true'. The object of study, as well as the evidence admitted, has changed through the ages; therefore what 'language' is, has also changed.

Since present-day linguistic theories interpret more phenomena than did their predecessors, it might be thought that the serious student of linguistics need concern himself only with the contemporary scene. But it may be contended that some knowledge of the history of a subject, and what might be called its philosophy, is essential to a full appreciation of it. 'The Goddess of Learning', according to the Indian proverb, 'does not smile upon those who neglect the Ancients.' Moreover, students who begin linguistics are usually acquainted with earlier views about language, absorbed informally or encountered formally in other classrooms; the nature of these theories must be made explicit. This is not, for example, the case with students of chemistry, who will normally be fairly ignorant about alchemy.

We begin, therefore, by dealing briefly with three earlier approaches to language, and only in Chapter 6 do we embark on 'linguistics' as the word is usually understood. But any informed view of human language must be aware of the interpretations expounded in Chapters 2 to 5. In terms of our above argument, linguistics does not necessarily interpret better those things that were interpreted by earlier views of language; but it interprets many more. It is not, therefore, a corrected version of an old theory; it is a different type of theory, it is a more *powerful* theory. [4]

2. Primitive Notions

Primitive notions about language appear in very early written texts (especially those of a religious nature) and in oral traditions (legends, poems and hymns). Many such views are remarkably similar, although we find them among peoples widely separated by time and location. All contain references to magical or supernatural forces. Nevertheless, similar notions are still current in twentieth-century Western society, and it is important that we recognise them for what they are. In general these views take cognisance only of the native language of the theorist and are in no way concerned with anything we might call the 'structure' of the language, for example its grammar. Instead, they concentrate on some or all of the following three points: the origin of language; the connection between names and things; and the power of language.

The origin of language is frequently attributed to supernatural activity: for example, in Genesis 2 : 19, the Deity gives mankind the power of naming. (Interestingly, in this account a period is envisaged in which mankind existed, but without language.) Sometimes the origin of writing was explained in a like manner, as in the Chinese legend of the turtle that appeared bearing a written character on its back.[1]

It is felt that there is a necessary and inevitable connection between a name and the person or thing that bears it. The name cannot be other. Therefore, examination of a name can reveal something of the nature of the bearer or his origin. In Genesis 2 : 7, mankind /ˈaːdaːm/ is formed from the dust /ădaːˈmaːh/, and his Hebrew name will forever show that this is so. Consequently, if a person's nature or status is changed, so too is his name. In the New Testament, Simon became Peter, and Saul became Paul, on their respective assumptions of new roles.

Language is felt to possess a power and the utterance of words may have a force that can be creative. In Genesis 1 : 3, an utterance is the agent of the Deity: 'God said, "Let there be light", and there was light'. Significantly Hebrew /ˈdaːvaːr/ means both 'word' and 'deed'. Indeed in some traditions it would appear that language is prior even to God or the gods. St John's Gospel opens with the words (translated by Moffatt) 'When all things began, the Word

3

was at the creation'. This idea of language preceding even the gods is found in religious traditions as diverse as those of Indian mythology and of a tribe of Central America, the Uitoto.[2] To possess language, therefore, is to possess power. Magic may be worked simply by knowing the correct spells, as any reader of *Tales of 1001 Nights* knows: only the words 'Open, sesame' could effect the desired result. Such power may also be attributed to the written forms of language; many religions have holy books which are venerated visibly and ceremonially.[3]

It follows that the knowledge of the *correct* name is of the utmost importance. The use of the name of a supernatural being may be considered to release the power of its bearer, hence the importance of the formula 'In the Name of the Father, the Son and the Holy Ghost' in the Christian liturgies. But conversely the possession of a name can confer power *over* its bearer. In Egyptian mythology, the sun-god Ra told his name to Isis with the result that she gained power over him and all the other gods.[4] Similarly, in many folk tales, for example that of Rumpelstiltzkin, the discovery of a name neutralises the evil power of its owner. Because they possess such great power, certain names must not be uttered, a phenomenon known as *taboo* (or *tabu*).

Some taboos affect the names of gods or others over which it is quite inappropriate to have power. Thus the personal name (probably *Yahweh*) of the Deity in the Hebrew Bible was virtually forbidden to be spoken, with the result that the original pronunciation became lost. (The alleged pronunciation *Jehovah* is demonstrably nonsensical.[5]) On the other hand, the power of a name may be so terrible that it becomes taboo. Thus the Greeks called the goddesses of revenge (the *Erinnyes*, that is 'Furious Ones', or 'Furies') by the euphemism of *Eumenides*, that is 'Gracious Ones'. In the same vein, an object may be so unclean that its correct name must not be uttered.

Such primitive views persist today. They are not taught formally, but we absorb them as we grow up. It must be admitted that outside religious communities the idea of a divine origin of language may not be very widely held now. Nevertheless, the view is still found that at some time mankind, hitherto dumb, developed the power of speech. But a connection is still felt between a name and that to which it refers. To the naive mind the words of a native language appear natural and inevitable, while foreign words appear perverse or idiotic; probably any learner of foreign languages has his favourite example. Within a language personal names may suggest certain types of individual: such statements as *She doesn't look like a Patricia* are frequently heard. Carlo Levi in his novel *Cristo si è fermato a Eboli* recounts the attitude of Southern Italian peasants to his dog Barone ('baron'). Because it bore such a superior type of name they expected that it would be a superior type of dog, and of course they did not disappoint themselves.

A change of name may accompany a change of official status (for example, on becoming a Member of the House of Lords), or of religion. Or a name may be changed if it could suggest an inappropriate nature: actors equip themselves with names considered to be romantic or attractive and naturalised persons may take a new name to indicate solidarity with their adopted country. There are cases where a change of name is made as slight as possible, presumably to show. that no change of nature is involved: for example, the English politician George Brown became Lord George-Brown.

The power of the spoken word is still evident, not only in religious ceremonies, but also in such activities as declaring war or being married, where an utterance constitutes an act. Modern instances of the veneration of the written word may be seen in attitudes to the physical embodiments of words such as *The Thoughts of Chairman Mao*. The obverse of such attitudes, namely the fear of the physical existence of the written word, is seen in the banning or even burning of books.

Taboo persists in our society: in English names of certain parts of the body, sexual activities and excretory functions come under taboo. During the nineteenth century, virtually the entire body between the chin and ankles was taboo in Britain and the United States, hence such euphemisms as *ankle-chin* ('the human abdomen') and *dark meat* and *white meat* (respective 'legs' and 'breast' of poultry). Such areas of taboo vary from country to country: in Italy religious terms and in Denmark certain names for the devil come under strong taboos. During war, the name of the enemy may come under taboo, giving rise to terms such as *Huns* and *Boches*, or the metamorphosis of the *German Ocean* into the *North Sea*. Another major area of taboo is that of certain dread diseases and of dying itself. The precise words under taboo may change. The word *leg* is no longer taboo for example. Conversely euphemisms may themselves acquire taboo: *lavatory* is considered indelicate in some quarters. And there may be degrees of taboo. Indeed some humour depends on the breaking of a mild taboo.

However irrational a taboo may be, its power is undeniable. It is therefore naive to break a verbal taboo and then pretend to be surprised at the power released, that is, the shock created.

FURTHER READING
Cassirer 1953; Firth 1964; Hawakawa 1965.

5

3.   Traditional Grammar

3.1 Greek origins. By 'traditional grammar' we mean that type of analysis which until recently characterised all school grammar-books (of English and of foreign languages) and which remains that most commonly found in language-teaching. Indeed many people are under the impression that it reveals the 'real' structure of language. (An explanation of key terms used here will be found in the glossary on p.xiv.) An unbroken line of descent connects the origins of this tradition in Ancient Greece with the present day.

The first Greek grammarians were philosophers, for philosophy embraced all scholarly investigation. In the fifth century B.C. the question arose whether certain institutions were grounded in the nature of things or were the result of some hypothetical tacit agreement among men: 'nature' was thus opposed to 'convention'. Applied to language this meant: *was* there an inevitable connection between a word and that to which it referred? For the first time the primitive assumption was questioned.

Naturalists advanced demonstrations of the naturalness of words. For example, a word might be imitative of a sound (cf. *crash*); or an imitative name might be applied to the source of the sound (cf. *cuckoo*); or the sound of an individual letter might be symbolic: it was suggested that the Greek letter L (*lambda*) denoted smoothness, as in /leîos/ 'level'.[1] Again the meaning of a word might be extended by metaphor, as the *foot* of a hill. Or one word might be derived from others because of some appropriate connection of meaning: the Greek word /ánthro:pos/ 'man', was regarded as derived from /anathrô:n hà ópo:pen/ 'considering what he sees' (animals do not consider what they see!). Indeed, a word might be derived from another precisely because the meaning of one virtually contradicts that of the other; /líthos/ 'stone' could therefore be traced back to /lían théein/ 'to run too much'. This remarkable type of explanation became later known by the Latin tag *lucus a non lucendo*, that is, 'a grove (*lucus*) is so called because it does not shine (*lucere*)', woods being dark places![2] In his dialogue *Cratylus*, Plato (429–347 B.C.) illustrates this controversy: in it the character Cratylus is a naturalist, while Hermogenes is a *conventionalist*, maintaining that

6

'there is no name given to anything by nature; all is convention and habit of the users'.[3]

In the second century B.C. this debate gave way to another between *analogists* and *anomalists*. The analogists held that language was basically regular, as could be seen in the declensions and conjugations of Greek (a parallel in English would be the huge numbers of words of the pattern *jump/jumped*); the anomalists, believing that language was irregular, laid stress on irregular forms (an English example would be *buy/bought*) and on such curiosities as the fact that in Greek the word for 'Athens' is plural. Neither side could be correct, for Greek like many other languages is (in this sense) predominantly regular, but with its share of irregularities; so in time the controversy was forgotten. But it was significant that patterns were now being studied, not merely single words.

The main investigators of Greek grammar were the Stoic philosophers, founded ca. 300 B.C. For the Stoics right conduct was living in harmony with nature; correct knowledge therefore would be a congruence of ideas with nature; and language ought to be words that express such ideas.[4] In part, the problem of language was: *how* and how *well* does language express thoughts? Notice the contention that thoughts were prior to, and could exist without, words; it persisted, and is with us still.

The Stoics wrote much about language; although their works have been lost, we have accounts of them from later writers.[5] Their philosophy forced them to make a clear distinction between the form of a word and its meaning, a fact that contributed to the view of meaning associated with traditional grammar (see Chapter 15). The analogist-anomalist controversy led them to pursue the examination of the patternings of Greek and in time they recognised five 'parts of speech'[6] (noun, proper noun, verb, conjunction and definite article), cases, transitive and intransitive verbs, active and passive voices, and perfect and non-perfect aspects. This analysis found its way into all subsequent grammar-books.

Another contribution, which determined the *attitudes* of traditional grammar, began in Alexandria in the third century B.C. Alexandria was a centre of great literary activity; this included the collation of manuscripts of the *Iliad* and the *Odyssey* (dating from at least the fifth century). As happens in the copying of manuscripts, mistakes had occurred, and so attempts were made to establish which was the original of two or more variant readings. It was easy to adopt the view that change in language must be corruption and that the earlier stage of the language is better or 'purer'. Moreover, 'cosmopolitan' Greek, the /koiné:/, spoken in contemporary Alexandria differed from the written Old Ionian of the manuscripts;

7

given the veneration in which the Homeric epics were held, the written form was almost inevitably considered to be the 'true' language, and the spoken form a sometimes variable derivation from it. Similar views showed great resilience down the ages.

In Alexandria, about the first century B.C., the first comprehensive grammar in the Western world was compiled; this was the *Grammar* (*Téchnē grammatikē*) of Dionysius Thrax, and it consisted of only twenty-five short paragraphs. Very little of any theoretical importance, with one exception, was added to grammar in the following centuries. Dionysius Thrax defined grammar as 'the technical knowledge of the language generally employed by poets and writers'. He isolated eight parts of speech: noun, verb, conjunction, article, adverb, participle, pronoun and preposition; and he recognised case, gender, number, person, tense, voice and mood. In part at least, the definition of these referred to alleged meanings and thoughts: for example, 'The noun is a part of a sentence having case inflections, signifying a person or a thing'; 'The sentence is a combination of words that have a complete meaning in themselves'.

One lack in Dionysius Thrax was treatment of syntax: that is, how the various parts of speech combine and how sentences may be analysed. To a great extent this was supplied by the grammar of Apollonius Dyscolus, written in the first or second century A.D. The works of these two Alexandrians remained the model for almost every grammar-book of the next sixteen centuries.

3.2 The Romans and the mediaeval period. The Romans owed almost everything of any cultural value to the Greeks, and this debt included grammar. The least derivative of the Roman grammarians is the first, Varro (116–27 B.C.); but the influence of his *The Latin language* (*De lingua latina*) – of which less than a quarter has come down to us – was slight. In the first century A.D. the grammar of Dionysius Thrax was translated by Remmius Palaemon; thereafter, Latin grammarians did their best to adapt the terminology and categories of Greek grammar to Latin.

It is a coincidence from the viewpoint of cultural history that the structures of Greek and of Latin are remarkably similar. Yet this coincidence had an important and lasting effect: it strengthened the notion that there was a universal grammar that reflected thoughts. Greek technical terms were therefore given Latin equivalents (although accompanied by some misunderstandings); these are the ancestors of the names used in English: for example, Greek /ónoma/, /antoːnymiaː/, /sýndesmos/ and /aitiaːtikè: ptôːsis/ became in Latin *nomen, pronomen, coniunctio, casus accusativus*,[7] and so in English *noun, pronoun, conjunction* and *accusative case*. Latin grammars typically consisted of three parts dealing with: the definition of grammar and the alphabet; the parts of speech; and mistakes to be avoided, style and sometimes verse-forms. Astonishingly, such a tripartite arrangement may be seen in modern grammars.[8]

The most influential of the Latin grammars were those of Aelius Donatus and of Priscianus, which served as textbooks for the entire mediaeval period, that is, for the next thousand (!) years. The *Grammar* (*Ars grammatica*) by Donatus, dating from the fourth century A.D., is a short school-book suitable for beginners, but *The Principles of Grammar* (*Institutiones rerum grammaticarum*) of about 500 A.D. by Priscianus is the most complete description of Latin that has come down to us. A Latin-speaker teaching Greeks in Constantinople, Priscianus applied to Latin all the possible appropriate categories of Apollonius Dyscolus and Thrax.

During the Dark Ages the work of the grammarians represented one of the defences of the classical heritage against the confusion of the times; Priscianus and Donatus were therefore accorded an authority of almost Biblical proportions. Not only was the analytical framework of traditional grammar preserved, but its underlying attitudes towards language became reinforced by practical circumstances.

Until the Renaissance Latin was the language of all scholarship in the Western world. It was no-one's native language therefore had to be taught; hence the attitude was strengthened that it was the grammarian's task to teach how to speak and write 'correctly' – grammar was *prescriptive*. Moreover, since the 'best' Latin was held to belong to the 'Golden Age' (late first century B.C.) and to the 'Silver Age' (first century A.D.) of Latin literature, this reinforced the opinion that the 'purer' language belonged to an earlier epoch. And since the various European nations pronounced Latin in slightly different ways although the written forms remained the same everywhere, the view was strengthened that the 'real' language was the written form.

The most significant development of the Middle Ages was the production of a number of *speculative* grammars, that is, treatises with the title *The modes of signifying* (*De modis significandi*) or some variant of it. The most famous is that by Thomas of Erfurt, dating from the first half of the fourteenth century, although a grammar of this type had been written by Roger Bacon at the end of the thirteenth. The various writers, the Modistae, represented substantially the same theoretical point of view, though the details varied. The problem they had set for themselves was to give a philosophical explanation for the categories of grammatical description. In the Modistic system things exist in various ways or modes: for example, they may possess the property of permanence, or they may undergo changes in time. Such are the 'modes of being'. Human understanding and language reflect these modes in appropriate categories.[9] The details of such systems were elaborated with enormous subtlety and intricate complications, but the principle is always the same, that language appropriately reflects the different aspects of reality. Hence the name 'speculative', from the Latin *speculum*, 'a mirror'.

In such a context, the concept of an underlying universal grammar was made explicit: Roger Bacon wrote that grammar was the same in all languages in substance, surface differences between them being merely accidental variations. From our point of view the importance of speculative grammar is that it reinforces the Stoic belief that the world contains classes of entities, human thought corresponds to these natural classes, and that language then clothes thoughts in words.

3.3 From the Renaissance to the present day. Until the late Middle Ages, a handful of grammars of languages other than Latin and Greek had been produced in the west, but from the Renaissance onwards an increasing number began to appear.[10] The majority of them applied Latin grammar to the description of other languages (see Chapter 6); in addition, the attitudes of traditional grammar were widely accepted, and again circumstances appear to conspire to strengthen them.

Speculation by such philosophers as Bishop Wilkins (1614–72), who postulated a universal thought structure possessed by mankind and therefore independent of any language, reinforced the notion of the priority of thought. This attitude is also found in the grammars of the Port-Royal schools in France (1637–61), for example the *Grammaire générale et raisonnée* by Arnauld and Lancelot (1660).

Practical considerations strengthened the belief that every language possessed one correct form and that it was the duty of the grammarian to teach it. The invention of printing made for the establishment of fixed spelling conventions. The increased geographical and social mobility of populations (especially after the Industrial Revolution) led to textbooks that prescribed standards of pronunciation, grammar and vocabulary so that the traveller or the social climber should not appear ridiculous or unintelligible.

Some communities established bodies to decide what would be 'correct', for example the Accademia della Crusca (1582) in Italy, and in France the Académie française (1636). No such body existed for English-speaking countries. Authority was here found in the works of self-appointed experts, two of the most influential being

10

3. Traditional Grammar

Samuel Johnson's *Dictionary* (1755) and Bishop Lowth's *A Short Introduction to English Grammar* (1762). Johnson's aim was to write 'a dictionary by which the pronunciation of our language may be fixed and its attainment facilitated; by which its purity may be preserved, its use ascertained and its duration strengthened'. To this end, 'I have studiously endeavoured to collect examples from the writers before the restoration, whose works I regard as *the wells of English undefiled*, as the pure sources of genuine diction'. Lowth equally took it upon himself to lay down some usages and forbid others. For example, writers at that time commonly used *You was*; Lowth prescribed *You were*; his lasting success is obvious.

In the later eighteenth and the nineteenth centuries an increasing stream of such prescriptive works appeared, two of the most notable being those of Lindley Murray and William Cobbett. Murray published an *English Grammar* in 1795, intended for a readership among whom he wished 'to promote the cause of virtue, as well as of learning'. Its debt to Lowth and Johnson is acknowledged, while its structure recalls that of Roman grammars. In 1819 Cobbett published a *Grammar of the English Language*, cast as a series of letters, 'more especially for the Use of Soldiers, Sailors, Apprentices and Ploughboys', that is, for newly literate classes. These two works share the traditional categories and, in their efforts to inculcate a socially acceptable standard, are prescriptive to a degree.

In the present century countless grammars of this type have been published, each intended to promote the learning of a foreign language or the study of the mother-tongue. Virtually all employ the terminology whose history has been sketched. Since language, it is believed, gives names to things and clothes our thoughts in words, language itself is analysed in terms of thoughts and things; so we find such definitions as 'A *sentence* . . . may be called a group of words which makes complete sense and expresses a complete thought' and 'A noun . . . is a word which is the name of a person, place or thing'.[11] It is still commonly held that there is a 'correct' form of the language and that it is the job of a grammarian to teach it. This correct form is held to be more 'logical', a view reflected in such judgements as 'It is illogical to blame a thing on a person, as "I blame it on him".' (We are advised to say 'I blame him for that'.)[12] The earlier stages of a language are regarded as better and change is resented, as may be seen in the correspondence columns of the British press where complaints against innovations in pronunciation or usage can frequently be found. Finally, it may still be observed that Latin and Greek are credited with more 'logic', 'economy', 'clarity', 'ability to express ideas': 'The linguistic

11

training of Latin emphasising as it does constant processes of analysis and synthesis, teaches clarity and precision of thought.'[13] An interesting blend of these attitudes may be found in the following question 'Is it because . . . they have not learnt . . . any Latin or Greek, that cultured, supposedly well-educated and logically minded people still use such constructions as "different to", "like I did"?'[14]

FURTHER READING
Arens 1969, 1–34; Dinneen 1967, chs 4–5; Ivić 1965, 1–21, 26–30; Michael 1970; Robins 1967, chs 1–4; Waterman 1963, 1–10.

4. More Languages, More Problems

4.1 The increase of data. The Greeks considered other languages as unworthy of notice; and so during the formative period of traditional grammar 'language' *was* Greek. Varro doubled the scope of language-study by describing Latin, and in the centuries following more and more languages were investigated, thus extending the scope still further – and raising problems.

The Christian Church has been concerned with languages since its beginning. Translations of its Scriptures are the earliest written records of many languages, and the production of these often entailed the design of an alphabet, as in the case of the translation into Gothic by Ulfilas (fourth century). (That reportedly invented by SS. Kyrillos and Methodios (ninth century) for writing Old Church Slavonic, the 'Cyrillic', is still used by Russian and many other languages.) Later missionary activity resulted in the investigation of many exotic languages, mainly under the auspices of the *Congregatio sacra de propaganda fide* (established in 1522) and the Society of Jesus (1540). For example a description of Aztec (Mexico) dates from 1529, and is followed in the next two centuries by investigations of Quechua (Peru), Chinese, Konkani (South India), Coptic (Egypt), Ethiopic, Guarani (Paraguay), Vietnamese, Tibetan, Burmese, and many, many more. Subsequently, organisations such as the British and Foreign Bible Society became responsible for many translations. During the twentieth century the Wycliffe Bible Translators and their associated training centres, the Summer Institute of Linguistics, have evolved training-schemes for translators and have contributed to linguistic theory.

Hebrew was known by a few Western scholars since the time of S. Jerome (fourth and fifth centuries), the translator of the Bible into Latin. In the later Middle Ages and during the Renaissance it became widely studied, and grammars were compiled, for example, by Roger Bacon, the first European Christian to do so. Little work had been carried out on European vernacular languages although noteworthy are treatises on Irish, on Icelandic and on Provençal. But towards the end of the Mediaeval period there was a spectacular increase in such works. Dante Alighieri's *Vernacular eloquence* (*De vulgari eloquentia*) (1303), which states that the 'mother-tongue' is

13

nobler than Latin, may have encouraged the investigation of Southern European languages, as may also his sublime use of such vernacular in *The divine comedy* (*La commedia*). Grammars of Italian and Castilian Spanish appeared in the fifteenth century and a French one in the sixteenth. Use of vernacular languages in writing was helped by the rise of nation-states and by the Reformation. From this period onwards a steady stream of vernacular grammars developed, English examples being by William Bullokar (1586), by Ben Jonson (1640), and by John Wallis (1653).

The development of trade necessitated the study of foreign languages, and grammars and dictionaries began to be produced to meet this need: introductions to French by Alexander Barclay (1521)[1] and J. Palsgrave (1530) mark the beginning of French studies in England. Above all the invention of printing facilitated the distribution of both native and foreign grammars. The era of exploration begun by Marco Polo and Columbus was marked by linguistic data brought back as souvenirs, in the form of manuscripts or of word-lists or observations about languages. For example a Flemish diplomat, Ogier Ghiselin van Busbecq, in Constantinople from 1560 to 1562, recorded and published a list of words in Gothic as it had survived in the Crimea. A fashion grew up of publishing language 'museums' containing specimens of as many languages as possible: for example, C. Gesner's *Mithridates* (Zürich 1555) with 22 languages. Such endeavour reached its climax with a *Catalogue of the Languages of all Known Peoples* (1800–5) by a Spanish Jesuit, Lorenzo Hervás y Pandura, with more than 800 languages.

Thus by the end of the eighteenth century the number of languages known of and described, if only to a minimal extent, was of the order of 1000. (Today it is estimated that there are 3000–5000 in the world.) This increase in data brought problems (as does the admission of any new data in a study) of which the outstanding three are:

(1) Which of these languages is the oldest, and how did it originate?
(2) What kinds of relationship exist among all these languages?
(3) Is the descriptive apparatus of traditional grammar, once held to be universal, adequate to handle all of them?

The first question, as we see in this chapter, does not admit of an answer. An answer to the second was provided by comparative philology, which we sketch in Chapter 5. The answer to the third is in the negative, and one reason for the development of linguistics was to try to provide such a descriptive framework; virtually the rest of this book, from Chapter 6 onwards, is devoted to this problem.

4.2 The 'original' language. The notion that some extant languages are 'older' than others appears to make sense to the naive mind; and the claim has been made that one is older than *all* others and is the 'original' language. Various contenders for this status have been proposed.

The question apparently occurred first to an Egyptian king, Psammetichus,[2] who decided that Phrygian was the oldest language – by having two new-born infants isolated from human contact and observing their first utterance *bekos*, the Phrygian word, he was assured, for 'bread'. Later, Hebrew was regarded as the 'original' language. Thus Isidore of Seville (seventh century) who wrote an etymological dictionary, held that Hebrew was the language of God and so the first language on earth. James IV of Scotland (1488–1513) repeated Psammetichus's experiment and reported that *his* two children 'spak very guid Ebrew'. But there were other opinions: Chinese was the first language;[3] Dutch was the first, because it was the most 'perfect';[4] there were eleven unrelated original tongues;[5] in the Garden of Eden, God spoke Swedish, Adam Danish and the serpent French.[6]

The truth is that scholars could not prove or disprove such theories until they had a generally accepted notion of how languages are related.

4.3 The origin of the first language. For long, language had generally been held to be the direct gift of God, either because of its 'complexity and perfect ordering'[7] or because the dilemma had been recognised that man needs *language* in order to think, but also *thought* in order to have something to say. Which therefore came first, language or thought?[8] By the latter part of the eighteenth century scholars began to wonder *how* language came into being, supposing it were *not* a direct gift from God.

A prize was offered by the Prussian Academy for an essay answering the question whether mankind alone could have evolved language. It was won by J.G. Herder (1744–1803) for *The origin of language* (*Über den Ursprung der Sprache*) (1772). He denies that language is the direct gift of God. God, to be sure, gave man the impulse to speak, but man used this impulse in his own way. He observed recurring phenomena and named them; the sense of hearing was the first to be used; then followed names for things recognised by other senses. Thus a simple vocabulary arose, confined to observable things. In time, as man's ability to think developed,

15

more diversified words and complex grammatical categories appeared. This is an advance on previous views, since Herder postulates a parallel development of the powers to speak and to think: so in a sense, he envisages a changing, evolving, mankind. During the eighteenth, nineteenth and even twentieth centuries, further theories explaining the origin of language were advanced. These were later given nicknames as follows:

(a) The *bow-wow* theory: primitive words were imitative of sounds; for example man copied the barking of dogs and obtained a word which meant 'dog' or 'bark'.[9]

(b) The *pooh-pooh* theory: language is derived from instinctive cries called forth by intense emotion.[10]

(c) The *ding-dong* theory: every substance has a natural resonance when struck; when man is struck by an impression (for example, the sight of a sheep), he will emit the appropriate vocal resonance, that is, the word 'sheep'.[11]

(d) The *yo-he-ho* theory: under strong physical effort, man will emit noises from his vocal tract; these became language, so the first words will mean 'heave' or 'haul'.[12]

(e) The *ta-ta* theory: man makes gestures appropriate to certain situations, for example waving when taking leave; the tongue may duplicate the manual gesture, and striking the roof of the mouth, will utter the sound *ta-ta*.[13]

(f) The *ta-ra-ra-boom-de-ay* theory: language arose from ritual dance and incantation.[14]

Entertaining as these speculations are, it is impossible to see how they could be proved or disproved. But even if we admit that any one might be tenable, this would only account for a tiny part of the repertory of human language. Furthermore we cannot use two approaches cited by Herder: the study of primitive languages and the study of how children learn language. Contrary to belief, there are *no* primitive languages to be found, either in the very earliest written records, or in the least accessible corners of the globe. How children acquire language has become an important investigation in recent years, but it cannot tell us anything directly about the origin of language, only about how a child learns the language by which it is already surrounded.

Scholars eventually realised that such theories were untestable: when the Linguistic Society of Paris was founded in 1866, its rules forbade discussion of the origin of language, although this did not discourage speculation. Recently, more light has been cast on the problem by the consideration of the anatomical and psychological attributes necessary for the production of human language and of the

16

differences between animal communication and human language. These differences appear to constitute a developmental chasm as great as that which separates animals from plants. The safest thing that can be said at present is that it is impossible to conceive of mankind existing without language, that is, language developed when man himself developed.[15]

FURTHER READING
Arens 1969, 62–133; Firth 1964, 53–73; Robins 1967, chs 5–6; Waterman 1963, 11–17.

5. Relationships between Languages: Comparative Philology

5.1 Babel. One account of the relationship between languages is found in the story of the tower of Babel in Genesis 11:

> Once . . . all the world spoke a single language . . . Then the Lord . . . said . . . 'Come, let us . . . confuse their speech, so that they will not understand what they say to one another.' So the Lord dispersed them from there all over the earth.

This view, supported by the authority of Scripture, that the relationship was *confusion*, remained dominant until the end of the eighteenth century and inhibited the search for systematic relationships.

Scholars were aware of similarities between languages. Dante knew that words for 'yes' in certain Northern European languages were forms of '*io*' (*ja*, *yes*) and that Spanish, Italian and French were to some extent similar; an Italian, Filippo Sassetti, travelling in India between 1583 and 1588, observed that the numerals of Sanskrit (see 5.2) and of Italian resembled each other; Claudio Tolomei (1492–1555) described the correspondences between Latin *plenus* 'full', *clavis* 'key' and *afflatus* 'blown' and their counterparts *pieno* /'pjeno/, *chiave* /'kjave/ and *fiato* /'fjato/ in the Italian of Tuscany. But no conclusions were drawn.

In general it was held that the first language had given rise to others by haphazard change. For example, in 1606 Etienne Guichard[1] contended that the relationships between words had to be sought 'by the addition, subtraction, transposition, and inversion of letters', which is understandable since 'Hebrews write from right to left, and Greeks and others from left to right'. (Notice the assumption that the written form is prior.) A late example of this view is found in Gesenius's *Hebrew Lexicon* (1834), where the Hebrew root /kalaːv/ (allegedly 'to knock' or 'to weave') is identified with the German *klopfen* /'klɔpfən/ 'to knock' and also ('with the letters transposed') *flechten* /'flɛxtən/ 'to weave'. And indeed to jumble letters would have been a good way for the Lord to confuse a written language.

A letter, written in 1767 by a missionary at Pondicherry, G.L. Coeurdoux, is perhaps the last word from this period. Coeurdoux notices resemblances between Sanskrit and Western languages, and offers two explanations: firstly, that the confusion at Babel was not total, for 'some common terms remained in the new languages'; and secondly, that having begun their wanderings, the tribes remained for some time in mutual contact and borrowed words from each other's languages.

5.2 Sanskrit and Sir William Jones. The Babel-based explanations of such scholars as Coeurdoux were superseded by *comparative philology*. The beginning of this period coincides with the spread of interest in Sanskrit among the scholars of Europe. Sanskrit is an Indian language whose earliest religious poems, date back beyond 1000 B.C. Later a writing-system was evolved but the spoken language continued to change, developing from 300 B.C. onwards into forms known as Prakrits. These in turn became the ancestors of many Northern Indian languages of today. Sanskrit, however, remained as a learned language, comparable to Latin in Europe, and is still one of the official languages of India. By 400 B.C. schools of grammarians came into existence to elucidate the old religious texts. The most famous of these grammarians was Pāṇini.

In Sanskrit, words undergo regular variations in sound when they are brought into different combinations, for example *vayam* 'we' and *ca* 'and', but *vayañca* 'and we' (see p.76 and p.101). These changes are noted in Sanskrit spelling. Pāṇini lists all such changes in instructions for building words. They take the form of 4000 rules that must be applied in a strict order and are characterised by meticulous economy. Statements are never repeated, and algebraic symbols and abbreviation devices appear wherever possible (even a zero-symbol is used: cf. p.97). It is difficult to imagine anything more unlike a traditional grammar; in no sense is it a teaching or prescriptive grammar. It is a mathematically concise statement of facts, a description.

Obviously Sanskrit was the language of an ancient culture with its own grammatical tradition, both totally independent of Graeco-Roman counterparts. More importantly, the language itself was striking in its resemblances to certain European languages. Compare two sets of words in Table 1.

Such similarity, not only of roots but of inflections, was so abundant that it could no longer be dismissed by appeal to a divine confounding followed by short cultural contact. Another answer had to be found.

British scholarship first spread the knowledge of Sanskrit in Europe. Among such scholars was the Englishman Sir William Jones (1746–94). A judge in Calcutta from 1783 onwards, he was also a brilliant student of languages (he had studied twenty-eight!) especi-

5. Comparative Philology

Table 1

English	Latin	Greek	Russian	Sanskrit
mother	matrem (acc.)	mḗtéra (acc.)	matjerji (gen.)	matáram (acc.)
two	duo	dúo	dva	dvaú
('house')	domus	dómos ('hut')	dom	dámas
mouse	mus	mûs	miʃ	mûs
three	tres	trêis	trji	tráyas

	Latin	Ionian Greek	Sanskrit
('I am')	sum	eimí	ásmi
('thou art')	es	éssi	ási
('he is')	est	estí	ásti

ally Oriental ones, and knew Sanskrit. On 2 February 1786 Jones uttered the famous words:[2]

The *Sanscrit* language . . . is of a wonderful structure; more perfect than the *Greek*, more copious than the *Latin*, and more exquisitely refined than either, yet bearing to both of them a stronger affinity, both in the roots of verbs and in the forms of grammar, than could possibly have been produced by accident;
. . . no philologer could examine them all three, without believing them to have sprung from some common source, which, perhaps, no longer exists: there is a similar reason . . . for supposing that both the *Gothick* and the *Celtick* . . . had the same origin with the *Sanscrit*; and the old *Persian* might be added to the same family.

Three things are important: Jones groups only a selection of languages as having a common origin; Hebrew is not included, nor are Arabic and Chinese (although he was familiar with all three); his criteria include not only roots, but similarities of inflection; he considers the possibility that the original source language no longer exists, that is no written records remain. Jones's statement is generally considered to mark the beginning of comparative philology.[3]

European scholars took up language-comparison with excitement as they realised possible advantages. Friedrich von Schlegel expressed his anticipation in *The language and wisdom of the Indians* (*Über die Sprache und Weisheit der Indier*) (1808): 'But the decisive point, which will clarify everything, is the inner structure of languages or comparative grammar [i.e. philology] which will lead us to quite new conclusions about the genealogy of languages. . . .'[4]

Once begun, comparative philology progressed by dint of immense

20

labour on the part of innumerable scholars. We now describe three stages: the observation of correspondences; the interpretations of this data; the Neogrammarian period.

Table 2

Latin	English	Latin	English
pater	father	*	*
tres	three (i.e. [θ])	decem	ten
cordis (gen.)	heart	genu	knee (i.e. [k])

*There is no example of an initial [b], but one may quote the correspondence /kannábis/ (Greek) and *hemp*.

5.3 The observation of correspondences. Fundamental principles of comparison were laid down in 1814 by Rasmus Rask (1787–1832) although they were not published until 1818. He stressed the importance of comparing inflectional endings to establish relationships between languages. Similarities of vocabulary were not necessarily reliable since they might be due to borrowing; however, if there were systematic correspondences between sounds of the 'most essential, concrete, indispensable words' of two languages, then one could speak of a fundamental relationship between these languages. He noted such correspondences between sounds of certain 'essential' words in the Germanic languages and their equivalents in Latin and Greek: for example the initial sounds in *pater = father*; *pauci = few*; *pes = foot*; *piscis = fish*, to take English examples. The credit for this is generally and (unfairly) given to Jakob Grimm (1785–1863). In 1822 Grimm gave an exposition of systems of correspondences between certain consonants in words in Germanic languages and consonants in Greek or Latin equivalents. We illustrate this in Table 2, using English examples. These correspondences are taken to mean that certain sounds in Germanic languages have shifted from their original values but have remained unaltered in certain other languages, such as Latin. To such phenomena Grimm gave the name *sound-shift* (*Lautverschiebung*). The process affecting Germanic is symbolised as

(a) p > f   (b) b > p
    t > θ   d > t
    k > h   g > k

5. Comparative Philology

This symbolisation does *not* imply that the Germanic word is derived from the Latin.

A third set of correspondences (in which the unshifted sounds remain in Sanskrit but not in Latin or Greek) can be grouped with the above. Grimm called these three the *first Germanic sound-shift*. He associated it with a second sound-shift confined to German, and not found in, for example, English.

Grimm noticed that sometimes a sound had not changed as expected, for example in the following words for 'brother', 'father': Gothic /bro:θar/, /fadar/ and German *Bruder, Vater* compared with Latin *frater, pater* and Sanskrit *bhrātā, pitā*. We would expect the medial consonant to be the same in the two Gothic words and the same in the two German words. Grimm concluded that sometimes words remained with unshifted sounds; in other words, sound-shifts were liable to exceptions.

During the remainder of the century, language-study was characterised by the comparison of languages both living and dead, and by painstaking plotting of correspondences, vocalic as well as consonantal.

5.4 Interpretation of correspondences: language-families. Scholars had apprehended that languages might be separated into different groups, but now systematic correspondences led to precise criteria for grouping into *families*. An individual family would show such correspondences, but no resemblances would be discernible between different families. So the task of classifying languages began. Some families showed branches or sub-groups; some languages could not be shown to be related to any other and so were single-member families. The most intensively studied was the Indo-European family, that is, that to which belonged Latin, Greek, Sanskrit and most of the languages of Europe and Northern India.

The examples given in Table 3 illustrate the principle, and evidence of a few sound-shifts may be seen. Only words from languages not written in the Latin alphabet have been transliterated: normal orthography, more conservative than pronunciation, may reveal correspondences not immediately obvious from a comparison of spoken forms.

It is impossible here to give a full account of contemporary opinion on the number, members and geographical distribution of language-families, but the short list below will be useful for reference († means that the language is no longer spoken). Some of the allocations are a matter of continuing debate.

5. Comparative Philology

A. INDO-EUROPEAN FAMILY:

(a) *Germanic branch*: English; Dutch, Afrikaans; German, Yiddish; Icelandic; Norwegian, Swedish, Danish; †Gothic.
(b) *Celtic branch*: Breton, †Cornish, Welsh; Irish, †Manx, Scots Gaelic.
(c) *Italic branch*: †Oscan, †Umbrian; †Latin and its descendants, the 'Romance' languages viz. French; Spanish, Portuguese, Catalan, Provençal; Sardinian; Italian; Rumanian.
(d) *Balto-Slavonic branch*:
   (i) *Baltic group*: Latvian; Lithuanian.
   (ii) *Slavonic group*: Polish, Czech, Slovak; Russian, White Russian, Ukrainian; Slovene, Croatian, Serbian; Macedonian, Bulgarian.
(e) †Ancient Greek, Modern Greek.
(f) Albanian.
(g) Armenian; †Phrygian.
(h) *Indo-Iranian branch*:
   (i) *Iranian group*: †Avestan, †Pahlavi, Persian, Kurdish, Pashto.
   (ii) *Indic group*: †Sanskrit; Hindi, Urdu, Bengali, Punjabi, Gujerati, Marathi, Sinhalese, etc.
(i) †*Anatolian branch* (Asia Minor): †Hittite; †Luvian, †Lycian; †Lydian.
(j) †*Tocharian branch* (Chinese Turkestan): †Tocharian A (Eastern Tocharian, Turfanian); †Tocharian B (Western Tocharian, Kuchean).

B. HAMITO-SEMITIC (or AFRO-ASIATIC) FAMILY:

(a) *Semitic branch*: †Classical Hebrew, Modern Hebrew; †Syriac, †Aramaic; †Akkadian, †Ugaritic, †Classical Arabic, Modern Arabic colloquials, including Maltese; †Classical Ethiopic (Ge'ez), Amharic, Tigre, Tigrinya.
(b) *Cushitic branch* (E. Africa): Beja; Afar; Galla; Somali.
(c) *Berber branch* (N. Africa): Tuareg; Kabyl.
(d) †Ancient Egyptian, Coptic.
(e) *Chad branch* (W. Africa): Hausa.

C. FINNO-UGRIAN (or URALIC) FAMILY (Europe and Siberia: Finnish, Estonian, Lapp; Hungarian; Ostyak; Cheremis; Samoyed.

D. Basque.

E. CAUCASIAN LANGUAGES:

(a) *Northern Caucasian* branch includes Lezgian, Kabardian, Circassian.
(b) *Southern Caucasian* branch includes Georgian and Mingrelian.

23

5. Comparative Philology

Table 3

A. INDO-EUROPEAN FAMILY

1. Germanic branch				2. Celtic branch	
				Scots	
English	Dutch	German	Danish	Gaelic	Welsh
one	een	eins	en	aon	un
two	twee	zwei	to	dà	dau
three	drie	drei	tre	trì	tri
four	vier	vier	fire	ceithir	pedwar
five	vijf	fünf	fem	cóig	pump
mother	moeder	Mutter	mor	màthair	mam
brother	broeder	Bruder	bror	bràthair	brawd
hand	hand	Hand	hånd	làmh	llaw
water	water	Wasser	vand	uisge	dwr

3. Slavonic branch			4. Romance branch		
				Portu-	
Russian	Czech	Bulgarian	Latin	guese	Rumanian
odjin	jeden	edin	unus	um	un
dva	dva	dva	duo	dois	doi
trji	tři	tri	tres	três	trei
tʃetirje	čtyři	tʃetiri	quattuor	quatro	patru
pjatj	pět	pet	quinque	cinco	cinci
matj	matka	majka	mater	mãe	mama
brat	bratr	brat	frater	irmão	fratele
ruka	ruka	ruka	manus	mão	mâna
voda	voda	voda	aqua	água	apa

F. ALTAIC FAMILY: (Asia Minor, Central and East Asia):
  (a) *Turkic branch*: Turkish; Uzbek, Kazakh, Kirgiz.
  (b) *Mongolian branch*: Mongolian (Khalkha); Buryat.
  (c) *Tunguz branch*: Tunguz; Manchu; Evenki, Goldi.
  (d) Korean.

G. NIGER-CONGO FAMILY:
  (a) *West Atlantic branch* (Senegal, Gambia, N. Nigeria):
    Wolof; Fulani.
  (b) *Kwa branch* (Ghana, Nigeria): Gã; Yoruba; Igbo;
    Ewe; Efik.

24

5. Comparative Philology

Table 3 (continued)

B. SEMITIC FAMILY

	Classical Hebrew	Classical Arabic	Maltese	Classical Ethiopic	Amharic
'mother'	ʔeːm	ʔumm	omm	ʔimm	ʔinnat
'brother'	ʔaːħ	ʔax	ħu	ʔix	wəndim
'hand'	jaːd	jad	id	ʔidd	ʔiddʒ
'water'	majim (pl.)	maːʔ	ilma	mij	wuha
'blood'	daːm	dam	demm	daːm	dəm
'head'	roːʃ	raʔs	ras	riʔis	ras
'heart'	leːvav	lubb		libb	libb
'heart'		qalb	qalb		
'sea'		baħr	baħar	baːhir	bahir
'sea'	jaːm	jam			
'star'	koːxav	kuːkab	kewkba	kaːkəb	kokəb

C. MALAYO-POLYNESIAN FAMILY

	Hanunoo (Philippines)	Indonesian	Maori	Samoan	Tongan
'one'	usa	satu	tahi	tasi	taha
'two'	duwa	dua	rua	lua	ua
'three'	tulu	tiga	toru	tolu	tolu
'four'	upat	empat	wha	fa	faː
'five'	lima	lima	rima	lima	nima
'six'	unum	enam	ono	ono	ono
'seven'	pitu	tudjuh	whitu	fitu	fitu

(c) *Benue-Congo group*: this includes the Bantu languages, e.g. Swahili; Kikuyu; Zulu; Xhosa.

H. KHOISAN GROUP (S.-W. Africa):
Bushman; Hottentot.

I. DRAVIDIAN FAMILY (S. India):
Tamil, Malayalam; Telegu.

J. SINO-TIBETAN FAMILY:
(a) *Tibeto-Burman branch*: Tibetan; Burmese.
(b) *Sinitic branch*: most Chinese 'dialects', e.g. Cantonese; Taiwanese; Shanghai Chinese; Mandarin dialects, including Pekingese, Szechuan dialect, Nanking Chinese.

25

5. Comparative Philology

K. TAI FAMILY:
Thai (Siamese); Laotian; perhaps Vietnamese.

L. MON-KHMER FAMILY:
Mon (Burma, Thailand); Cambodian; perhaps Vietnamese.

M. Japanese.

N. MALAYO-POLYNESIAN FAMILY:
(*a*) *Malay branch*: Malagasy; Malay, Indonesian; Javanese; Sundanese; Tagalog; Hanunóo.
(*b*) *Polynesian branch*: Samoan; Fijian; Maori; Tongan; Hawaiian.

O. American Indian languages number hundreds; the suggested numbers of language *families* are of the order of between 25 and 50 in North America, around 20 in Central America and 108 (!) in South America. Noteworthy names are: Eskimo; Nootka; Navaho; Hopi; the Algonquian family (including Cree, Fox, Menomini, Ojibwa); Maya; Quechua; Guarani.

P. The languages of Borneo, New Guinea and Australia have been little investigated up to now, but work has begun. It is said that the Australian indigenous languages all belong to one family, but that the other territories appear to contain large numbers of language-families.

5.5 Interpretation of correspondences: proto-languages. In the nineteenth century, particularly between 1850 and 1870, much thought was given to drawing inferences from correspondences. In this section, and the following two, we examine three topics: reconstruction of a parent language; family-tree theory; wave-theory. We confine ourselves to examples from Indo-European, but the arguments could apply to any language-family.

In the case of at least one sub-group of the Indo-European family, the Romance languages, written records of a parent language, Latin, existed. It was postulated that an equivalent parent language of every other sub-group had existed, but by accident had not attained written form (for example, Proto-Germanic (or Primitive Germanic), Proto-Celtic, Proto-Slavonic), and alleged forms of these parent languages were 'reconstructed' by comparing forms attested in the descendants. For example, English *mother*, Old English *mōdor*, Old Norse *mōðer*, Old Frisian *mōder*, Old Saxon *mōdar* and Old High German *muoter* were all traced back to a hypothetical, Proto-Germanic *asterisk-form* *mōder (these 'reconstructions' were usually marked with an asterisk).

26

5. Comparative Philology

Since it was assumed that the entire family was derived from one parent language, this was given the name Primitive Indo-European (P.I.-E.) and its forms were also 'reconstructed' in a similar fashion. Thus the Proto-Germanic form *$m\bar{o}der$, together with other appropriate asterisk-forms and the attested forms of other parents of branches (for example, Albanian *motre* 'sister', Old Armenian *mair*, Sanskrit *mātā*, Latin *māter*, Greek *mēter*) were all traced back to a P.I.-E. *$m\bar{a}t\bar{e}r$. The principle was that any feature common to all or most of the related languages must have been present in the parent. The word *etymology* came to be used for listing earlier forms of a word, comparing them with cognate forms in related languages, and deriving them all from reconstructed forms. August Schleicher (1821–68) went so far as to write a fable in P.I.-E., reconstructing not only words, but grammatical forms and even idioms.

5.6 Interpretation of correspondences: family-tree theory and wave theory. Schleicher also elaborated a theory of interrelationship of the various members of a family. He envisages the line of descent as being bifurcated whenever a sound-shift (or change in a grammatical feature) occurs among certain speakers but not others; this gives two languages where previously there had been one; each new language may be similarly split; and so on. This is the *family-tree theory* (*Stammbaumtheorie*). According to Schleicher,[5] the main branches (see 5.4) of the Indo-European family-tree are related as in Figure 1.

Unfortunately this arrangement cannot be reconciled with another constructed according to a division of the Indo-European family proposed originally by Franz Bopp (1791–1867) into a Western group (Greek, Italic, Celtic, Germanic) and an Eastern (Indic, Iranian, Armenian, Albanian, Baltic, Slavonic). The basis is that certain initial *k*-sounds (or *h*- derived from *k*-) in the Western languages are paralleled by *s*-sounds in the Eastern: cf. Latin *centum*, Scots Gaelic *ceud* /ˈkiət/ English *hund*(*red*) with Russian

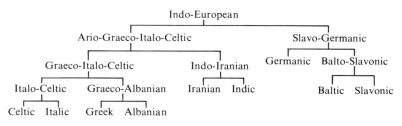

Figure 1

Figure 2

/sto/, Latvian *simts*, Sanskrit *śatám*, Old Persian /satem/. The Western group hence became known as *centum*-languages and the Eastern as *satem*-languages. This division is shown in Figure 2.

Compare the relative positions of Germanic and Balto-Slavonic, of Greek and Albanian, and of Indo-Iranian and Greek in the two family-trees. Moreover Figure 1 can take only partial account of grammatical features peculiar to: (*a*) Germanic and Balto-Slavonic (certain case-endings in common); (*b*) Italic and Celtic (a passive voice ending in -*r*, cf. Latin *mordeor*); (*c*) Greek, Armenian and Indo-Iranian (certain past tenses with prefixed *e*-); (*d*) Italic and Greek (certain feminine nouns with masculine suffixes); (*e*) Italic and Germanic (a perfect tense is used as a non-perfect past). We conclude that no one family-tree can be drawn in such a way that the arrangement of the branches takes account of all Indo-European correspondences.

This difficulty entraps the constructor of perhaps all linguistic family-trees, whether of branches within a family, of sub-branches, of languages or even of dialects.[6] Furthermore, allegedly distinct languages may turn out in practice to merge into one another. For example, Dutch and German are reckoned to be distinct branches of a West German family-tree, yet a trip down the Rhine reveals a gradual change from Swiss German (High German) to Dutch (Low German); there *is* no sharp break. How can this be handled by a family-tree?

A solution was advanced by Johannes Schmidt (1843–1901) in his *wave-theory* (*Wellentheorie, Ausbreitungstheorie*). This visualises sound-changes operating geographically, beginning at a point and spreading outwards; then the sound-shift ceases, leaving an area of shift surrounded by an area where the shift has not operated.

This may be seen in dialect situations. The difference between High German and Low German is sometimes stated as though a sharp division had taken place (a bifurcation on a family-tree) summed up in the sound-change: Low German [p, t, k] > High German [pf-, ts-, kx-] and [-f, -s, -x]. (This is Grimm's *second sound-shift* mentioned above in 5.3.) Viewed geographically the situation is more complicated; at least seven sound-shifts seem to have spread northwards from the Swiss area, each halting on a different

28

Table 4

	'child'	'pound'	'that'	'on'	'village'	'make'	'I'
Zürich	Kchind	Pfund	das	auf	Dorf	mache	ich
Freiburg	Kind	,,	,,	,,	,,	,,	,,
Heidelberg	,,	Punt	,,	,,	,,	,,	,,
Trier	,,	,,	dat	,,	,,	,,	,,
Luxemburg	,,	,,	,,	op	,,	,,	,,
Aachen	,,	,,	,,	,,	Dorp	,,	,,
Düsseldorf	,,	,,	,,	,,	,,	make	,,
Kaldenhausen	,,	,,	,,	,,	,,	,,	ik

line and so giving rise, not to a sharp division but to a gradual dialect change. The details, involving seven test words quoted in ordinary orthography (*ch* = /x/), are shown in Table 4.[7] Indeed at the western end the change [-k-] > [-x-] has halted before [-k] > [-x], giving in Düsseldorf *ich make*; further east [-k] > [-x] halted before [-k-] > [-x-], giving in Berlin *ik mache*. This dialect scene is enlivened by three independent sets of vowel-shift that spread out from different points in the middle of the area. To try to construct a family-tree to take account of all ensuing dialects is to invite frustration. The wave-theory allows us to plot differences *and* similarities.

The application of this theory to the above Indo-European phenomena provide us with the overlapping 'ripples' illustrated in Figure 3.[8]

Hittite and the Tocharian languages, discovered in the twentieth century, are centum-languages and have a passive in *-r*; this makes it difficult to maintain the notion of a basic East-West satem-centum division – unless we postulate that the Tocharian-speakers migrated eastwards after the split. The wave-theory suggests that the satem-change spread outwards from a point, but stopped before it reached the periphery of the Indo-European area.

Two languages affected by a wave-change need not be mutually intelligible, which adds to the credibility of the theory applied on a large scale. A well-known example is the change from a tongue-tip [r] to a uvular 'gargled' [ʀ] or [ʁ], begun in Paris in Molière's time; it spread to most of France, and now is found among speakers of Dutch, German, Danish, Swedish, Norwegian and even Italian and Icelandic. Grammatical features, too, may spread from language to language. For example, a suffixed definite article appears in Rumanian (*om, omul*), Bulgarian (/tʃovek/, /tʃovekət/) and Albanian (*burr, burri*) (each pair meaning 'man', 'the man', respectively); yet

5. Comparative Philology

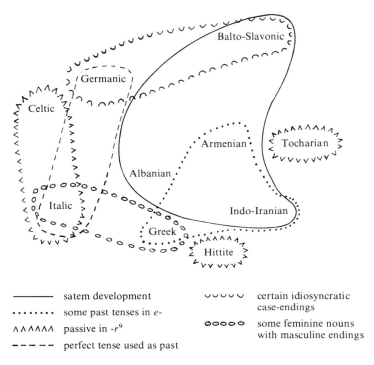

——————	satem development	⌣⌣⌣⌣⌣	certain idiosyncratic case-endings
········	some past tenses in *e-*		
ΛΛΛΛΛΛ	passive in *-r* [9]	ooooo	some feminine nouns with masculine endings
– – – – –	perfect tense used as past		

Figure 3

the form of the article is peculiar to the language. This phenomenon does not appear in other Romance or Slavonic languages.

5.7 Neogrammarians. The years between 1875 and the early 1890s saw the appearance of the group styled Neogrammarians (Junggrammatiker); [10] there were four members, August Leskien (1840–1916), Berthold Delbrück (1842–1922), Hermann Osthoff (1847–1909) and Karl Brugmann (1849–1919), but other names have become associated with them. They are generally (and unfairly) remembered for pronouncements on sound-shifts. Grimm had accepted that sound-shifts were liable to exceptions; the Neogrammarians claimed that apparent exceptions could always be explained, usually in one of three ways.

The conditions for the sound-shift might be formulated more precisely. Karl Verner (1846–96) showed that /bro:θar/ and /fadar/ (see 5.3) were regular by taking into account the stressed syllable in

30

Sanskrit. In Sanskrit we have *'bhrātā* but *pi'tā*; in the development from P.I.-E. to Germanic, certain consonants remained voiceless (see p.48) after the stressed vowel, but became voiced elsewhere, hence the Gothic forms. (A similar phenomenon may be seen in *luxury* with [kʃ], but *luxurious* with [gʒ].) Later in Germanic the stress on the word for 'brother' moved to the first syllable.[11] This explanation, Verner's Law, shows that some apparently anomalous consonantal alternations in Germanic and other languages[12] are quite regular.

A second explanation is a pressure towards analogy. For instance in Latin there had been a change: intervocalic [s] > [r]. Therefore **honosis* (genitive of *honos* 'honour') became *honoris*, giving a pattern *honos : honoris*. In the course of written Latin, we find that *honos* has suddenly become *honor*; it thus appears as though a final [s] has become shifted. However, it is explicable by assuming that since there also existed words with the pattern *orator : oratoris* 'orator', the speakers of Latin replaced *honos* with *honor* to 'bring it into line'.

The third explanation is that, a word was borrowed at a particular date. The Latin *philosophus* 'philosopher' does not appear as **philorophus* because it was borrowed from Greek /philósophos/ *after* the sound-change intervocalic [s] > [r] had operated. Sound-shifts appear to work themselves out completely so that no unshifted sound remains; but if thereafter a borrowing is introduced that contains the previously 'sensitive' sound, this remains unshifted. For this reason the German *Pforte* 'gate' (< Latin *porta*) is found beside *Person* 'person', (< Old French *persone*), the first borrowed before the seventh century, the second in the twelfth century.

Since sound-shifts apparently never admitted of exception, they became known as *sound-laws*: for example, the First Sound-shift became Grimm's Law. The Neogrammarian position is seen in Brugmann's dictum on the 'absence of exception in sound-laws': 'it must be expected that a sound-change . . . should manifest itself without exception in all cases which satisfy the same conditions',[13] that is, the same sound in the same environment will always develop in the same way in the same dialect.

5.8 Comparative philology. It is impossible to overestimate the contribution made in the nineteenth century to the study of languages. An appreciation had developed of sound-change and of analogy; ways had been suggested in which relationships between languages could be formulated; and massive progress had been made in classifying the world's languages. The leading scholars were intellectual giants and their capacity for work is staggering. In addition, comparative philology had attained the status of a science, as the term was understood: hypotheses (asterisk forms, family-tree theory, wave-theory and sound-laws) were advanced to account for the data, hypotheses that could be tested (unlike the story of Babel). And comparative philology reflected the intellectual preoccupations of the late eighteenth and the nineteenth centuries, namely historical development (cf. Lamarck, Wallace, Darwin and Mendel) and classification (cf. Linnaeus and Mendeleyev), while the Romantic movement encouraged the study of mediaeval manuscripts and languages.

But of course the hypotheses of comparative philology are not 'truth'. It is impossible to assert that asterisk forms are words that were ever spoken by anyone; they represent an algebra by which we can derive attested forms, given the appropriate rules, that is, the sound-shifts required. The premise, that a feature common to the related languages must have been present in a parent language, is demonstrably suspect. For example, seventeenth-century English and modern German show the forms *thou thinkest* and *du denkst*, respectively; we would therefore conclude that a common ancestor would have a corresponding ending *-st*. Luckily we possess written records of Old English and Old High German, and in them we find *θu θinkes* and *du denkis* respectively; the *-t* has developed *independently* in German and in English. Another example is the futures of verbs in Romance languages: these, apart from Rumanian, show close resemblances: for example, French *chanterai* /ʃɑ̃tre/, *ferai* /fəre/ and Italian *canterò* /kanteˈrɔ/, *farò* /faˈrɔ/ ('I shall sing' and 'I shall make'); yet the Classical Latin forms are *cantabo* and *faciam*. Clearly Classical Latin is not the immediate ancestor of the Romance languages. How sure may we then be about the reconstructed forms of P.I.-E.?[14]

The forms of P.I.-E. were liable to change when a new Indo-European language was taken into account and so P.I.-E. developed greatly! For example, the P.I.-E. ancestor of English *wot* ('know'), German *weiß* /vaɪs/ was *vaida* according to Bopp but *γwoidxe* according to Edgar Sturtevant (1875–1952). A natural language exhibits regional differences of sound-system, grammar and vocabulary, yet the algebraic formulae of P.I.-E. are homogeneous and 'monolithic'; it is improbable that they coincide with anything that was a language. Furthermore P.I.-E. cannot be 'original' except in that it is the convergence of lines that we project backwards in time: there is no reason to suppose that a tribe suddenly appeared on this planet speaking P.I.-E. Unfortunately, some histories of particular languages inform us, as though it were a matter of fact, that P.I.-E. possessed certain sounds, which then developed in various ways;[15]

32

such a presentation misrepresents the status of P.I.-E. For these reasons, conjecture about the 'original' habitat of the Indo-Europeans, about their way of life or religious beliefs, on the basis of words found in attested languages[16] is pointless, unless one can assign a date to this 'original' period.

The nature of the conjecture in both theories is easily demonstrated: if Latin had disappeared, how would we deal with the modern Romance languages? In a family-tree they would appear in the *satem* branch (though French is more *satem* than Italian) with no affinities to the Celtic group or Greek (since they have lost the passive in -*r* and most feminine nouns with masculine suffixes). According to a wave interpretation, they would be affected by the advance of *satem* development, which would be seen to have encircled *centum* Sardinian. Our historical knowledge refutes these suggestions. Clearly, in making conjectures about non-attested languages, every possible relevant evidence, linguistic and non-linguistic, must be used – loan-words in other languages (which may preserve an older pronunciation), migrations, place-names, subjugations of peoples, political alignments, even archaeological evidence.

The criticism is sometimes made of comparative philology that it is 'atomistic' in that fractions of the language (single sounds, grammatical terminations or single words) are inspected with little regard for the overall configuration of languages or their systems; the import of this criticism will become clear in the next chapter (6.2). Nevertheless, it may be argued that this approach is inevitable initially. The descriptive apparatus of traditional grammar was preserved: Schleicher, for example, uses a ready-made battery of categories little different from those of Dionysius Thrax. Again it may be contended that in dealing with Indo-European there was little reason to depart from previous practice.

The concern with 'sounds' stimulated scholars such as Sievers and Sweet (see p.46) to develop a sophisticated framework for describing sounds, as opposed to written symbols. But in other quarters there was ignorance or even hostility, for example, in the case of Grimm himself or August Pott (1802–87), on the grounds that what was important was the letter! The result is that even now there is confusion between sound and symbol: some alleged sound-changes are no more than changes in writing-habits,[17] while in some text-books the explanation of sound-changes may degenerate into what Sweet described as 'the mechanical enumeration of letter-changes'.[18] Finally, the overwhelmingly historical approach to language-relationship led to confusion between the description of affairs at one point in time and the history of these details, both being handled in the same statement.[19]

33

5. Comparative Philology

The work of the Neogrammarians did not mark the end of the collection, collation and interpretation of new data; this has continued ever since.[20] But theoretical development slackened, for the energies of scholars began to be directed to other aspects of language. In retrospect, we see that this new movement was under way by the turn of the century. However, in due course attention was again given to the theory of language-change, and we indicate something of this in Chapter 18.

FURTHER READING
Arens 1969, 155–399; Jankowsky 1972; Jespersen 1922, 32–99; Lehmann 1967; Meillet 1925; Pedersen 1959; Robins 1967, 164–97; Waterman 1963, 18–60.

6. The Beginning of Linguistics

6.1 A shift of interest. Development in any study depends on proposed solutions of problems. Some problems whose proposed solutions formed the new 'linguistics' were of a practical nature; but others were posed by intellectual curiosity and creativity. Such questions had been raised during the era of comparative philology by men like Wilhelm von Humboldt (1767–1835) and Hugo Schuchardt (1842–1927) and were variations of a basic question: 'What *is* human language?' (The use of 'language' rather than 'languages' is significant. One source of impetus in language-study is the tension between focus on 'language' and on 'languages'.) These debates had not been vigorously pursued because the majority of scholars were more interested in relations between languages and in sound-changes. But towards the end of the period we find individuals aware of dimensions other than the historical and they may be regarded as bridges between comparative philology and linguistics. The spiritual home of comparative philology had been Germany (in spite of the contributions of the Danes, Rask and Verner); but the new pioneers were of diverse nationalities. They include the American, W.D. Whitney (1827–94), the Pole, Jan Baudouin de Courtenay (1845–1929), the Englishman, Henry Sweet (1845–1912), the Swiss, Ferdinand de Saussure (1857–1913), the American, Franz Boas (1858–1942), the Dane, Otto Jespersen (1860–1943) and the Czech, Vilém Mathesius (1882–1946). The title 'father of linguistics' is generally given to de Saussure. Invidious though this is, there is justification in that he produced a short, comprehensible 'system', and exerted a virtually unbroken influence on linguistics in Europe.

6.2 Ferdinand de Saussure. Ferdinand de Saussure taught philology in Paris and in Geneva, where in 1906, 1908 and 1910 he gave courses on 'General Linguistics'. After his death, students' notes were collected, together with what could be found of his own notes, collated and made into a book, 'his' *Cours de linguistique générale*, published in 1916. In spite of inconsistencies (and it is not clear whether these are due to de Saussure or his editors), we may trace the features of his linguistic system. These underlie much of twentieth-century linguistics, although it is not always possible to tell whether the later appearance of a 'Saussurean' notion is indebtedness to de Saussure or an independent cogitation.

De Saussure is celebrated for drawing the distinction between *langue*[1] (the system according to which speakers in a speech-community speak) and *parole* (utterances in that system). He was influenced by the sociologist Emile Durkheim who had claimed that a 'social fact' is anything that 'exercises external constraint over the individual' and is general throughout a given society. *Langue* according to de Saussure is such a social fact. Language-study may be concerned with various things, for example meaning, historical development or phonetics, but de Saussure states that his linguistics is concerned with *langue*, the system. (He also uses a term *langage* to refer to the faculty of speech, that is, *langue* plus *parole*.)

A second distinction is between the *synchronic* axis of *langue* and the *diachronic*. The synchronic is the state of affairs at one point in time (an 'état de langue'), the diachronic is the historical axis along which one element of *langue*, such as the form of a word, might be studied. For example, the relationship between *foot* and *feet* is sychronic, a relationship (singular v. plural) on an axis of simultaneity; but the relationship of Proto-Germanic **fōt* to *foot* is diachronic, as is that between **fōti* and *feet*. Some confusion had been apparent in philological works between these axes, for example, in the statement that 'When Latin *facere* "to make" is compounded with a preposition it becomes *-ficere*, e.g. *perficere* "to achieve".' But this is not a synchronic fact; it is diachronic since **perfacere* > *perficere* by a Latin sound-change: non-initial [a] > [i]. Therefore the Saussurean system makes a distinction between diachronic linguistics (an elaboration of a comparative philological approach) and synchronic linguistics, the new dimension in language-study. His book devotes a roughly equal amount of space to each, but we describe only his innovatory synchronic linguistics.

An important element is the concept of the *linguistic sign*, for example, a word. This is thought of as existing in the mind of each speaker and as consisting of two parts, *concept* (the *signified*) and *sound-image* (the *signifier*); the concept may be paraphrased as 'what one understands by the word' and the sound-image as 'one's memory of the sound of the word'. Since there is no natural connection between the two (de Saussure would have been a conventionalist – see p.61) he describes the sign itself as *arbitrary*.

A *langue* is a system of such signs – by 'system' he implies an underlying organisation. Signs not only possess a *signification* (the property of 'standing for an idea'), but a *value*, derived from their place in the system. Thus the signification of French *mouton* /mutɔ̃/

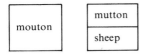

Figure 4

may, in one utterance, be the same as English *sheep*, but the value can never be the same; for English possesses an item *mutton* that has no counterpart in the French system (see Figure 4). The system of a *langue* is therefore something peculiar to itself; the values of its signs are derived from the system, not from the substance. (The roles of 'system' and 'substance' may be seen in the example of the 8.25 a.m. train to Paris which on two successive mornings may consist of different rolling-stock, though it is the 'same' train in terms of system; it could happen that an afternoon train was in terms of substance the 'same' train as the morning express; the substance serves only to expound the system.)

It is this aspect that allows de Saussure's work to be called *structuralist*, and we can illustrate the pervasiveness of his insight from other areas of language. In Figure 5 two more examples of different word-values are shown.

	English	French	German
'timber'	wood	bois /bwa/	Holz /hɔlts/
'small wooded area'			Wald /valt/
'large wooded area'	forest	forêt /fɔrɛ/	

	English	French
'to be acquainted with'	know	connaître /kɔnɛ:tr/
'to know (that . . .)'		savoir /savwar/
'to know (how to . . .)'	can	
'physically to be able to'		pouvoir /puvwar/

Figure 5

	English	Scots	Latin	German	French
'near the speaker'	this	this	hic		
'near the person spoken to'		that	iste	dieser /ˈdizər/	ce /sə/
	that				
'remote from speaker and hearer'		yon	ille	jener /ˈjenər/	

Figure 6

English	French	German
I *visit* my grand-mother in hospital	Je *rends* visite à ma grand'mère . . .	Ich *besuche* meine Oma . . .
I *am visiting* my grand-mother in hospital	/ʒə rã vizit a ma grãmɛr/	/ɪx bə'zuxə maɪnə 'oma/

Figure 7

The principle can be applied to grammatically important words, such as the demonstrative adjectives in Figure 6, and even to grammatical categories such as those in Figure 7. Indeed a structuralist principle may be applied to the sound-system of a language. For example, it makes no difference in Italian if the nasal sounds in *ancora* [aŋˈkora] 'yet' and *ingente* [inˈdʒɛṇṭe] 'huge' are interchanged: the words sound odd but no confusion could occur; but one cannot interchange the same two nasals in English *sin* [sɪn] and *sing* [sɪŋ].

Finally, we notice de Saussure's distinction between two types of relationship between linguistic signs. Any stretch of language of more than one unit may be called a *syntagma*, for example *re-read*; *God is good*; *if the weather is good, we shall go out*. The elements in a syntagma do not merely 'bring their meaning with them', but are mutually defining, a principle we may illustrate by considering the different meanings of *in* followed respectively by *the box*, *the street* and *earnest*. The relations involved here, that is, those contracted between the elements of a syntagma, 'along the line', are *syntagmatic*.

With these de Saussure contrasts a set of *associative* relations. These he envisages as existing between any word and others associated with it in the mind because of similarity of meaning, root, grammatical formation or even sound, as in Figure 8.[2] The elements of a syntagmatic relation occur 'in praesentia', in a fixed order, and are of a limited number; the elements of an associative relation are 'in absentia', in no fixed order, and are of an unlimited number.

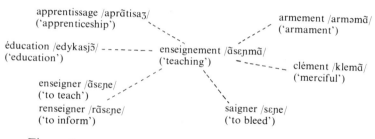

Figure 8

Unfortunately this is useless, since every item in a vocabulary can stand in an associative relation to any other. But de Saussure actually uses a more refined idea, which we may call *paradigmatic relations*. These are the relations between elements that may occur at the same point in a given syntagma – what we may describe as alternative 'fillers' for the same 'slot'. Thus *in* and *from* stand in paradigmatic relationship, since we find *in the street* and *from the street*; and so do *the* and *that*; but not, for example, *from* and *that* since we do not find **in from street* or **the that street*.[3]

De Saussure visualises the mechanism of *langue* as the interplay of these axes. Thus the analyst may divide syntagmas into constituent parts, examine the syntagmatic relations between these and classify them on the basis of paradigmatic relations with possible substitutes. The fruitfulness of this approach may be seen in its applications in Chapters 7, 8 and 9.

But not only did de Saussure clarify distinctions essential to the theory and methodology of linguistics, he enunciated goals 'The task of linguistics will be:

(*a*) to make the description of and trace the history of every language that it can study, which means in effect writing the history of each language-family and, as far as is possible, reconstructing the parent languages of each family;

(*b*) to look for those forces permanently and universally operative in all languages, and to deduce the general law to which may be attributed every individual phenomenon;

(*c*) itself to fix its boundaries and frame its definition.[4]

Each of these has been the concern of later linguists, although not all have received the same degree of attention from any one individual. Other aspects have been added, as we shall see; yet de Saussure's three goals, including the last, continue to be of the greatest importance.

6.3 Practical problems. However, development of linguistics has also been due to practical circumstances. The grammatical apparatus of Thrax was inadequate to analyse any language but Greek. Applied to other languages, either the descriptive framework was changed, or the analysis was imperfect, or both. In Latin grammar the framework was expanded to include an ablative case; in Bullokar's *Bref grammar for English* the author does not dare add to the classical eight parts of speech, and so the indefinite article *a* is treated merely as a 'marker'. Even in later grammars of English, we rarely find treatment of countable nouns and mass nouns,[5] or of the word-class 'particle', or of the tense system (thus *I shall scream* is a 'future tense' but *I'm going to scream* has no particular name). Nevertheless, the application of Greek grammar to Indo-European languages did not give rise to insuperable difficulties, since their structure was not wildly different from that of Greek. Adjustments were even made for Semitic languages by Arabic and Greek grammarians.

But difficulties became acute whenever traditional grammar was confronted with a language so different from Greek that no adjustment was possible. In Eskimo *takusariartorumagaluarnerpâ* 'do you think he really intends to go to look after it?' can be analysed into: *takusar* 'he looks after it'; *iartor* 'he goes to'; *uma* 'he intends to'; *galuar* 'he does so – but!'; *ner* 'you think he'; and (*p*)*â* 'the sign of a question'.[6] A Thrax-type grammar cannot handle such situations.

We assume that pre-twentieth-century investigators of exotic languages had met such difficulties, but had had to solve them as best they could individually. However, at the end of the nineteenth century a 'confrontation' took place between scholars trained in the philological tradition and indigenous languages of North America. These proved so intractable to traditional analysis that new methods had to be found. A milestone was reached in 1911 with the first part of the *Handbook of American Indian languages*;[7] this contained an introduction by Boas that amounts to a treatise on language in general and American languages in particular. In discussions of such topics as race and language, phonetics, grammatical categories, and language and thought, Boas formulates ideas that were developed by later American linguists; indeed his influence on linguistics in North America was as powerful as that of de Saussure in Europe.

One practical reason that encouraged development of language-study in Europe was the desire for improved teaching of foreign languages, especially pronunciation. In the twentieth century other stimuli have contributed to linguistics: interest in links between languages and cultures on the part of anthropologists, it being

40

impossible to understand the structure or workings of a society without a knowledge of its language; investigation of thought-processes and perception by philosophers and psychologists, and the links between these topics and language; work of communications engineers, not only on acoustics of spoken language, but on efficiency of language as a means of communication; activity of translators and of those whose ambition is the construction of translating-machines; and comparison of animal signalling-systems with human language.

6.4 The development of linguistics. We therefore date the beginning of linguistics from the first decade of the twentieth century. That de Saussure delivered his lectures and Boas wrote his introduction at virtually the same time illustrates a common phenomenon. An intellectual climate may predispose scholars independently to suggest the same solution to a problem, or to make distinct proposals that are later integrated as components of a new approach. (An example is the work of Wallace and Darwin on natural selection.)[8] It is remarkable that the first decade of the twentieth century saw three great pioneers of linguistics. The third was Vilém Mathesius who in February 1911 delivered in Prague a lecture the title of which is translated as 'On the potentiality of the phenomena of language'. We say something about this in Chapter 18. He not only seems in some respects to have anticipated de Saussure's principles but is more perceptive and subtle. Unfortunately since Mathesius gave the lecture in Czech it attracted less attention outside Czechoslovakia than it deserved. (We may compare Rask's overshadowing by Grimm for the same kind of reason.)

The years following saw work carried out in many countries on topics that proved to be of importance. Research and theorising has continued up to the present: the entire field is in a state of continual activity. In the following chapters we concentrate on developments in Great Britain and the U.S.A. that afford us a useful descriptive apparatus and form a convenient standpoint from which to view other approaches. A few of these are named in Chapter 18.

Some twenty years after these works of Boas, Mathesius and de Saussure, scholars had reached some sort of agreement on the shape of linguistics and the problems it should be tackling. Declarations of faith and intent were made in a series of international conferences, chief among which are the First International Congress of Linguists (The Hague 1928), the First International Congress of Slavicists (Prague 1929) and the (first) International Congress of Phonetic Sciences (Amsterdam 1932). In 1933 appeared Leonard Bloomfield's *Language*. This was epoch-making for two main reasons: it marshalled components that had been the subject of discussion and assembled them into one framework: and Bloomfield was sufficiently individual to encourage both dissent (always a good thing) and enthusiastic continuation of his lines of thought.

Noteworthy centres of linguistic research up to the present include Prague and Vienna (especially in the inter-war period), Copenhagen, London, Paris, Edinburgh (from the 1950s onwards) and institutions in the U.S.A. and the Soviet Union.

6.5 Linguistics as a 'scientific' study. During the twenty or so years in which the guide-lines laid down by Bloomfield were dominant in the United States, it became fashionable to define linguistics as 'the science of' or 'the scientific study of language' as though this were sufficient explanation; to be sure, Bloomfield refers to 'study in a scientific way, by careful and comprehensive observation'[9] but this does not take us very far and there was coyness in explaining why linguistics was a science or why a linguist should be called a scientist.

A clarification was made later by the distinguished English linguist, R.H. Robins,[10] who tells us that linguistics is scientific in that it '. . . deals with a specific body of material, namely spoken and written language, and that it proceeds by operations that can be publicly communicated and described, and justified by reference to statable principles and to a theory capable of formulation . . . In its operations and statements it is guided by three canons of science:

'1.   Exhaustiveness, the adequate treatment of all relevant material;
'2.   Consistency, the absence of contradiction between different parts of the total statement, and within the limits imposed by the two preceding principles;
'3.   Economy, whereby, other things being equal, a shorter statement or analysis employing fewer terms is to be preferred to one that is longer or more involved.'

Such characteristics are important in serious study. Nevertheless, whether or not they distinguish a 'science' is a matter of debate within the philosophy of science. Yet even so, these principles are thought-provoking for it is debatable whether we *can* know when two of these canons have been observed: exhaustiveness and economy. It may be contended that no study of language(s) is exhaustive and so progress is made by seeking more comprehensive theories; and it may not be possible to decide which of a set of descriptions is the more economical, for example a reduction in the number of technical terms may be achieved at the expense of greater length of statement.[11]

Robins further claims that linguistics '. . . is an empirical science, in that its subject matter is observable with the senses, speech as heard, the movements of the vocal organs as seen directly or with the aid of instruments, the sensations of speaking as perceived by speakers, and writing as seen and read'. The nature of empirical observation may again be discussed within the context of the philosophy of science: but even in Chapter 13 we shall see that developments pose the question whether empirical observation is all that the linguist admits as evidence.

The requirement that linguistics be justified by reference to a theory is of prime importance; there is interaction between general theory (the domain of *theoretical linguistics*) and description of individual languages (the domain of *descriptive linguistics*); neither is possible without the other and there is constant reappraisal of one in the light of the other. To take a hypothetical example, we may say that the sound-system of a language consists of five vowels and ten consonants: this piece of descriptive linguistics presupposes the theoretical statement that sound-systems of languages are describable in terms of vowels and consonants; but it may become apparent that in the description of another language we require a third category, which we then call 'bloodges', and so we change our theoretical statement to include a category of 'bloodges'; something comparable happened when Roman grammarians recognised an ablative case.

6.6 Some assumptions and recognised problems in linguistics. Linguists are in agreement that languages, wherever spoken and by whomever, are equally 'language', as are all styles, dialects and accents; there is no hierarchy of 'good' and 'less good'; all natural languages are within the linguist's scope and he does not tell speakers that they ought to give up saying one thing and say another: linguistics is not prescriptive.

The relationship of spoken language and written form has been the subject of differences of attitude among linguists. The spoken form is historically prior, as far as the language-community is concerned and as far as the individual is concerned. It is also more complicated. For these reasons, emphasis is placed on study of the sound-systems of languages and this has led some linguists to describe the spoken form as 'language' and the written form as 'written language'. We adopt the view that both are equally examples of language. The relationship is not a straightforward case of deriving the written from the spoken; moreover once a written form comes into being, it seems to live a life of its own and acquire or preserve usages different from the spoken – written French possesses a tense (the 'past definite') absent from the spoken, written Arabic diverges even more from the spoken form, and written and spoken Chinese are sometimes described as though they had nothing at all in common. The position is complicated in practice because many who claim to be discussing the spoken form give the impression of dealing with written language!

Linguists can observe only *parole*. If therefore we claim, as did de Saussure, that we are studying *langue* or system, then we are faced with the problem of how we *can* when we have no direct access to it; somehow or other the picture of the system is built up from knowledge of utterances.

The bulk of linguistic theorising in the first half of this century was in the domain of synchronic linguistics; but in recent years theoreticians' attention has happily been turned again to diachronic processes. It would seem, however, that any statement of language-change must presuppose a synchronic description of two 'états de langue', even such a simple statement as 'p > pf'; to that extent the synchronic study is prior.

There is an individual aspect of language; it is voluntary human behaviour, that is, a set of habits that may be exercised. But there is also a social aspect; normally we use language so that others see or hear the result – it is part of human interaction.

An utterance may be regarded as linear or unidimensional in time or space; it is a sequence of happenings (in spoken language) or of shapes. Such unidimensionality means that language conveys meaning in a way different from that of the two-dimensional map or the three-dimensional scale model; it also means that a sequence of one kind (for example, noises) may be converted into a sequence of another kind (for example, letter-shapes, Morse-code symbols, Braille) and even into a third (for example, flashed Morse, semaphore). Because of unidimensionality, utterances may be segmented into units (for example, words or noises) that recur. We shall find that such units may be regarded as falling into different classes (for example, vowels and consonants, or nouns and verbs) that can only be placed in certain sequences.

All human languages must be similar (otherwise a general theory could never apply); linguistics is therefore regarded by some as a 'search for universals of language'. On the other hand, all languages differ to some extent, otherwise individual descriptions would be unnecessary; each language is therefore unique. It is also the linguist's job to provide these descriptions.

Many, perhaps all, languages exist in different *styles* or *registers*,

44

as well as in various kinds of regional and even social variations. We cannot discuss these in this book, but the existence of this problem must be indicated: it is not at all clear what constitutes a natural language.

6.7 A three-pronged approach. Language is normally produced in order to convey meaning. We therefore distinguish two planes, that of the meaning (or content) and that of the form (or expression or substance) in which the meaning is carried, that is the sound of the voice, or the shape of the letters. The study of the meaning or content-plane is *semantics*.

The form of a spoken utterance may be studied as noises and as noise-patterns; this is the realm of *phonetics* and of *phonology*. (By the same token we can study the shapes and patterns of the letters of written language.) However, phonetics and phonology are not sufficient to account for all the patternings in a natural language: for example, *unnecessary be ungealding the would* is a sequence of English letters, and English sounds can be found to pronounce them, yet neither sequence, letters or sounds, would be acceptable as English. We therefore recognise a second level of patterning, that of grammar, which will study *which* sequences of letter-patterns and sound-patterns are possible. These two levels, phonetics and phonology on the one hand and grammar on the other, constitute the double articulation of language.[12] Thus linguistics is generally accepted as falling into three main areas: phonetics and phonology, grammar, and semantics, descriptions in each area being carried out in terms of some general theory. We examine now these areas in turn, beginning with phonetics.

FURTHER READING
Arens 1969, 1–34; Bloomfield 1933; Boas 1911, 1–83; Culler 1976; Dinneen 1965, chs 1, 3, 7, 8, 9; Ivić 1965, 37–185; Lyons 1968, chs 1, 2; Robins 1964, 1–75; Saussure 1916.

7. Phonetics

7.1 The scope of phonetics. The Graeco-Latin tradition had little interest in observing speech-sounds, so that clumsy descriptive terms survived to be used by Grimm (to the detriment of his work) and even later scholars. But an awakening interest in the sounds of speech is observable in England and in Scotland from the time of W. Bullokar for a variety of reasons – elocution (for social advancement or public speaking), spelling reform, the teaching of the deaf, and the design of shorthand systems. Huge progress was occasioned at the end of the eighteenth century by those who drew attention to the Sanskritic scholars of two thousand years before, for the latter included phoneticians of a sophistication surpassing anything achieved in the Western tradition.[1] In the nineteenth century, contributions to the study of speech were made by researchers in various fields: physiologists, investigators of sound-changes, physicists, neurologists, language pathologists and psychologists.[2] Four outstanding pioneers of phonetic theory of this period were A.J. Ellis (1814–90), Alexander Melville Bell (1819–1905), Henry Sweet (1845–1912) and Eduard Sievers (1850–1932). In 1886 an association of teachers of languages was founded, subsequently to become the International Phonetic Association; its moving spirit was Jespersen and other prominent members included Paul Passy (1859–1940) and later Daniel Jones (1881–1967). Thus phonetics was the first area of linguistics to attract general attention and indeed popularity, with emphasis on its use in language teaching.

Phonetics seeks to provide a descriptive terminology for the sounds of spoken language. Traditionally this has been achieved by classifying them in terms of their physiological production – the realm of articulatory phonetics. But phoneticians have other concerns: they use instrumental techniques for investigating the production of speech and the acoustic qualities of its sound (instrumental phonetics), they attempt the artificial production of speech (speech synthesis) and they explore the aesthetic qualities of spoken language, the relation between spoken and written language, and the extent to which speech reveals characteristics of its speaker.

A linguist must be able to use and to assess the principles and procedures of phonetics. Phonetics, Sweet proclaimed on many occasions, is the indispensable foundation of all study of language. Therefore a serious student must proceed to a textbook wholly devoted to this branch of linguistics[3] (and if possible find a good teacher).

Phoneticians require to record analyses in written form; we use the alphabet of the International Phonetic Association, which is that most widely employed. An explanation of its symbols used in this book is given on p.xi.

7.2 The production of speech-sounds. Human speech is produced by organs of speech. These fall into three groups (Figure 9). The first is the *lungs* and their associated muscles, the *bronchial tubes* and the *trachaea* (wind-pipe). The second is located at the opening of the trachaea into the throat (in men its situation is indicated by the Adam's apple): this is the *larynx*. Its important component may be visualised as a slit formed by two muscles, covered with mucous membrane, lying side by side: these are the *vocal folds* (or *vocal bands* or *vocal cords*), roughly 2.3 cm. long in men, and 1.7 cm. in women. The space between the vocal folds is known as the *glottis*. The third set, the *articulators*, consists of the various components of the mouth described below.

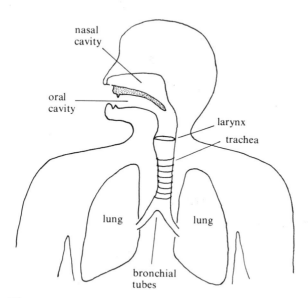

Figure 9

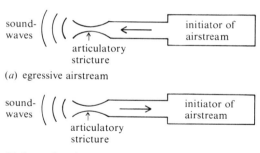

(*a*) egressive airstream

(*b*) ingressive airstream

Figure 10

All speech-sounds are produced according to the same principle: movements of articulators are made audible by a flow of air, either going in (*ingressive*) or out (*egressive*) (Figure 10). We consider first sounds made with air from the lungs, the *pulmonic egressive airstream*. In this case, two further factors contribute to the speech-sound: the *state of the glottis* and the *state of the velum*, terms that we now elucidate.

The vocal folds may occupy different postures relative to each other (Figure 11) and these states of the glottis impose different qualities of sound (*phonations*) on the airstream.

(*a*) *Open glottis* is the state in which the vocal folds are widely separated so that the passage of air through the glottis is as free as possible. *Voiceless* sounds are made with an open glottis; [s] of *sue* is an example.

(*b*) When the glottis is *in vibration*, it is rapidly opened and closed (a minimum of seventy times per second); *voiced* sounds are made with the glottis in vibration, e.g. [z] of *easy*. If you repeat [z] and [s] alternately, passing from one to the other without interruption, you will hear the voicing being 'switched on and off'.

(*c*) A third state is *closed glottis*; the vocal folds are brought together so that the pulmonic airstream is interrupted; such an interruption is a *glottal stop* [ʔ]. It may be heard in English: in Cockney ['tɒʔnəm] *Tottenham*, or Glaswegian ['waʔɪr] *water*.

(*d*) The glottis is in *whisper* position when the folds are fairly close together so that a hissing sound results when a pulmonic airstream passes through. If you whisper (in its popular sense) the word *zoo* and isolate the first sound, prolonging it, you

48

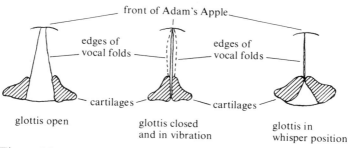

Figure 11

will be able to contrast this *whispered* sound with voiceless [s] and .voiced [z]. Whispered sounds occur in most accents of English, for example in the last sound of *dogs* when a pause follows.

(*e*) When the glottis is in position for *breathy voice*, it is not fully closed during vibrations; the result is a kind of murmured sighing, an effect often adopted by would-be 'sexy' ladies in films, though not by Miss Mae West.

(*f*) For *creaky voice* the folds operate in such a manner that as well as voice there is audible a low regular vibration or *creak*; creak has been compared to the noise of a stick being drawn along railings.

The pulmonic airstream leaving the larynx enters the *pharynx* (see Figure 12) and thence may enter either only the mouth or both the mouth and the *nasal cavity*; whether it does the first or the second depends on the *state of the velum*. The *velum* is the membranous part of the roof of the mouth, known also as the *soft palate*; this can be lifted and drawn back by muscles, in which case the entrance to the nasal cavity is blocked and an egressive airstream can only enter the mouth (Figure 12*a*), this being described as the *raised* state or *velic closure*; at other times the velum may hang down inertly (in its *lowered* state or *velic opening*) so that egressive air enters the nasal cavity as well as the mouth (Figure 12*b*). In breathing out normally, with the mouth closed, air can only escape through the nostrils; the velum is therefore lowered. If you pretend that you are going to pronounce [p] (the initial sound of *pig*) and try to do so, but do not open your lips, air can no longer escape through the nostrils but is building up pressure in the mouth; the velum has become raised. Speech-sounds are made with the velum either lowered or raised. If it is raised, oral sounds result, in which case air enters only the mouth, for example [s] as in *see*. If the velum is lowered, air enters

49

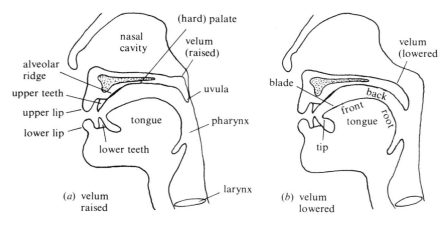

Figure 12

the nasal cavity as well; if then air escapes through both mouth and nostrils *nasalised* sounds are produced, for example French [œ̃], that is *un* 'one'; but if there is a closure in the mouth and air can escape only through the nostrils then a *nasal* is produced, for example [m] as in *me*.

Two articulatory factors contribute to the quality of speech-sounds: the articulators employed and the degree of narrowing or *stricture* between them. The location of the articulators may be found by referring to Figure 12 while prodding the inside of the mouth with tongue or finger or examining it by means of a mirror. We divide the roof of the mouth into four zones: the back is the soft palate or velum, as we have seen; the velum terminates in a blob of flesh, visible in a mirror, the *uvula*; towards the front of the mouth, the velum gives way to a rigid, bony surface, the *hard palate* or simply the *palate*; and at the front of the palate, just behind the upper front teeth, is a convex ridge, the *alveolar ridge*. If you say *Aah* the back wall of the pharynx will be visible in a mirror, beyond the uvula. The lips and the teeth are also reckoned among the articulators.

The *tongue* does not show any helpful visible features according to which we could segment it; we therefore divide it into zones mainly with reference to the roof of the mouth, assuming that the tongue is in a position of rest. The *tip* (or *point*) is that part touching the two middle upper teeth; the *blade* lies under the alveolar ridge, the *front* (N.B.!) under the palate and the *back* under the velum; the *root* faces the back wall of the pharynx.

50

7.3 The classification of speech-sounds: consonants. We pretend that the movements of the speech-organs are not continuous but a succession of discrete *postures*. This allows us to split up the flow of speech, or *speech-chain*, into a succession of speech-sounds that we classify.

An intermediate stage in such analysis is provided by the consideration of *syllables*. Most speakers of English will agree on the recognition of syllables in speech, for example *ran* consists of one syllable but *ransom* of two. We assume that the *segmentation* of syllables is possible, each *segment* being describable in terms of a posture of the vocal organs.[4] These segments may be divided into *vowels* and *consonants*. During the production of any one syllable, there will be a moment during which the vocal tract is narrowed least; this is the *nucleus* of the syllable, the 'bearer' of the syllable pulse, or a vowel, thus in the word *stumps*, the noise represented by *u* is the vowel. Syllables may be released and/or arrested by articulatory movements that impede the airflow to a greater extent; segments made by such movements are consonants, for example the sounds represented by *m*, *p*, *s* and *t* in *stumps*. A syllable with no arresting consonant, for example the word *high*, is an *open syllable*; one which does have an arresting consonant (or more than one), for example *hide* or *stumps*, is a *closed syllable*.

In the production of any consonant the crucial factors include airstream; states of glottis and velum; articulators and stricture between them. The most extreme degree of stricture is complete closure, which allows no air to escape through the mouth: the releasing and arresting consonants of *bait* are produced with such a stricture; so also is the initial consonant of *mate*, although here air escapes through the nostrils by way of lowered velum. A lesser degree of narrowing is involved in the initial consonant of *fate*: the articulators allow air to pass between them, but are so close together that audible friction or 'hissing' occurs; this is the stricture of *close approximation*. A still lesser degree of narrowing is responsible for the releasing and arresting consonants of *wail*; here no friction is caused but a distinctive quality is imparted to the voicing; this stricture is *open approximation*. (The difference between open approximation and close is adjudged according to the *auditory* impression.)

Two types of stricture are not strictly speaking postures but involve movements of the articulators. The first is *intermittent closure*: complete closure alternates very rapidly with opening. Examples of consonants produced with intermittent closure are the rolled *r* of stage 'Scotsmen' of a byegone age and the gargling noise with which some French cabaret singers pronounce a French *r*.

Another is made by a *ballistic* movement, that is, a muscular movement of an articulator (usually tongue-tip) that meets no resisting second articulator; examples are the *tap* and *flap* described below.

The information we possess about the articulation of any consonant may be summed up in a three-term label whose parts specify (*a*) state of the glottis; (*b*) articulators involved, that is place of articulation; (*c*) manner of articulation.

The state of the glottis is described as *voiced, voiceless, whispered, breathy-voiced* or *creaky-voiced* as necessary.

The place of articulation is indicated by an adjective in most cases derived from the Latin name of one of the articulators:

ADJECTIVE	ARTICULATORS INVOLVED
bilabial:	both lips, e.g. the initial sound of *bait*;
labiodental:	lower lip and upper teeth, e.g. the initial sound of *fate*;
dental:	tip or blade of tongue and back of upper teeth, e.g. the initial sound of *those*;
alveolar:	tip or blade of tongue and alveolar ridge, e.g. the initial sounds of *toe, so* and *low* in many accents of English;
post-alveolar:	tip of tongue and border of alveolar ridge and palate, e.g. the initial sounds of *try*;
palatal:	front of tongue and palate, e.g. the initial sound of *yes*;
retroflex:	tip of tongue (curled back so that it points almost vertically) and palate, e.g. the English West Country and some American pronunciations of *-er* in *butter*;
velar:	back of tongue and velum, e.g. the initial sound of *cat*;
uvular:	back of tongue and uvula, e.g. the common pronunciation of French *r* as in *rouge* or *quatre*;
pharyngal:	root of the tongue and pharynx; such sounds produced with strictures of close or open approximation, are found in certain Semitic languages, e.g. Arabic.

The *manner of articulation* is indicated by the third term, which specifies the degree of stricture and also, on occasion, other information. A list of these follows.

A *stop* is made with a stricture of complete closure and with velic closure. A stop released by a pulmonic egressive airstream is a *plosive*: the voiced bilabial plosive [b] in *be*.

A *nasal* is made with a stricture of complete closure and with velic opening; for every plosive there is a corresponding nasal: to [b] corresponds the voiced bilabial nasal [m].

A *trill* or *roll* is made with intermittent closure alternating with open approximation, for example the above mentioned noises of stage 'Scotsmen' (voiced alveolar trill [r]) and French cabaret singers (voiced uvular trill [ʀ]).

A *fricative* is made with close approximation: the voiceless labiodental fricative [f] in *fee*.

An *approximant* is made with open approximation: the voiced palatal approximant [j] in *you*.

A *lateral* is made with central closure but lateral open approximation; if the tongue is involved, part of the central lengthwise portion of its surface makes complete closure with the roof of the mouth, and one side of the tongue is lowered (or both sides may be) to form a stricture of open approximation, allowing the airstream to escape laterally without audible friction; such a sound is the voiced alveolar lateral [l] in *laugh*. Proof of its lateral articulation is the sensation of cold air at the side of the mouth if one tries to produce [l] with a pulmonic ingressive airstream. Such sounds might be less economically described as *approximant-laterals*.

It is possible to lower the side(s) of the tongue to form close approximation, so that the airstream escapes with audible friction; such a sound is a *fricative-lateral*, for example the voiceless alveolar fricative-lateral [ɬ] in Welsh *llan* [ɬan], 'church'. This may be learned by producing a long [l] and trying to substitute voicelessness for voice, on the analogy of [zzzsss]. The resulting increase in flow of breath should ensure friction.

The trills above are alternations of complete closure and open approximation; however, it is possible to alternate between complete closure and close approximation, thus producing a *fricative-trill*. The auditory effect is of a simultaneous fricative and trill. A pair of alveolar fricative-trills occur in accents of Czech, both represented in spelling by *ř*, for example voiced [ɼ] in the name Dvořák, voiceless [ɼ̥] in *před* 'in front of'.

A *tap* is a ballistic movement, equivalent to 'one strike of a trill'; for example, a voiced alveolar tap [ɾ] is made by flicking the tongue at the alveolar ridge, forming momentary complete closure. It may be heard in some accents of English as a pronunciation of *r*, such as in many Scottish accents and in South African English (as in *brown*) and in accents of American English, as a pronunciation of *t* in *getting*.

53

A more ambitious ballistic movement is responsible for a *flap*. A voiced retroflex flap is made by placing the tongue in position for a retroflex approximant, then 'flapping' the tongue on to the floor of the mouth so that it strikes the alveolar ridge in passing. This sound occurs in Northern Indian languages and in dialects of Norwegian.

Certain consonants are not produced with a pulmonic airstream, but with a *glottalic* or a *velaric*. In the case of the glottalic airstream, the vocal folds are brought together and the entire larynx moves upwards or downwards, like the piston of a bicycle pump. If there is a stricture, for instance of complete closure, the air trapped in the mouth and pharynx is either rarefied or compressed; if then this stricture is released, the pressure is equalised with a 'popping' sound. When the larynx is raised the trapped air is compressed, and if released, escapes as an egressive airstream; sounds made with such a glottalic egressive airstream are *ejective*. *Ejective stops*, or *ejectives*, occur sporadically in accents of individual speakers of English or French as 'varieties' of *p*, *t* and *k*. In many languages ejectives are used as normal speech sounds and may contrast with voiced and voiceless plosives, for example Amharic [t'ɨwat] 'morning'. But if the larynx is lowered, the trapped air is rarefied so that when the stricture is released, an ingressive airstream results; noises made in this way are *implosive*. Such *implosive stops*, or *implosives*, are used in some Central American languages, for example Tojolabal.

In the *velaric* airstream mechanism, the back of the tongue makes a complete closure against the velum while a second closure is made further forward, for example by the lips; the air thus trapped is rarefied by a backward and downward movement of the tongue; if the forward closure is released, an ingressive airstream and a popping noise result. Such sounds are *clicks*. In English clicks are used as interjections, for example a bilabial click (a 'kissing' noise) to attract the attention of domestic animals, an alveolar click ('tut-tut') to express dismay and a lateral click ('gee-up') (alveolar central closure with lateral release) to encourage horses or express enthusiasm. As language sounds, clicks occur in Bushman, Hottentot and some southern Bantu languages, such as Zulu and Xhosa.

The production of certain consonants is due to two airstreams. For example, the vocal folds can be in vibration (with a pulmonic egressive airstream) and at the same time the larynx may be pulled downwards so that a glottalic ingressive airstream also occurs; the amount of air from the lungs is not sufficient to counteract the rarefaction. Noises made in this way are *voiced implosives* and are commoner than the (voiceless) implosives described above, being

54

used in many African and American Indian languages in contrast with plosives: in Noho (Cameroons) [mɓoa] 'prisoner' but [mboa] 'horse'. Similarly, the vocal folds may be in vibration during the production of a click, either with raised velum, giving a *voiced click*, or with lowered velum, giving a *nasalised click*. These are used as distinct speech-sounds in certain languages that possess simple clicks.

7.4 Vowels. Vowels are produced by using the mouth as a resonating chamber; alterations in its shape affect the sound produced when, for instance, the vocal folds are in vibration. The oral cavity may assume an infinity of shapes and therefore an infinity of vowel-qualities can be made. The problem is how to classify this infinity of vowel-qualities. The usual solution is in terms of mouth-shape. We assume that three variables affect the shape of the cavity, namely the posture of the lips and the position and shape of the tongue. The next step is to assume that the tongue is always humped or convex, and that if the position of the hump or highest point is specified, then the shape and position of the rest of the tongue can be taken for granted. Two axes are sufficient to plot the position of this highest point: a vertical and a horizontal. On the vertical axis, the highest point may be nearer the roof of the mouth (as in the *close* or *high* vowel of *see*) or nearer the floor (as in the *open* or *low* vowel of *balm*). On the horizontal axis, the highest point may be nearer the front of the mouth (as in the *front* vowel of *red*) or nearer the back (as in the *back* vowel of *bud*). As for the lips, they may be relatively rounded (as in the *rounded* vowel of *pool*) or relatively unrounded (as in the *unrounded* or *spread* vowel of *leave*). These three – the shape of the lips and the two axes of the highest point of the tongue – are used to produce a three-term label system for classifying mouth-shapes and hence vowel-qualities.

The number of points on each axis is infinite, but the following arbitrary conventional positions are distinguished:

(*a*) *lips*:	(i)	*rounded* as in *goose*;
	(ii)	*unrounded* as in *geese*.
(*b*) *vertical axis*:	(i)	*close* as in *goose*, *geese*;
	(ii)	*half-close* as in most Scots English *ray* and *rope*, French *été* and *chaud*, German *Schnee* and *rot*;
	(iii)	*half-open* as in *get*, *thought*;
	(iv)	*open* as in *halve*, *crass*.
(*c*) *horizontal axis*:	(i)	*front* as in *see*, *get*, *crass* and Scots English *ray*;

(ii)   *central* as in RP[5] *learn*, Scots *gude*;
(iii) *back* as in *pool*, *bud*, RP *halve*, Scots
       English *rope*.

These positions may be used as components of descriptive labels: for example, *see* contains an unrounded close front vowel, *get* an unrounded half-open front vowel, RP *learn* an unrounded half-open central vowel, *but* an unrounded half-open back vowel. This system can specify twenty-four vowel qualities and is useful for many purposes. Yet it is somewhat Procrustean and is inadequate to furnish as meticulous a description as may be necessary.

A more precise instrument is Daniel Jones's system of *cardinal vowels*, that is a series of eight vowels used as reference points. Jones chose these by establishing the closest front vowel it is possible to make, namely [i] (were it any further forward, it would become a voiced palatal fricative), and the lowest possible back vowel, namely [ɑ] (were it any lower it would become a voiced pharyngal fricative). Between these two points Jones chose three vowels [e], [ɛ] and [a] such that the steps between all five were *auditorily equidistant* in his estimation. Moreover, these vowels were peripheral: a vowel area may be traced out by the possible positions of the highest point of the tongue – for the tongue to go outside this area either results in close approximation or is a physical impossibility; *peripheral* vowels are on the edges of this area. Jones then added three vowels [ɔ], [o], [u] of increasingly close quality on the back edge of the periphery, which continued (he claimed) the series of auditorily equidistant steps. These last three are rounded while the first five were unrounded. The eight together form the *primary* cardinal vowels.

Another eight, the *secondary* cardinal vowels, were established by retaining the tongue position of the primary cardinal vowels but with the alternative selection of lip posture; thus to the five unrounded vowels [i], [e], [ɛ], [a] and [ɑ], correspond the rounded vowels [y], [ø], [œ], [ɶ] and [ɒ]; while to the three back rounded vowels [ɔ], [o] and [u], correspond the unrounded [ʌ], [ɤ] and [ɯ].

These sixteen vowels were assigned to positions on a *vowel diagram* derived from a stylisation of the shape of an individual's vowel area (charted from X-ray photographs). The relationship of these shapes, and the positions of the cardinal vowels, are shown in Figures 13*a*, *b*, and *c*.

Another six cardinal vowels, three pairs of unrounded and rounded, have been proposed for the central area; we cite the unrounded member of each pair first (see Figure 13*d*).

The sixteen primary and secondary cardinal vowels must be

56

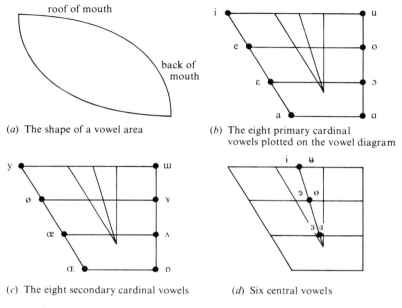

(a) The shape of a vowel area

(b) The eight primary cardinal vowels plotted on the vowel diagram

(c) The eight secondary cardinal vowels

(d) Six central vowels

Figure 13

learned by the phonetician who wishes to use this system and he must learn from a competent teacher to recognise and to produce them; it is impossible to do so from a book, or from records, since it is vital that the lips be observed. The tongue position only is plotted on the chart and it is possible to be seriously misled about this in the absence of the visible clue of lip-posture.

If a vowel sound from a natural language is to be described, it is plotted on the diagram relative to cardinal qualities: for example, if it is similar in quality to a cardinal vowel, but is closer and further back, it will appear upwards and to the right of the cardinal position. The vowels of *fit* and *feet* as pronounced by the writer appear in Figure 14. Part of the training of the phonetician consists in learning to compare vowel sounds in terms of their positions on the axes described and to plot them on a diagram. The technique works fairly successfully in practice and no suggested improvement has been generally adopted.[6] Each cardinal vowel symbol may be regarded as possessing a 'domain' and may be used to transcribe any vowel that falls within that domain. Diacritics may be added, for example [e̞] indicates a vowel closer than Cardinal 3. If two or more vowel qualities have to be distinguished within a domain, then

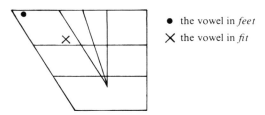

● the vowel in *feet*
✗ the vowel in *fit*

Figure 14

recourse may be had to a set of 'float' symbols that themselves have no cardinal definition: for example, [ɪ] may be used for any unrounded frontish, closish vowel.

The vowels of natural languages may be divided into *monoph-thongs* (in which the posture of the tongue and lips is assumed to be static) and *diphthongs* (in which the posture of either or both is continuously changing); both occupy the nucleus of a syllable. On the vowel chart, diphthongs may be represented by a line indicating the path of the highest point between the beginning of the segment and the end. In transcription we indicate them by two symbols, namely, those appropriate for the posture at the beginning of the movement and at the end. (This notational practice, and the fact that the orthographies of many languages employ a similar device, does not imply either that a diphthong is a *succession* of sounds or that a diphthong necessarily occupies a greater duration of time than a monophthong.) An example appears in Figure 15.

During the production of a diphthong, the posture of the lips may be static (spread as in [aɪ] of *tie* or rounded, as in [ɔY] of German *scheu*) or it may change (becoming rounded as in [ay] in some pronunciations of Dutch *huis* or unrounded as in RP [ɔɪ] of *boy*).

We have assumed that vowels are produced with the vocal folds in vibration. But voiceless vowels occur in English, for example between voiceless plosives preceding the stress as in RP *potato* [pə̥'teɪtʒɑ]; in French they may be heard in pre-pausal position as varieties of [i], [y] and [u]: *c'est tout* [sɛ 'tṳ]. A common sequence in English is a syllable-initial voiceless vowel followed by a voiced vowel that forms the nucleus of the syllable: *heed, head* and *hood* (respectively [i̥id], [ɛ̥ɛd] and [ṳud]). And breathy-voiced and creaky-voiced vowels are found, for instance in Hindi and Thai, respectively.

Vowel and consonant were defined above in terms of their function within a syllable. This is not completely satisfactory, since we classified [l] as a consonant yet it can function as the bearer of a syllable-pulse in *bottle*, as can [r] in Serbo-Croat *krv* [krf] 'blood'.

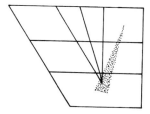

The diphthong [aɒ] in an
RP pronunciation of *house*

Figure 15

Conversely [w] and [j] function as releasing consonants in *wet* and *yet*, but in articulatory position resemble the vowels of RP *full* and *pit*. Moreover, the initial segment of such words as *heed* and *hood* have been described above as voiceless vowels, yet they function as releasing consonants of syllables. This situation has given rise to the term *semi-vowel* for such segments as [w] and [j].

The situation can be clarified by drawing on a distinction made by K.L. Pike.[7] *Vocoids* are defined as all central (i.e. not lateral), resonant (i.e. without audible friction) oral segments, such as [w], [j], [ɛ], [ʌ], etc. and *contoids* as all others, such as [l], [b], [ʃ], etc. A segment of each class may then be further classified as *syllabic* or *non-syllabic*, thus giving a fourfold distinction between syllabic vocoids, as in *yell*; syllabic contoids *sh!*, *little*, *krv*, etc.; non-syllabic vocoids, as in *yell*; and non-syllabic contoids, as in *little*, *dog*, *krv*, etc. Unfortunately the traditional terminology of 'vowel' and 'consonant' is so entrenched that often the terms 'vocoid' and 'contoid' are used only where ambiguity might result.

7.5 Greater precision in segmental description. It is necessary of course to combine in further ways the above categories. Phoneticians have recognised for example, voiced labiodental plosives (in some pronunciations of *obvious*), *linguolabial* stops (in Lutoxo, spoken in Sudan), flaps made by drawing the lower lip past the upper teeth (in Margi, a Chad language), voiceless nasals (in Burmese and Icelandic), voiceless alveolar trills (in Welsh), voiced velar laterals (in some American and London accents), bilabial laterals (in some accents of Irish), voiced alveolar fricative-laterals (in Zulu) and a whole range of approximants, corresponding to every possible fricative.[8]

Yet to describe the sounds of even one language requires still more detail. Certain places of articulation are extensive areas and strictures may be made towards the front of them or towards the back: contrast the fronted or *advanced* velar plosive of *key* [k̟i], the *retracted* velar plosive of *caw* [k̠ɔ], and the intermediate or 'neutral'

 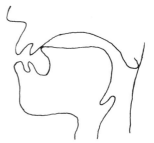

(*a*) posture of tongue in
articulation of palatalised
alveolar lateral

(*b*) posture of tongue in
articulation of velarised
alveolar lateral

Figure 16

velar plosive of *cool* [kul]. It may be necessary to distinguish *apical* articulation, involving the tip of the tongue (e.g. the common *apico-alveolar* pronunciation of English *t*) from *laminal*, involving the blade (e.g. the common *lamino-dental* pronunciation of French *t*). Or lateral tongue-shape may be important: for [θ] and [ð] (dental *flat* fricatives) the surface of the front of the tongue is flat while for most English [s] and [z] (alveolar *grooved* fricatives) it is grooved; however, some English speakers pronounce all four as dental fricatives, the former pair flat and the latter grooved.

In some sounds there is not only a significant primary narrowing of the vocal tract but a second narrowing elsewhere (usually of open approximation), termed a *secondary articulation*. Various types are recognised.

labialisation is open approximation between upper and lower lips, not necessarily with rounding and protrusion; *lip-rounding* definitely implies the latter.[9] In some English accents [ʃ] and [ɹ] are always *lip-rounded*: *sheep* [ʃip] and *reap* [ɹip].

palatalisation is open approximation between the front of the tongue and the hard palate (see Figure 16*a*). In some English accents a voiced alveolar lateral is *palatalised* syllable-initially: *laugh* [l̡ɑf]; in some Irish English accents this is the only pronunciation of *l*. The English fricatives [ʃ] and [ʒ] are often produced with a primary post-alveolar stricture and a secondary palatal one and hence are classified as *palato-alveolar*. This palatalisation may be the only difference between [ʃ] and [ɹ]: *cheat* [tʃit] and *treat* [tɹ̥it].

velarisation is open approximation between the back of the tongue and the velum (see Figure 16*b*). Russian uses a *velarised* voiced alveolar lateral as in [dɑɫ] 'gave'.

pharyngalisation is the retraction of the root of the tongue to make open approximation with the back wall of the pharynx.[10] RP uses a *pharyngalised* voiced alveolar lateral syllable-finally as in *eel* [iɫ]; some Scots and American accents use this as the only pronunciation of *l*.

Other secondary articulations include: *alveolarisation*, as in the *alveolo-palatal* (with primary palatal and secondary alveolar articulations) fricatives [ɕ] and [z] of Polish and Pekingese Chinese – try them by making [ç] (as in *hue*) and [s] or [z] simultaneously; *labiodentalisation* as in some Gaelic [ɫ] and some 'defective' [ɹ] in English; and *lateralisation*, a contraction of the tongue producing lateral open approximation, as in the voiced lateralised alveolar taps and retroflex flaps of some Japanese accents and Gujerati, respectively.

Double articulation occurs when two simultaneous strictures have the same degree of narrowing: for example: the voiced *labial-velar* plosive [g͡b] in the name of the language Igbo, the simultaneous glottal stops and oral plosives of Cockney, as in ['kɒʔpə] *copper*, and the rounded labial-velar approximant [w] in *we*.

We may include here *nasalisation*, in which velic opening allows air to escape through both nose and mouth. *Nasalised* voiced vowels are heard in, for instance, French and Scots Gaelic, nasalised breathy-voiced vowels in Hindi and nasalised whispered ones in Chatino (Mexico). Nasalised voiced labial-velar approximants, alveolar laterals, velar fricatives and retroflex flaps are heard in Scots Gaelic, some Edinburgh accents of English, Japanese and Gujerati respectively.

Some vowels are produced with the tongue tip curled back into a retroflex position: such *retroflected* or *r-coloured* vowels are found in Pekingese Chinese and some American accents (e.g. in *err*). The quality of some vowels may be due to a *sulcalised* position of the tongue, that is, there is a longitudinal central groove; the vowel in North Welsh *du* [di] 'black' may be an example. It is possible to bunch up the tongue lengthwise (pulling the root forwards) so that the vocal tract, especially the pharynx, is enlarged: vowels produced with this enlargement are termed *wide* and may contrast, for example in Twi, with *narrow* vowels in which there is no pulling-forward of the tongue-root.[11]

Some plosives may have to be described by specifying how the closures are made or are released, thus:

affricated plosive: the articulators open so slowly that brief friction is heard: Cockney *a cup of tea* [ə 'kˣʌp əv 'tˢi];

aspirated plosive: after a voiceless plosive a puff of voiceless vowel is heard before the glottis vibrates: RP *tar* [tʰɑ];

unaspirated plosive: the release of the articulators coincides with the onset of voicing: some Scots English *tar* [ṯar];
preaspirated plosive: a puff of voiceless vowel precedes the voiceless plosive, *aspiration* and *preaspiration* are heard in most Scots Gaelic *cat* [kʰaʰtʰ] 'cat';
unexploded stop: the plosive is not released by a vowel but is replaced by a second closure elsewhere in the vocal tract: the [k˺] in R P *act* [ak˺tʰ], cf. French *acte* [akʰtʰ] 'act';
laterally exploded stop: the plosive is released by lowering the side(s) of the tongue: most English *bottle* ['bɒtˡl], (however some speakers have ['bɒtəl]);
nasally exploded stop: the oral closure is retained and the velum lowered, resulting in a nasal: frequent English *open* ['əʊpᴺm], (however some speakers have ['əʊpən]);
prenasalised stop: the central closure occurs with initial temporary velic lowering, resulting in a nasal too brief to be reckoned an independent segment: Tiv [áⁿdèrà] 'he began'.[12]

A final point is that in some languages long segments may have to be distinguished from relatively short ones: Scots English *brood* [brud] and *brewed* [bruːd], Hungarian *hal* [hɒl] 'fish' and *hall* [hɒlː] 'hears'.

7.6 Dynamic features. Some features cannot be assigned to one place in a sequence of segments: these are *dynamic* (or *suprasegmental* or *prosodic*) features and include voice quality, stress, rhythm and speech melody.

Voice quality is due to the shape of a speaker's anatomy and also to factors that he can control. One such is the volume of noise, for speech-communities differ about what is 'normal' loudness in speaking. Another factor is that the larynx can be displaced relatively upwards or downwards during speech: an upwards displaced larynx gives the voice a measure of 'stridency' (as in some German speakers), a downwards displaced one a 'relaxed' quality (typical of some R P speakers). A further important contribution is made by the articulatory setting used.[13] This refers to such matters as whether the jaws open more or less widely, whether lip-rounding is vigorous or weak, whether the cheeks are relaxed or tense, and whether the tongue is typically anchored to the roof or the floor of the mouth. A particular articulatory setting tends to be a community feature, so that differences of setting account in great measure for the variety of auditory impression made by different languages and also for the typical facial expressions which characterise their speakers (contrast the overall sounds of French and R P and the stereotyped French and English 'faces'). A particular case is the presence of a permanent secondary articulation, for example the velarisation and pharyngalisation typical of some Liverpool English. The type of phonation employed also contributes to the voice quality. In R P, creak as well as voice may be used if the pitch falls below a certain level (e.g. at the end of sentences) and breathy voice may be employed when certain speakers wish to convey intimacy or encouragement.

Although there is no universal agreement among phoneticians on what constitutes a syllable,[14] speakers of the same language generally agree on how many syllables to recognise in a given stretch of speech. Certain syllables moreover are *stressed*, such as the first syllable of *'ransom*. Unfortunately the nature of *stress* is also in dispute[15] yet it too is recognised by speakers. In English, stressed syllables occur at more or less regular intervals of time, *isochronously*, as may be demonstrated by tapping audibly whenever a syllable is stressed, for example in the pronunciation of *A 'funny thing 'happened to me on the 'way to the 'theatre*: such isochronicity of stress characterises a stress-timed language. Obviously the relative length of syllables varies, depending in part on the number between stresses. But in certain other languages such as French and Italian *syllables* occur at isochronous intervals and are of the same relative length: in such syllable-timed languages stresses occur irregularly, either as properties of words (as in Italian) or of 'sense-groups' (as in French). Sometimes when we expect a stressed syllable the articulators remain closed and a pause or *silent stress* results, for example at the ends of lines of verse: *There 'was an old 'man of Nan'tucket ∧ Who 'hid all his 'cash in a 'bucket*. Silent stresses in English enter into the same isochronous pattern as audible stressed syllables.[16] Audible stress may be used to convey distinctions of meaning: *im'port* (verb) and *'import* (noun), Italian *principi* ['print∫ipi] 'princes' and *principi* [prin't∫ipi] 'principles'. Silent stresses may distinguish such constructions as *The four ladies ∧ who were wearing trousers ∧ were not introduced to the Archbishop* from *The four ladies who were wearing trousers ∧ were not introduced to the Archbishop*; the former, a *non-restrictive relative*, means here '. . . who incidentally were . . .' and the latter, a *restrictive relative*, means '. . . and only the four who were . . .'. Even the relative length of syllables may carry meaning, as in the R P examples *Take Grey to London* and *Take Greater London*; the segmental analyses are identical, ['teɪk-'greɪ-tə-'lʌndən], but the rhythms are different.[17]

The glottis may vibrate relatively more quickly or slowly, resulting respectively in a higher or lower pitch of the voice. During speech, the speed of glottal vibration fluctuates continually, with corresponding continual variation of pitch; the pitch-variation is not random but occurs in a language according to a system – such organised pitch-variation is *speech-melody*.[18] Some languages distinguish words by means of pitch-variation, for example Pekingese Chinese [bā] ('high level') 'eight' but [bǎ] ('low fall-rise') 'to hold' and Urhobo (spoken in Nigeria) [ācicā] ('high-low-high') 'chewing-gum' but [acica] ('low-low-low') 'umbrella';[19] languages of this type are tone-languages. In others, such as English, 'tunes' are distributed, as it were, over sentences; such languages are sentence-intonation languages. Speech-melody can function in some of these to indicate different sentence-types: *You're not going* (a statement, with a falling tune on any one of the words) but *You're not going?* (a question with a rising tune). Some tone-languages (e.g. Chinese and many West African languages) show a certain amount of sentence-intonation as well; other languages, such as Norwegian, make only a limited use of speech-melody to distinguish words.

Native speakers of a language may be very conscious of dynamic features, using them to interpret the speaker's attitude, provenance or status. But the phonetic investigation of them has lagged behind that of segmental postures: among other things, a satisfactory examination of them demands the solution of difficult technical problems in instrumental phonetics. The temptation to pretend that these features do not exist faces those who concentrate mainly on written language; some temptations should not be resisted, but this one ought to be fought, fiercely.

7.7 Instrumental phonetics. The categories of articulatory phonetics have been established principally by direct visual observation and by *kinaesthesis*, that is, the observer's awareness of the muscular effort involved in his own articulation. Human speaking is also investigated by laboratory techniques. These form part of the province of *instrumental phonetics* (or *experimental phonetics*).

Ciné-photography (particularly in slow-motion) with a synchronised sound-track is of value in investigating those organs of speech which are directly visible. Still X-ray photographs can reveal the postures of articulators and ciné X-ray films would provide invaluable information about the changing shape of the vocal tract and the co-ordination of movements – phenomena which are normally hidden. But the intensity of radiation has prevented the making of such X-ray films on any extensive scale. Now, however, the use of a television camera equipped with a device to intensify weak images has made it possible to X-ray as much as two minutes of continuous speech and record it on videotape rather than film.[20] The amount of information derived from analysing this is huge.

Another method of observing that which is normally hidden is to

64

look at the larynx by means of a *laryngoscope*, essentially a mirror placed at the back of the mouth; unfortunately this interferes with normal speech. But by passing a *fibre-optic bundle* (a pliable assemblage of glass fibres that can transmit light round curves) into the nose and through the nasal cavity so that the end can look down into the pharynx, it is possible to photograph the movements of the vocal folds, allowing the subject virtually complete freedom of phonation and articulation.[21]

Information about the tongue muscles, lip muscles, or the muscles associated with the lungs may be gained from *electromyography*, a technique of placing electrodes on or into muscles so that as muscular electrical energy is generated in speaking, the particular muscles involved may be identified.[22]

The contact made by the tongue against the roof of the mouth may be investigated by *palatography*. A false palate (like a dental plate without teeth) can be sprayed with powder, inserted into the mouth and, when the subject has made an articulation, removed again. The 'wipe-off', where the tongue has removed powder, shows the place and extent of articulation. Or the subject's own palate may be sprayed directly and the 'wipe-off' photographed by means of a mirror; this not only permits a much more natural articulation but enables velar articulations to be examined. Articulatory movements on the roof of the mouth may be observed by means of *dynamic palatography*. In this technique the subject has a false palate into which are set a series of electrodes; these are sensitive to tongue contact and, by means of a wire from the subject's mouth, display tongue movements as lights on a screen.[23]

Another type of investigation, using mouth-pieces and nose-pieces, notes changes in pressure and in direction of air from mouth and nostrils. A third record, derived from a throat microphone, can be added to show larynx activity. An early device in which such information is conveyed and traced pneumatically and mechanically is a *kymograph*. Much more sophisticated versions have been developed in which the information is processed electronically (sometimes with the aid of a computer). These instruments permit the observation of aspiration, onset and cessation of voice, and nasalisation, as well as the measurement of the relative duration of these phenomena and of certain individual segments.[24]

There is a further area of instrumental phonetics concerned not with speaking but with sound, that is with acoustic phenomena rather than articulatory. Sound is due to a sequence of regular and irregular variations in air pressure, picked up by the ear-drum and 'heard' by the brain. These variations may also be picked up by a microphone and made visible, for example as a wavy line on an oscilloscope screen. The number of complete repetitions of air pressure variations in one second is the *frequency* of the sound in question. Frequencies are interpreted by the listener in terms of pitch, that is whether a sound seems relatively higher or lower than its neighbours. Intonation patterns consist in changes in the pitch of the voice. Pitch-meters can display intonation patterns (e.g. as wavy lines) since they measure changing frequencies.

Differences in the quality of individual sounds are due to different frequencies being present simultaneously, for example vowels contain a fundamental frequency (heard as the pitch at which the vowel is spoken) and three or more higher bands of pitches or *vowel-formants*. A recurring individual vowel sound is characterised by the same set of formants regardless of different fundamental pitches.

The *sound spectrograph* interprets speech by giving a visual account of component frequencies; this is a *spectrogram*, a two-dimensional picture in which the vertical axis represents the frequency and the horizontal axis represents time. The relative *intensity* (the acoustic measurement of loudness) attributed to each frequency shows up as relative darkness, so that each spectrogram consists of patches of greys and blacks. Vowel formants, for instance, appear as horizontal bands. The trained observer can recognise the distinctive shapes of classes of sounds, not only of vowels but of stops, fricatives and laterals, amongst others. However, the acoustic structures of consonants are more complex than those of vowels, for example all voiceless stops look alike during the period of closure (since this is actually silence) and the different qualities audible show up as differences in the formants of adjacent vowels.[25] It is conceivable that some classificatory system for vowels, more precise than the Cardinal Vowel system, can be evolved from plotting relative positions of vowel formants.

Instrumental phonetics underlines not only the complexity of speech-production but the subtlety of the human brain in interpreting a constantly changing flow of acoustic data as recognisable speech-sounds. In particular the correlation between acoustic quality, auditory perception and articulatory position is revealed as by no means straightforward and presents an area of research of interest to phoneticians, psychologists and even philosophers.

A Note on Terminology. The technical terms used in this chapter are those used in the *Principles of the International Phonetic Association* – with the exception of 'approximant' (suggested originally by Peter Ladefoged) for which the *IPA* uses *frictionless continuant* and *semivowel* and 'tap', which the *IPA* does not distinguish from 'flap'. But the student may encounter other terms in phonetic and philological writings:

> *breathed* (/brɛθt/): voiceless;
> *cacuminal*: retroflex;
> *dorsal*: ambiguous, either 'laminal' or 'made with back of tongue';
> *glottalised*: in American writings frequently 'ejective', in British usage usually 'with simultaneous glottal closure';
> *guttural*: covers velar, uvular, pharyngeal and glottal;
> *lingual*: often refers to sounds made with alveolar strictures;
> *liquids*: covers alveolar trill and lateral;
> *occlusives*: stop consonants, usually plosives;
> *resonants*: often covers laterals, nasals, approximants;
> *sibilants*: usually means [s], [z], sometimes also [ʃ] and [ʒ];
> *sonants*: voiced sounds;
> *spirants*: fricatives;
> *surds*: voiceless sounds.

We dispense with two pairs of terms in fairly frequent use: *lax* and *tense*, and *lenis* and *fortis*. 'Lax' and 'tense' refer to the relative muscular tension during articulation; whether this difference actually exists or not is in some doubt. 'Lenis' and 'fortis' refer to the relative force of articulation, but this seems to be attributable always to the presence or absence of aspiration.

FURTHER READING
Abercrombie 1967; Catford 1977; Henderson 1971; Ladefoged 1975; Lass 1976; O'Connor 1973; Malmberg 1963, 1968; Pike 1943; Wang 1974.

8. Phonology

8.1 Phonology and phonemic analysis. General phonetics classifies the speech-sounds of all languages; but any one language uses only a selection of the possibilities available: the study of this selection of sounds and how they are used is the *phonology* of the language in question. Various types of phonological statement exist that process the same phonetic data in different ways. The choice among them depends on the predilection of the phonologist and his evaluation in terms of appropriateness for a particular task and of such criteria as exhaustiveness, consistency, economy and (we would hope) clarity. In this chapter we deal mainly with one kind of phonology, *phonemic analysis* or *phonemics*, though we glance at another type. (In Chapter 16 we describe a further approach, *generative phonology*.)

In any one accent of a language, the number of phonetically distinct segments can approach two hundred or even more. These can be arranged into a much smaller number of groups. For example, the initial segments of the English words [i̯id], [ɛ̯ɛd], [a̯ad] and [u̯ud] are clearly different yet they can be grouped together. It is relevant that all are represented by *h* in spelling: *heed, head, had* and *hood*. The English-speaker will not recognise sequences such as [u̯id] and [i̯ud] as anything but odd pronunciations of *heed* and *hood* respectively, if indeed he recognises them at all; the point is that they could not be conceivable English words in their own right.

Such a group of sounds constitutes a *phoneme* of the language, and the individual sounds in the group are the *allophones* of that phoneme.[1] A phoneme can therefore be regarded as a group of sounds that are different from the point of view of phonetic classification, but that have the same function phonologically, that is in their language-bearing capability. The allophones of a phoneme show phonetic similarity to each other, thus the allophones of the phoneme /h/ just illustrated are all voiceless non-syllabic vocoids. (Symbols representing phonemes appear between slant lines, those representing allophones between square brackets.)

Phonemes: (i) Phonemes are abstractions or elements of form since each is the result of grouping concrete sounds;[2] and they are *unpronounceable*, for it is impossible to pronounce a group of sounds simultaneously. A phonemic symbol is therefore pronounced

68

by phonologists as an arbitrary sound, for example /h/ as 'aitch', or as one allophone plus a vowel if necessary, for example /t/ as [tʰi]. (ii) Any accent possesses a list of phonemes, the *phonemic system*; most languages have between twenty-five and fifty items in their phonemic systems. (iii) Phonemes in a language differentiate words, cf. /fat/ *fat*, /hat/ *hat* and /kat/ *cat*. (iv) In a given language, the same 'slot' in a particular environment may be 'filled' by members of different phonemes, for example /_at/ by /f/, /h/ or /k/; /f_t/ by /a/ or /i/; /fa_/ by /t/, /d/ or /n/. Phonemes may therefore be described as occurring in *parallel distribution* in their language.

Allophones: (i) Allophones are pronounceable in the sense that any single speech-sound is an allophone of some phoneme;[3] they are elements of substance, the exponents or realisations of abstract phonemes. (ii) Different allophones of one particular phoneme cannot be used to differentiate words in their language; the sole result of such attempts is a distorted pronunciation, as we saw in the case of /h/. (iii) No allophone ever occurs in the same phonetic environment as any other allophone of the same phoneme: thus *heed* /hid/ can only be [i̥id], not [y̥id]; hence allophones of the same phoneme are said to be in *complementary distribution*. (iv) Therefore we can set up rules for the occurrence of the allophones of a language. Given that a certain phoneme is going to occur in an environment, the particular allophone that realises it can be predicted from that environment.

In English we can formulate a rule that states that the allophones of the phoneme /h/ are voiceless vocoids *homorganic* with (i.e. pronounced with the same articulatory posture as) the voiced vocoids that follow them; given this rule, then /hid/ can be only [i̥id]. It may be very economically written as a *context-sensitive* rule

/h/: [i̥]/_i
     [ɛ̥]/_ɛ
     [ḁ]/_a
     etc.

This may be read 'The phoneme /h/ is realised as [i̥] in the context where it precedes /i/, as [ɛ̥] where it precedes /ɛ/, as [ḁ] where it precedes /a/, etc.' The rule may be simplified by using V for any voiced and V̥ for any voiceless vocoid, and requiring that the articulatory value of V and V̥ should be the same in any one application of the rule, thus:

/h/: [V̥]/_V

It is obvious that the phonetic environment is crucial in specifying allophonic conditioning; but *which* particular features of the environment are relevant differ in individual cases. The selection of a particular allophone may be associated with such factors as:

69

A. *Place in the word*: ⎫
   Place in the syllable: ⎬ initial, medial or final?

   Occurrence only in   first, second, second-last, final, etc.?
   certain syllables:

B. *Adjacent sounds*:   preceded or followed (or both) by a
                              vowel or a consonant?

C. *Adjacent vowel*:   always of one quality, or from a
                              restricted group (which may have
                              some characteristic in common)?

D. *Adjacent consonant*:   always of one quality, or from a
                              restricted group (which may have
                              some characteristic in common)?

E. *Stress*:   always in a stressed syllable, or an
                              unstressed one, or only before or
                              after stress?

F. *Tone*:   does it occur only in a syllable with
                              a particular tone?

These principles are seen in the following examples of (partial) specification of phonemes.

(*a*) *Spanish*   /b/:   [b]/# _   (# = word-boundary)
                              [b]/m _
                              [β]

(The first line specifies the context as word-initial. These rules are to be read in order; the last therefore specifies the context 'elsewhere', i.e. occurring in all contexts not specified by the preceding rules.)
Example. [biˈβir] *vivir* 'to live' = /biˈbir/; [beˈβɛr] *beber* 'to drink' = /beˈber/; [ɛmˈbjar] *enviar* 'to send' = /emˈbjar/.

(*b*) *English* (RP) /l/:   [l]/_ V   (V = any vocalic phoneme)
                              [ɫ]

thus [ˈlʌɫ] *lull* = /lʌl/; [ˈbɒtɫ] *bottle* = /ˈbɒtl/; [fɪɫd] *filled* = /fɪld/.

(*c*) *French*   /r/:   [χ]/Ç _   (Ç = any voiceless consonant)
                              [ʁ]

Example. [pχɔpχ] *propre* 'clean' = /prɔpr/; [ãkχ] *encre* 'ink' = /ãkr/; [ɛtχ] *être* 'to be' = /ɛtr/; [ʁut] *route* 'way' = /rut/; [bʁœ̃] *brun* 'brown' = /brœ̃/.

(*d*) *Amharic*   /ɜ/:   [ɛ]/j _
                              [ɜ]/w _
                              [ɜ]

Example. [jɛt] 'where' = /jɜt/; [wɜd] 'to' = /wɜd/; [ˈfɜrɜs] 'horse' = /ˈfɜrɜs/.

(*e*)   *Japanese*   /h/:   [a̬]/_a
                               [e̬]/_e
                               [o̬]/_o
                               [ç]/_i
                               [ɸ]/_ɯ
Example. [a̬a] 'tooth' = /ha/; [e̬eja] 'room' = /heja/; [o̬o]
'sail' = /ho/; [çi] 'sun' = /hi/; [ɸɯde] 'writing-brush' = /hɯde/.

(*f*) *German*   /x/:   [ç]/+_   (+ = syllable-boundary)
                               [x]/a, ɔ, u, aʊ_
                               [ç]
(The first rule specifies the context 'syllable-initially'.)
Example. [çe'mi] *Chemie* 'chemistry' = /xe'mi/; [bux] *Buch*
'book' = /bux/; ['byçɐʁ] *Bücher* 'books' = /'byxər/; [zɔlç] *solch*
'such' = /zɔlx/.

Certain sequences of phonemes may be mutually conditioning: in
the Persian phrase [tʃ0NGɑ:'zi] 'when the judge . . .', [NG] is
phonemically /nq/, since the rules for these phonemes contain the
specifications /n/: [N]/_q and /q/: [G]/n_. It may be that a particular
phoneme is realised by a set of allophones with no consistency of
selection: the present writer realises /r/ in English indifferently as
[r], [ɾ], [ɹ], [ɻ] or [ɽ]; such allophones are in *free variation*, not
complementary distribution. Sometimes reference is made to
'marginal phonemes', classes of sounds found only in words
obviously borrowed from a foreign language, such as [ɥ] and [ã] in
English, on the grounds that some speakers employ them in pronunciations such as [nɥãs] for *nuance*. But there seems to be no
good reason to treat these sounds as phonemes, whether 'marginal'
or not, of English at all. Pronunciations such as [nɥãs] may best be
regarded as non-English insertions and described in terms of the
phonology of the parent language, here French.
   No predictions are possible about which sounds will occur in an
accent of a language, or how they will be grouped into phonemes.
Both the phonemic system and the allophonic specification of the
individual phonemes will be peculiar to that accent – a thoroughly
Saussurean notion. For example, in 6.2 we referred to nasals in
Italian and English; we may now interpret that observation in
terms of phonemic theory: [aŋ'kora] *ancora* 'yet' and [in'dʒɛnte]
ingente 'huge' are phonemically /an'kora/ and /in'dʒɛnte/, respectively, since
   Italian   /n/:   [ŋ]/_k, g
                    [n]/_tʃ, dʒ
                    [n]
But [sɪn] *sin*, [sɪŋ] *sing* and [naɪn̪θ] *ninth* are /sɪn/, /sɪŋ/ and /naɪnθ/,

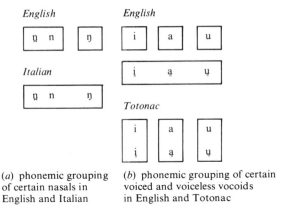

(*a*) phonemic grouping of certain nasals in English and Italian

(*b*) phonemic grouping of certain voiced and voiceless vocoids in English and Totonac

Figure 17

respectively, since [n] and [ŋ] belong to independent phonemes in English (Figure 17*a*) and :

English   /n/:   [ṇ]/_θ
                    [n]

Similarly, comparable sets of voiced and voiceless vocoids are found in English and Totonac (Mexico).[4] The allophonic specification of English /h/ has been given above. The specification for Totonac voiced and voiceless vocoids is :

/V/:   [V̥]/_♯   (♯ = word-boundary)
         [V]

The first line specifies the context as 'when the vocoid is word-final'. Thus Totonac [ʃumpi̥] 'porcupine', [tsilinksḁ] 'it resounded' and [stapu̥] 'beans' are /ʃumpi/, /tsilinksa/ and /stapu/ respectively. There is no equivalent to English /h/ (Figure 17*b*).

Since only phonemes can differentiate words in a language, an ideal alphabetic writing system requires symbols only for phonemes. A native reader would inevitably pronounce them as the appropriate allophones. But this situation is seldom found in natural languages. The need to encompass several different accents (see 8.6), historical change, the presence of borrowed words in their original spelling – these and similar factors make for confusion. Nevertheless, some languages (for certain of their accents) are blessed with nearly phonemic alphabets, for example Spanish, Welsh and German; the alphabets of others, such as English, Danish and French, are much less so.

Sounds in foreign languages seem to be perceived in terms of the 'nearest' phoneme of the native language; borrowed words therefore may be remodelled: *nuance* is often /nju'ans/ in English and *manager* may turn up as /'mɛnɛtʃɐʁ/ in spoken German.

8.2 Phoneme theory. The use of phonemic analysis is ancient;[5] 'phonemic intuitions'[6] seem to have been drawn on when alphabets were developed: witness the genesis of the Greek alphabet based on a Semitic writing-system.[7] But the first *explicit* formulation of a phoneme theory was made only in the 1870s by Jan Baudouin de Courtenay and his student Mikołaj Kruszewski (1851–87) at Kazan.[8] The name *phonème* had already been invented, probably by the Frenchman, A. Dufriche-Desgenettes, with the meaning of 'speech-sound', in which sense de Saussure and other French-speaking writers continued to employ it.

Thereafter the idea was developed in many centres, especially (*a*) in London by Daniel Jones, between ca. 1911 and 1950; (*b*) by the Prague School, particularly by N.S. Trubetzkoy between 1923 and 1938 in Vienna; (*c*) among American linguists, of whom Boas and Sapir may be said to have apprehended the theory; Bloomfield to have formally enunciated it; and B. Bloch, Y.R. Chao, C.F. Hockett, M. Swadesh, H.L. Smith, G.L. Trager and W.F. Twaddell to have contributed significantly to its character, especially from the mid-1930s to the early 1940s. The areas of discussion included (*a*) the nature of the phoneme; (*b*) what were eligible for consideration as phonemes; (*c*) whether there could be more than one phonemic analysis of a language.

The question of the nature of the phoneme, that is, what sort of an entity a phoneme essentially is, was hotly debated. Jones defined it as a class or family of sounds – a 'physical' view. Against this various 'abstract' views were proposed. A 'mentalistic' view regarded it as a psychological entity, an 'ideal' sound at which the speaker aims or which he recognises in his language: this was the view of Baudouin de Courtenay and of Sapir. The 'functional' or 'structural' view of Trubetzkoy and the Prague School regarded phonemes essentially as 'differentiating signs' realising distinctions within a particular *langue*. And Twaddell in 1935 suggested that the phoneme was an 'abstractional, fictitious unit', invented as it were for the purpose of describing languages and having no existence. For the practical task of describing sound-systems, this question is of little importance, since identical phonemic analyses of a language might be made by holders of any of these views. Such discussion belongs to the realms of theory about theory, or metatheory, and it is difficult to maintain that any one view has a monopoly of the truth.

Here we rest content with the illustration of the phoneme given and avoid further definition. We restrict phonemes to vowels and consonants; dynamic features are considered in a different section of our phonology. Furthermore in listing phonemes and describing their allophones we limit ourselves to words in isolation (hence word-spaces may appear in any phonemic transcription we make). Later we describe briefly a type of phonemic analysis that differs in these two respects.

8.3 Dynamic features. The dynamic features to which we have denied the status of phonemes include speech melody, stress, rhythmic organisation, length and syllabicity; yet any of these may be phonologically significant for the language being described.

In our phonological treatment of meaningful speech-melody, we assume that in a sentence-intonation language it may be necessary to enumerate a set of 'tunes', each of which can extend over a *tone-group*. Our examples on p.64 illustrate a fundamental opposition in the intonation of English sentences, namely between those whose tunes rise towards the end and those whose tunes fall. In certain tone-languages we can group the tones into families analogously to the grouping of speech-sounds into phonemes; these families are *tonemes*, consisting of *allotones*. In Cantonese Chinese one toneme is called 'high-falling' since a frequent allotone is a high-falling pitch: [tɔ̂] 'much' (= /tɔ̂/); but if it is non-final the toneme is realised as a high-level pitch: [tɔ̄tɔ̂] 'very much' (= /tɔ̂tɔ̂/).[9]

We have given examples (pp.62, 63) of linguistic distinctions being carried by the presence or absence of stress, by rhythmic differences and by variation in the lengths of vowels or consonants. Therefore, if appropriate, the possibilities under these headings too must be listed in a phonological description of an accent and the relevant distinctions marked in any phonological analysis. Moreover, pairs of words in a language may be segmentally identical, apart from the fact that a particular segment syllabic in one word is non-syllabic in the other. In RP *lightning* /'laɪtnɪŋ/ may be distinguished from *lightening* /'laɪtn̩ɪŋ/; in some accents of American English *string* is /stɹɪŋ/ while *stirring* is /'stɹ̩ɪŋ/. This kind of difference must also be recognised by the phonology of English.

It appears then that at least *five* sets of significant variables may have to be stated in addition to the system of segmental phonemes to yield the list of basic 'building-blocks' of a language's phonology. These possibilities must therefore find a place in a general theory of phonology. (Admittedly English does not make much use of distinctive rhythmic variation or syllabicity; but they exist and we cannot assume that English is the only language to employ them for linguistic purposes.)

74

8.4 Structure. A phonemic system emphasises discrete positions on a 'horizontal' line and enumerates all possible paradigmatic fillers for them, but it says nothing about the syntagmatic relations, that is the permissible sequences of phonemes, or about the shapes of larger units of utterance; this is the realm of *structure*. Restrictions are imposed on sequences of phonemes by such things as (*a*) the position of the phoneme in its syllable; (*b*) the phonological length of the vowel in the syllable; (*c*) whether the word is monosyllabic or polysyllabic; (*d*) the presence of other phonemes in the word or adjacent syllables. Examples follow.

Syllable-initially in English /h/ is permitted (as in *hat*) but /ŋ/ is not (there is no conceivable word **ngat*). If a cluster of two consonants releases a syllable, /s/ is permissible as the first (as in *spoon*), but not /θ/, /f/ or /ʃ/ (there are no possible words **thpoon, *fpoon* or **shpoon*, although all are perfectly easy to pronounce). In many accents of English /ŋ/ occurs syllable-finally, but /h/ does not, thus *fling* but not **flih*. Only a few clusters that occur syllable-initially are found syllable-finally (e.g. /sk/ as in *scan* and *task*), otherwise the set of syllable-final clusters possible is different from that of syllable-initial and is larger, including such items as /lkt/ *baulked*, /ndʒd/ *hinged*, /lvz/ *shelves* and /ksθs/ *sixths*.

In RP /ŋ/ occurs after a short vowel, but not after a long vowel or diphthong, thus *sing* occurs, but not **seeng* or **sowng*.

In RP syllabic ļ occurs only in polysyllabic words and then after the stress. In Scots English /x/ (found in hundreds of personal and place-names) can release syllables only within words: *Lochee* /lɔ'xi/, *Acharacle* /ʌ'xarakļ/. In Finnish, syllables may be released only by single consonants and arrested only by single consonants, apart from the first syllable of polysyllabic words, which may be arrested by two-consonant clusters: for example *lapsissame* /lɑp-sis-sa-me/ 'our children' but *lamppu* /lamp-pu/ 'lamp'.

Successive syllables may not begin with aspirated plosives in Greek; many Greek verbs reduplicate the first syllable in the formation of the perfect tense, thus /lúoː/ 'I loose' and /léluka/ 'I have loosed' but /tʰúoː/ 'I sacrifice' and /tétʰuka/ 'I have sacrificed'. In Turkish, Hungarian, Finnish and many other languages, words are characterised by *vowel-harmony*, that is, all the vowels in a word must be of one phonetic type: for example, back or front, rounded or unrounded, close or open; thus Turkish *elim* /elim/ 'my hand', *gözüm* /gøzym/ 'my eye', *kolum* /kolum/ 'my arm' and *başım* /baʃɯm/ 'my head'.

Not only segmental phonemes but other phonologically relevant features may obey structural limitations. In tone-languages poly-syllables may use only some of the conceivable tone-patterns, for example in Urhobo syllables may be of relatively low, mid or high pitch but in nouns of two and three syllables mid tones are limited to a final syllable preceded by a high tone. Similarly, there may be restrictions on the possible stress-patterns in words; in English, for example, the final syllable of a five-syllable word may not be stressed. Structural rules are peculiar to individual languages, indeed to individual accents. Certain other languages will therefore tolerate structures forbidden to English. Syllables may be released with /ŋ/ in Swahili, such as *ngombe* /ŋombe/ 'cattle' and arrested with /h/ in Finnish, such as *tohtori* /tohtori/ 'doctor'. Releasing clusters in French include /pn/ as in *pneu* /pnø/ 'tyre' and in German /kn/ as in *Knie* /kni/ 'knee' and /sts/ as in *Szene* /'stsenə/ 'scene'. Some languages are of extremely simple phonological structure: Maori words consist of sequences of (C)V: *tokomauri* 'hiccup'. Others, as in English, have relative complex structural possibilities. Some idea of the possible variation in the length of statement necessary is seen in the fact that the structure of the Japanese word may be described in eight simple rules, while the structure of the English word required twenty-two *pages* in a monograph on English phonology.[10]

Adult speakers of a language know the structural rules subconsciously and all coined words (trade-names, Lewis Carroll-type inventions, neologisms) will obey these restrictions, *Kodak*, *chortle*, *gimmick*. Borrowed words may be remodelled to fit the structural rules of the recipient language: the usual English pronunciations of *zeppelin*, *psychology*, *bdellium*, *Knorr* do not permit the original releasing clusters /ts/, /ps/, /bd/ and /kn/. Some languages alter the spelling to conform to the new pronunciation: Finnish *Ranska* 'France', *Tukholma* 'Stockholm'. Structural rules may change during the history of a language; this may be betrayed by a conservative spelling, as in English *wretch*, *knee*, *gnaw*.

8.5 Segmental features of connected speech. Certain phonological facts of importance may emerge only when pieces of connected speech, that is, groups of words, are studied. This clearly applies to such dynamic features as intonation and rhythmic organisation. (Incidentally, it ought not to be necessary to point out that, contrary to popular legend, we do not normally pause between words in connected speech.) But the selection of allophones and phonemes may also be influenced when words are used in groups rather than cited singly. Segmental alternation at word-boundaries – *sandhi* to use a term from the Sanskrit grammarians (see 9.6) – and within words occurs in many languages. It can be used to avoid particular sequences of segments. Thus certain French words contain a /ə/ that is dropped in connected speech unless it results in an unacceptable group of consonants: *je* /ʒə/ 'I', *ne* /nə/ 'not', *le* /lə/ 'it', *repète* /rə'pɛt/ 'repeat', but *je ne le repète pas* /ʒə n lə rpɛt pɑ/ 'I do not repeat it' and *quand je ne le repete pas*/kɑ̃ ʒ nə l rəpɛt pɑ/ 'when I do not repeat it'.[11] Similarly in Amharic the vowel /ɨ/ is inserted to prevent the occurrence of three consonants at word boundaries, thus /k'ɨrb/ 'nearby', /hotel/ 'hotel' but /k'ɨrbɨ hotel/ 'nearest hotel'. A different kind of sandhi-form occurs in Italian when word-initial consonants are doubled when preceded by one of a restricted set of words: *che?* /ke/ 'what?', *farò* /fa'rɔ/ 'I shall do' but *che farò?* /ke ffa'rɔ/ 'what shall I do?'.

Phonology being the study of what may be termed the sound-patterns of a language, the above phenomena are relevant in a full phonological description of that language. There is, however, another side to this coin, revealed in Chapter 9.

8.6 Accent. We shall consider how the phonological framework just described may be applied to a language, English. First we draw attention to a feature of spoken languages that has so far been ignored: differences of 'accent', a term we have used without explanation. A given language can be realised in sounds: any one system of such sounds and their combinatorial possibilities constitutes an accent of that language. A language may have more than one accent, just as it may be realised visually as different styles of print or handwriting. (Therefore it is quite impossible to 'speak without an accent'.)

We reserve the term *dialect* for differences in the systems of grammar or vocabulary: *dove* v. *dived*, *his* v. *one's*, *fender* v. *bumper*. No rigorous distinction can be drawn between a 'language' and a 'dialect'; thus different 'languages' may be mutually intelligible, as are to a great extent, Danish, Norwegian and Swedish; on the other hand, some spoken 'dialects' or 'colloquials' of Chinese or Arabic are mutually incomprehensible (the written forms are themselves further dialects or languages). In countries where one form is recognised by government or educational system as the official language, any other related form which diverges in grammar or vocabulary may be called a 'dialect': there is, however, no *linguistic* reason for this.

Individual groups of speakers may be delimited by the possession of roughly similar accents; within each group increasingly smaller sub-groups may be recognised on the grounds of slight differences of accent between them. The smallest such unit is one individual speaker, who may indeed change his accent according to his surroundings. Therefore the logical conclusion of differentiation of accents is that of one individual speaking in one style, an *idiolect*. From a linguist's point of view, all accents are equally 'good', 'bad', 'educated' or 'vulgar'; to apply such descriptions indicates either prejudice or that a judgement about a speaker has been transferred to his speech. Equally it is impossible to set up some aesthetic scale according to which one may judge the euphony of an accent. There is therefore no reason to prefer any accent of a language to another. In certain circumstances, however, notably the teaching of a second language, one accent must be selected as the model pronunciation to be imitated; appropriate practical criteria must then be employed, such as intelligibility over a wide area, relative simplicity of system and structure, similarity of the sound-system to that of the learner's mother-tongue, and even social judgements such as relative popularity in relevant surroundings.

We shall assume that there is a language, Standard English, fairly homogeneous in grammar and vocabulary but spoken in a variety of accents, for instance Australian, Canadian, Indian, London, New Zealand, South African, Scots, West African, Yorkshire. It is impossible to talk about the phonology of English without specifying the accent(s) under discussion, for no one accent is 'the' accent of English.

Most accents of Standard English belong to geographical areas of various sizes. Those of the U.S.A. are grouped into three main types: Eastern (Maine, New Hampshire and the eastern parts of Vermont, Massachusetts and Connecticut), Southern (the Southern states) and General American (the rest of the Union). Scots English (spoken by most of the inhabitants of Scotland) is an instance of a fairly homogeneous accent covering a much smaller country.

Within England (but not the other countries of the British Isles) the situation is complicated by the existence of Received Pronunciation or RP. This grew up in the 'public' (i.e. exclusive boarding) schools of England, which, until the advent of broadcasting, remained virtually the only source of its propagation. It cannot, however, be held to be 'the educated' accent of England: many highly educated Englishmen use other accents.[12] RP was brilliantly investigated by Daniel Jones (among others) and publicised as a model for foreign learners. But Jones himself declared that learners should feel free to adopt any other accent they chose.[13] And RP does have disadvantages: phonetic complexity, unpopularity in England itself[14] and abroad, and the fact that it is very much a minority accent. As are all accents, RP is continuously changing (witness English films made in the 1950s) so that the pronunciation heard now from some RP-speakers differs somewhat from that described in older textbooks; it *may* be that a convergence is taking place between R P and educated accents of London and South-east England generally.[15] R P is sometimes termed 'Standard English' (which we reserve for the language, not an accent), 'Southern English', 'Southern British' (both of which suggest a regional accent) or 'Southern British Standard' (which suggests several things, all misleading). Few (if any) other language-communities show equivalents to R P.

A phonological description of an accent would encompass: (i) phonemic system; (ii) allophonic realisations and their distribution; (iii) significant dynamic features; (iv) phonological structure; (v) segmental features occurring in connected speech. We take examples from General American (probably the accent spoken by the greatest number of native speakers), Scots English (perhaps that with the simplest phonemic system) and R P.

(*a*) *The Consonant Phonemes of General American,*
     Scots English and RP

				/w/ *wail*
/p/ *pie*	/b/ *buy*	/m/ *my*	/f/ *foal*	/v/ *vole*
			/θ/ *thigh*	/ð/ *thy*
/t/ *toe*	/d/ *doe*	/n/ *no*	/s/ *seal*	/z/ *zeal*
		/l/ *law*		
		/r/ *raw*		
		/j/ *yaw*		
			/ʃ/ *she*	/ʒ/ *measure*
/k/ *sack*	/g/ *sag*	/ŋ/ *sang*		
		/h/ *hay*		

These twenty-two consonants are common to all three accents, but Scots English has two extra items: /ʍ/ as in *whale* (found also in many accents of American and Canadian English) and /x/ as in *loch*; this last occurs so frequently in personal and place names as well as, for some speakers, in words such as *parochial* and *technical* that it cannot be considered a 'marginal phoneme'.

(*b*) *The Vowel Phonemes of General American* (15 vowels)

/i/ *bead*				/u/ *pool*
/ɪ/ *bid*				/ʊ/ *pull*
	/eɪ/ *gate*	/ɝ/ *bird*	/oʊ/ *goat*	
/ɛ/ *bed*		/ə/ *but*		/ɔ/ *caught*
/a/ *bad*	/aɪ/ *file*	/aʊ/ *fowl*	/ɔɪ/ *foil*	/ɑ/ *bomb*

(*c*) *The Vowel Phonemes of Scots English* (13 vowels)

/i/ *bead*		/u/ *pull*
	/ɪ/ *bid*	

79

8. Phonology

/e/ gate	/ɔe/ foil	/o/ goat
/ɛ/ bed	/ʌu/ fowl	/ɔ/ not
	/ʌi/ side	/ʌ/ but
/a/ calm	/ae/ sighed	

(d) The Vowel Phonemes of RP (21 vowels)

/i/ bead				/u/ pool
/ɪ/ bid	/ɪə/ beer		/ʊə/ poor	/ʊ/ pull
	/eɪ/ gate	/ə/ above	/ɜʊ/ goat	
/ɛ/ bed	/ɛə/ bear	/ɜ/ bird	/ɔə/ pore	/ɔ/ caught
			/ɔɪ/ foil	/ʌ/ cut
	/aɪ/ file			/ɒ/ cot
/a/ bad		/aʊ/ fowl		/ɑ/ cart

Our phonemic symbols give some clue to the allophones involved, but the complete description of the phonology of an accent would of course require their precise phonetic specification in various environments.
The types of relevant dynamic features would have to be enumerated. For example, our two-part division of English intonation-tunes (either 'rising' or 'falling') is inadequate: for RP more sophisticated accounts list between five and eleven tunes.[16] In this connection possible stress-patterns have to be stated: for example, a word may have as many as three stressed syllables ('inter'nationali'sation) in deliberate speech but two or one ('internationali'sation,internationali'sation) at a quicker speed; indeed a word may have no stressed syllable in connected speech (contrast 'under but ∧ He 'fell under the 'train).

The structural description of the English word is so complex that the problem arises of how best to set it out. One possibility is simply to list consonantal clusters and indicate their permissible positions;[17] another is to attempt a more 'general' formula that shows some system behind all the individual restrictions. A formula of this type was devised for the American English monosyllable by B.L. Whorf;[18] it represents a vocalic nucleus, flanked by possible types of releasing and arresting clusters. The number of possible monosyllables specified is around 100,000, including those that could be conceivable words, such as /frɛlkt/ (frelked?), but excluding simple non-English structures, such as /θna/.

Various phenomena have to be included among the segmental features of connected English speech. Conditioning factors of allophones may operate across word-boundaries: compare nine /naɪn/ [naɪn] with nine things /'naɪn 'θɪŋz/ ['naɪn̪ 'θɪŋz]. Changes of phoneme may be involved: some fifty words in RP have a strong form when stressed and a weak one when unstressed, for example,

80

8. Phonology

from as in *Trains to and from Paris* /ˈtreɪnz 'tu ŋ 'frɔm 'parıs/ but *He's come from Paris* /ʌ hɪz ˈkʌm frəm 'parıs/. Two (or more) different phonetic or phonological forms may represent the 'same' word as far as grammar and meaning are concerned; we may then view the *relationship* between them as a fictitious *process* and derive one from the other. For example, *assimilation* may be defined as the replacement of one phoneme by another under the influence of a neighbouring segment, as when *have to* optionally /ˈhav tə/ is pronounced /ˈhaf tə/ (assimilation of voicelessness). *Elision* is the omission of a segment that may be optionally pronounced, or is regularly pronounced in a different context, such as *sit* /sɪt/ but *sit down* /sɪ 'daʊn/. A striking sandhi-form (see 9.6) occurs in RP when a word ending in one of certain vowels is followed by a word beginning with a vowel: a *linking-r*, /r/ usually [ɾ], is inserted, thus *far* /fɑ/ but *far off* /ˈfɑr ɒf/: if an *r* does not appear in the spelling, this linking-r is termed an *intrusive r*, as in *law and order* /ˈlɔr ən 'ɔdə/.

8.7 The phonology of a natural language. The phonologies of various English accents may be compared and contrasted; differences can be seen in every area described. We draw attention to them to show the complexity in the overall phonology of a natural language, for languages less geographically widespread than English exhibit comparable phenomena. The three accents exemplified clearly differ in their vowel systems. The relationship between them is brought out in Figure 18 (p.82).[19] These by no means exhaust variations in system.[20] Other accents (e.g. types of American, Scottish, South African, Welsh and Yorkshire) possess extra phonemes that divide a single area of the systems illustrated. Conversely, some systems (e.g. North of England and Jamaica) have only one phoneme where all our exemplificatory accents have two. The English-speaker exploring his own accent should not therefore be puzzled if he discovers that he does not have distinctions between words that, according to some authority or other, are pronounced differently 'in English' or that he makes distinctions between words allegedly pronounced the same 'in English'.

When we look at the different allophones that realise the phonemes of the systems we find a very intricate picture. Over the whole English-speaking community differences in realisations of vowel-phonemes are vast, even though the systems of two accents are identical. Similar (though less extensive) variation is found in consonants.

Dynamic features vary from accent to accent. English has several sets of intonation tunes, differing in the number available and in their 'shapes'. The stressing of individual words can differ: for

81

Stressed vowels

	General American	Scots English	RP
bead	i	i	i
bid	ɪ	ɪ	ɪ
bay	eɪ	e	eɪ
bed	ɛ	ɛ	ɛ
bad	a	a	a
balm	ɑ	a	ɑ
not	ɑ	ɔ	ɒ
nought	ɔ	ɔ	ɔ
no	oʊ	o	ɜʊ
pull	ʊ	u	ʊ
pool	u	u	u
bud	ə	ʌ	ʌ
side	aɪ	ʌi	aɪ
sighed	aɪ	ae	aɪ
now	aʊ	ʌu	aʊ
boy	ɔɪ	ɔe	ɔɪ

Vowels plus r

	General American	Scots English	RP
first		ɪr	
pearl	ɻ	ɛr	ɜ
word		ʌr	
hear	ɪɻ	ir	ɪə
fair	ɛɻ	er	ɛə
hard	ɑɻ	ar	ɑ
forty		ɔr	
four	ɔɻ	or	ɔ
poor	uɻ	ur	ʊə

Unstressed vowels

	General American	Scots English	RP
chin*a*	ə	ʌ	ə
fath*er*	ɻ	ɪ	
pitt*ed*	ə		ɪ
pit*ied*	ɪ	e	

Figure 18

example, *magazine* is stressed on the last syllable in RP and Southern England but on the first in North America, Northern England and Scotland. Syllabification may vary: in Scots English consonants can 'jump' across word-boundaries to release syllables (e.g. *West End* /'wɛs 'tɛnd/) but not normally in other accents. In General American and RP monophthongs are inherently long or short but in Scots English all monophthongs are short (except /iː/ and /uː/, which contrast with /i/ and /u/). And rhythmic organisation varies: *meter* will have syllable-lengths (not vowel lengths) of 'long-short' in some American and Yorkshire, 'short-long' in Scots English and some West Indian, and 'equal-equal' in RP.

One structural difference makes for an important dichotomy, namely whether /r/ is permitted post-vocalically (in *r-pronouncing* or *rhotic* accents) or not (in *non-r-pronouncing* or *non-rhotic*). The former include General American, Canadian, Scottish, Irish, Northumberland, North Lancashire, the English West Country, most Indian and some Welsh; the latter include RP, London, English Midlands, most Northern English, West Indian, South African, Australian and most New Zealand. But other structural

82

differences are found: in most General American /ɛɹ/ is permitted but not /eɪɹ/ or /aɹ/, so that *merry*, *Mary* and *marry* are pronounced alike.

Segmental features of connected speech vary: some accents have no weak forms contrasting with strong; differing types of assimilation occur; even the use of linking-r is not the same in all relevant accents.

A final type of possible difference is selection of phonemes. Given that certain phonemes in two accents are comparable, these accents may use non-corresponding phonemes in particular words: a once-popular song celebrated the difference between General American /təˈmeɪtoʊ/ and R P /təˈmɑtɜʊ/, both *tomato*. Sometimes a regularity is discernible: General American and Northern English /a/ but R P /ɑ/ in *path*, *laugh*, *brass*, and so on.

These considerations pose the important problem of whether we can in fact talk of 'the phonology' of English (or any other language), meaning thereby one single underlying scheme rather than a collection of phonologies of separate accents. It would appear unlikely that we can. The question also arises of how speakers of one accent can understand speakers of another. Both points are touched on in Chapter 18.

8.8 Alternative interpretations of segmental phonemes. The phonemic interpretation of segments is on occasion dubious, and alternative solutions may suggest themselves. Such cases are of various well-known types.

(1) The grouping may be in dispute: are English [h] and [ŋ] members of the same phoneme since they are in complementary distribution? Appeal may be made here to 'phonetic similarity' in reaching a negative conclusion. Are German [x] and [ç] members of different phonemes because of such pairs as *tauchen* [ˈtaʊxən] 'to dive' and *Tauchen* [ˈtaʊçən] 'small rope'? Here we may try to argue (not very convincingly) that the syllabification of the words is different so that the allophonic specification given on p.71 still holds, or else we may simply observe that the diminutive termination -*chen* /xən/ is always [çən], thus using information from grammar to make a very particular allophonic specification.

(2) A sequence of segments may be interpreted as one phoneme. *Chew* and *Jew* begin with the sequences [tʃ] and [dʒ]; are they each one phoneme or two? Both solutions are found; however, the structural rules must be appropriately framed for each case. The sequences [tɹ] and [dɹ] of (in many accents) *true* and

83

drew are also plosive-plus-fricative and hence phonetically similar to [tʃ] and [dʒ], but they do not occur syllable-finally; to treat them as single phonemes would involve adding to the structural rules (specifically to exclude them from syllable-final position) and so they are always regarded as sequences of two phonemes.

While we are on the subject of reducing two distinguishable sounds to one phoneme, notice that General American and RP [pʰɪn] *pin* is /pɪn/, the voiceless vowel being treated as part of the consonant; this interpretation is odd phonetically, but it adds an extra allophone to only three consonants (/p/, /t/ and /k/) rather than to every vowel phoneme.

(3) One sound may be interpreted as two phonemes. Diphthongs may be transcribed as two vowel symbols (/aɪ/, /aʊ/, etc.) and are then usually regarded as single phonemes written with a digraph; but they may also be written as /aj/, /aw/, etc., with consonantal second elements, and in this case they very often are treated as sequences of two phonemes. The French nasalised vowels /ɛ̃/, /œ̃/, /ɑ̃/ and /ɔ̃/ may be written as digraphs /ɛŋ/, /œŋ/, /ɑŋ/ and /ɔŋ/, and again, though single sounds, may be interpreted phonologically as sequences of vowel plus /ŋ/; this approach may not endear itself on phonetic grounds to teachers of French pronunciation, but it is conceivable as phonology. A further case is the [ʍ] of some North American and Scots English, occasionally interpreted as /hw/; this solution simplifies the structural rules but may run counter to the intuition of the native speaker.

(4) General American and RP possess a set of vowels each of which is inherently longer than members of a second set. Each vowel of the long set may be paired with a vowel from the short set on the grounds of rough phonetic similarity, for example the vowels of RP *fit* and *feet, Sam* and *psalm, not* and *nought, pull* and *pool, cupboard* and *bird*. Various interpretations and transcriptions can follow from this.
(i) Each vowel is regarded as an independent phoneme with its own symbol, e.g. *fit* /fɪt/, *feet* /fit/, *Sam* /sam/, *psalm* /sɑm/, etc., or *fit* /fɪt/, *feet* /fiːt/, *Sam* /sam/, *psalm* /sɑːm/, etc.
(ii) Or each pair of vowels may be regarded as sharing the same phoneme, so reducing the vowel system considerably, thus

(*a*) *fit* /fit/, *feet* /fiːt/, *Sam* /sam/, *psalm* /saːm/, etc.
(*b*) *fit* /fit/, *feet* /fiit/, *Sam* /sam/, *psalm* /saam/, etc.
84

(c) *fit* /fit/, *feet* /fijt/, *Sam* /sam/, *psalm* /sahm/, *pull* /pul/, *pool* /puwl/, etc.[21]

We see that the phonologist has a degree of choice in the phonemic analysis. It may be possible to reduce the size of a phonemic system but at the cost of more complex structural rules. Requisite adjustments must then also be made to the allophonic specifications. In no case is one solution indubitably right. The phonologist must make his choice according to the relative weight he attaches to such things as the desire to avoid possible phonetic misrepresentation, tradition, economy and simplicity of typographical symbol, the symmetry of the phonemic system, the balance of complexity between system and structural rules and the degree to which he wishes one accent to resemble another in either system or structure. Thus a phonological analysis is revealed to be not only a *discovery* but a *creation*.

8.9 American phonemic phonology. Many American works use a type of phonemic phonology that differs from the above model; the details vary but not sufficiently to obscure a family resemblance. The beginning of the tradition is marked by Bloomfield's *Language*.

Bloomfield divides his phonemes into *primary phonemes* (written with single symbols) and *compound primary phonemes* (combinations of symbols which represent diphthongs and certain long vowels). The latter employ the 'consonantal' notation, thus /baj/ *buy* and /sij/ *see*; this caused comment at first (although it was by no means an innovation, being used by Sweet) but it became widely adopted. To these he adds a set of *secondary phonemes* to indicate stress, syllabic consonants and sentence-intonation. (Tones of tone-languages are primary phonemes since they can distinguish words.) He describes virtually all the phonological variables (except rhythmic variation) and deals with differences of syllabification and segment-length such as distinguish *an aim* from *a name*. And he devotes almost an entire chapter to phonological structure. In the light of later developments, it should be pointed out that Bloomfield holds that phonology 'involves the consideration of meanings'; this knowledge is assumed on the part of the phonologist and it includes knowledge of where one word ends and another begins.

After Bloomfield[22] the 'consonantal' interpretation of long vowels was extended to [ɑ] and [ɔ], analysed as /ah/ and /oh/. Consequently the number of vowel phonemes in General American could be reduced to six, /i/, /e/, /a/, /o/, /ə/ and /u/; phonetic long vowels, diphthongs and retroflected vowels were regarded as phonological sequences of a vowel and one of /w/, /j/, /h/ and /r/. Syllabic consonants were held to consist of a phonological sequence of /ə/ and a consonant, for example *middle* ['mɪdl̩] was interpreted phonemically as /'mɪdəl/, hence the syllable-marker was no longer required as a phonological sign.

Increasingly, phonemic analysis was carried out within a total scheme of linguistic description, involving grammar as well as phonology. It came to be believed that no grammatical information could validly be drawn upon in phonemic analysis: thus the phonemicist had to pretend that he did not know where word-divisions or sentence-divisions were (although allophonic variation could depend on such information). For example, the difference between *an aim* and *a name* could no longer be attributed to a word-boundary. The solution was to attribute such allophonic variation to the different location of a *plus-juncture* / + /, thus *an aim* /ən + ehm/ but *a name* /ə + nehm/. This is an imaginary device whose sole purpose is to 'explain' allophonic variations; it appears most often at word-boundaries. Other terminal junctures were said to be necessary, such as *single-bar* / | /, *double-bar* / ‖ / and *double-cross* / # /; these specify that the preceding pitch-level respectively remains level, rises or falls.

Degrees of stress were recognised: primary /´/, secondary /^/, tertiary /ˋ/ and weak /˘/, all four allegedly occurring *élēvàtŏr-ôpĕràtŏr*. It seems that a syllable marked by 'primary stress' is the bearer of the most important pitch-change in an intonation tune; in the terms introduced in Chapter 7 we would therefore interpret both 'primary stress' and 'secondary stress' as *stress* but 'tertiary stress' and 'weak stress' as *lack of stress*; in distinguishing 'tertiary' and 'weak' phonologists were probably responding to different syllable-lengths imposed by the rhythm.

Changes in pitch were handled in terms of the relative pitch of each individual syllable. Four such pitch levels, marked by numerals, were held necessary in the phonemic description of English. The effect of this is to present tunes as sequences of discrete pitches (modified perhaps by one of the terminal junctures). Indeed, it was explicitly stated that the phonemicist had no business to be concerned with tunes; these were held to be the province not of phonology but rather of syntax or some other area of linguistic description.[23]

The result of these developments is that phonemes came to embrace not only segmental features but other phonologically relevant phenomena; a phonemic system in this tradition contains not only vowels and consonants but also phonemes of stress, pitch and juncture. A final requirement was that the symbols of a phonemic analysis (given the allophonic specifications) had to be unambiguous and directly readable as sounds; conversely any one sound had to have one and only one symbol. Consequently any recurring sounds regarded as 'the same' phonetically had to belong to the same phoneme when they occurred in the same phonetic environment.[24]

8.10 Trubetzkoy, distinctive features and archiphonemes. Trubetzkoy's *Principles of phonology* (*Grundzüge der Phonologie*) of 1939 is the major contribution of the inter-war 'Prague School' to phonological theory. Trubetzkoy regarded phonemes as being composed of a number of phonologically significant distinctive features (such things as voice, aspiration, nasality, place of articulation, etc.). Each distinctive feature stands in opposition to its absence (or to the presence of another feature) in at least one other phoneme in the language, for example English /t/ possesses the distinctive feature of alveolarity or dentality as opposed to velarity in /k/ or bilabiality in /p/. Thus, phonemes are seen to possess similarities as well as differences, and they can therefore be grouped, for example /p/, /t/ and /k/ in English have lack of nasality (or presence of plosion) and lack of voice in common, and differ only in place of articulation. The differences between allophones (being non-distinctive) are ignored: in dealing with /t/, for instance, we ignore that it is sometimes aspirated, sometimes unaspirated, sometimes lip-rounded, sometimes lip-spread; indeed even though its place of articulation is distinctive we disregard the fact that it is allophonically sometimes dental or alveolar or post-alveolar and subsume these three different places as 'the same' place of articulation, let us call it 'front'. And 'frontness' is recognised because it is neither bilabiality nor velarity, which characterise /p/ and /k/ respectively.

bilabiality		frontness		velarity	
nasality		nasality		nasality	
voice		voice		voice	
/m/		/n/		/ŋ/	
/p/	/b/	/t/	/d/	/k/	/g/
bilabiality	bilabiality	frontness	frontness	velarity	velarity
no nasality	no nasality	no nasality	no nasality	no nasality	no nasality
no voice	voice	no voice	voice	no voice	voice

Figure 19

As a result, the phonemic system of a language may be arranged in patterns that show such relationships: English plosives and nasals, for example, may be arranged as in Figure 19. Such patterns often turn out to be symmetrical, for example the Italian vowel

8. Phonology

(a)	i	u	(b)	p	ph	t	th	c	ch	ʈ	ʈh	k	kh
	e	o		b	bɦ	d	dɦ	ɟ	ɟɦ	ɖ	ɖɦ	g	gɦ
	ɛ	ɔ		m		n		ɲ		ɳ		ŋ	
	a												

Figure 20

system (Figure 20*a*), and the Hindi plosive and nasal system (Figure 20*b*).

The Italian system is describable in terms of five distinctive features (openness, half-openness, half-closeness, closeness, frontness) and the Hindi of eight (bilabiality, dentality, palatality, retroflexion, velarity, voice, aspiration and plosion). The Italian /a/ does not draw on the possibility of the presence or absence of frontness in that it stands in opposition to no other open vowel and its allophones are fairly central; hence its *only* distinctive feature is openness. Phonemic systems were thus revealed as arrangements of 'oppositions' possessing an inner form rather than as random collections of items.

Systems are found where the symmetry is marred by gaps: expected phonemes do not exist. RP monophthongs require the recognition of a feature of rounding (to describe the oppositions /ʌ/, /ɔ/ and /ɑ/, /ɒ/), yet a possible series of front rounded vowel phonemes is missing, as are two non-rounded vowels in opposition to /u/ and /ɷ/. Arabic plosives and fricatives require a feature of voice in order to describe the oppositions of /t/ v. /d/ and /s/ v. /z/, yet the system contains no /p/ or /tʃ/, though the voiced correlates are found, and no /v/, /ʒ/, /g/ or /G/ in spite of the presence of their voiceless correlates. German possesses /ʃ/ but no /ʒ/; French /ɲ/ but no /ʎ/ and /g/ but no /ŋ/; Spanish /tʃ/ but no /dʒ/. However, gaps of this kind make an important contribution to the efficiency of the language and to its intelligibility when spoken, as we explain in Chapter 18.

Since articulatory distinctive features had long been used in the phonetic classification of speech-sounds, Trubetzkoy's advance was in the application of such a technique to phonemes, necessarily entailing idealisation or abstraction.[25] The advantages were that not only were relationships between phonemes revealed but the number of basic phonological elements was reduced: the above twenty-five Hindi consonants can be regarded as arrangements of only eight distinctive features.

Yet this very analysis uncovers further complexity in the interrelationship of system and structure: phonological units enter into different oppositions at different positions in structures. For example, in English /s/ and /z/ stand in opposition, word-initially and intervocalically (as in *sue, zoo* and *racer, razor*), yet word-finally after a plosive they do not; the only possible grooved alveolar fricative in this position must have the same voicing as the preceding plosive[26] (e.g. *backs* /baks/, *bags* /bagz/, but not */bakz/ or */bags/) and to this extent these voiced and voiceless fricatives are comparable in this position to the allophones of *one single phoneme*. In other words, in the alveolar fricatives in English, distinction between voice and lack of voice is non-existent after word-final plosives; the opposition is said to be *neutralised* and the only relevant distinctive features are alveolarity and friction. Those phonological units that occur in positions of neutralisation are termed *archiphonemes* by Trubetzkoy and consist only of features still distinctive in such positions. On occasion we may symbolise them by capital letters, thus /bakS/ and /bagS/. Such archiphonemes are found in many languages, perhaps all. For example, Spanish /ɾ/ and /r/ contrast intervocalically but not word-finally or word-initially; French /e/ and /ɛ/ contrast pre-pausally, that is in stressed position, but not elsewhere; German voiced and voiceless plosives do not contrast in word-final position; Italian /e/, /ɛ/ and /o/, /ɔ/ contrast only in stressed position.

The implication of Trubetzkoy's reasoning is that rather than to postulate *one* phonological system in the analysis of an accent, it might be less misleading to draw from a series of systems composed of phonemes and archiphonemes in opposition, each system being appropriate to a given point in structures.

8.11 Firth and prosodic analysis. Phonemic analysis is one way of looking at the sound-patterns of a language, but though useful it invites comment.

(1)   The emphasis on the distinction between system and structure is misleading. These are not independent but interdependent: different formulations of system require different structural rules.

(2)   Trubetzkoy's systems of archiphonemes and of phonemes destroy confidence in the notion of *one* phonemic system and hence in that of the phoneme itself.

(3)   To treat all phonological phenomena in terms of phonemes assigns inappropriate places in a transcribed linear sequence to essentially dynamic features.

(4)   A sequence of segmental phonemes can misrepresent phonetic data, for example when Arabic [saːrʌ] 'he marched' and [sɑːrʌ] 'he became' are phonemicised as /saːra/ and /saːra/ respectively;

yet the difference in the initial syllables is at least as audible in the vowels as in the consonants.

(5) Not to admit a knowledge of grammar not only results in the invention of juncture phonemes, but makes it impossible to state in the phonology of English that (i) virtually all word-final sequences of voiced plosive plus alveolar fricative are either singular verbs or plural nouns (/rʌbz/ *rubs*, /rɪbz/ *ribs*); (ii) word-final sequences of nasal plus fricative or plosive are homorganic (/tɛnθ/ *tenth*, /θʌmp/ *thump*, /sɪŋk/ *sink*) except in verbs and plural nouns (/hʌmd/ *hummed*, /haŋz/ *hangs*, /θɪŋz/ *things*); (iii) word-initial /ð/ occurs in only a tiny set of grammatically important words such as *this, the, then, there, though*.

(6) It is misleading to regard the vocabulary of English (and some other languages) as a set of items all obeying the same phonological rules. For example, final /ʒ/ is found only in words borrowed from French (*rouge, beige*); initial /w/ betokens a 'native' Germanic word (*water, wine*) but initial /v/ a later borrowing (*vast, vortex, vine*); certain consonant clusters appear only in words borrowed from Greek (*sphinx, sclerosis, rhythm, spasm*); the interjection *boing* contains (unusually) a diphthong preceding a velar nasal. And some words must be reckoned exceptions to general rules, such as *adze* (not a plural noun) and *vixen* (a Germanic word).

Criticisms of this kind were made about phonemic phonology by J.R. Firth (1890–1960) of London, and he elaborated an alternative, *prosodic analysis*. This uses two descriptive categories: the *prosody* and the *phonematic unit*. A prosody is a feature of importance in a stretch of utterance: it may be a segment, a component of a segment (e.g. nasality), a tone, an intonation tune, or the occurrence of stress; and it marks some syntagmatic or grammatical aspect of the stretch (which may be of any length from part of a syllable to a sentence). Thus in English [h] has relevance for any syllable in which it occurs since it marks the syllable-release; word-initial [ð] has relevance for the word in which it occurs since it marks it as one of the grammatically important words just mentioned; 'frontness' (here frontness of vowel and palatalisation of consonant) is of relevance to the Russian word [mʲatʲ] 'to crumple' since it characterises every segment (in contrast to the 'backness' of [mɑt] 'checkmate'.

Previously we have talked of intonation tunes as though they could be removed from utterances, leaving behind sequences of pitchless segments. Similarly 'frontness' and 'backness' may be

abstracted from [mạt] and [ɐɑt] respectively to leave *MAT*, a
sequence of abstract units, namely articulatory positions unspecified
as to palatality or velarity. Such abstract units are phonematic
units. The prosodies of 'frontness' and 'backness' may be shown by
the indices ʸ and ʷ respectively, thus ʸ*MAT*ʸ = [mạt] and
ʷ*MAT*ʷ = [ɐɑt]. (Phonematic units are conventionally written on
the lowest line and the prosodies on higher lines.)

The approach is 'ad hoc': the prosodic analyst selects prosodies
according to the aspects of the language he wishes to illustrate (thus
in dealing with the phonology of the syllable he will not require
sentence-prosodies), for he is concerned minutely to examine
circumscribed areas rather than to give an overall phonological
description of an accent.[27] Moreover, this approach is polysystemic
in that it recognises that sets of items, such as grammatical classes,
borrowings or idiosyncratic words may exhibit characteristic phonological features; such different sub-systems are recognised explicitly
in the phonology. This involves a principle of *congruence with
grammar*, for the prosodist will unhesitatingly draw on grammar to
explain his phonological distinctions. One result of this approach is
that 'the same' sounds from the point of view of phonetic description
or a reading transcription may turn out to be different from the
point of view of phonology, for example [n] of [ən] *an* is different
from [n] of [man] *man*, the former being a junction prosody peculiar
to the indefinite article, the latter a phonematic unit.

Conversely, different phonetic segments may be 'the same' at the
phonematic level. The eight Turkish vowels [i] [y] [e] [ø] [ɯ] [u] [ɑ] [o]
may be analysed in terms of two pairs of prosodies *front* v. *back*,
unrounded v. *rounded* (respectively ᶠ, ᴮ, ᵁ, ᴿ) and two phonematic
units *I* (a relatively close vowel) and *E* (a relatively more open
vowel).[28] Thus the four Turkish words exemplified in 8.4 may be
analysed as

ᶠᵁ*ElI*m	ᶠᴿg*EzI*m	ᴮᵁb*EʃI*m	ᴮᴿk*ElI*m	
elim	gøzym	baʃɯm	kolum	(transcription)
elim	*gözüm*	*başım*	*kolum*	(orthography)
'my hand'	'my eye'	'my head'	'my arm'	

This analysis emphasises that each word is characterised by a
phonetic feature that persists throughout (so-called 'vowel-
harmony', although it affects consonants also, such as in the matter
of lip-rounding), that different phonetic vowels share the same
phonematic feature and that the form of the first-person possessive
suffix may most economically be stated at the phonological level
as -*I*m.

91

8. Phonology

8.12 The nature of phonological theory. Prosodic analysis may appear cumbersome, but it emphasises that a single-system, segment-by-segment analysis such as phonemic theory provides (or generative phonology, introduced in Chapter 16) is in no sense 'natural', though our alphabetic writing-system may predispose us to think so; communities who use other types of writing system find the idea of indicating discrete vowels and consonants very strange.[29] (Undeniably of course the phonemic approach is of value in devising alphabets for unwritten languages and for elementary pronunciation-teaching.)

If we demand one 'correct' phonological approach, with no reference to practical aims, then an answer is impossible. It is conceivable that the same information can ultimately be given by every available phonological theory, each in its own way (allowing a phonemic approach to use grammatical information). It is perhaps necessary to point out that we cannot define the best phonological analysis as that 'most in accord with phonological facts': there are no phonological facts; there are only the workings of the phonologist's imagination.

FURTHER READING
Bolinger 1972; Bronstein 1960; Fischer-Jørgensen 1975; Fudge 1973; Gimson 1970; Gussenhoven and Broeders 1976; Jones and Laver 1973; Kenyon 1946; Makkai 1972; O'Connor 1973; Palmer 1970.

9 Structuralist Grammar: Morphology and Syntax

9.1 The scope of grammar. Grammar deals with the structure of stretches of utterance that cannot be described in phonology; we may assume that it will identify recurrent elements, classify them and study the relationships which these elements enter into with each other. The word 'grammar' both is the name of a general study and also refers to conditions in a given area; such double usage is commonly the case with the names of technical subjects, such as chemistry, harmony, phonology; we may speak of grammar in general and English grammar in particular. While it may be helpful to define grammar as 'the study of how words are put together' or 'the study of sentences', this to some extent begs the question, since *word* and *sentence* can be defined only within grammar: therefore this definition itself presupposes some knowledge of grammar.

In grammar we must make a clear distinction between data and structure. In many forms of 'communication', human beings recognise structures (patterns or forms) beyond and different from the data (concrete exponents or substance), yet contained in them. But two dissimilar pieces of data may embody the same structure, for example the hand-written and printed shapes of the same word. Conversely the same piece of data may contain two or more possible competing forms; puns and ambiguous utterances are of this nature: *George likes amusing girls.* The task of grammar therefore involves the development of a technique that can describe structures, and that includes giving different descriptions to all different structures contained in one set of data. In this sense grammar is the study of the invisible, the abstract.

There are more than half a dozen different approaches to grammar within modern linguistics. In the next chapters we deal with one tradition, certain other approaches being named in Chapter 18. Here we are concerned with a development in the U.S.A. between the early 1930s and the early 1960s; it falls into two parts, a post-Bloomfieldian structuralist and a transformational-generative, which we consider in turn.

Post-Bloomfieldian structuralism was dominant in the U.S.A. in the 1930s, 1940s and early 1950s; the beginning is marked by Bloomfield's *Language* and the tradition was developed by B. Bloch,

93

9. Structuralist Grammar : Morphology and Syntax

H.A. Gleason, A.A. Hill, C.F. Hockett, H.L. Smith and G.L. Trager among others; Zellig Harris's *Methods in structural linguistics* (1951) could be considered the climax. The adjective 'post-Bloomfieldian' makes clear that it is not the 'structuralism' of a Saussurean European tradition and also reminds us that features of this American tradition are attributable not to Bloomfield but to later linguists. Having made these points, we shall refer to the tradition under discussion simply as *structuralism*. With this type of grammar is associated the phonology outlined in 8.9. In the present chapter we illustrate, as far as possible without comment, an analysis typical of this approach, leaving until Chapter 10 the discussion of certain beliefs which came to characterise it.

9.2 Morphs. If we examine samples of any language, we discover that they are composed of repeated appearances, in various orders, of the members of a closed set of sequences of phonemes or written symbols; this set may also include certain single phonemes. Any utterance may be split to reveal such sequences, for example the phonemes corresponding (in any accent of English) to *sudden-ly-the-over-excit-ed-lectur-er-astonish-ed-his-sleep-y-hear-er-s*. Such sequences are *morphs*. Other sequences, although equally congruent with the rules of phonology or orthography, do not belong to the set of morphs, such as in English, *b, ug, modge, trinkle*. There is no universal phonological shape by which we may recognise morphs: in the English example just quoted we find (in the writer's accent) C, V, CV, VC, CVC, CVCC, CCVC, VCVC, VCCVC, VCCVCVC, CVCCCVC. Morphs are the minimal visible or audible exponents of grammar; if we attempt to split them we find only phonemes or sequences of phonemes with no grammatical significance, for example /sli/ or /lɛk/ from *sleep* and *lecture*. We leave until Chapter 10 the question of how we recognise morphs; for the moment we assume that there is a closed list for every language and that any element quoted here as a morph *is* a member of such a set.

Morphs enter into structures with each other in utterances. Since these are not random, if we alter a structure at one point this may entail a further change at another point; by a process of substitution we may therefore investigate groupings of morphs and the nature of structures. For example, the sequence *the-cat-is-black* may occur, but if we change *is* to *are* we can find only a sequence *the-cat-s-are-black*.

The morph *cat* is found in a variety of environments, *the-cat-is-black*, *I-dis-like-your-cat*, *a-black-cat-screech-ed*, etc. Such a morph is a *free morph*. Contrasted with this is the type represented by *s*;

94

this is a *bound morph*, found only in a given position relative to any of the morphs with which it must co-occur; *s* always occurs after a morph such as *cat*. *Cat* however could begin an utterance: *cat-s-are-loath-some*.

Bound morphs, such as *s*, that appear after the element with which they must co-occur are *suffixes*. Those that appear before the element with which they co-occur are *prefixes*, such as English *un*. Bound morphs that appear inserted into the element with which they co-occur are *infixes*, such as /um/ in Bontoc (Philippines) /fumikas/ 'he is becoming strong' (contrasted with /fikas/ 'strong'). Infixes occur in many languages of the Pacific and America; there is a relic of a once-active present-tense nasal infix in English *stand* v. *stood*.

Prefixes, suffixes and infixes may be classed as *affixes*. Those morphs that are not affixes are *roots*. (Not all roots are free morphs; some are bound: *ceive* in English *per-ceive-s, con-ceive-d, re-ceiv-ing, de-ceiv-er*.)

An affix may be a repeated part of the root with which it occurs, a phenomenon known as *reduplication*. Greek /léluka/ 'I have loosed' shows a reduplicated prefix, cf. /lúo:/ 'I loose'. In Samoan the plural of adjectives shows a reduplicated prefix, for example *puta* (singular) v. *puputa* (plural) 'fat'. Sometimes an entire root may be reduplicated: Maori *wera* 'hot' v. *werawera* 'warm' (this last an exception to a tendency for reduplication to indicate some kind of intensification). The reduplicated affix may be an infix: Samoan *fagota* 'he fishes' v. *fagogota* 'they fish'.

The root into which an infix is inserted is a *discontinuous morph*, for example Bontoc *fumikas* 'he is becoming strong' may be analysed as the infix *um* inserted into the discontinuous morph *f..ikas*. The grammars of certain languages show an abundance of discontinuous morphs. In the Semitic languages, utterances largely consist of two simultaneous series that 'mesh' like the teeth of gear-wheels, namely of roots (each normally three consonants) and of affixes (vowels and occasional consonants). Examples are the borrowings from Arabic *Muslim, Islam*, and *salaam*, all containing the root SLM. Likewise from the root KTB we find in Arabic /'kataba/ 'he wrote', /'jiktubu/ 'he is writing', /ki'ta:b/ 'book', /'kutub/ 'books', /'ka:tib/ 'scribe', /'maktab/ 'elementary school', and many others. Borrowings may exhibit the same behaviour: Maltese *kitla* 'kettle' v. *ktieli* 'kettles'.

9.3 Allomorphs and morphemes. Using the substitution approach outlined above, we consider the following frameworks (in the writer's accent): (1) /ðɪ-kat-ɪz-blak; (2) /ðɪ-dɔg-ɪz-blak/; (3) /ðɪ-hɔrs-ɪz-blak/. These are identical apart from /kat/ ~ /dɔg/ ~ /hɔrs/. If we carry out the same substitution on all three, namely /ar/ for /ɪz/, we find (4) /ðɪ-kat-s-ar-blak/; (5) /ðɪ-dɔg-z-ar-blak/; (6) /ðɪ-hɔrs-ɪz-ar-blak/. The replacement of /ɪz/ by /ar/ requires the presence of an additional element and it is reasonable to conclude that it is the same grammatical element; we therefore group the morphs /s/, /z/ and /ɪz/ into a set, exponents of this abstract element. Such a grammatical element is a *morpheme*.

Morphemes can never be directly observed but are represented in utterances by morphs. They are the basic grammatical elements. We symbolise them by brace-brackets enclosing capital letters that have mnemonic significance: the morpheme represented by /s/, /z/ and /ɪz/ could be symbolised as {S} or {PLUR}. When a morph represents only one morpheme, it may be termed an *allomorph* of that morpheme; thus /s/, /z/ and /ɪz/ are all allomorphs of {S}.

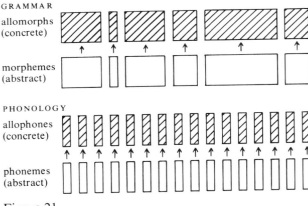

GRAMMAR
allomorphs (concrete)

morphemes (abstract)

PHONOLOGY
allophones (concrete)

phonemes (abstract)

Figure 21

It was tempting for structuralists to hope that the one-to-one relation of phoneme and allophone would be repeated at the grammatical level by a one-to-one relation of morpheme and allomorph, as in Figure 21; indeed to *some* extent such a situation is found in English.

Sometimes the occurrence of one allomorph rather than another depends on the phonological environment: normally after a root ending with /s/, /z/, /ʃ/ and /ʒ/, the allomorph of {S} is /ɪz/; after a voiceless plosive /p/, /t/, /k/ it is /s/; elsewhere it is /z/. These are *phonologically conditioned* allomorphs. (Reduplicated affixes are therefore phonologically conditioned allomorphs.)

But it may be that the correct allomorph is unpredictable in terms of phonology; in that case it is a *grammatically conditioned* allomorph. For example, *the ox-en-are-black* reveals *en* or /ŋ/ as a grammatically conditioned allomorph of {S}, and the comparison of *jump*, *jumped*, *sleep* and *slept* shows that *sleep* /sliːp/ and *slep* /slɛp/ are grammatically conditioned allomorphs of {SLEEP}.

allomorphs

/kat/ + /s/   /dɔg/ + /z/   /hɔrs/ + /ɪz/   /ɔks/ + /n/   /ʃip/ + ∅
  ↑   ↑   ↑   ↑   ↑   ↑   ↑   ↑   ↑   ↑
{CAT} + {S}   {DOG} + {S}   {HORSE} + {S}   {OX} + {S}   {SHEEP} + {S}

morphemes

Figure 22

However, sometimes a one-to-one relationship can be recognised only by drawing on the notion of a *zero exponent* (a device introduced by Pāṇini!). In English we find *the-sheep-is-black* and *the-sheep-are-black*; if we wish to maintain that all *are*-structures must involve {S}, then we could say that {S} has here a grammatically conditioned *zero allomorph*, written ∅ by the analyst, thus *the-sheep-∅-are-black* (see Figure 22). This is a case where the behaviour of morphemes is different from that of phonemes.

But cases are frequent in English where analysis into allomorphs proves even trickier, for example *man* v. *men* or *sing* v. *sang*, where an *internal* difference distinguishes the two forms. Various solutions were suggested to this problem;[1] we illustrate two (see Figure 23):

(i)   The allomorph of {MAN} before {S} is /mɛn/, but elsewhere /man/; the allomorph of {S} after {MAN} is ∅. Thus {MAN} is represented by /man/; {MAN} + {S} by /mɛn/ + ∅.

(ii) The sequence of {MAN} and {S} combines in an indivisible morph /mɛn/ in which it is impossible to say which part represents which morpheme; elsewhere the allomorph of {MAN} is /man/. Given this solution we cannot always assign a place in sequence to allomorphs of those morphemes we recognise; moreover some morphs cannot now be regarded as single allomorphs. Thus again the parallelism of phonemes and morphemes is incomplete.

allomorphs: /mɛn/ + ∅   /mɛn/
                ↑   ↑   ⌣‾‾‾‾‾⌣
             {MAN} + {S}   {MAN} + {S}
             Solution (*a*)   Solution (*b*)

Figure 23

Certain morphemes never appear singly as allomorphs, but always and only as components of indivisible morphs. For example, *s* in *wants* represents {PRESENT} and {SINGULAR}, neither of which ever appears by itself, unlike *na* in Swahili *anataka* 'he wants', which represents only {PRESENT}. Similarly *em* in Latin *urbem* 'city' contains {ACCUSATIVE}, {FEMININE} and {SINGULAR}, which again are never found in isolation; by contrast /ɛt/ in Hebrew /ɛt ha ʔiːr/ 'the city' is an allomorph of {ACCUSATIVE} only.

The particular branch of grammar dealing with the concrete appearance of the allomorphs or morphs representing morphemes is sometimes known as *morphophonemics* or *morphophonology*.

A certain effort went into the search for *base forms*, that is allomorphs or morphs in a language from which related allomorphs and morphs could be regularly predicted. For example the morpheme {LOAF} has two allomorphs *loaf* and *loave* (as in *loaves*): *loaf* is the base form since the voicing of the final fricative before {S} is fairly regular. This approach may be useful in simplifying particular aspects of language-learning.[2] But although on occasion a single base form may be found from which all other related morphs can be derived, this base form is not a morpheme, which we are regarding as abstract. Often indeed no base form can be found, witness the three 'principal parts' of the English verb (e.g. *eat*, *ate*, *eaten*).

9.4 Typological interlude. The distinctions between morpheme and morph, and between bound morph and free morph, illuminate *language typology*. Here we are concerned with grammatical similarities whose description dates back to F. Bopp, W. von Humboldt and A.W. Schlegel. The presentation varied somewhat, but a fourfold system has come down containing the following categories: (i) *analytic* or *isolating* languages; (ii) *agglutinative* or *agglutinating* languages; (iii) *inflecting* or *synthetic* or *fusional* languages; (iv) *polysynthetic* or *incorporating* languages.

Analytic languages are those with no overt grammatical links between words and with only invariable words. This means that all words are root morphemes, there being no bound morphs. Classical Chinese is often cited as *the* example of such a language. Another is Vietnamese: *Anh ãy đã xem nhiều người lính đi qua đấy* /⌐aːɲ ′ei ′dɑ ⌐çɛm _ɲieu _ŋɯɔi ′liɲ ⁻di ⁻kwa ⁻dei/, that is 'Brother that past see many man soldier go pass here = 'He saw a number of soldiers going past'.[3]

Agglutinative languages are those in which the relationships between words in the sentence are marked by affixes with quite clear functions; in our terms there are no indivisible morphs. Turkish, Japanese, Swahili and Hungarian are among the languages most often called agglutinative. For example, Turkish:

/jɯl/	'year'	/jɯla/	'to year'
/jɯllar/	'years'	/jɯllara/	'to years'
/jɯlɯn/	'of year'	/jɯldan/	'from year'
/jɯllarɯn/	'of years'	/jɯllardan/	'from years'

Inflecting languages fuse roots and affixes into variant forms, that is they are rich in indivisible morphs. Russian, Greek, Latin and Sanskrit are of this type. For example, Latin:

annus	'year'	*dies*	'day'
anni	'years'	*dies*	'days'
anni	'of year'	*diei*	'of day'
annorum	'of years'	*dierum*	'of days'
anno	'to year'	*diei*	'to day'
annis	'to years'	*diebus*	'to days'
anno	'from year'	*die*	'from day'
annis	'from years'	*diebus*	'from days'

In the Turkish example we see clearly which allomorphs represent {PLURAL}, {OF}, {TO} and {FROM}. It is impossible to see this in the Latin where, moreover, the same combinations of morphemes are represented by quite different morphs in conjunction respectively with {YEAR} and {DAY}, while conversely the same morph may represent different combinations of morphemes, for example *anni, anno, dies, diei.*

◄ *Polysynthetic* languages are traditionally those in which one word may express what in other languages would require a sentence. They include Eskimo and other American languages, for example Menomini (an Algonquian language) /akuapiːnam/ 'he takes it from the water', that is root {AKUA} 'removal from a medium' plus suffixes {EPI} 'liquid', {EN} 'act on object by hand', and {AM} 'third person actor'.[4]

These labels only indicate tendencies and are not a rigid scheme of classification (cf. 'industrial' and 'residential' as descriptions of towns). Thus analytic languages may have occasional bound morphs. Agglutinative languages may show fusional tendencies: Swahili prefix *m* represents either {SINGULAR} + {m-/mi-GENDER} or {SINGULAR} + {m-/wa- GENDER}. Inflecting languages can show agglutinative forms: Latin *abire* 'to go away', *inire* 'to go into'. French verbal formations are agglutinative complexes: /ʒedi/ 'I said', /ʒənləlɥiepɑdi/ 'I didn't say it to him', although conventionally written as independent words *j'ai dit, je ne le lui ai pas dit.*

The category 'polysynthetic' seems unnecessary, these being extreme examples of agglutinative languages. Eskimo for one may have more than one word in a sentence.[5] On the other hand, agglutinative languages may show one-word sentences of extreme length: thus in a Turkish *First Reading and Writing Book* (1939) we find *Şöhretlendirmediklerinizdendir* /ʃøhretlendirmedikleriniz-dendir/, 'he belongs to those who have not made you (pl.) famous'.[6]

It may well be that there are no 'pure' types of language in terms of the above typology. English shows analytic features: *The cow startled the monk* and *The monk startled the cow*; agglutinative features: *un-eat-able*; and fusional features: *go* v. *went*. But the terms are useful to give an immediate rough description of the grammar of a language.

9.5 Words. It is usual to recognise the *word*; since it is a grammatical unit, any definitions in terms of meaning or of phonological structure are inappropriate. (The traditional definition of word as 'a unit of meaning' is absurd: the same meaning can be conveyed by one word or more, for example *his reappearance* and *his turning up again*, apart from the difficulties of deciding what a 'unit' of meaning might be.)

In English and other languages, certain morphs and certain sequences of morphs continually recur in diverse environments; these are never interrupted by another morph. Such morphs and sequences of morphs are *words*. Thus in *the-goal-keep-er-dis-lik-ed-the-rat-catch-er* we recognise as words *the, goal-keeper, disliked* and *rat-catcher*: firstly because they appear in other environments, such as *in-the-early-morning, the-judge-was-great-ly-dis-lik-ed, he-is-not-their-best-goal-keep-er, an-un-skill-ed-rat-catch-er-is-a-menace*; secondly because we cannot find in English **a-goal-young-keep-er*, **the-rat-old-catch-er*, **dis-much-lik-ed.*

Words may therefore be defined as morphs or sequences of morphs that are characterised by potential external mobility within larger structures and by internal stability, which implies indivisibility by other morphs and the maintenance of the same sequence.[7] Certain difficulties arise in connection with the recognition of words, which will be mentioned in Chapter 10; perhaps because of these difficulties some linguists have envisaged discarding the unit completely. We retain it because there do seem to be a natural unit recognised by speakers of a language: Sapir's American Indian informants had no difficulty in dictating word-for-word[8] and in

9. Structuralist Grammar : Morphology and Syntax

Cratylus Plato cites and discusses words, although a grammatical definition was not available at the time. Moreover, a category of 'word-class' membership (see 9.9) allows us an additional grammatical descriptive dimension.

An utterance can therefore be split into words that may be cited as strings of symbols, so that *I hastily put it behind the book-case* consists of seven orthographic words. Words cited as strings of phonemic symbols (or in some other form of transcription) will be phonological words, for example /ɪt/.

However, certain phonological or orthographic words may be analysable in more than one way; *put* is one word orthographically or phonologically, but it represents three sets of morphemic constituents: *I put [v. throw] it away every Monday*, *I put [v. threw] it away last Monday*, and *I have often put [v. thrown] it away*. Such constituent morphemes form grammatical words; *put* therefore represents three grammatical words.

In some languages phonological words have some characteristic feature. In Polish, Welsh, Swahili, Zulu, Sundanese and others the second-last syllable is stressed (at least in citation forms); in Hungarian the first syllable is stressed; in Italian words may end only in a vowel or one of a small set of consonants; in certain tone-languages words may be characterised by one of a set of tonal patterns, as in Serbo-Croatian. On the other hand, the syllabification of languages may conflict with grammatical word-boundaries, as in French *les enfants* 'the children' /le-zã-fã/.

The writing system of a language may mark word-boundaries, by spaces, by pairs of dots (as in Amharic) or by different letter-shapes initially, medially and finally (as in Arabic). Both the orthographic marking of word-boundaries and the fact that a speaker *may* pause at a word-boundary are possible only because there is prior recognition of the word-boundary by the writer or speaker; they cannot be a primary reason for recognising the unit 'word'. Indeed some languages, such as Japanese, do not mark word-boundaries in writing.

9.6 Types of variable words. We have seen that different grammatical words can appear as the same phonological word; conversely the same grammatical word can appear as different phonological words. This phenomenon embraces *phonologically-conditioned word-variation* or *sandhi*, and includes the examples quoted on pp.77 and 81; but it is now viewed from the point of view of grammar and so also includes features peculiar to individual items of vocabulary. Allophonic variation at word-boundaries, assimilation, English linking-r, Italian word-initial consonant-doubling, Amharic vowel-insertion and the elision of French /ə/ are all relevant here. Other examples are English *a man* v. *an apple*; Welsh *y dyn* /ə diːn/ 'the man' v. *yr afal* /ər 'aval/ 'the apple'; French *il aime* /i lɛm/ v. *aime-t-il?* /ɛm til/ 'does he love?'; Arabic /al 'walad/ 'the boy' v. /ar 'radʒul/ 'the man'; the forms of unstressed *is* namely /s/, /z/ and /ɪz/ found respectively in *Dick's a linguist*, *Bob's a linguist* and *Liz is a linguist*; and the alternative forms of certain Italian pronouns: *le* and *glie-* as in *le diedi la busta* /le 'djɛdi la 'busta/ 'I gave her the envelope' and *gliela diedi* /'ʎela 'djɛdi/ 'I gave it to her'.

A language may show sets of grammatical words in which part, the root, remains constant while variations in the other parts, affixes, are matched by identical variations in sets containing other roots: *walk, walks, walking, walked*; *snort, snorts, snorting, snorted*; *jump, jumps, jumping, jumped*. These may be called *grammatically variable* words, the variations being relevant to the grammatical structures in which the words occur.

The entire series of forms of a grammatically variable word may be called a *lexeme*,[9] thus *sing, sang, sung*, and so on. The conjugations and declensions of traditional grammar are ordered displays of lexemes. Because we cannot pronounce all forms of a lexeme simultaneously we choose an arbitrary name for it, often the form of the infinitive mood or nominative case if these exist in the language. Since it refers to an entire set, it is helpful to indicate this in some way. We use capital letters enclosed by angled brackets; this avoids confusion in such statements as 'The infinitive of ⟨BE⟩ is *be* and its past tense singular is *was*'.

A particular type of grammatical variation occurs in the Celtic languages where certain forms of lexemes are characterised by different initial sounds, the selection depending upon grammatical factors; this phenomenon is *mutation*. These grammatical factors may be of quite diverse types, for example Scots Gaelic: (i) *taigh* /tʰəi/ 'house' but *mo thaigh* /mɔ həi/ 'my house'; (ii) *toilichte* /'tʰɔliçtə/ 'pleased' but *glé thoilichte* /kleː'hɔliçte/ 'very pleased'; (iii) *tog!* /tʰok/ 'lift!' but *thog mi* /hok mi/ 'I lifted'; (iv) *Tómas* /'tʰoːmʌs/ 'Thomas' but *a Thómais!* /ə 'hoːmɪʃ/ 'Thomas!' (vocative).

9.7 Problematical words. There are several well-known cases of words whose freedom in larger structures is so restricted that a case could be made for treating them as bound morphs, for example French personal pronouns *je* /ʒə/ 'I', *tu* /ty/ 'you', *il* /il/ 'he' and *ils* /il/ 'they': we may have *il est là* /i lɛ la/ 'he is there' and *Jean est là* /ʒɑ̃ ɛ la/ 'John is there', but whereas *c'est Jean* /sɛ ʒɑ̃/ 'it is John' is possible, **c'est il* is not; 'it is him' must be *c'est lui* /sɛ lɥi/. There is an even greater case for treating the pronouns *le* /lə/ 'him', *la* /la/ 'her', *y* /i/ 'to it' and *en* /ã/ 'of it' as bound morphs incorporated into agglutinative verbal complexes (cf. p.100), since their position relative to the verb is quite precisely determined. A similar dubiety characterises *'s* in such formations as the *President of the Royal Society's speech*; in some sense it appears to belong to *President* rather than *Society*, yet it cannot be a normal bound morph since it is separated from it (see further p.117). Such cases are solved on fairly arbitrary grounds; traditionally (probably because of orthography) these French pronouns are treated as words, and the English *'s* as a bound morph with the idiosyncrasy that it may be separated from its root. These are so very few that they by no means weaken the *usefulness* of the concepts of word and morph in investigating the grammar of the two languages; but obviously the boundary between them is not clear-cut.

9.8 Morphology and syntax. The study of the grammatical structure of words is *morphology*; the study of structures larger than words is *syntax*. Traditional grammar devotes much space to morphology and relatively little to syntax. It also distinguishes between *accidence* (or *inflection*) and *derivation*, giving great attention to the former and much less to the latter. Inflection is the study of the various forms of lexemes (e.g. of ⟨SING⟩: *sing, sings, singing, sang, sung*) while derivation is concerned with the relation between one lexeme and another root-related one, such as between ⟨SING⟩, ⟨SINGER⟩ (*singer, singers*) and ⟨SONG⟩ (*song, songs*).

We proceed now to the study of syntax, first dealing with relations into which words enter with each other within larger structures and then with the shape of these larger units themselves. The investigation of syntactic relationships and structures is facilitated by drawing upon the Saussurean paradigmatic and syntagmatic axes.

Samples of any language reveal pairs of utterances, identical apart from the fact that a given position is occupied in one utterance by one element, and in the other utterance by another: *The village was flooded* and *The farmhouse was flooded*. The two elements in question, *village* and *farmhouse*, may be regarded as being in a relationship of substitutability.[10] This is a paradigmatic relationship and is covert, that is not visible in any one utterance but only in a comparison of utterances. Naturally the meanings of the utterances, and hence of the mutually substitutable elements, are not necessarily the same; *farmhouse* does not mean *village*. Elements consisting of different numbers of morphemes or words may be mutually substitutable, for example, *The quaint old English village* and *The village*; therefore it may be necessary to specify that investigation of a particular kind of substitutability requires us to limit substitutions to those containing the same number of morphemes or words.

Elements of a certain type may require or permit the occurrence of elements of another particular type whenever they appear, for example a word such as *the* is always accompanied by a word such as *man*; the relationship between the class represented by *the* and the class represented by *man* is a *co-occurrence* relationship. The existence of a co-occurrence relationship does not necessarily imply any particular sequential order; *often* co-occurs with a word such as *come* but we find both *Do you come here often?* and *Do you often come here?*

If two co-occurring elements must appear in a certain sequence, then they are also in a relationship of *fixed sequential position*; *the* must always precede the word with which it co-occurs.

9.9 Word-classes. Reference to paradigmatic and syntagmatic relationships helps us to illustrate how the words of a language fall into groups or word-classes. Some structuralists tried to show this by the use of specimen frameworks with 'slots' or gaps.[11] In the following examples the slot, which must be filled by a single word, is marked by X: optional elements in the framework are enclosed in parentheses; and the 'alternative sign' ∼ means that either of the elements it separates may be chosen. Each slot can be filled, it is claimed, by words drawn only from a particular word-class.

(*a*) *X hat is on the table* illustrates a class *the, a, that*, etc., of *Determiners* (abbreviated Det).

(*b*) (*Det*)*X* ({S}) is ∼ *are good* illustrates a class *man, oats, New York, fortitude, John*, etc., of *Nouns*. (But see p.122.)

(*c*) (*Det*) *Noun X* ((*Det*) *Noun*) illustrates a class *is, sings, smokes, makes*, etc., of *Verbs*.

(*d*) *Det X Noun* illustrates a class *big, green, brackish, gibbous*, etc., of *Adjectives*.

(*e*) *Det Noun is X Adjective* illustrates a class *too, very, badly, amusingly, misguidedly*, etc., of *Adverbs*.

(*f*) *X Verb (Det) Noun* (where X ≠ Noun) illustrates a class *I, you, he*, etc., of *Pronouns*.

(*g*) *Noun Verb Pronoun X* (where X ≠ Adverb) illustrates a class *up, over, out*, etc., of *Particles*.

(*h*) *Det Noun Verb X Det Noun* (where X ≠ Adverb) illustrates a class *into, under, up*, etc., of *Prepositions*.

For the moment we accept that this type of illustration is illuminating to a certain extent. But a rigorous interpretation of such frameworks poses formidable problems, as we shall see in Chapter 10. Since these classes are not defined in terms of alleged classes of meaning (e.g. in terms of 'objects' or 'actions' or 'qualities') but are *distributional* groups, structuralists did not expect to find a universal set of word-classes. Of course in the particular case of Latin and Greek it may turn out that the traditional grammarian's analysis in terms of 'parts of speech' reveals the same groups as a structural analysis in terms of word-classes; this is scarcely surprising since traditional grammar *is* essentially a grammar of Latin and Greek. What is important is the kind of definition and the lack of preconception about the number and alleged meaning of word-classes in languages, especially those whose structures are far removed from the model of Latin and Greek, for each set of frameworks will be peculiar to one language.

In fact the numbers of word-classes vary: German has a single class corresponding to English *adjective* and *adverb*; French has no equivalent to English *particle*; Chinese has no equivalent to English *preposition*; Japanese, Armenian and Georgian have no equivalent to English *adjective*; English has no equivalent to the Arabic, Hebrew and Scots Gaelic *prepositional pronoun*. Languages have been analysed in terms of nineteen classes (English by C.C. Fries), twelve (Vietnamese by P.J. Honey) and two (Nootka by C. Hockett);[12] objections may be made to these particular analyses, but the point is that there is no expectation about the number of word-classes.

Since we are not dealing in terms of entities allegedly grouped in the world outside language, such as 'persons', 'animals', 'actions', 'qualities' and 'relationships', we do not expect that word-classes necessarily reflect any such categories. For example, the division between 'things' and 'actions' may not be mirrored by a language in terms of word-class: Nootka allegedly has no word-class distinction between what we would consider a noun and what we would consider a verb, thus /ʔatḥija/ may be translated as 'night time' but /ʔatḥijama/ (another form of the same lexeme) 'he does it at night'.[13]

It does no harm to retain the familiar names, such as 'noun', of traditional 'parts of speech' for the word-classes at least of Indo-European languages, although a structuralist would stress the claim that he had arrived at the classification on distributional grounds.

All members of a word-class *may* show identical morphological behaviour in taking the same set of affixes. But the syntactic relationships exhibited by a word are the primary considerations in

105

its allocation to a class; where they appear to conflict with a proposed morphological requirement, they take precedence. Thus *grotesque* is allocated to the same class as *loud* even though we have *louder* but not **grotesquer*.

It may happen (especially in a language with little morphological variation) that the same phonological word may appear in more than one word-class. This phenomenon was called *class-cleavage* by Bloomfield. Thus English *round* is a member of five classes, as in (1) *a round of golf*; (2) *a round table*; (3) *we round off our meetings with a reading from the Gilgamesh epic*; (4) *Egbert is coming round the corner*; (5) *she came round when they loosened her stays*. All these may be reckoned to be different grammatical words and representatives of different lexemes.

All the members of a word-class may not show precisely the same syntactic behaviour. Thus certain verbs appear only in a pattern *Noun – Verb – Noun*: *He is making a noise* (never **He is making*); others appear either in a pattern *Noun – Verb* or a pattern *Noun – Verb – Noun*: thus *He is smoking a pipe* or *He is smoking*; others again appear only in a pattern *Noun – Verb*: thus *He is giggling* (never **He is giggling a noise*).[14] This allows us to make a division between transitive verbs, transitive verbs that allow of object deletion and intransitive verbs.

Such a process of splitting up a major class into subclasses is *subcategorisation*. It may be applied to almost any major class in English.

(a) *Nouns.* Some nouns never appear without a determiner in the singular (*countable nouns*): *The table is* . . . never **Table is*; some may or may not appear with a determiner in the singular (*mass nouns*): *The wine is* . . . or *Wine is*; and some never appear with a determiner in the singular: *Hawaii, Radnorshire, Lycidas* (*proper nouns*). Mass nouns do not normally appear in the plural (but see later).

(b) *Adjectives. Four pretty little French girls* exhibits four subclasses of adjective isolated on the grounds of their respective sequential position; or *The main function of linguistics is to edify* and *The important function of linguistics is to edify* contain adjectives of two different subclasses, since we may have *The function is important* but not **The function is main*.

(c) *Adverbs. She sings unbelievably badly* and *She sings very badly* show two subclasses of adverb since we can find *She sings unbelievably* but not **She sings very*. Similarly a comparison of *She sings there* and *She sings badly* reveals a further subclass, since we cannot find **She sings very there*.

9. Structuralist Grammar : Morphology and Syntax

Having established a normal allocation of word to word-class, we recognise that on occasion a word may appear in the 'wrong' class or subclass: thus mass nouns may appear in the plural as though they were countable nouns, for example *The wines of Yugoslavia, The imbecilities committed by the Senatus.* (There may be a readily observable change of meaning involved, that is 'kinds of . . .' or 'instances of . . .'.) Similarly, proper nouns may behave syntactically like countable nouns: *The Bertha Tosh whom Vera tried to murder was not the Bertha Tosh who painted my portrait.* This phenomenon may be called *recategorisation*.

It is conceivable that there may be division of opinion about what constitutes a class and what a subclass: for example, whether particles should be regarded as a separate class (*up, round, off,* etc.) or whether they are a subclass of preposition (*up, round, off,* etc. plus *of, into,* etc.); whether there *is* a class 'adverb' or whether there is more than one class (allowing class-cleavage in the case of *unbelievably,* etc.). Assuming that the same syntactic behaviour is ultimately specified, then all these approaches are possible; any preference between them is to be decided in terms of 'economy', 'precision', 'power', certainly not of 'right' v. 'wrong'. Different grammarians may take note of the same phenomena in different ways. But we see in Chapter 10 that there may be uncertainty about *which* phenomena are relevant, that is which co-occurrences to take into consideration.

9.10 Grammatical categories. Syntactic relationships between members of certain word-classes may be accompanied by specific morphological forms in some or all of the variable words involved. Thus *John sees me* involves one syntactic relation between ⟨SEE⟩ and ⟨I⟩, *I see John* involves another; they are accompanied in the one case by the form *me,* and in the other the form *I.* Such variations are attributable to the presence of a different member of a grammatical category. A *grammatical category* is a closed set of morphemes the occurrence of which depends on syntactic relationships, and which may or may not appear as distinct allomorphs. Languages vary considerably in the number and nature of grammatical categories used. These do not necessarily reflect any clear-cut fields of meaning and the occurrence of a member of a category need not, by itself, convey any information; the categories are distinguishable primarily because they enter into syntactic relations.

Probably no category in any one language corresponds precisely to a category in any other language; nevertheless similarities in the word-classes involved or in the syntactic relations concerned allow us to use the same name to describe categories in different languages.

9. Structuralist Grammar : Morphology and Syntax

We enumerate some of these, though the list is not exhaustive. No category need appear in a language, above all any which Indo-European speakers might regard as essential, such as number, tense and person; the numbers of members of comparable categories vary from language to language.

Number may be a feature of word-classes comparable to English nouns, verbs, adjectives and pronouns and is associated with the meanings of 'one' versus 'more than one'. Many languages, such as English, have two members, *singular* and *plural*. Yet by themselves they do not act as exponents of the meanings 'one' and 'more than one'. For example, English *many a*, French *maint* /mɛ̃/ 'many a', Italian *qualche* /'kwalke/ 'several' are all grammatically singular but mean 'more than one'. Conversely *scissors* and *trousers* are grammatically plural but mean 'one' or 'non-plural'. Classical Greek, Arabic, Gothic and Samoan, among others, have three members of this category, namely singular, *dual* and plural; other languages, such as Fijian, have four, including a *trial* (associated with 'three') or a *paucal* ('a few'). On the other hand, Chinese and Japanese do not have a category 'number': Chinese /jǒu rén lái/ means 'A man has come' or 'Some men have come'.

Gender may be a feature of nouns, adjectives and verbs; it may be associated with the meaning of sex differences, different shapes or some other characteristic. English has three genders, *masculine*, *feminine* and *neuter*,[15] revealed in co-occurrences with *his*, *her*, *its* and *himself*, *herself* and *itself*. These correlate with the natural division into 'male', 'female' and 'sexless' to a great extent but not completely, since, for instance, *ship* may be feminine while *baby* may be neuter. Latin, Russian, German, and Greek also have three genders; French, Italian, Scots Gaelic, Welsh have two. In these languages, masculine and feminine words refer to sexless objects, apportioned arbitrarily to their classes: German *der Mond* /dɛr mont/ 'the moon' (masculine), *die Sonne* /di 'zɔnə/ 'the sun' (feminine), but Welsh *y lleuad* /ə 'ɬəɪad/ 'the moon' (feminine), *yr haul* /ər haɪl/ 'the sun' (masculine). Living persons may be categorised by a gender inappropriate to their sex: German *das Weib* /das vaɪp/ 'the woman' (neuter), French *la sentinelle* /la sɑ̃tinɛl/ 'the guard' (feminine), Italian *la guida* /la 'gwida/ 'the guide' (feminine), *il soprano* /il sop'rano/ 'the soprano' (masculine). In Amharic, a masculine noun may be made feminine to indicate 'relative smallness' and a feminine made masculine to indicate 'relative largeness'; /bet/ 'house' is masculine and /kokəb/ 'star' is feminine, thus /bet nəw/ 'It's a house', /kokəb nat/ 'It's a star'; but /bet nat/ 'It's a small house', /kokəb nəw/ 'It's a large star'. These examples stress that gender may not have a visible allomorphic

108

exponent in the noun, (e.g. *Weib* and *Mond*) but may only be revealed in a syntactic relationship (*das Weib, der Mond*). Chinese, Japanese, Indonesian and Navaho reveal gender in this way, namely in the form of a word inserted between any preceding numeral and the noun: Indonesian *supuluh* 'ten', *India* 'an Indian', *pisau* 'a knife' but *supuluh orang India* 'ten Indians' and *supuluh bilah pisau* 'ten knives'. Such inserted words are *classifiers* or *measure-words*. In these languages gender is associated with heterogeneous kinds of meanings, for example in Indonesian with human beings, animals, large things (e.g. 'houses'), long cylindrical things (e.g. 'trees'), flowers, and so on. Yet even this kind of gender does not convey any meaning by itself: in Indonesian 'thought' appears in the 'large object' gender. The Bantu languages show a gender-category that appears together with number in bound morph prefixes: Swahili *kisu* 'knife', *jiwe* 'stone' but *visu* 'knives', *mawe* 'stones'; again one type of gender does not completely correlate with one meaning.

The phenomenon of grammatical gender is extremely common and few languages are without it. But one group of geographically contiguous genderless languages consists of Armenian, Persian and Turkish; in these even the third person singular pronoun means 'he', 'she' or 'it'.

Some languages exhibit a second or even a third gender-like category. *Animateness* is a category of this type that must be recognised in, for example, Russian; there are two members *animate* and *inanimate*, thus /'sputnik/ 'fellow-traveller' is animate but /'sputnik/ 'artificial satellite' is inanimate. Yet this category does not necessarily correspond to a natural distinction: one word for 'corpse' /mert'yets/ is animate and another /trup/ inanimate. *Humanness* is another gender-like category, observable in Spanish, for instance, in the occurrence of a particle *a* before the 'human' object of a transitive verb.

Dependence is a category in Algonquian languages. *Dependent* nouns occur only with a possessive: Menomini /neːk/ 'my dwelling', /keːk/ 'your dwelling' – it is impossible to say 'dwelling'; *independent* nouns may appear without a possessive: /netoːs/ 'my canoe', but also /oːs/ 'canoe'.[16] The phenomenon may reflect something recognised in other ways by other languages, including some European (see p.252).

Definiteness or *determination* is a category whose members appear in co-occurrence with, for example, the presence or absence of a definite article; in German and Danish it characterises adjectives, in Arabic nouns and adjectives, and in Hungarian verbs. There are often only two members, *definite* and *indefinite* and the selection of them varies from language to language: German *dein großes Haus*

/daɪn 'grosəs haʊs/ (indefinite) but Danish *dit store hus* /did 'sdoʔrə hus/ and Arabic /'baituka lka'biːru/ (both definite); all mean 'your big house'.

Case, found in nouns, adjectives and pronouns, consists of morphemes indicating types of grammatical relationships to verbs, prepositions and nouns. English pronouns display a *nominative* case (in e.g. *I*) before verbs and an *accusative* (in e.g. *me*) after verbs and prepositions. The number of cases varies: Hindi has two, Latin seven and Finnish fifteen. Chinese lacks the category completely. The meanings associated with cases are extremely diverse; they may indicate subjects, objects of transitive verbs, directions, positions of rest, recipients, possessors, instruments – or nothing at all. Seldom does a particular case in a language have one single function or a clearly definable meaning; moreover the meanings and uses of cases to which we apply the same name are never identical in different languages, for example *dative* in Greek, Latin and German.

We must beware of the assumption that the case-systems of Latin and Greek embody some universal logic. For example, it is sometimes accepted as 'logical' that the subject in a sentence should be marked by the nominative case and the object by the accusative, and that the complement after ⟨BE⟩ appears in the nominative: Latin *Petrus* (nom.) *advenit* 'Peter has arrived'; *Iohannis* (nom.) *Petrum* (acc.) *docet* 'John is teaching Peter'; *Petrus* (nom.) *erat mercator* (nom.) 'Peter was a merchant'. Other languages deploy their cases differently. Arabic ⟨BE⟩ is followed by an accusative: /'kaːna 'zaidun/ (nom.) 'taːdʒiran (acc.)/ 'Zaid was a merchant'. In Basque the subject of an intransitive verb may appear in the same case (the nominative) as the object (!) of a transitive verb: *Bettiri* (nom.) *ethorri da* /beṭiri ethori da/ 'Peter has arrived' but *Joanesek argitzen du Bettiri* (nom.) /joaneṣek argitsen du beṭiri/ 'John is teaching Peter'. In fact it is misleading to apply 'subject' and 'object' with their Graeco-Latin connotations to Basque, Eskimo, Tongan and many other languages. It could be argued indeed that (in the above example at least) Basque reflects reality more subtly, for 'teach' can be regarded as a *causative* verb (i.e. 'cause to learn') and there is a special case for the agent of such an action, the *ergative*, denoted by the suffix -*ek*; since Peter is doing the learning, it is appropriate that he should appear in the nominative case!

Tense places an event in time relative to the speaker: *I watch television a lot* v. *I watched television last night*. But the category may be entirely absent as in Chinese or Indonesian: Indonesian *Ali tertawa* 'Ali is laughing' or 'Ali laughed';[17] any indication of location in time felt to be necessary can be added as the equivalent of an adverb or adverbial phrase. When tense is a grammatical category in a language, the number of members varies: English, German and Russian have a two-way system, *past* v. *non-past*; Latin has *past, present, future*. Yet again the meaning of a tense may not be always that typically associated with it: English *Did you want to go there?* is not necessarily past in meaning.

Aspect has to do with whether an action was completed or not, whether it happened once or frequently, whether it occupied a point in time or a stretch of time. In Russian there is a distinction between completed action (*perfective*) and non-completed action (*imperfective*): /prətʃi'tat̪/ 'to read to the end' and /tʃi'tat̪/ 'to read without necessarily finishing'. English has two co-existent choices of aspect, namely (1) *continuous* denoted by the presence of {ING}, *I am writing*, and *non-continuous, I write*; (2) *perfect* denoted by the presence of {EN}, *I have written*, and *non-perfect, I write*. They require the presence of the 'empty' lexemes ⟨BE⟩ and ⟨HAVE⟩ respectively and co-occur with one or other of the tenses giving such forms as *I had written, I was writing* and (together) *I have been writing*. Again languages do not show complete consistency in the partnering of category-member and meaning: in Biblical Hebrew the imperfective and the perfective aspects reverse their meanings after the conjunction /wə/ 'and'.

Mood is associated with different degrees of reality, or of possibility, or of desirability. Greek has four moods, traditionally *indicative* (for facts), *imperative* (for commands), *subjunctive* (for possibility) and *optative* (for wishes), though in fact the meanings are never as clear-cut as this. Latin has three: indicative, imperative and subjunctive as have German, French, Italian and Spanish. Some of these appear automatically according to syntactic rules and therefore have no meaning. Hence it is not surprising to find differences of usage: German *Er sagte, seine Frau sei* (subj.) *müde* /ɛr 'zaktə zaɪnə 'fraʊ zaɪ 'mydə/ and Italian *Ha detto che sua moglie era* (indic.) *stanca* /a 'dɛtto kes swa 'mɔʎʎe era 'stanka/; both meaning 'He said that his wife was tired'. English possesses an indicative mood (*Homer nodded*), an imperative (*Vote for me*) and traces of a subjunctive (*If I were a blackbird . . ., God save the Queen!*). The *infinitive* (e.g. Greek /einai/, Latin *esse*, both meaning 'to be') is sometimes also reckoned to be a mood; while the infinitive in some Indo-European languages may show tense (Latin has three), in few of them is it inflected for person or number.[18]

Voice (a category of verbs) involves such things as 'who did the action?', 'who was at the receiving end?', 'who benefited by it?'. English has no voice (see 11.3). Latin has two: an *active* (*puella amat* 'the girl loves') and a *passive* (*puella amatur* 'the girl is loved'). Ancient Greek has three including a *middle* or *self-benefactive*:

111

/phulássomai/ 'I watch for my own interests', that is 'I guard against'. More complicated systems are found: Amharic *active* /ləkk'əmə/ 'he picked'; *passive-reflexive* /tələkk'əmə/ 'he was picked'; *causative* /aləkk'əmə/ 'he himself made someone pick'; *effectuative* /asləkk'əmə/ 'he caused others to make someone pick'; *adjutative* /alləkk'əmə/ 'he helped to pick'.

Person is a category of pronouns and verbs associated with a classification of entities relative to the speaker (the *first person singular*) and the addressee (the *second person*). Anything other than speaker or addressee is in many languages the *third person*, hence a system such as the English *I*, *you* and *he*. These three persons may appear in pronominal forms as bound morphs containing a gender morpheme: frequently in the third person, such as *he*, *she*, *it*, but also in the second, as Arabic /anta/ 'you' (masc. sing.) and /anti/ 'you' (fem. sing.). Forms occur that also contain plural morphemes, such as *we*, *you* and *they* and dual morphemes, as Arabic /huma:/ 'they two' and /antuma:/ 'you two'. (The phonological word *you* represents two grammatical words because of the different relationships to *yourself* and *yourselves*.)

Distinctions may be made in the case of 'first' person plural and other 'more-than-one' forms between those which do not include the hearer, *exclusive* ('I and he'), and those which do include the hearer, *inclusive* ('I and you'). Thus Neo-Melanesian of New Guinea (a 'descendant' of English) has exclusive *mipela* 'we' and inclusive *yumi* 'we'. A distinction is made in the Algonquian languages in the category of things other than speaker and addressee: we find a third person and a *fourth person* (or *obviative*), a person or object distinct from one already referred to in the third person; a distinction of this kind is visible in, for instance, Latin *suus* 'his' (i.e. of the subject of the sentence) and *eius* 'his' (of someone other than the subject).

The correspondence between meaning and grammatical person may not be constant: in English the third person may appear where the first is expected (*One felt very honoured to be invited*), the first where the second is expected (*Have we had any more trouble with the knee?*), and the second where the first or the third would be more 'appropriate' (*Being addressed as 'Doctor' makes you feel very proud*).

9.11 Concord and government. Syntactic co-occurrence relations involving grammatical categories fall into *concord* (or *agreement*) and *government*. In concord-relationships the same member of a grammatical category is the property of all the word-classes involved in the relationship, such as {PLUR} in *these men*. In government-relationships the relevant grammatical category is not a property of

112

9. Structuralist Grammar : Morphology and Syntax

one of the classes, for example in *from me* case (here {ACC}) is contained in *me* but not in *from*.

Concord-relationships involving number are common: between determiners and nouns (*this man* v. *these men*); between adjectives and nouns (French *un livre ennuyant* /œ̃ livr ɑ̃nɥijɑ̃/ 'a boring book' v. *des livres ennuyants* /de livrə zɑ̃nɥjɑ̃/ 'boring books'); and between nouns, pronouns, and verbs (*The politician is dishonest* v. *The politicians are dishonest*). In some types of English the verb agrees with the nearest noun whether or not it is the subject: *The delusiveness of Bolingbroke's repeated observations are transparent enough*.[19] Also common are concord-relations involving gender: between adjective and noun in French *des champignons dangereux* /de ʃɑ̃piɲɔ̃ dɑ̃ʒrø/ 'dangerous mushrooms' but *des liaisons dangereuses* /de ljɛzɔ̃ dɑ̃ʒrøz/ 'dangerous relationships'. Gender-concord between nouns and verb is also found: Arabic /'kataba mu'hammad/ 'Muhammad wrote' but /'katabat 'fatimah/ 'Fatima wrote'. In spoken Italian the verb may agree in number and person with its subject, and in gender and number with its object: *Io la pacificazione gliela darei* /'io la patʃifika'tsjone 'ʎela da'rɛj/ 'I'd give him peace all right!';[20] the object-agreement is revealed in a prefixed form *la*, the subject-agreement in the ending of the verb. A comparable double agreement is found in Swahili and other Bantu languages.

Concord of case is found between determiner, adjective and noun in German: *der gute Mann* /dɛr 'gutə 'man/ 'the good man' but *des guten Mannes* /dɛs 'gutən 'manəs/ 'of the good man'; and between adjective and noun in Latin and in Russian. There may be concord of person between a possessive adjective and the following noun: Welsh *tŷ* /ti/ 'house' but *fy nhŷ i* /vən 'hi i/ 'my house' and *dy dŷ di* /də 'di di/ 'your house'. Comparative adjectives in Scots Gaelic agree in tense with the main verb of the sentence: *Tha Seumas nas motha na Màiri* /ha 'ʃemʌs nas 'mɔʌ na 'mãːɾi/ 'James is bigger than Mary', but *Bha Seumas na bu mhotha na Màiri* /va 'ʃemʌs na pu 'vɔʌ na 'mãːɾi/ 'James was bigger than Mary'. Concords can involve several categories simultaneously: French adjectives show concord of gender and number; Latin adjectives concord of gender, number and case; German adjectives concord of gender, number, case and definiteness.

There is nothing 'logical' or 'natural' about concord; therefore there may be differences between languages that exhibit similar categories. French adjectives agree in number and gender with nouns both when immediately adjacent to them and also in the 'predicate' when separated by a 'copula' (⟨BE⟩, ⟨SEEM⟩, ⟨BECOME⟩, etc.): *la petite maison* /la ptit mɛzɔ̃/ 'the little house'

113

and *la maison est petite* /la mɛzɔ̃ ɛ ptit/ 'the house is small'; but German adjectives agree only when they precede nouns while Hungarian adjectives agree only in the predicate. One kind of concord that may seem inevitable to speakers of Indo-European languages is that between numeral and noun: *one man* but *four men*. However, this kind of concord is entirely absent in, for example, Turkish and Hungarian, and also in Basque when no article is present: *bat gizon* /bat gison/ 'one man', *lau gizon* /lau gison/ 'four men', *lau gizonak* /lau gisonak/ 'the four men'.

Government is found typically in relations between verb or preposition and following noun or pronoun; the noun or pronoun exhibits the variation: Latin *Miles necavit decanum* (acc.) 'The soldier killed the dean' but *Miles pepercit decano* (dative) 'The soldier spared the dean', and *In urbem* (acc.) 'Into the city' but *Ab urbe* (abl.) 'From the city'. The phenomenon is seen in English pronouns: *I saw him, He saw me, I took it from him* and *He took it from me*. Exactly the same relation is seen in the requirement that certain conjunctions 'take' certain moods: *jusqu'à ce que* /ʒyskaskə/ 'until' 'governs' the subjunctive in schoolbook French; /lam/ 'not' the jussive in Arabic, and so on. Ordered sets of government are found in some types of spoken English: *from us* but *from we academics*, and *from me* but *from you and I*.

The importance of concord and government is not their conformity to a natural state of affairs. There is a different kind of reason for attributing importance to such relationships: they contribute to the efficiency of a language in use, as will be indicated in Chapter 18.

9.12 The sentence. The largest structural unit normally recognised by grammar is the sentence. Any attempt to define a sentence as, for example, 'containing a complete thought' is nonsensical. (It may be that the grammatical completeness of sentences was recognised by traditional grammar and ascribed to a 'thought' contained in the sentence.) Nor is any definition tolerable that insists that a sentence must contain a verb: there are many languages in which sentences are formed without verbs: for example, Russian /i'van fsa'du/ 'Ivan is in the garden' (literally 'Ivan in garden'). It may be that every utterance must contain at least one sentence, which could lead to a definition in terms of 'a minimum independent unit of utterance' (or some such formulation); but this is scarcely a structural definition.[21] Indeed there is no universally valid shape that we could use as the basis of a definition.

Bloomfield pointed out that in every language there is a very limited number of favourite sentence-types to which most others

114

can be related. They vary from language to language. English has been said to contain the following four types,[22] represented by (1) *John sang*; (2) *Sing!*; (3) *Did John sing?*; (4) *What did John sing?*. Other languages may use different types: Latin *Beatus ille qui . . .* 'Blessed is he who . . .', literally 'Blessed he who . . .'; Russian /dom nof/ 'The house is new', literally 'House new'; Italian *Cantava* /kan'tava/ 'He used to sing', literally '3rd.-sing-used-to-sing'; German *Mir ist kalt* /mir ɪst kalt/ 'I am cold', literally 'to-me is cold (adj.)'.

Certain utterances, while not immediately conforming to one of the favourite sentence-types, can be expanded in their context to become unambiguously one sentence of a quite regular type (see p.127). These can be called referable utterances: *Got a light?* can only be *Have you got a light?*; *No* (or *No, I haven't*) in that context can only be *No, I haven't got a light*. Given a preceding context *When is Aunt Martha coming?*, *Tuesday* can be expanded only to *Aunt Martha is coming on Tuesday*. Other utterances that do not conform to the favourite sentence-types may reveal obsolete sentence-types; these are often proverbial sayings and can be called *gnomic* or *fossilised* sentences, for example *The more, the merrier*; *Easy come, easy go*. A very small number of utterances not conforming to the favourite sentence-types are found in quite strictly prescribable social situations, such as *Hullo!*, *Cheerio!*.

9.13 Immediate constituent analysis. This type of sentence-analysis became popular in American structuralism. With this method, any sentence can be regarded as a string of morphemes, for example *The-lone-ly-police-man-ate* (= {EAT} + {PAST}) *-a-boil-ed-egg*. Such morphemes can be called the *ultimate constituents* of the sentence. But some morphemes 'cohere' or belong more closely to each other than to other morphemes: for example, *lone-* and *-ly* belong more closely together than either does to *-ed*. The test of such mutual coherence is whether or not such a group is syntactically replaceable by a single element: *lone-ly* could be replaced by the monomorphemic *sad*. (It is not necessary that the replacement should have the same meaning.) Often, but not always, words are the result of the first grouping of ultimate constituents, such as *lonely*.

This process may be repeated successively until the entire original sentence is reduced to a sentence of a favourite type. Thus *police-man* may be replaced by *man*; *lone-ly* and *boil-ed* by *sad* and *large* respectively; then *the man* by *John* and *a(n)-egg* by *chocolate*; finally *ate chocolate* by *sang*. Thus the utterance is seen to belong to the favourite sentence-type *John sang* (Figure 24). Such a procedure

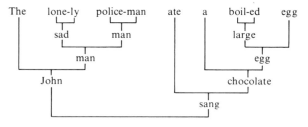

Figure 24

reveals a hierarchically ordered set of structures. The sentence is seen to fall into two main parts *The lonely policeman* and *ate a boiled egg*, each being ultimately reducible to one word. Each main part then falls into two parts: on the one hand *The* and *lonely policeman*, on the other *ate* and *a boiled egg*. And so on, until we arrive at the ultimate constituents.

It is convenient to define a sentence or any significant group of words or morphemes as a *construction*.[23] A *constituent* is a construction or a word or morpheme that enters into a larger construction. An *immediate* constituent (or IC) is one of the constituents of which any given construction is directly formed. Thus *The lonely policeman* and *ate a boiled egg* are the ICs of the sentence above.

An *endocentric* construction may be replaced by one of its immediate constituents (*lonely policeman* by *policeman*) or by a member of the same major word-class as one of its immediate constituents (*the man* by *John*; both are nouns, though in different sub-classes). A *co-ordinative* endocentric construction is one in which both or all of the immediate constituents may replace the whole construction: thus *ladies and gentlemen* may be replaced by either *ladies* or *gentlemen*. A *subordinative* endocentric construction is one in which only one of the immediate constituents can stand for the whole: *bald gentleman* can be replaced by *gentleman* but not by *bald*. In a subordinative endocentric construction, the immediate constituent that can stand for the whole construction is the *head*: *gentleman* is the head of *bald gentleman*; that which cannot is the *modifier*: *bald* is the modifier to the head *gentleman*.

An *exocentric* construction is one which cannot be replaced syntactically by any of its immediate constituents, or by a member of the same major word-class as one of its immediate constituents. Thus, *on the buses* cannot be replaced by anything but an adverb (e.g. *there*), and this is not an immediate constituent of the construction. Phrases consisting of preposition plus noun (e.g. *on*

116

the buses) and subordinate clauses in English are exocentric: *When she got there* . . .; . . . *that he had won a Nobel prize*; *Because she was so helpful.* . . . The basic sentence-types in a language are also exocentric, for instance *John sang.* A translation equivalent in Italian *Giovanni cantò* /dʒoˈvanni kanˈtɔ/ is endocentric, being reducible to *cantò*; therefore what is exocentric and endocentric depends on the language.

In a linear sequence, a constituent may be interrupted by another element. Thus, in Figure 25, the ICs are *John* and *often sang.* The latter, however, is interrupted by *John*; this type of element is a *discontinuous* constituent.

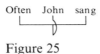

Figure 25

Sometimes a constituent analysis cuts into a word and assigns one or more morphemes to another word to form a construction; the word boundary therefore conflicts with a constituent-analysis. Such a phenomenon is called *cross-cutting.* An example is Turkish *yüksek sesli adam* /jyksek sesli adam/ 'a man with a loud voice' (Figure 26*a*), and the English literal translation exhibits the same thing (Figure 26*b*). IC analysis is even applicable to the groupings of morphemes within words: compare Figure 26*c* and *d*.

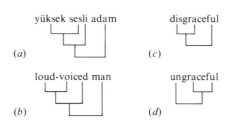

Figure 26

The importance of IC analysis is that it clearly demonstrates that sentences are not mere left-to-right linear sequences of elements; on the contrary the elements enter into relationships of great complexity and varying kinds, as in Figure 27. (Here an 'equals' sign indicates co-ordinative constructions; an arrow points from modifier to head in subordinative constructions; an exocentric construction is marked by *ex*; and a loop indicates discontinuous morphemes.[24]) By using an IC technique grammatical descriptions may be made of

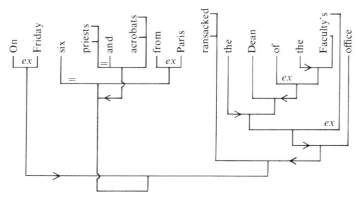

Figure 27

different interpretations of some ambiguous utterances, as in Figures 28(*a*), (*b*) and (*c*).

Having established a definition of general constituent types (exocentric, endocentric, head, modifier, etc.), some linguists began the task of classifying the particular varieties of these found in natural languages.[25] Although the alleged principle of analysis and the terminology are different, the results of this procedure are similar to those of sentence analysis (into subject and predicate, etc.) and the classification of various types of clauses and phrases in traditional grammar.

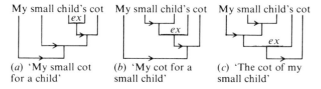

(*a*) 'My small cot for a child'

(*b*) 'My cot for a small child'

(*c*) 'The cot of my small child'

Figure 28

FURTHER READING
See Chapter 10.

10. Structuralist Grammar: Theory and Problems

10.1 Aims and principles. American scholars in the era of which we speak prided themselves on the elaboration of a linguistics founded on 'scientific', 'objective' principles. The ramifications of phoneme, morpheme, word-class, grammatical category, concord, government, sentence and immediate constituent form a typical post-Bloomfieldian structuralist descriptive framework, employed to achieve the goal of a contemporary linguist, namely the investigation of a language by *classification*. 'When the observer has determined the phonemic structure of a language, and has classified all its constructions, both morphological and syntactic, the resulting description will be an accurate and usable grammar of the language, accounting in the simplest way for all the utterances of the speech community, and presenting the clearest possible summary for the use of students and scientific linguists alike.'[1] Structuralists of this tradition shared to a greater or lesser extent a set of articles of faith, underlying principles that determined their view of the nature of linguistics and also how they undertook the task in hand (or how they imagined they were undertaking it).

American structuralists consciously used a corpus-approach: the linguist based his description on a corpus, a set of data or texts in the language under investigation recorded usually either in phonetic transcription or on disks, the size varying from a few words or sentences to a large number of books. There were both practical and theoretical reasons for this. Infrequent or difficult access to native-speaking informants often made it necessary or convenient to amass a fair amount of material before beginning work on it. And in accordance with the enthusiastic labelling of linguistics as 'scientific' and 'objective', it seemed necessary to have an actual object, the corpus, to study.

Structuralist grammar tended to be formal in the sense that it was concerned with phonological and grammatical, but not semantic, considerations and that it did not assume that particular word-classes or grammatical categories (corresponding, for example, to some natural classification) would necessarily appear in every language.[2] It was also distributional for it was assumed that there are recurrent elements of different types (e.g. word-classes) that

119

exhibit different conditions of distribution (e.g. as was shown in the word-class frameworks).

As time went on, one goal of linguists, and indeed increasingly the *chief* goal, was held to be construction of a discovery-procedure, a technique for uncovering the structure of a language. An analyst would apply such a procedure to any corpus and automatically arrive at the grammar of the language in question. Again there were reasons. One was the laudable aim of helping to 'reduce the impression of sleight-of-hand and complexity which often accompanies the more subtle linguistic analyses' and to replace a 'hit-or-miss intuitive technique'[3] by describing the activity of a grammarian in terms of a rigorously formulated programme of successive steps to be followed. Apart from that, many exotic languages had to be analysed for the first time and on occasion by those whose interests were not primarily linguistic, such as missionaries and Bible-translators; in the interests of kindness and efficiency these analysts had to be trained, and the training was essentially the imparting of a discovery-technique.

A popular ingredient of a discovery procedure and of a linguistic description was the separation of levels; the levels included phonology and grammar, the separation involved the order of investigation. So 'firstly the phonological elements are determined or described and the relations among them investigated; then the grammatical elements are determined, and the relations among them investigated'.[4] If this is rigorously maintained, it is quite impossible to make use of grammatical information in investigating or describing phonology, and it goes without saying that no phonological or grammatical classification could be justified by appeal to categories of meaning.

Some effects of structuralism were salutary. The insistence on distributional criteria meant that definitions had to be justified in terms of visible behaviour of the units under discussion (e.g. phonemes, morphemes or words); and because this was by no means an easy task, one result was a constant reappraisal of the bases of grammatical definitions.

The emphasis upon a corpus meant that at least in some cases natural language *was* examined, rather than what the analyst imagined to be natural language; this applied to colloquial and alleged 'substandard' forms of familiar languages as well as to exotic ones. Published works analysed not only great numbers of unfamiliar languages for the first time but also, from the new point of view, languages described many times previously.[5]

The descriptive framework made it inevitable that if two languages were compared, it was the differences between them which were

120

stressed, that is the differences between phonemic, morphological and word-class systems, between the grammatical categories and the members thereof, between syntactic relations and between sentence-types. Such differences were the very stuff of *contrastive linguistics*, that is, comparisons of pairs of languages made to assist language-learners by identifying areas of expected error.[6]

But (with hindsight!) we recognise limitations in the structuralist approach – inadequacies in the available descriptive frameworks, problems in definition, and inconsistency, even contradiction, between theory and practice.

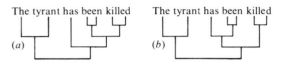

Figure 29

10.2 Inadequacy in syntactic description. In our account little space has been devoted to sentence structure; while structuralists wrote much about phonology and morphology, they were less forthcoming when faced with syntax. Immediate constituent analysis shows the hierarchical structure of certain sentences, but it presents some obvious weaknesses. The requirement that every element must be a constituent means that, for example, *and* in *ladies and gentlemen* is treated as though it were of the same type as *ladies* and *gentlemen*, yet it is neither head nor modifier, since it can appear only when both alternative heads of the co-ordinative construction are present; similar reasoning applies to *when, unless*, and so on. Such words are not merely meaningful, each seems to be of crucial relevance to the grammatical structure in which it is found; it is tempting to apply to them some 'dynamic' term such as 'operator'. It is difficult to see the correct allocation of *there* and *it* in *There is a balm in Gilead* and *It's a long way to Tipperary*; are they discontinuous constituents grouped respectively with *balm* and *way*, or modifiers to *is*, or immediate constituents of their respective sentences? Furthermore, it is not clear how we impose an IC analysis on unambiguous verbal forms such as *has been killed*. Do we analyse as Figure 29(*a*) or (*b*)?

In 9.1 we required that alternative analyses account for grammatical ambiguities; to some extent structuralism can do this in terms of constituent relations and of word-classes. Yet not in all cases; many utterances in English that are ambiguous cannot be given alternative grammatical descriptions within structuralist grammar. Consider the following:

121

(i) *Norah's writing occasioned him some surprise.*
(ii) *Fifi left her mother to attend to the injured man.*
(iii) *Mr Prendergast is one of our biggest tulip-growers.*
(iv) *Look, there's one of the Chinese lecturers!*
(v) *Aunt Bella's shooting kept us amused all afternoon.*
(vi) *Isn't the missionary ready to eat yet? He has been cooking for two hours.*

Their ambiguity is obvious, but it is an ambiguity not attributable to accidental double or triple meanings of individual words; alternative *grammatical* analysis would be desirable.

10.3 Word-classes. In the specification of word-classes suggested in 9.9 the presentation in frameworks is a convenient, but not completely successful, way of indicating distributional criteria; the following observations apply also to allegedly more rigorous definitions.

The question arises of whether the list of definitions should be ordered (as in our example) or not. If it is ordered, then the first framework must consist of actual lexical items rather than other word-class names (to avoid intolerable circularity or complete mystery). Yet however general a first framework we choose, we cannot guarantee that every syntactically relevant example will be acceptable, because of possible semantic incompatibility. If we rely on the ability of our reader to ignore meaning and insert syntactically permissible examples, then we are relying on his prior recognition of the very word-class we are attempting to define. And if the framework is made sufficiently general to admit all members of the class in question, it may admit members of the wrong word-class. For example, in the definition of noun, a preceding determiner has to be optional in order to admit proper nouns; but this allows the definition to include pronouns, as does our own in fact, as *He is good.*

We may note that certain words display such idiosyncratic behaviour that it might be best to place them in one-word classes. For example, *and, but, although* and *because* could be regarded as 'conjunctions' since they can all appear in the framework *Gwen sang X Malcolm danced.* Yet only *and* can appear in *Gwen X Malcolm danced,* and only *although* can appear in *X singing, Gwen danced;* of the remaining two, only *because* can appear in *X Gwen sang, Malcolm danced.* And these words have great importance in English syntax. Furthermore some classes, such as pronouns, might be most clearly defined by enumerating them – which would not be a distributional definition.

We could suspect that the notion of distributionally defined word-class may not in fact be very helpful. Thus to read a distributional analysis of word-classes of a totally unfamiliar language is meaningless until the reader has become acquainted with the sentence-structure of the language sufficiently to understand the role of the word-classes and this (an important point) involves understanding the sentences.

10.4 Identification and definition of basic units. Much discussion took place about morphs and morphemes and different definitions of them were proposed, for certain problems recurred. Firstly, there is dubiety about the identification of morphs. Should a sequence (e.g. *whortleberry*), containing a form (*berry*) appearing in other environments and a form (*whortle-*) appearing only in this, be segmented into morphs or regarded as one morph? Or if a recurring sequence has apparently two different meanings, as *goose* and the first syllable of *gooseberry*, do we treat it as two different morphs or as the same morph? And if we consider borrowed words containing more than one morph in the original language, do we, for example, segment *hippopotamus* because of *Mesopotamia*? Such cases are few and frankly it matters little whether we analyse *hippopotamus* as one morph or three (whereas it would be highly uneconomical and obscure vital facts about English grammar if we did not treat such forms as *hits* as composed of two morphs); nevertheless, the fact that these questions arise is revealing. They arise in part because we are not sure whether certain recurring sequences have meaning, grammatical significance, or neither. A second source of difficulty is the necessity for distinguishing the abstract morpheme (which need never appear uncombined) from the concrete morph. Thirdly, the preoccupation with discovery-procedures led some framers of definitions not only to say what a morpheme was, but how an utterance should be segmented into morphs and how morphemes should be recognised.

Some definitions,[7] such as those of Bloomfield and Hockett, allowed the analyst knowledge of whether two forms had roughly the same meaning or grammatical significance; others, such as that of Harris, did not. If we do not admit to this knowledge, it is difficult to justify such statements as that in English some recurring groups of phonemes (e.g. /skr/ in *scratch*, *screen*, etc.) are not morphs while some single phonemes (/t/, /d/) or single letters (*s*, *y*) are morphs. The problem is: how does the analyst possess this knowledge when all that his discovery-procedure allows him to know at this stage is the phonology?

Many structuralists required that morphemes should have con-

123

crete exponents. This posed difficulty in the case of indivisible morphs: much ink was used in, for example, attempting to isolate an actual past tense marker in *sang* and curious non-traditional analyses were made such as that by Hill[8] of Latin *amavissem* (1st person singular pluperfect subjunctive of ⟨AMARE⟩ 'to love') as: *ama* (base) + *vis* (aspect) + *s* (tense) + *e* (mood) + *m* (person).

The recognition of words by discovery-procedure was also difficult and the problem is made no easier by the fact that single-morph words occur in English and other languages; for example, if *obtain* and *able* are recognised as words, and if *un-obtain-able* and *un-able* are found, then these could be held to be sequences of three and two words respectively. The speaker of English would presumably reject this. It may be that the recognition of words is dependent upon something other than distributional criteria and the suspicion increases that in the grammatical investigation of a corpus distributional criteria are simply not adequate.

It appears that while it is satisfactory to define *morpheme* as 'the basic grammatical unit' and *morph* as 'the minimum concrete exponent of grammar', the actual isolation of morpheme and morphs in a language can only be carried out by someone *who knows the language*. (This would of course have appeared self-evident before the notion of discovery-procedure was introduced.)

There is a certain circularity in the definitions of grammar, a fact which ought not to disturb us unduly. There is, for example, a circularity in defining grammar as (essentially) 'the study of morphs (i.e. sequences of phonemes which cannot be accounted for by phonology)' and morphs as 'the smallest grammatically relevant sequence of phonemes'. Similarly there is circularity in the definitions of bound morph and of word, since the recognition of bound morphs implies the recognition of word, but the recognition of word implies the prior recognition of bound morph. And if a word is a cohesive group of morphemes mobile within larger grammatical structures, then that can only mean within 'structures of words'.

However, the definitions of any study are probably circular in the sense that we can make *reductiones ad absurdum* of them: *Chemistry studies chemical elements and compounds* or even *Linguistics studies those things of interest to linguists*. This observation is not made cynically; the situation may be characteristic of all systems of descriptive categories. The problem of the existence of primitive terms, that is those that do not have to be defined, is a philosophical one. But even the most immediately circular definition fulfils the function of opening up a universe of discourse; the hearer has some idea of what is being talked about and more details can then be given to him. The solution (or amelioration) of the frequent situation of circularity is to make the circle as wide as possible, to insert as many terms as possible between successive occurrences of the identical item. It may in fact be argued that progress is dependent on the use of undefined terms. Physicists are not in the habit of worrying about the definition of terms such as *energy* and *light*, yet the most extensive knowledge we have is in the physical sciences. Armed with this fact, we may accept that we can define linguistics as the *study of language* and thereafter proceed to discuss what *language* may be: difficulty in framing an unassailable definition of a term does not necessarily invalidate the usefulness of that term – and this applies to *morph, morpheme* and *word*.

10.5 Discovery procedures. A critical problem of a discovery procedure is: how can the analyst know which structures to compare to reveal grammatical entities when the only thing so far available to him is the phonology (if indeed that)?

If the analyst does not admit a knowledge of meaning, distributional criteria are then entirely responsible for discovery and it is highly doubtful whether this could work in practice. For example, why should we not analyse *spend* and *lend* as the morphs *sp + end* and *l + end*, given that the surrounding contexts may be identical as in *He is quite ready to spend ~ lend money*? It might seem reasonable, but not to the person who knows English. Unfortunately it is quite unclear how we could give any precise directions about how to use meaning in a discovery-procedure, even if we wanted to; for one thing, we have not so far elaborated any theory of semantics, and neither had the structuralists; for another, it is possible to know the meaning of an utterance but not of its constituent parts; for a third, 'morphemes do not always have meaning, and even when they do, the meaning is not always clear',[9] witness English {CEIVE}.

When we come to allocate words to word-classes, there may well be complete uncertainty about which co-occurrence relations to take into consideration; for once the process of subcategorisation has begun, it may be continued apparently indefinitely by observing the co-occurrence of successive sub-classes. For example, we may place *man, baby, table* and *storm* in different sub-classes of noun on the grounds of the occurrence or non-occurrence of *The baby which . . ., The table which . . ., The man who . . ., The baby chuckled, *The table chuckled, The table was covered with a cloth, *The storm was covered with a cloth.* Given these sub-categorisations we could then put the verbs *collapse, admire, terrify* and *happen* into different sub-classes because of *The man collapsed, The table collapsed, The man admired the view, *The storm admired the view, The storm terrified the man, *The storm terrified the table, The storm happened* *on Wednesday, *The table happened on Wednesday.* And so on.

There appears to be no reason on distributional grounds why we should ignore any one environmental factor while taking note of another, and thus we could continue until every word in a corpus was in a sub-class of its own, defined in terms of its distribution. Such a conclusion would obscure any *general* statements we might wish to make about grammar. Thus a genuinely distributional grammar would take account of every visible co-occurrence in the corpus; if it drew the line anywhere, then there would be no distributional reason for doing so, the decision would be arbitrary.

Yet in practice grammarians seemed to agree very closely on where to draw the line; they drew it after the sub-categorisation of verbs into transitive, transitive allowing of object-deletion and intransitive, and after that of nouns into proper, countable and mass. They might therefore – wittingly or not – be bringing some other factor to bear that a completely distributional analysis overlooks. It is possible to suggest what such a factor might be.

We group words not only on positive evidence, but on negative. *Cat* and *on* appear in different word-classes because we find *The cat is behind the desk* but not *The on is behind the desk. Committee* and *man* are in different sub-classes since we find *The committee are . . .* but not *The man are. . . .* We could place *ice* and *water* in different sub-classes because we find *Boiling water . . .* but not *Boiling ice . . .* – yet we do not. There is a difference in type between the latter two instances of negative evidence: one may be described as ungrammatical and the other as meaningless. Co-occurrences may not be found because they are meaningless or because they are ungrammatical. Unfortunately a distributional approach may not ask the question 'Is this ungrammatical or is this meaningless?' It can only ask the question: 'Is this found?'

What is meaningful may not be grammatical (a fact of enormous value to users of second languages): *Me want eat*; conversely what is grammatical need not be meaningful: *Obese cupboards feel aggrieved.* Meaningfulness may be very much conditioned by the situation: *Heard melodies are sweet, but those unheard are sweeter* would scarcely be regarded as meaningful if one were having one's ears tested. Furthermore, meaningfulness may be quite doubtful: *Three-toed sloths have a better sense of irony than squirrels*; and it could be contended that 'meaningfulness v. meaninglessness' shades into 'true v. false', for example theological assertions viewed from different standpoints.

It seems certain that grammarians concentrate on the question of 'grammaticality v. ungrammaticality' and ignore 'meaningfulness v. meaninglessness'. It is hard to resist the opinion that in doing so, they are already bringing to their corpus a knowledge of what is grammatically relevant and what is not, that is a knowledge of grammar. Evidence for this may be seen in the fact that we talk of major word-classes. Why do we postulate a major class 'noun' and then subdivide it? We claimed that it was done on the basis of a frame (*Det*) X ({S}) *is* ~ *are good.* Yet how did we construct such a frame? It was not on statistical grounds, for there is no reason to equate grammatical priority and statistical frequency. Somehow we had the knowledge that *is* ~ *are* is more important in a framework than, for instance, *whistled.*

Much of discovery-procedure theory was written before computers were widely used; yet a computer would seem to be ideal for testing a discovery-procedure. But how could it be programmed? It would surely produce our final and undesirable stage, the specification of a different environment for every word (if it could recognise words). How then could it be told how to carry out a subsequent grouping into word-classes? It could not be given an instruction that *is* ~ *are* is more important than *whistled* since the programme must be applicable to any corpus in any language and therefore the computer would have to work out its own frameworks. It appears increasingly certain that *the peculiar knowledge possessed by a human speaker is necessary in the investigation of a language.*

Our instinctive rejection of some purely distributional classifications may be taken as further confirmation. Few speakers of English would take kindly to the isolation of *un* as a word because of the series *able, obtain, obtainable, unable* and *unobtainable* or to Hill's analysis of both *svelte* and *potato* as bimorphemic on phonological grounds.[10]

At the beginning of the previous chapter we referred to alternative structures recognisable in a single set of data. A truly distributional analyst would be limited to the data; only one with a knowledge of the language would be aware of the structures. Towards the end of the same chapter we quoted different descriptions of the structures present in *My small child's cot* in terms of immediate constituents; if the level of grammar is recognised only because phonology cannot deal with all restrictions operating on sequences of sounds, then there is no *need* to offer two different explanations in this particular case. One may indeed query whether the procedure of IC analysis, depending as it does on syntactic replaceability, is at all possible without a knowledge of the language including certainly syntactic possibilities and perhaps also semantic interpretations. Similarly unambiguous expansion of referable sentences (see p.115) cannot be achieved by distributional analysis. It seems probable also that a distributional approach that admitted no semantic knowledge would not be able to recognise that there are important relations between, for example, *I* and *my*, *he* and *his*, and so on. The nature of the corpus itself is dubious. However big, it is still a random set of accidentally overheard utterances or a perhaps less random set of elicited responses; can there be any guarantee that all relevant grammatical phenomena will be found in it? Clearly there is no such guarantee. A corpus can be only a sample of a language. The question arises: what then *is* the language? For it is the language that the linguist seeks to describe. It is tempting to say that some structuralists ignored the Saussurean distinction between *langue* and *parole* and seemed to mistake utterance for system.

The conclusion of the arguments in this chapter is that while it is possible to recognise morphs, words and word-classes in a corpus, this is not done simply by applying a discovery-procedure couched in distributional terms. It may be that in examining a corpus the investigator *learns* the language to some extent and thereafter makes explicit the grammar he then has in his head. Evidence for this is visible in the instructions of certain theoreticians, such as Harris (1952): 'The corpus does not, of course, have to be closed before analysis begins'; and Gleason (1955):[11] 'A linguist, therefore, strives to obtain a corpus that will be representative in the minimum total bulk'. (How does he *know* it will be representative if it is his sole object of study?) Hall (1964) seems to concede our point, 'The best situation is that in which the linguistic analyst is also a native speaker of the language he is working on; in this case, he has at his disposal an unlimited knowledge of what is and what is not normal in the language'. In other words, one tailors the corpus so that it exhibits all the grammatical features being described. At that rate the corpus is no longer the object of study but the *evidence*. This may be efficiently economical, but it makes nonsense of any subsequent claim that a discovery-procedure was applied to that particular corpus.

If the suggestion is correct that the analyst at least partly learns the language before giving an analysis 'of a corpus', he must have some knowledge of the meaning of the language; there can be no guarantee that he does not draw on this knowledge in the elaboration of the grammar. Such a self-limitation must furthermore be an impossibility in the case of a fluent or native speaker.

10.6 Scientific revolutions. We have devoted considerable space to structuralist grammar for several reasons. The technical terms, with or without structuralist definitions, are still indispensable parts of the linguist's vocabulary. The nature of the innovations to be

128

described in the next chapters is not comprehensible save against the background of structuralism. And the gradual recognition of problems and inadequacies in the approach is not peculiar to post-Bloomfieldian structuralism but is a universal feature of any study which has a stated theory or methodology.

Here it is relevant to mention the bare bones of a view of scientific development that we drew upon in the opening chapter of this book, that of Thomas Kuhn.[12] The progress of a science is not a simple process of additions to what is already known; it proceeds in periods during which most practitioners have coherent traditions about, for example, what it is they are studying, how they set about studying it, and what the main problems are that have to be solved. Before the emergence of a model for such a tradition (Kuhn's *paradigm*), only a number of facts may be known, with no notion of their relative relevance or importance, an un-ordered morass. But once a paradigm has been established, a selection of facts is made and a structure imposed on them; thereafter the practice of the science proceeds until anomalies are observed in its theory. These increase, and finally the science can progress no further, impeded by its own inadequacies like a snow-plough stuck in an immovable snow-drift.

Eventually perhaps, a new paradigm is initiated. It may come about by reason of a new discovery, or an influential publication, but at any rate by an act of creative thought. This entails a reappraisal of a previous theory; the actual subject-matter may be changed, or the methods, or the goals, or the type of data that may be offered in evidence, or familiar observations may be seen to possess quite different implications. As we pointed out, during the lifetime of a paradigm, the methods employed are no more or less 'scientific' than those of a later paradigm and the theory may accord very well with initial observations. It is only when existing theories fail that a search is made for new ones. And a new paradigm heralds a scientific revolution.

Parallels to this can be seen in the study of language. The era of Plato's *Cratylus* and the naturalist-conventionalist controversy can be seen as a pre-paradigmatic period; Thrax's *Téchnē grammatikē* established the paradigm of traditional grammar, which continued successfully for nineteen hundred years or so. Anomalies and discrepancies were noticed from the beginning of the writing of vernacular grammars, but these problems were not acute until the late nineteenth century. True, comparative philology followed another paradigm, but this in effect incorporated that of Thrax. Then a paradigm appeared in the work of de Saussure, Boas and Mathesius that was more powerful than either of these. Bloomfield's

10. Structuralist Grammar : Theory and Problems

Language initiated yet a further paradigm that worked apparently successfully until the accumulation of problems and inadequacies catalogued above prevented further development. Kuhn's views have been challenged and questioned[13] and in any case the application of them to the study of language is debatable. Nevertheless our over-simplification is helpful in an initial account, and the notion of scientific revolution was embraced enthusiastically in some linguistic quarters. We have described in this chapter problems in post-Bloomfieldian structuralism that seemed insurmountable (or at least do so in retrospect). The next paradigm, it was claimed, was established by the publication in 1957 of Noam Chomsky's *Syntactic structures*.

FURTHER READING
Bazell 1952 (a stimulating contemporary criticism of some aspects of American structuralism – and of other things); Bloch and Trager 1942; Bloomfield 1933, esp. chs 10–16; Fries 1957; Gleason 1955; Hall 1964; Harris 1951; Hill 1958; Hockett 1958; Joos 1957 (see esp. papers by Harris 1942, 1946; Haugen 1951; Hockett 1942, 1947, 1954; Nida 1948; Wells 1947).

11. Transformational-Generative Grammar: an Introduction

11.1 The *Syntactic Structures* tripartite model. Noam Chomsky's *Syntactic Structures* introduced not only a different technical mechanism but also a different conception of grammar; the ramifications extend to a reappraisal of the nature of linguistic theory and to conjectures concerning the nature of human language and of the human mind.

This type of grammar is *generative*. This means that a grammar will give a description of every sentence in a specific language; it may be regarded as a non-mechanical device, the product of any one operation of which is a sentence. The form of this particular generative grammar is that of a set of *ordered rules*; these may be regarded as instructions to be followed. In fact we have already introduced the idea of such ordered rules in our specifications of allophones in Chapter 8. The set of rules in the *Syntactic Structures* model of grammar falls into three parts.

The first part is the *Phrase-Structure* (or PS) component. Let us illustrate how it works before we proceed to a more formal description. A helpful preamble is to take an IC analysis, such as Figure 30. Given that we know the word-classes and morphemes involved, we can state our information as 'The sentence consists of two constituents: a noun phrase and a verb phrase; the verb phrase consists of a transitive verb followed by a further noun phrase; both noun phrases consist of a determiner followed by a noun; the verb consists of a verb stem followed by a tense morph'. (*Phrase* is used here for any small group of words of syntactic significance; phrases may be further described as noun phrases, verb phrases, and so forth, according to the word-class of the head of an endocentric construction or, in the case of an exocentric construction, according to the word-class of a possible replacement (e.g. adverb phrase) or of an existing component (e.g. preposition phrase). The actual

The lady alarmed the horse
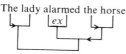

Figure 30

131

terminology is of little importance from the point of view we are going to adopt, as we shall see; apparently at first it had mnemonic value only in this brave new world.)

The above information can be stated succinctly as:

Example 1
(1)   S → NP + VP
(2)   VP → Vtr + NP
(3)   NP → Det + N
(4)   Vtr → Vs + Tns
(5)   Tns → *ed*
(6)   Vs → *alarm*
(7)   N → *horse, lady*
(8)   Det → *the*

(The meaning of the abbreviations is obvious from the preceding paragraph.) Our analysis has thus been cast as a set of PS rules; the PS components of more elaborate grammars do not differ in principle from the above.

The PS component therefore consists of a set of ordered *rewrite rules*; such rules contain an instruction to rewrite the symbol on the left of the *rewrite arrow* as the *string* of symbols on the right-hand side. In PS rules, only *one* symbol at a time may be rewritten. Apart from the initial symbol S, every symbol appearing on the left of the arrow must have appeared previously on the right-hand side. No symbol may be used on the left-hand side more than once. The symbols which are not written out again constitute the *lexicon*. In the lexicon, and at other places in such grammars, a comma indicates that a choice must be made from the items separated by it.

The grammar produces its output by a step-by-step application of the rules. The possibility of choosing (cf. Rule 7) allows us to generate not one but four sentences; thus even this simple grammar has the capacity to generate beyond the original data, that is to project. (*The horse alarmed the horse, The lady alarmed the lady, The lady alarmed the horse, The horse alarmed the lady.*)

```
                   S
(1)       NP    +    VP
(2)       NP + Vtr   +   NP
(3)    Det + N + Vtr + Det + N
(4)    Det + N + Vs + Tns + Det + N
(5)    Det + N + Vs + ed + Det + N
(6)    Det + N + alarm + ed + Det + N
(7)    Det + horse + alarm + ed + Det + lady
(8)    the + horse + alarm + ed + the + lady
```

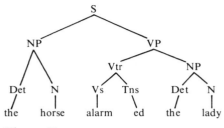

Figure 31

Notice that the grammar not only generates the sentence but also assigns to it a constituent structure, as in Figure 31. This derivational tree consists of *phrase-markers* (*P-markers*); the bifurcation of a P-marker is a *node*.

We recommend that those coming to this type of grammar for the first time take paper and pencil and produce write-outs similar to the above of the further examples in this chapter. In these – and in 'real life' grammars – there is no 'helpful preamble'; the initial symbol S is really the starting point and the subsequent adventures of the P-markers are dependent only on the rewrite rules. It is for this reason that we described the 'actual terminology' (which is the same thing as 'the shape of symbols') as of little importance; the definition of these essentially arbitrary shapes *follows* their first appearance in the course of their rewriting.

All the symbols we have used in the above grammar are abstract; those that appear in the lexicon can be regarded as morphemes. That they are written in their normal orthographic form is for our convenience; a concrete form must finally be assigned to them if we are attempting to describe natural language. This assigning of a concrete form takes place in the *morphophonemic component* of the tripartite grammar; it is in fact the third section of it. The morphophonemic component for the above rules would consist of further rules of the form:

(9)   *the*   → ðι   OR   (9a) *the*   → the
(10) *horse* → hɔrs   (10a) *horse* → horse
(11) *lady* → lede   (11a) *lady* → lady

(The phonemes in the left-hand column are those of the writer.) The right-hand set of rules might be called *morphographemic*.

However, not all morpheme write-outs can be of this simplicity: for example '*see + ed* → seeed' does not give an acceptable form. This can be handled by a rule such as

(12)   *see + ed* → sɔ   OR   (12a) *see + ed* → saw

This introduces a new type of rule, namely one in which *more than one* symbol appears on the left-hand-side of the arrow. Such rules must be ordered, that is such 'irregular' rules as (12) must come before 'regular' forms such as

(13) *alarm* → alarm   (14) *ed* → ed

It is also necessary to order morphophonemic rules differently from morphographemic.

Strictly speaking, *every* morpheme must be rewritten into a concrete shape via the morphophonemic component. As a short cut, we shall assume that the orthographic shape of items in the lexicon *is* their final orthographic shape, as is the case in rules (9a) to (11a) and in this chapter we shall use morphophonemic rules only to specify indivisible morphs containing more than one morpheme. In a *Syntactic structures* model of grammar the items in the lexicon (and any new symbols subsequently introduced in the second section of the grammar) are abstract – they could be listed as serial numbers or as arbitrary shapes – and there must therefore be some component that assigns a concrete shape to them. In a later model of transformational-generative grammar the listing of lexicon items does not regard them as abstract in the above sense and therefore the morphophonemic component is quite different (see p.208).

In our phrase-structure and morphophonemic components we allow the grammar the possibility of scanning the string in which a symbol is found in order to rewrite the symbol according to the context. The grammar is therefore *context-sensitive*; this concept is familiar to us from our specification of allophones in Chapter 8 and the symbol employed, a slant line /, is the same. A context-sensitive grammar is more efficient and takes a more general view of grammatical phenomena than a *context-free* one.[1]

We have illustrated the form of the first and the third portions of our grammar but have said nothing about the second. We now reveal the mystery. If we attempt to generate *Yesterday John sang* and *John sang yesterday* in one and the same grammar, we find that this is most efficiently done if we generate the first via the underlying form of the second. Thus

Example 2
(1)   S → NP + VP
(2)   VP → Vintr + Adv
(3)   Adv → *yesterday*
(4)   Vintr → *sang*
(5)   NP → *John*
          134

Topt
(6)   NP + Vintr + Adv → Adv + NP + Vintr

Rule (6) is of a form not permitted in the PS-rules; it operates on a string of symbols rather than on one only. Such a rule is a *transformational rule* and the string on the right of the arrow may be called the *transform* of the string on the left. Transformational rules make up the second part of a *Syntactic structures* grammar.

The effect of (6) is to convert the string of lexicon-items *John sang yesterday* into *Yesterday John sang*. The form of the rule refers to pre-lexicon symbols. We permit our grammar the capacity not only to scan the string in which is found the symbol to be rewritten but also to refer back to the derivational history of the sentence it is producing. (In a fuller grammar of English, we would have to allow other adverbs to behave in this way; we must not restrict the possibility to *yesterday*.) A transformational rule such as this, which rearranges the elements in the string, is a *permutation* rule. Unlike PS-rules, this particular transformational rule need *not* be applied; such rules are *optional transformational rules* and are marked accordingly as *Topt*.

Other transformational rules *must* be applied if the conditions specified in the string on the left arise. Such rules are *obligatory* transformational rules and are so marked, as *Tob*. The difference is shown by considering:

(1)   *I wound the watch up*
(2)   *I wound up the watch*
(3)   *I wound it up*

Assuming that *wind up* comes from Vtr → V + Part, then (1) and (2) arise from a rule:

Topt
V + Part + Noun → V + Noun + Part

and (3) from a rule:

Tob
V + Part + Pron → V + Pron + Part

We have introduced thus far a device, a grammar, that can specify sets of sentences; it consists of three successive parts, namely a PS-component, a transformational component and a morphophonemic component. As an illustration of these points, consider

Example 3
(1)   S → NP + VP

(2)   VP → VPhr + Adv

(3)   VPhr → Vtr + $\left\{ \begin{array}{l} \text{NP} \\ \text{Pron} \end{array} \right\}$

(4)   Vtr → V + Part

(5)   NP → Det + Noun

(6)   V → Vs + Tns

(7)   Vs → *wind*

(8) Noun → *man, clock*

(9)   Det → *the*

(10)   Part → *up*

(11)   Pron → *it*

(12)   Adv → *usually*

       Topt

(13) NP + VPhr + Adv → Adv + NP + VPhr

       Topt

(14) V + Part + NP → V + NP + Part

       Tob

(15) V + Part + Pron → V + Pron + Part

(16) *wind* + Tns → wound

Rules (1)–(12) constitute the phrase-structures rules, (7)–(12) being the lexicon. The transformational component is represented by rules (13)–(15), both (13) and (14) being optional and (15) obligatory: all three are permutation transformations. The morphophonemic component is rule (16).

The grammar specifies or produces a 'language', consisting in this case of the following strings:

(1) *The man wound up the man usually*

(2) *The man wound up the clock usually*

(3) *The clock wound up the man usually*

(4) *The clock wound up the clock usually*

(5) *The man wound it up usually*

(6) *The clock wound it up usually*

(7) *The man wound the clock up usually*

(8) *The man wound the man up usually*

(9) *The clock wound the clock up usually*

(10) *The clock wound the man up usually*

(11) *Usually the man wound up the man*

(12) *Usually the man wound up the clock*

(13) *Usually the clock wound up the man*

(14) *Usually the clock wound up the clock*

(15) *Usually the man wound the clock up*

(16) *Usually the man wound the man up*

(17) *Usually the clock wound the man up*

(18) *Usually the clock wound the clock up*
(19) *Usually the man wound it up*
(20) *Usually the clock wound it up*

It is noteworthy that such a lengthy output can be produced from a sequence of short rules. Were we to introduce more lexicon-entries (e.g. *a, this, boy, girl, watch, time-piece, blow, mess*, etc.) then the extent of the product would be impressively multiplied. Notice also that some of the above sentences are semantically odd from the point of view of the speaker of English.

We can now define a language as the output of such a grammar: so we come to a novel idea, namely that *a language is defined by its grammar*.

It is now possible to envisage a situation in which the output of a theoretician's grammar would be identical with the set of sentences used by the speakers of a natural language. If this situation should ever come to pass, then the generative grammarian will be able to write a specification, a grammar, of a natural language.

Our first task is to investigate whether such a grammar can encompass the features we have observed in natural languages.

11.2 Some features of PS-rules and transformational rules. As already stated, phrase-structure rules operate on one symbol only; this is rewritten as a string of one or more symbols. The formal relationship between the symbols on the right-hand side of a PS-rule may be one of a very limited set of types. These relationships mirror syntactic relationships holding between elements of natural languages, as follows.

They may exhibit a relationship of *simple* (*unidirectional*) *dependency*:

Example 4
    $a \rightarrow b(c)$

The brackets indicate that *b* is obligatory but *c* is optional (hence dependent upon *b*). Thus if *b* is a VP, then *c* might be Adv (Adverb) or PP (Preposition phrase). This rule describes the structure of:

> *Maude sang*
> *Maude sang incessantly*
> *Maude sang in her bath*
> . . . etc.

They may exhibit a relationship of *mutual* (*bidirectional*) *dependency*:

Example 5
    $a \rightarrow b + c$

both *b* and *c* being obligatory (hence dependent upon each other) and occurring in that sequence. Thus if *b* is NP, *c* might be VP; or if *b* is Vtr, then *c* might be NP. Such rules will specify both *Hermione swooned* (S → NP+VP) and *Benjamin painted the porch* (S → NP+VP; VP → Vtr+NP).
They may exhibit a *mutually exclusive relationship*:

Example 6

$$a \to b, c \quad \text{OR} \quad a \to \begin{Bmatrix} b \\ c \end{Bmatrix}$$

that is the choice must be made between *b* and *c*. Thus *b* might be Vintr and *c* might be Vtr+NP: for example, either *swooned* or *painted the porch*. This rule of course applies to lists of lexical choices, for example one of *Flossie, Fanny, Agnes, Roberta* or one of *ran, jumped, walked, postured*.
They may exhibit a *context-sensitive dependency*, such as rule (3) in

Example 7

(1) $a \to b+c$ (1) $N \to Ns+G$

(2) $b \to d, e$ e.g.   (2) $Ns \to Ns_1, Ns_2$

(3) $c \to \begin{Bmatrix} f/d\_ \\ g \end{Bmatrix}$ (3) $G \to \begin{Bmatrix} G_1/Ns_{1\_} \\ G_2 \end{Bmatrix}$

Rule (3) exhibits both mutually exclusive relationship and (at least) a simple dependency relationship. As the example shows, the output of a rule which assigns the correct gender to sub-classes of nouns illustrates this kind of relationship. If we are considering French, this Ns_1 would include *garçon* 'boy', *soleil* 'sun', *livre* 'book', etc., and Ns_2 *fille* 'daughter', *lune* 'moon', *livre* 'pound', etc.
Notice that in PS-rules a *zero write-out* (or *null-string*), such as $\varnothing$ in

$$*a \to \varnothing$$

is not normally permissible as the only symbol on the right-hand side. It will be found that there is no reason to have introduced *a* in the first place; alternatively the rewritings of *a* will be found to include various (probably context-sensitive) possibilities, only one of which is zero.
Transformational rules (which operate on strings of 'more than one' symbol) equally show formal differences of this kind. There appear to be only three possibilities.
Permutation transformations (already illustrated) have the effect of rearranging the order of symbols on the left-hand side into a different order on the right-hand side. These rules deal with optional or obligatory discontinuity of constituents. Such is (3) in

Example 8

(1) $a \rightarrow (b)c$	(1) $VP \rightarrow (Neg) V$
(2) $b \rightarrow d+e$	(2) $Neg \rightarrow ne+pas$
Tob e.g.	Tob
(3) $d+e+c \rightarrow d+c+e$	(3) $ne+pas+V \rightarrow ne+V+pas$

This will be necessary in the specification of French *Il ne rit pas* /in ri pɑ/ 'He is not laughing'.

Deletion transformations have the effect of removing one or more symbols from the string on the left-hand side so they do not appear on the right-hand side. Thus:

Example 9
$$a+b \rightarrow b \quad \text{e.g.} \quad NP+VP \rightarrow VP$$

This type of rule is used in the specification of such sentences as Italian *Cantò* /kan'tɔ/, literally '3rd-person-singular sang'. The original NP has fulfilled its function, so to speak, in specifying the number and person of the verb (the concord being achieved by a transformational rule of adjunction, to be described immediately below) and may consequently be deleted in this language. An example of optional deletion in an English grammar is in rule (13) of 11.3.

Adjunction transformations have the effect of adding a symbol (or more than one) to the left-hand string to form the right-hand string. The added symbol may have appeared before in the grammar, for example:

Example 10
$$a+b+c \rightarrow a+b+c+b$$

(as in the example of concord specification below), or it may not have appeared previously:

Example 11
$$a+b \rightarrow a+b+c$$

as in rule (15), *Topt Neg*, of 11.3.

The co-occurrence relations of concord and government are specified by rules of the above kinds. The definition of government as 'x governs y if a member m of the grammatical category c must occur in y whenever y occurs with x' may be 'translated' into a context-sensitive rule. For example, the Latin preposition *contra* 'against' governs the accusative case (*contra hominem* 'against the man') while *pro* 'for' governs the ablative (*pro homine* 'for the man'). This can appear as

139

Example 12
(1)   PP → Prep + N
(2)   Prep → *contra, pro*
(3)   N → Ns + Ca
(4)   Ca → $\left\{ \begin{array}{l} \text{Acc}/contra + \text{Ns}_- \\ \text{Abl} \end{array} \right\}$

or more generally, encompassing other Latin prepositions, as

Example 13
(1)   PP → Prep + N
(2)   Prep → Prep$_1$, Prep$_2$
(3)   N → Ns + Ca
(4)   Ca → $\left\{ \begin{array}{l} \text{Ca}_1/\text{Prep}_1 + \text{Ns}_- \\ \text{Ca}_2 \end{array} \right\}$

In a similar way, the definition of concord as '*x* agrees with *y* if, whenever *x* occurs with *y*, whatever grammatical categories are properties of *y* are also properties of *x*' may be 'translated' as an adjunction transformation. For example, Latin adjectives agree with the nouns they modify in gender, number and case, as in *regum bonorum* 'of good kings', both words being masculine plural genitive. This can appear as

Example 14
(1)   NP → N + Adj
(2)   N → Ns + Af
(3)   Ns → Ns$_1$, Ns$_2$, Ns$_3$
(4)   Af → G + Nu + Ca
(5)   Nu → Sing, Plur
(6)   G → $\left\{ \begin{array}{l} \text{Masc}/\text{Ns}_{1-} \\ \text{Fem } /\text{Ns}_{2-} \\ \text{Neut} \end{array} \right\}$
(7)   Adj → A
      Tob
(8)   Ns + Af − A → Ns + Af − A + Af

The effect of (8) is to convert '*reg* + Masc + Plur + Gen − A' into '*reg* + Masc + Plur + Gen − A + Masc + Plur + Gen'. The use of a hyphen rather than a plus is simply a convenient reminder of groups of constituents; it does not add any new information. The use of the most general symbol, that is the earliest to be introduced in the grammar, in this instance Af, makes unnecessary the individual specification of every possible combination of the categories involved (amounting here to 36); one general rule therefore appears instead of thirty-six independent ones. In any one application of the rule the value already assigned to the general

140

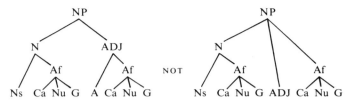

Figure 32

symbol in the left-hand string should be assigned to all repetitions of it in the right-hand string.

The apparently pointless rule (7) is necessary to provide a node so that the correct constituent structure will be assigned to the NP, as in Figure 32. Rule (6) illustrates how the correct inherent gender may be assigned to nouns; should a noun possess more than one possible gender, this may be specified by listing the noun-stem in more than one sub-class.

The above two grammars are of course only fragments of a grammar that would generate the sentences of the natural Latin language. Theoretical discussion makes frequent use of such incomplete sets of rules. One obvious omission is that of the morphophonemic component; in a synthetic language such as Latin one conceivable presentation would resemble very closely the paradigms of declensions and conjugations of traditional grammar. This illustrates a striking difference between a transformational grammar of a *Syntactic structures* variety and the layout of a traditional grammar; in the latter the listing of inflectional forms precedes the syntactic section that describes how these are joined together in sentences. In the Chomskyan model these inflections arise as a consequence of prior syntactic relations.

A second omission in our two fragments is that of the correct case-endings of the subject and object of sentences. These are of crucial importance for understanding the syntax of Latin since word-order cannot be relied upon; for example, the sentence quoted on p.114, *Miles necavit decanum*, might easily appear in any of the five other possible sequences of these words. The fact that we must generate every sentence in a single word-order first of all, given the restrictions imposed by our rewrite rules, allows us to suppose a stage NP + Vtr + NP in the generation of this particular sentence.

The situation is slightly more complicated since three cases are governed by Latin verbs; we therefore require three sub-classes of transitive verbs. We may then proceed to the allocation of case by a set of rules such as

Example 15

(1) S → NP + VP

(2) VP → $\begin{Bmatrix} \text{Vintr} \\ \text{Vtr} + \text{NP} \end{Bmatrix}$

(3) Vtr → V_1, V_2, V_3

(4) NP → N + Ca

(5) Ca → $\begin{Bmatrix} Ca_1/V_{1-} \\ Ca_2/V_{2-} \\ Ca_3/V_{3-} \\ Ca_4/_-VP \end{Bmatrix}$

(For the sake of clarity the specification of gender and number has been omitted; it can be achieved exactly as in rules (2)–(5) of Example 14. In a complete grammar of Latin the specification of case following prepositions, on the lines of rule (4) of Example 12, could be incorporated into an extended rule (5) of Example 15.)

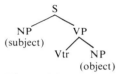

NP (subject) VP Vtr NP (object)

Figure 33

Having then achieved a sequence of stems and their appropriate case-morphemes, for example, the underlying morphemes of *Miles necavit decanum* and *Miles pepercit decano*, we may specify the range of possible word-orders by means of optional permutation transformations. The effect of this procedure is ultimately to define *subject* of a sentence as 'the NP dominated directly by the node S' and *object* as the NP dominated directly by the node VP, as in Figure 33.[2] There is thus no reference to such notions as 'the person or thing we are talking about' or 'the person performing the action' or 'the person or thing to which the action is directed'.

11.3 A section of a grammar for English. The following grammar, adapted from *Syntactic structures*,[3] illustrates some of the above general types of rule; the sentences generated are a sub-set of the sentences in the English language.

(1)   S → NP + VP
(2)   VP → Vtr + NP
(3)   NP → Det + Noun
(4) Noun → Ns + Nu
(5)   Nu → Sing, Plur
(6)   Vtr → Aux + V

(7)   Det → *the*
(8)   Ns → *man, letter*
(9)   V → *write*
(10) Aux → C (M) (*have* + *en*) (*be* + *ing*)
(11)   C → Pres, Past
(12)   M → *will, shall, may, can, must*
(13) *Topt Pass*
$$NP_1 + Aux + V + NP_2 \rightarrow NP_2 + Aux + be + en + V \ (by + NP_1)$$
(14) *Tob Concord*
$$Ns + Nu - \begin{bmatrix} Pres \\ Past \end{bmatrix} \rightarrow Ns + Nu - \begin{bmatrix} Pres \\ Past \end{bmatrix} + Nu$$
(15) *Topt Neg*
$$\begin{bmatrix} NP - C + Nu & -V \\ NP - C + Nu + M & \rightarrow X \\ NP - C + Nu + have - X \\ NP - C + Nu + be & -X \end{bmatrix} \rightarrow \begin{bmatrix} NP - C + Nu & +n't - V \\ NP - C + Nu + M & +n't - X \\ NP - C + Nu + have + n't - X \\ NP - C + Nu + be & +n't - X \end{bmatrix}$$
that is
$$X_1 - \quad X_2 \quad -X_3 \rightarrow X_1 - \quad X_2 \quad +n't - X_3$$
(16) *Topt Tq*
$$\begin{bmatrix} NP - C + Nu & (n't) - V \\ NP - C + Nu + M & (n't) - X \\ NP - C + Nu + have(n't) - X \\ NP - C + Nu + be & (n't) - X \end{bmatrix} \rightarrow \begin{bmatrix} C + Nu & (n't) - NP - V \\ C + Nu + M & (n't) - NP - X \\ C + Nu + have & (n't) - NP - X \\ C + Nu + be & (n't) - NP - X \end{bmatrix}$$
that is
$$X_1 - \quad X_2 \quad -X_3 \rightarrow \quad X_2 \quad -X_1 - X_3$$
(17) *Topt Tw* (conditional on Tq)
   (i) Tw_1 X − NP − Y → NP − X − Y
                  (X or Y may be null)
   (ii) $Tw_2 \begin{bmatrix} NP_{an} \\ NP_{in} \end{bmatrix} - X \rightarrow \begin{bmatrix} who \\ what \end{bmatrix} - X$
(18) *Tob Taux*
     Af − v → v   − Af ‡
          (v = V, M, *have, be*
          Af = C + Nu, *en, ing*)
(19) *Tob T word-boundary*
     X − Y → X − ‡ Y
          (X − Y ≠ v − Af
          Y ≠ *n't*, Nu)
(20) *Tob*
     S → ‡ S ‡
(21) *Tob Tdo*
     ‡ Af → ‡ *do* − Af

The particular syntactic phenomena correctly specified by this grammar include complex verbal forms (i.e. all combinations of tense-morphemes and the two kinds of aspect), negative verbal forms, passive sentences and two types of interrogative sentences ('yes-no' questions and some kinds of *wh*-questions). The specified sentences amount to no fewer than 756, none of this variation being attributable to difference in lexicon choice; these rules therefore represent a most important section of a full grammar of English. The diversity of forms range from the simple *The man writes the letter* to *Isn't the man writing the letter?*, *Did the man write the letter? Couldn't the letter have been being written?*, *Who was the letter written by?* and *What did the man write?*. Already we see that this grammar can give a structural description, couched in terms of the rules necessary for their generation, of those verbal forms which proved intractable to IC analysis (see Figure 29).

We now illustrate the working of these rules by producing eight sentences. Each line represents a string produced by the part of the grammar up to and including the rule whose number appears at the beginning. The necessity for a morphophonemic component to specify the correct surface forms of, for example, *write + Past + Sing* is obvious.

(*a*) *The man wrote the letters*
(9) the + man + Sing + Aux + write + the + letter + Plur
(10) the + man + Sing + C + write + the + letter + Plur
(11) the + man + Sing + Past + write + the + letter + Plur
(14) the + man + Sing + Past + Sing + write + the + letter + Plur
(18) the + man + Sing + write + Past + Sing + the + letter + Plur
(19) the ♯ man + Sing ♯ write + Past + Sing ♯ the ♯ letter + Plur
(20) ♯ the ♯ man + Sing ♯ write + Past + Sing ♯ the ♯ letter + Plur ♯

(*b*) *The man didn't write the letters*
(14) the + man + Sing + Past + Sing + write + the + letter + Plur
(15) the + man + Sing + Past + Sing + n't + write + the + letter + Plur
   (Rule (18) cannot be applied since *n't* comes between *Af* and *v*.)
(19) the ♯ man + Sing ♯ Past + Sing + n't ♯ write ♯ the ♯ letter + Plur
(21) ♯ the ♯ man + Sing ♯ do + Past + Sing + n't ♯ write ♯ the ♯ letter + Plur ♯

(*c*) *Must the man write the letters?*
(9) the + man + Sing + Aux + write + the + letter + Plur
(10) the + man + Sing + C + M + write + the + letter + Plur
(12) the + man + Sing + Pres + must + write + the + letter + Plur
(14) the + man + Sing + Pres + Sing + must + write + the + letter + Plur
(16) Pres + Sing + must + the + man + Sing + write + the + letter + Plur

144

(18) must + Pres + Sing + the + man + Sing + write + the + letter + Plur

(*d*) *The letters are being written*
(9) the + man + Sing + Aux + write + the + letter + Plur
(10) the + man + Sing + C + be + ing + write + the + letter + Plur
(11) the + man + Sing + Pres + be + ing + write + the + letter + Plur
(13) the + letter + Plur + Pres + be + ing + be + en + write
(14) the + letter + Plur + Pres + Plur + be + ing + be + en + write
(18) the + letter + Plur + be + Pres + Plur + be + ing + write + en
    (Each of the three original sequences of *v* − *Af*, namely
    Pres + *Plur* − *be*, *ing* − *be*, *en* − *write* has been reversed.)
(20) ♯ the ♯ letter + Plur ♯ be + Pres + Plur ♯ be + ing ♯ write + en ♯

(*e*) *Did the man write the letters?*
(14) the + man + Sing + Past + Sing + write + the + letter + Plur
(16) Past + Sing + the + man + Sing + write + the + letter + Plur
(20) ♯ Past + Sing ♯ the ♯ man + Sing ♯ write ♯ the ♯ letter + Plur ♯
(21) ♯ do + Past + Sing ♯ the ♯ man + Sing ♯ write ♯ the ♯ letter +
    Plur ♯

(*f*) *Who wrote the letters?*
(16) Past + Sing + the + man + Sing + write + the + letter + Plur
(17) (i) the + man + Sing + Past + Sing + write + the + letter + Plur
(17) (ii) who + Past + Sing + write + the + letter + Plur
(18) who + write + Past + Sing + the + letter + Plur
    (The application of rule (17) simply undid the work of rule
    (16); this was due to our selection of the NP to be permuted.
    The different selections in (*g*) and (*h*) do not have this effect.
    The rule therefore,-so far from being pointless, proves to be
    of general value.)

(*g*) *What did the man write?*
(16) Past + Sing + the + man + Sing + write + the + letter + Plur
(17) (i) the + letter + Plur + Past + Sing + the + man + write
(17) (ii) what + Past + Sing + the + man + write
(21) ♯ what ♯ do + Past + Sing ♯ the ♯ man ♯ write ♯

(*h*) *Who were the letters written by?*
(11) the + man + Sing + Past + write + the + letter + Plur
(13) the + letter + Plur + Past + be + en + write + by + the + man +
    Sing
(14) the + letter + Plur + Past + Plur + be + en + write + by + the +
    man + Sing
(16) Past + Plur + be + the + letter + Plur + en + write + by + the +
    man + Sing
145

(17) (i) the + man + Sing + Past + Plur + be + the + letter + Plur +
en + write + by
(17) (ii) who + Past + Plur + be + the + letter + Plur + en + write + by
(18) who + be + Past + Plur + the + letter + Plur + write + en + by
(20) ♯ who ♯ be + Past + Plur ♯ the ♯ letter + Plur ♯ write + en ♯ by ♯

In getting to grips with the above grammar the reader is urged not to be a cursory one; the apparent complexity of the workings of the rules is due to unfamiliarity and an unhurried experimentation with the aid of paper and pencil will expose the essential simplicity of each individually in a surprisingly short time. The beginner should not rest content with the above examples; greater enlightenment will come by going on to produce one's own applications of the rules. A start could be made by observing only the minimum obligatory elements and then gradually testing the effects of the different optional contents of the grammar; finally a search should be made for the most complicated single output of the rules, which will be something like *Who couldn't the letters have been written by?* (Apropos this last sentence and the output of (*h*), Chomsky's grammar produces the alleged 'colloquial' form; the rules would have to be extended to produce the 'correct' *By whom were the letters written?* The reader is invited to work out the changes necessary.)

The grammar then is remarkable for its 'power', its shortness compared with its massive output. But we can see a further feature of importance characteristic of transformational-generative grammars: it shows clearly that sentences that are of different surface appearance may in fact be closely related. This might have been expected in the case of, for example, *The man wrote the letters* and *The letters were written by the man*, differing only in that the second requires the application of the optional rule (13). (It was for this reason that we stated in 9.10 that there was no category of voice in English; passive sentences are achieved by a syntactic process rather than by the presence of a 'passive' morpheme. But on this particular point there is much food for thought, see Chapter 16.) It may be more surprising to observe that *What did the man write?* and *Who wrote the letters?* are produced by the application of exactly the same rules and that a close connection exists between interrogative sentences and negative sentences in English, visible in the tripartite structure of the left-hand string in rules (15) and (16) and in the consequently obligatory insertion of *do* (rule (21)) in certain clearly defined cases.

FURTHER READING
See Chapter 13.
146

12. Generalised Transformations

12.1 Singulary and generalised transformations. Chapter 11 illustrated grammatical phenomena handled by PS-rules and transformational rules. So far, all the transformational rules shown have operated on one string, that is on only one output of the PS-rules: they may therefore be termed *singulary* or *single-based* transformations. But many phenomena are explicable (in the *Syntactic structures* model) only in terms of transformations which operate on two strings, generated independently in the PS-rules; these are *generalised* or *double-based* transformations.

The first string generated is, as it were, 'held' until the second string has been generated and is ready to be combined with it. After the combinatory rule has been applied, the resulting string of abstract morphemes may undergo further transformations, finally to progress through the morphophonemic component to achieve concrete shape. The ordering of generalised transformations with respect to each other and to singulary transformations gives rise to some difficulty, but this need not concern us. In *Syntactic structures*, the varieties of types of and the formulations of generalised transformations are not elaborated upon to any great extent, although they play an important part in Chomsky's theorising. We present therefore in this chapter an illustration of different types of generalised transformation possible within the *Syntactic structures* model, but very informally. For the most part we illustrate the strings of morphemes under discussion not as abstract symbols but as orthographic words 'smuggled' through the morphophonemic rules; nor do we present rigorous formulations of the generalising rules. It is sufficient that the principles are grasped.

12.2 Conjoining transformations. Generalised transformations fall into two types, *conjoining* and *embedding*, the criterion being the hierarchical relationship of the two input strings in the output. Conjoining transformations combine two input strings in such a way that we may talk of them as being 'added' together; both are of equal 'importance' in the output: neither underlying string (represented here by the nodes S_1 and S_2) 'dominates' the other, as in Figure 34. An example would be *Charlie told stories and Robert*

147

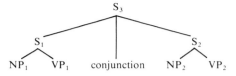

Figure 34

sang ballads resulting from the conjoining of '*Charlie told stories*' (S_1) and *Robert sang ballads* (S_2) by a rule:

$$S_1 + S_2 \rightarrow S_1 + and + S_2$$

Other 'connectives' are of course possible, such as *but, or, either . . . or* in English. Such elements introduced in the transformational component must feed directly into the morphophonemic component; they do not appear in the lexicon of the PS-component.

There must be some similarity of derivational history in the strings being conjoined; such an output as **Who told stories and Robert sang ballads* must not be permitted. We do not deal with this aspect further. In actual language semantic appropriateness will be observed in conjoining; e.g. it is highly unlikely that **I am about to lecture and Vesuvius used to erupt frequently* will occur. But such restrictions cannot be written into grammar of this type.

If two strings to be conjoined are of the form $NP + VP$, and if $NP_1 = NP_2$, then the rule above may be applied, giving an output, for example

> *John ran and John played football*

though this is somewhat unusual. More frequently a rule of the form

$$NP_1 + VP_1 + NP_1 + VP_2 \rightarrow NP_1 + VP_1 + and + Pron + VP_2$$

is applied, producing *John ran and he played football* though gender-agreement has to be specified (by writing more precisely as $Ns + G - VP_1 - and - Prns + G - VP_2$). Often a conjoining rule completely deleting the second of the identical NPs,

$$NP_1 + VP_1 + NP_1 + VP_2 \rightarrow NP_1 + VP_1 + and + VP_2$$

is applied, to give *John ran and played football*.

In the same way, if two strings of the form $NP + VP$ are to be conjoined, and if $VP_1 = VP_2$, then the first occurrence of the identical VP may be deleted, thus

$$NP_1 + VP_1 + NP_2 + VP_1 \rightarrow NP_1 + and + NP_2 + VP_1$$

e.g. *John and Henry play football*. Notice that this conjoining rule must be applied *before* an agreement-in-number rule to avoid **John and Henry plays football*. Such strings may also be conjoined in a *Tso Topt* transformation, giving *John plays football and so does Henry*; this would have to be applied before the *T do Tob* rule, to avoid **John plays football and so s Henry*.

There are many instances of conjoining strings identical apart from the fact that where S_1 has x, S_2 has y; the principle is to link x and y by *and*, then to delete one occurrence of the identical portion. Such rules generate sentences of types like *The lamplighter turned the light on in the evening and off in the morning, Minnie cycled into and out of town, Boris walked and canoed across the island, Yootha was, and still is, a prude*. The constituents x and y must be of the same type; thus *I have lost the book on hang-gliding* and *I have lost the book I was reading* cannot be conjoined as **I have lost the book on hang-gliding and I was reading*. (Input strings of this type are themselves the product of generalised transformations, as we shall see.)

This is not the whole story on conjoining by any means. Another type of conjoining is necessary to explain *The car and the Black Maria collided*, for this cannot come from **The car collided* and **The Black Maria collided*. Similarly *Jason and Melanie were in agreement* poses difficulties. It is ambiguous; we may paraphrase the meanings as (i) that each was in agreement with the other; (ii) that each was independently in agreement with some other thing or person. The sentence which has the first meaning cannot be derived from *Jason was in agreement* and *Melanie was in agreement*. By the same token *Janet and Mike were playing squash* is ambiguous; *I loathe Gilbert and Sullivan* is understood differently from *I loathe Alain Fournier and Berlioz*; and *Doris jumped up and down* is not the same as *Doris jumped up, and down*.

The word *and* can indicate either the conjoining of two independently generated strings, or it can indicate what appears to be a conjoining of two NPs which together function as one element in the output sentence. (It is conceivable that a language could represent the English *and* in these two situations by two different surface words.) But it is not clear how the latter situation is to be handled in a grammar of the present type. It is impossible to conjoin NPs so that they appear as compound units in the lexicon, and therefore we seem to have only possibilities such as deriving from *The car collided with the Black Maria* (a singulary transformation) or from both *The car collided with the Black Maria* and *The Black Maria collided with the car*. But it is not clear how this suggested derivation can be applied to cases such as *Gilbert and*

Sullivan or *He gave a lecture on Goethe and Byron,* or to pairs of nouns connected by *between,* as in *Betsy explained the difference between crocodiles and alligators.* The conclusion is that further problems remain to be solved in constructing a grammatical model.

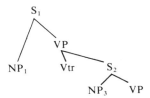

Figure 35

12.3 Embedding transformations. Embedding transformations combine two strings in such a way that in the output we may speak of one as being of greater 'importance' than the other: the less important has been inserted into the more important (the *matrix*). The more important S-node 'dominates' the others, as in Figure 35. This tree is the structure of *He told me Jo was ill* and it can be regarded as being derived from that in Figure 36 by the insertion or embedding of S_2 in place of NP_2. We could symbolise the derivation by means of a rule

$$\left.\begin{array}{l} S_1 = NP_1 + Vtr + NP_2 \\ S_2 = NP_3 + VP \end{array}\right\} \rightarrow NP_1 + Vtr + NP_3 + VP$$

that is, in this case:

$$\left.\begin{array}{l} S_1 = \textit{He told me } NP \\ S_2 = \textit{Jo cop ill} \end{array}\right\} \rightarrow \textit{He told me Jo was ill}$$

(The symbol *cop,* reminiscent of 'copula', is used here to represent an element which may appear in the final product as a part of ⟨BE⟩.)

Having illustrated the principle we demonstrate types of embedding transformations, using fairly loose formulations and a somewhat ad hoc terminology.

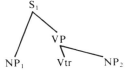

Figure 36

12.4 Adverbial replacements. One group of embedding transformations inserts an S in place of an adverbial in the matrix, for example:

$$\left. \begin{array}{l} S_1 = NP_1 + VbP_1 + Adv \\ S_2 = NP_2 + VP_2 \end{array} \right\} \rightarrow NP_1 + VbP_1 + when + NP_2 + VP_2$$

Thus, if S_1 is *The cupboard was bare* Adv and S_2 is *She got there*, then the output of the above is *The cupboard was bare when she got there*. Similar transformations in English employ *if*, *because*, *although*, *whenever*, *as*, *unless*, etc.

It is probable that the optional Adv in the PS-rules may be written out as

$$Adv \rightarrow (Adv_{Time})(Adv_{Place})(Adv_{Reason})(Adv_{Manner})$$

(using this notation to mean that all possible choices and combinations are possible). This has the advantages that various co-occurring adverbs in a simple write-out may be specified, that in embedding transformations various kinds of subordinate clauses may be attached and that by using an elaboration of the *Tw* transformation quoted in 11.3, we may generate *when?*, *where?*, *why?* and *how?* questions.

Outputs of the applications of the above rules may undergo the optional permutation of Rule (6) in *Example 2* of 11.1, giving *When she got there, the cupboard was bare*. Such a possibility must of course be specifically indicated in the grammar of a natural language: it cannot be taken for granted.

The rule may require restrictions on co-occurrence of tenses, as in English (we must exclude **The cupboard was bare when she gets there*). Similar rules in other languages may require permutation of word-order in the embedded sentence (as in German) or government of a particular mood in the embedded sentence (as in French, Latin, Italian, etc.). If the NPs of the matrix and the embedded sentence are identical in English, the NP in the embedded sentence may be deleted and the tense-marker of the verb in the embedded sentence replaced by *ing* in certain circumstances, for example:

Although arriving late, Mrs Spriddle entered noisily

(but not

*Because arriving late, Mrs Spriddle entered noisily).

Indeed no 'operator' need be used: *Arriving late, Mrs Spriddle entered noisily*.

12.5 Restrictive relativisations. A different type of embedding transformation is the set of restrictive relativising transformations; in these an NP in the matrix is identical with an NP in the S to be embedded: for example, S_1 is *The man shot the crocodile* (matrix) and S_2 is *The man alarmed Mrs Spriddle.* These may be combined as *The man who alarmed Mrs Spriddle shot the crocodile.* Similarly, *The man shot the crocodile which alarmed Mrs Spriddle* results from

S_1: *The man shot the crocodile* (matrix) and
S_2: *The crocodile alarmed Mrs Spriddle.*

The specification of such transformations may be treated in stages: first the replacement of the NP in the embedded S by a Pron., then the insertion of a WH- element into the matrix (after the appropriate NP) followed by the embedded S. But there is a third stage in English and other languages which requires that the pronoun be 'permuted' so that it follows the WH- and thereafter a morphophonemic rule assigns a shape to WH- + Pron. Thus:

Stage 1	S_1	*The man shot the crocodile*
	S_2	*Mrs Spriddle alarmed the crocodile* → *Mrs Spriddle alarmed it*
Stage 2		*The man shot the crocodile* WH- *Mrs Spriddle alarmed it*
Stage 3		*The man shot the crocodile* WH- *it Mrs Spriddle alarmed* (WH- + it thereafter → *which*)

But this additional stage is not found in many languages, which write out the WH- element in the surface and also the pronoun in its 'original' form. For example, Hebrew:

/ha- 'iʃʃa ʃɛ- da'viːd 'natan la   ɛt   ha- 'seːfɛr/
'the girl WH- David gave   to her (Acc) the book'

that is 'The girl to whom David gave the book'.

12.6 Adjectivalisations. Adjectivalising embedding rules insert an Adj adjacent to a Noun in the matrix; this Adj is the sole survivor of the embedded S of the form Noun + cop + Adj, the noun being identical to the one in the matrix. Thus:

$$\left. \begin{array}{l} S_1 = \text{Det} + \text{Noun} + \text{VP} \\ \quad \textit{The} \quad \textit{man} \quad \textit{sang} \\ S_2 = \text{Det} + \text{Noun} + \text{cop} + \text{Adj} \\ \quad \textit{The} \quad \textit{man} \quad \text{cop} \quad \textit{drunk} \end{array} \right\} \rightarrow \begin{array}{l} \text{Det} + \text{Adj} \; + \; \text{Noun} + \text{VP} \\ \textit{The} \quad \textit{drunk} \quad \textit{man} \quad \textit{sang} \end{array}$$

A similar type inserts a PP adjacent to the Noun, but in English the PP follows the Noun:

$$S_1 = Det + Noun + VP$$
The man sang
$$S_2 = Det + Noun + cop + PP$$
The man cop on the bus

$\rightarrow \quad Det + Noun + PP + VP$
The man on the bus sang

Such PPs may also appear at the beginning or end of an S if the NP which is deleted is identical with the subject NP of the matrix, so also may Adjs. Thus: *With his arm in a sling, the man sang*; *The man sang with his arm in a sling*; *Furious, the girl left the room*; *The girl left the room, furious.* Such usages are non-restrictive, that is they give additional information. Contrast *The man with his arm in a sling sang* and *The furious girl left the room.*

Thus grammatical ambiguities arise in the case of PPs at the end of Ss; semantically, the ambiguity may not be very important, or one alternative is so idiotic that the brain refuses to consider it (a most interesting property of human understanding of language). But consider:

(*a*)   *Szigeti played the violin with a broad grin*
($\leftarrow$ NP[= *Szigeti*] + cop + PP) (Non-restrictive)
(*b*)   *Szigeti played the violin with a loose bridge*
($\leftarrow$ NP[= *violin*] + cop + PP) (Restrictive)
(*c*)   *Szigeti played the violin with a new bow*
(No generalised transformations involved; PP is an expansion of Adv$_{Manner}$ present in VP).

The PP may be embedded in front of the Noun in the matrix with the deletion of the Prep. (but this is only permissible in the case of Preps. like *for, from, in, like, on, to, with*, etc., not *without*, etc.). Thus we can account for formations such as: *the ice-man* ($\leftarrow$ *the man* cop *with ice*); *the snow-man* ($\leftarrow$ *the man* cop *of snow*); *the ice-axe* ($\leftarrow$ *the axe* cop *for ice*); *the London correspondent* ($\leftarrow$ *the correspondent* cop *in London*). Sometimes semantic ambiguities arise, for example *the London train* (either $\leftarrow$ *the train* cop *to London* or $\leftarrow$ *the train* cop *from London*; *baby meringues* ($\leftarrow$ *of* or $\leftarrow$ *like* or $\leftarrow$ *for babies*).

On occasion the Noun from the PP, preceding the matrix Noun, that is in typical adjectival embedded position, may be given the termination of an Adj derived from a Noun, and will be given an acceptable surface adjectival form by the morphophonemic component. Thus: *medical student* ($\leftarrow$ *student of medicine*, NOT $\leftarrow$ *student* cop *medical*); *legal problem* ($\leftarrow$ *problem of law*, NOT $\leftarrow$ *problem* cop *legal*); *atmospheric scientist* ($\leftarrow$ *scientist of the atmosphere*, NOT $\leftarrow$ *scientist* cop *atmospheric*). Certain of such formations may be grammatically and semantically ambiguous, for example *French lecturer* (either ← *lecturer* cop *French* or ← *lecturer* cop *in French*); *religious leader* (either ← *leader* cop *religious* or ← *leader* cop *of religion*); *BBC's Chinese correspondent* (← *correspondent* cop *in China* or ← *correspondent* cop *Chinese*).

12.7 Factive ('that') nominalisations. Nominalisations are embedding transformations which insert a string in place of an NP in the matrix. Some writers include under nominalisations transformations which attach a string to an NP, so that what we termed 'adjectivalisation' would be regarded as a type of nominalisation.

Factive nominalisations involve the embedding of the string, introduced by *that*; the NP to which it is attached must be deleted unless it is one of a small set of nouns such as *fact, claim, lie, proposal, suggestion*, etc. Thus:

S_1 *The suggestion alarmed the vicar*
S_2 = *Queen Anne cop dead* (or with deletion of the NP)

→ *The suggestion that Queen Anne was dead alarmed the vicar*
→ *That Queen Anne was dead alarmed the vicar*

The string embedded in subject position may be permuted to the end of the new S, thus *The suggestion that Queen Anne was dead alarmed the vicar* → *The suggestion alarmed the vicar that Queen Anne was dead*. But the gap left by any deleted NP must be filled by *it*: *That Queen Anne was dead alarmed the vicar* → *It alarmed the vicar that Queen Anne was dead*.

The output of this type of transformation may bear a superficial resemblance to the output of restrictive relativising transformations; compare *The suggestion that he made amused Beth* and *The suggestion that he smoked amused Beth*. There may even be ambiguity: *The idea that he proposed made her laugh*.

In the case of the restrictive relativising and of the factive nominalising transformations, the *that* (arising in the one case from WH- + Pron and in the other from *that*) may be deleted. Thus both *The suggestion he made amused Beth* and *The suggestion he smoked amused Beth* are possible. But WH- + Pron may be written out by the morphophonemic rules alternatively as *which* (or *who* depending on animateness of Pron). Thus: *The suggestion which he made amused Beth* but NOT **The suggestion which he smoked amused Beth*.

12.8 Gerundial ('-ing') nominalisations. *Gerundial* nominalisations replace an NP in the matrix by an S in which Aux + Verb is converted to Verb + *ing*: the subject-NP of the embedded S becomes NP's or *of* NP. In the case of intransitive verbs:

154

12. Generalised Transformations

$S_1 =$ NP *was a distraction* $\left.\begin{array}{l} \\ \end{array}\right\} \rightarrow$
$S_2 = $ *The nurse* Aux $+$ *giggle*
(1) *The nurse's giggling was a distraction*
(2) *The giggling of the nurse was a distraction*

The original NP of the embedded string may be deleted: the resulting Noun may be a Mass Noun or a Count Noun. Thus:

(1) *The giggling was a distraction*
(2) *Giggling annoyed him*

In the case of transitive verbs there are several possibilities:

$S_1 =$ NP *is an eccentricity* $\left.\begin{array}{l} \\ \end{array}\right\} \rightarrow$
$S_2 = $ *The lecturer* Aux $+$ *wear a monocle*
(1) *The lecturer's wearing a monocle is an eccentricity*
(2) *The lecturer's wearing of a monocle is an eccentricity*
(3) *The lecturer's monocle-wearing is an eccentricity*

Here the subject-NP may be deleted from the embedded S, resulting in

(4) *Wearing a monocle is an eccentricity*
(5) *The wearing of a monocle is an eccentricity*
(6) *Monocle-wearing is an eccentricity*

In the case of transitive verbs allowing object-deletion, similar transformations occur:

The Queen Aux-*hunt foxes* →
(1) *The Queen's hunting foxes . . .*
(2) *The Queen's hunting of foxes . . .*
(3) *The Queen's fox-hunting . . .*
(4) *Hunting foxes* [*is unfashionable*]
(5) *The hunting of foxes* [*is unfashionable*]
(6) *Fox-hunting* [*is unfashionable*]

But the original object-NP may be deleted (unlike the case of transitive verbs) '*The Queen's hunting . . .*' or '*The hunting of the Queen . . .*'. Indeed the original subject-NP and object-NP may both be deleted: *Hunting . . .* [*is unfashionable*] or *The hunting . . .* [*was fast and furious*].

Transitive verbs of both types may undergo a passive transformation before the S_2 is embedded:

(a) $S_2 = $ *A monocle* Aux $+$ *be* $+$ en $+$ *wear by the lecturer* →
    The wearing of a monocle by the lecturer
(b) $S_2 = $ *Foxes* Aux $+$ *be* $+$ en $+$ *hunt by the Queen* →
    The hunting of foxes by the Queen

The *by* + NP may be deleted:

> *The wearing of a monocle . . .* AND *The hunting of foxes . . .*

Some forms therefore, such as *The hunting of the Queen . . .* are then semantically ambiguous, arising from either NP *hunts the Queen* (with passive transformation) or *The Queen hunts* NP.

The (passive) subject of the S_2 may be deleted: *Being worn by a lecturer* [*damages a monocle*] and *Being hunted by the Queen* [*is no fun*]. Both NPs may be deleted: *Being worn* [*damages a monocle*] AND *Being hunted* [*is no fun*].

12.9 Non-gerundial action-nominalisations.

Non-gerundial action-nominalisations are syntactically very similar to gerundial nominalisations: the difference is that the Aux (and any *be* + *en*) is replaced not by *ing* but by another nominalising element which is converted by the morphophonemic rules into a wide variety of phonological shapes. For example,

(*a*) (Intransitive verb)   *The earth* Aux + *revolve* →
                                      The revolution of the earth . . .

(*b*) (Transitive verb)   *The choir* Aux + *perform the cantata* →
                                        The choir's performance of the cantata . . .

It is possible to apply a passive transformation to transitive verbs before embedding, thus:

> *The cantata* Aux + *be* + en + *perform by the choir* →
>   *The performance of the cantata by the choir . . .*
> *The enemy* Aux + *be* + en + *defeat by the army* →
>   *The defeat of the enemy by the army . . .*

The choice of surface preposition to mark the underlying subject-NP and object-NP is very much as in gerundial nominalisations. In the case of an original intransitive verb, the underlying subject may be marked as either *of* NP or NP's, e.g. *The revolution of the earth . . .* or *The earth's revolution. . . .* If both underlying subject and object appear (without a passive transformation), the subject is normally marked as NP's and the object as *of* NP, e.g. *The board's promotion of Mr Bagshot.* If a passive transformation has been applied, then the original subject is marked as *by* + NP and the original object as either *of* + NP or NP's, for example *The promotion of Mr Bagshot by the board* or *Mr Bagshot's promotion by the board.*

Any underlying NP may be deleted. In the case of active verbs, (*a*) the original subject, (*b*) the original object or (*c*) both original subject and object are deleted in respectively:

12. Generalised Transformations

(a) NP Aux + *revolve*   → *The revolution* . . .
(b) NP Aux + *perform the cantata* → *The performance of the choir* . . .

AND

The choir's performance . . .

(c) NP$_1$ Aux + *perform* NP$_2$ → *The performance* . . .

In the case of strings which have undergone a passive transformation, (a) the original subject, (b) the original object or (c) both original subject and object may likewise be deleted as in respectively:

(a) *The cantata* Aux + be + en + *perform by* NP →
      The performance of the cantata . . .

AND

The cantata's performance . . .

(b) NP Aux + be + en + *perform by the choir* →
      The performance by the choir . . .
(c) NP$_1$ Aux + be + en + *perform by* NP$_2$ →
      The performance . . .

Such possibilities make for identical surface representations, for example

(a) *The choir's performance* . . .; *The performance of the choir* . . .
(b) *The cantata's performance* . . .; *The performance of the cantata* . . .

If the deleted NP (of either type) is animate, semantic ambiguity may result, for example especially if the retained NP appears as NP*'s* rather than *of* + NP: *Hermione's rejection shattered Lionel* and *Hermione's betrayal shattered Lionel*.

12.10 Underlying adverbs of manner. We have seen in 11.4 that an underlying VP must be expandable to include an optional set of adverbial elements, including one of 'Manner', thus

$$VP → VbP + Adv_{Manner}$$

This may of course be written out as a surface adverb (e.g. *He sang loudly*) and as *how?* via a Tw question transformation. Being optional it may not appear at all. In the two groups we have just discussed, gerundial and non-gerundial action-nominalisations, this underlying adverbial element must, if it appears, be written out as a surface adjective, thus

(a) *He sang loudly*   → *His loud singing* . . .
(b) *He performed his duties efficiently* → *His efficient performance*
                                                 of his duties . . .

The discussion in 12.7 and 12.8 assumed that this option was not taken up, that is that there was no selection of an underlying Adv_{Manner}. But it may be that the Adv_{Manner} is postulated, only to be deleted subsequently. This rather unexpected distinction allows us to give a regular syntactic explanation for the alternative understanding of these nominalisations as containing elements which can be paraphrased either as 'the fact that' or 'the manner in which'. Compare

(*a*) *His singing was an act of courage in view of his illness*
       The performance was a triumph over difficulties
(*b*) *His singing was excruciating*
       The performance could have been better

In (*b*) the nominalisations are derived from strings containing a deleted Adv_{Manner}, in (*a*) there is no such element. On occasions there is ambiguity: *Her driving terrified me*.

12.11 'To' nominalisations. A nominalisation similar to those described in 12.8 and 12.9 embeds a string in which Aux is replaced by *to*; this string may or may not have undergone passive transformation but in either case the immediately-occurring subject of the string to be embedded may be deleted. For example:

$$\left. \begin{array}{l} S_1 = NP \text{ *is quite normal*} \\ S_2 = NP_2 \text{ Aux-}dream \end{array} \right\} \rightarrow \text{*To dream is quite normal*}$$

It is applicable in the case of object-deleting and object-retaining transitives, to give for example *To sing madrigals is the mark of a gentleman*, *To sing is the mark of a gentleman* and *To back horses is not advisable*. After a passive transformation, the *original* subject-NP may be deleted (*To be knighted was his ambition*) or retained (*To be sentenced by the judge was his fate*). However, the immediately-occurring subject of the embedded string may be retained, preceded by *for*, as in *For Olga to have nightmares was not unusual*, *For the princess to be criticised by the bishop was a matter of public interest*.

Any *to*-nominalisation may be embedded as the complement (NP_2) of a $NP_1 + \text{cop} + NP_2$ sentence: *My secret dream is to keep bees*. Thereafter it may be permuted from subject-position in the output sentence to the end of the sentence with the insertion of an *It* to fill the consequent gap: *To watch trains fascinated Nigel* → *It fascinated Nigel to watch trains*. But as always care has to be taken in framing precise rules, for example to admit *I did not like Nigel to observe trains*, *My hope was for Cullis to be made leader* but to exclude **It fascinated me for Gregory to talk about linguistics* and **I didn't approve of Maggie to go to the Caribbean*.

12. Generalised Transformations

12.12 'Abstract' nominalisations. 'Abstract' nominalisations result from the embedding of a string of the form NP+cop+Adj into a matrix, via a nominalising element which is thereafter written out together with the adjectival component as a single lexical item by the morphophonemic rules; the subject-NP of the embedded string may be attached as NP's or *of* NP. For example,

$$S_1 = NP \; was \; remarkable$$
$$S_2 = The \; linguist \; was \; good$$

$\rightarrow$ *The linguist's goodness was remarkable*

AND

The goodness of the linguist was remarkable

The variety of surface forms is illustrated by the pairs *broad, breadth*; *charming, charm*; *erudite, erudition*; *idiotic, idiocy*; and *sober, sobriety.* Comparable nominalisations result from an embedded string $NP_1 + cop + NP_2$: *bachelordom, headmastership, knighthood, manhood, nationhood, spinsterhood, virginity.* The original subject-NP of the embedded string may of course be deleted, as in *Sobriety is to be recommended.*

12.13 Agentive nominalisations. A final group may be described as *agentive* nominalisations. In these a string $NP_1 + VP$ is embedded (to replace NP_2) in a string $NP_1 + cop + NP_2$, for example

$$S_1 = Egbert + Aux + giggle$$
$$S_2 = Egbert + cop + NP_2$$

$\rightarrow$ *Egbert is a giggler*

The Aux is deleted from the string to be embedded and replaced by an agentive nominalising morpheme very frequently written out as -*er* by the morphophonemic rules.

Should the string to be embedded be of the form $NP_1 + Vtr + NP_2$, then the object-NP (NP_2) may appear prefixed to the agentive noun without a preposition, or after it as *of* NP_2: *The lecturer is a monocle-wearer, Nellie is a bearer of tales.*

An Adv in S_1 may appear as a surface Adj. For example, *The entomologist is a secret drinker* is derivable from the embedded string *The entomologist* Aux *drink secretly*, and *not* from *The drinker cop *secret* as would be the case if it were an adjectivalising transformation. In this way we can indicate a clear syntactic difference between the sentences *Maria is an atrocious singer* and *Maria is a famous singer*, and between the two interpretations of *Maria is a beautiful singer.*

12.14 Recursiveness and the importance of generalised transformations. Certain types of generalised transformation are *recursive*,

159

12. Generalised Transformations

that is their output may be used as one input of a second application of the same rule, a new string forming the other input. For example

(1) S_1 = *The firm builds schools* ⎫
    S_2 = *The firm builds houses* ⎬ → *The firm builds schools and houses*

(2) S_1 = *The firm builds schools and houses* ⎫
    S_2 = *The firm builds offices* ⎬ → *The firm builds schools and houses and offices*

These recursive generalised transformations may be re-applied an unlimited number of times. Each of the following sentences results from the repeated application of an embedding rule:

(a) *When Queen Victoria sat on the throne and when cows grazed in Hyndland, there were eighteen theatres in Glasgow.*
(b) *A man wearing a blue anorak and carrying a small bomb entered the lecture-room.*
(c) *That large white expensive car belongs to my colleague.*

Generalised transformations may be combined to yield a richness and variety of sentence-type comparable to that found in natural languages. Examination of the following sentence by Charles Dickens[1] will demonstrate the application of the types of rule described in this chapter; those readers who care to count them may be surprised at the number of transformations detectable in a sentence of this length:

> *There was one little weazen, dried-apple-faced old woman, who took occasion to doubt the constancy of husbands in such circumstances of bereavement; and there was another lady (with a lap-dog) old enough to moralize on the lightness of human affections, and yet not so old that she could help nursing the baby, now and then, or laughing with the rest, when the little woman called it by its father's name, and asked it all manner of fantastic questions concerning him in the joy of her heart.*

Much longer sentences are found. Indeed the property of recursiveness means that there is *no* restriction on the length of sentences; consider the string:

> *I well remember the day when Churchill was buried because I was travelling from Glasgow to Edinburgh in one of the diesel trains which had been introduced in the 1950s as the use of steam-power was gradually abandoned, although it had proved its worth over the long years since its invention by Richard Trevithick, the illustrious son of Cornwall, where, as legend has it, Tristan and Isolde . . .*

160

12. Generalised Transformations

Such a string may be continued indefinitely by the continued application of recursive generalised transformations, although it must stop at *some* point in order to become a sentence. Therefore, as far as the grammar is concerned, a language contains an *infinite number of possible sentence-lengths*. As a consequence, the sentences of a language are also *infinite in number*.

Restrictions are imposed by limitations of human beings. In the same way, the rules of football do not exclude the possibility of a score of 1 million, but such a number of goals could not be scored in a match simply because human beings cannot move sufficiently rapidly. The physical limitations on the length of sentences are imposed by (*a*) the necessity of the body to eat, sleep, die, and so on; (*b*) the shortness of the short-term memory which very soon makes comprehension impossible. This is especially true of embedded structures, in particular 'nesting' structures, that is those which appear on the surface surrounded by the matrix, for example *The man that I came to see has not turned up*, and above all of self-embedding nesting structures, that is those in which structures are inserted into structures *of the same type*; in this case the limit of comprehension is very quickly reached. Examine the comprehensibility of the sentences:

> *This is the malt that the rat ate, This is the malt that the rat that the cat caught ate, This is the malt that the rat that the cat that the dog chased caught ate, This is the malt that the rat that the cat that the dog that the farmer bought chased caught ate. . . .*

The recognition of nominalisations contributes important advantages to this grammatical theory. Firstly we economise on lexicon entries: an enormous number of surface nouns are derived from underlying verbs and adjectives in this way. Consequently, secondly, order and syntactic regularity are observed where formerly the grammatical analysis saw thousands of unrelated dictionary-entries. Thirdly, the superficial similarity between such phrases as *The retreat of the English* and *The defeat of the English* is removed and the important underlying syntactic difference between them is recognised. Fourthly, many ambiguities, for example the utterance *Ptolemy Crunkhorn's appearance startled the audience*, are shown to be not haphazardly so because of the vague meaning of a word (in this case *appearance*) but predictably and quite regularly ambiguous for reasons of syntax, thus

(*a*)   ← *Ptolemy Crunkhorn* Aux-*appear*
      [It had been announced that his understudy was going to play instead.]

161

(*b*)   ← *Ptolemy Crunkhorn* Aux-*appear* Adv_{Manner}
          [He made his entrance as King Lear on a bicycle.]
(*c*)   ← *Ptolemy Crunkhorn* Aux-*appear* Adj
          [In the role of King Lear, he was dressed as Mickey Mouse.]

The embedding transformations thus demonstrate that the distinction between derivation and inflection is blurred in transformational-generative grammar. In this connection, it is interesting that the surface word-classes are not identical with the classes of morpheme in the lexicon, which for convenience we have been calling 'noun', 'verb', 'adjective' and 'adverb'; some lexicon 'nouns' appear as surface 'adjectives' e.g. *atmospheric scientist*, some lexicon 'verbs' and 'adjectives' as surface 'nouns' e.g. *smoker* and *idiocy*, and some lexicon 'adverbs' as surface 'adjectives' e.g. *heavy smoker*. Although the question goes beyond the scope of *Syntactic structures*, it could be discussed why it was helpful to apply these labels and to what extent this 'traditional' nomenclature could be justified in a modern grammar.[2]

FURTHER READING
See Chapter 13.

162

13. The Impact of Transformational-Generative Grammar

13.1 The importance of *Syntactic Structures.* In *Syntactic structures*, Chomsky has two main themes: the introduction of a new kind of grammatical model such as has been described; and a discussion of the nature and goals of linguistic theory. These themes are interlinked. His procedures are marked by extreme rigour of argument and of formulation, avoiding (he claims) 'obscure and intuition-bound notions', '*ad hoc* adjustments' and 'loose formulations'.[1] Indicative of this is the precise algebra of his rewrite rules.

The grammatical model introduced is clearly more powerful than either traditional grammar or structuralist grammar; differences are accounted for that are not clearly marked at surface level and for which traditional and structural grammars lacked a description. It will suffice to recall those ambiguities, quoted in 10.2, that defied analysis in a structural model of syntax; in all cases but two, transformational-generative grammar can give syntactic accounts of the different interpretations. Further evidence of the power of this grammar may be seen in the embedding transformations described in the previous chapter and the rules specifying verb-complexes and sentence-forms in 11.3.

But the grammar is not simply more powerful, it is of a different type altogether. We have seen that in the structuralist period, the task of the linguist was held to be that of taking note of observable facts, finding a technique for classifying them and then arranging them. This accords with the general tenor of science in the first half of the twentieth century, which may be regarded as classificatory. But as the emphasis in the natural sciences changed to become that of finding structures and rules for synthesising them (e.g. DNA in genetics and plate-tectonics in the earth sciences), this too was reflected in the new model of a grammar that would be generative. The grammar was now seen as the device that described the structure of all the grammatical sentences in the language and excluded all the ungrammatical ones.

The language was therefore seen to be the output of the grammar; and the sentences of the language were of an infinite number of lengths and themselves infinite in number. The problem was thus avoided of wondering whether to equate the language with the random set of utterances in a corpus (and, if not, wondering what on earth 'the language' was.) In retrospect, one may question whether the structuralists had an adequate definition of 'a language'. Turning his attention to the goals of linguistic theory, Chomsky considered the relationship between a corpus and a grammar. He completely rejected the contention that the task of a linguist was to formulate a discovery-procedure that could process any corpus and produce '*the*' grammar for that corpus. It is not denied that a grammar can be written from a corpus; but it is 'questionable that this goal is attainable in any interesting way'. (It is not 'interesting' because presumably it proceeds by trial-and-error, hunches, rule-of-thumb, tricks of the trade – and not according to any programme which can be rigorously formulated.) Chomsky's dismissal of discovery-procedures as a goal for linguists is very short, but he quotes the names of seven 'of the more careful proposals' whose explicit goal is the construction of a discovery-procedure (including one of his own four years previously) and concludes that what these works really do is to give directions for choosing the better of two possible grammars that have suggested themselves to the linguist. Thus he simply annihilated one ostensible aim of later structuralism.

In like manner the doctrine of the separation of levels was rejected as unnecessary; in fact the existence of a given number of different levels was rejected as false. For if we have given up the goal of a discovery-procedure, there is no need to define the morphemes in terms of the phonemes, but not vice-versa (which led to difficulties as noted in 10.4). Further, if we abandon the idea that any one level is literally constructed from a sequence of units of a lower level, we do not have to face the problem of locating the actual situation of morphemes in, for example, /man/ ~ /mɛn/ (cf. pp.97 and 124); the idea of an indivisible morph presents no obstacle. Finally, if we look at a transformational-generative grammar, we cannot discern the fixed number of levels of, for example, morpheme, word, phrase, clause and sentence; to presuppose this number is gratuitous. On the other hand, it may be convenient to distinguish levels of phrase structure and transformational structure: this conception of levels is very different from that of structuralist grammar.

It has been contended that one of Chomsky's important innovations was to recognise the role of intuition in linguistic description; indeed J.P. Thorne has said[2] that Chomsky has given formal shape to our intuitions. Much more discussion could be given to this question than can be accommodated in this book. However, the statement can be taken as true if we recognise what is meant by intuition in this context and if we recognise where the emphasis lies.

As we have seen (e.g. p.127), it seems impossible that a grammar can be written using only distributional criteria (as had been claimed). The writer of a grammar draws upon knowledge such as that certain utterances (e.g. *John left his brother to mend the puncture*) are ambiguous and that other pairs of utterances are connected in some way or other (e.g. *Caroline chased the mouse* and *The mouse was chased by Caroline*). Such knowledge is not available to the distributional analyst. But it is precisely this knowledge that is reflected in the grammar. With this interpretation we can accept the statement.

However, discussion is bound to arise since Chomsky rejects the idea that a grammar can be constructed by appealing to meaning; equally he concedes that ' "intuition about linguistic form" is very useful to the investigator of linguistic form (i.e. grammar)'; but states that 'the major goal of grammatical theory is to replace this obscure reliance on intuition by some rigorous and objective approach'. A formidable methodological obstacle, moreover, is the question of how to resolve the difference of opinion if two native speakers disagree about their intuitions.

At one point Chomsky introduces what might be seen to be alternatives to the tasks proposed by structuralists, although he does not dwell on these proposals. Given that a grammar is a device for producing grammatical sentences, then there are three main tasks to be carried out by the writer of grammars. First it is necessary to state precisely the 'external criteria of adequacy' for grammars (i.e. how to test that the sentences generated will be acceptable to native speakers). Secondly 'we must characterise the form of grammars in a general and explicit way so that we can actually propose grammars of this form for particular languages'. Thirdly 'we must define the notion of simplicity that we intend to use in choosing among grammars all of which are of the proper form'.

If the first and second tasks can be carried out, then it will be possible to write grammars the output of which will, for practical purposes, be identical with all the sentences that could conceivably be uttered by native speakers of a natural language. Each of these grammars will be generative and transformational, with the consequent advantages of such a form. The implication is that it is possible to write different generative grammars, each of which produces the same output. This puts paid to the idea that there can be one grammar, *the* grammar of a language. The third task then is to elaborate some system of choosing the best of these possible grammars. It is tempting to choose the most 'simple' – but 'simplicity' is not simple: do we measure it in terms of, for example, total length of explanation necessary or the number of *different* symbols or terms used? Hence the necessity for defining 'simplicity'.

Not one of these tasks has reached anything like completion; this we may ascribe to the nature of the world and of science.

13.2 Wider ramifications. The publication of *Syntactic structures* not only injected excitement into the field of linguistics: workers in other disciplines attempted to make use of transformational-generative grammar in a variety of investigations into, for example, the structure of the human brain; analogies between language and the output of certain types of computers; the nature of the algebra we need to describe deep grammatical structures; and the relationship between linguistics, psychology and philosophy. Four topics in particular beyond the field of description of individual languages attracted increased attention.

Universal grammar. Whereas a structuralist approach had laid stress on the differences between natural languages, we see now the enormous similarities, once we have penetrated the barrier of the surface appearance. 'There are grounds for believing that there are certain formal features which underlie all languages and which constitute a universal grammar.' 'Deep structures seem to be very similar from language to language, and the rules that manipulate and interpret them also seem to be drawn from a very narrow class of conceivable formal operations.'³ And in 11.2 we have seen seven such operations – no more appear to be possible: complicated transformational rules simply combine permutation, adjunction and deletion in different ways, without adding anything new. Thus it appears that the contention of such Modistic grammarians as Roger Bacon is confirmed, namely that the grammar of all languages is in essence the same, although different in appearance. On the other hand, the thought-framework of the Modistae (in terms of a distinction between 'accidents', the superficial appearance, and 'essence', the true nature), derived ultimately from Aristotle, is quite unlike that of Chomsky's rewrite rules. Further investigation of this problem will involve both consideration of the meaning of the phrase 'universal grammar' and decision as to whether the shapes of postulated individual grammars are sufficient to satisfy whatever definition we have proposed.

Psychological investigation of the understanding of sentences. Ambiguous sentences are not usually ambiguous in context. Why should the context cancel out the ambiguity? We can only begin to answer this question if we have adequately described the relation between the single surface structure and the various deep structures. Thus the formulation of a transformational-generative grammar is the first step in such an investigation.

Notice also that we have been considering 'idealised' utterances that we can directly analyse in terms of our grammar and phonology; yet human utterances are often 'degenerate' in that they contain coughs, hesitations, slips of tongue, incomplete sentences, anacolutha. A further problem of investigation is how to relate 'degenerate' actual utterances to the idealised sentences of linguistic theories.

There is a third area of interest. The term 'generative' is unfortunate in that the impression given to the unwary is that a generative grammar is a model of human mental processes that produce utterances. This is explicitly denied in *Syntactic structures*. Nevertheless, it is inevitable that the question must be investigated whether there are any analogies between a grammar and mental operations. Experiments were conducted[4] to test the proposal that when speakers produce complex sentences they do so by first generating a string and then applying a number of optional transformations, and conversely, that a listener who hears a complex sentence has to undo these optional transformations in order to understand. The experiments appeared at first to confirm this hypothesis, but only when language is being used artificially; in normal language semantic factors predominate and complicate the issue. This then is a continuing field of investigation.

Language acquisition. It is a common lay view that children in the process of 'learning to speak' produce a random deformation of the language of adults, due perhaps to 'faulty remembering'. However, it appears[5] that at the very beginning of patterned speech (18 months or so) children have a grammar with two word-classes. The complexity of the child's grammar increases with time and comes more and more to resemble the grammar of the language with which it is surrounded. Moreover, the number of different combinations heard from a child far exceeds anything it can have heard. The conclusion is that when a child learns its language, it develops an internal representation (allegedly!) of the rules of its language and constantly changes its internal representation until the output is consistent with the adult sentences it hears. But no one has told it to do this; such an activity can only be the result of an inbuilt theory of language and an inbuilt language-acquisition device whose properties can be stated.

Moreover, this ability is limited to human beings, it is species-specific; children in learning their native language are carrying out a procedure whose complexity is vastly beyond anything within the capabilities of the more independent young of other species, such as puppies and piglets.[6]

One investigatory task, therefore, for the stout-hearted is to chart the syntactic development over the years of as many children as possible and from as many language-communities as possible; in this way it may be discovered whether or not the children of one language-community all acquire their eventual mastery of syntax via the same sequence of stages and whether or not there is discernible any universal pattern of language acquisition common to all human beings.

Innate ideas. The above indications of the possibilities of universal grammar and an inbuilt language-acquisition device run contrary to the tenets of 'behaviourism', an approach to psychology that regards human beings as mechanisms that respond to stimuli. Language is seen by behaviourists as a series of learned responses to stimuli, which learning comes about by habit, association and conditioning.[7]

Chomsky joins battle with behaviourism, pointing out that the sheer number of sentences that we hear and understand yet have never previously heard and the sheer number that we utter without having previously heard, preclude learning by habit, association or conditioning. He maintains that in human beings the species-specific innate language-component not only allows us to learn a natural language but imposes firm restrictions on the type of grammar human beings may adopt. In this he sees himself as heir to the rationalism of Descartes and others who propounded a doctrine of innate ideas.

It is of course debatable whether Chomsky's view is sufficiently similar to that of the Cartesian philosophers to warrant a claim of kinship; moreover, it may be disputed how unanimous these philosophers were in those matters that have attracted Chomsky's interest and indeed whether these are genuinely 'Cartesian' rather than inheritances from a Mediaeval period.[8]

Each of the above interrelated problems is the subject of continuing investigation and no final conclusions can be formulated. Nevertheless, we have sufficiently indicated the astonishing result of the advent of transformational-generative grammar, that the study of grammar has expanded beyond the narrow aim of describing the workings of a natural language to become a tool in the investigation of the nature of man.

13.3 Not ultimate truth. The appearance of *'Syntactic structures'* had the effect of an explosion. It overturned fundamental tenets of post-Bloomfieldian structuralism, it provided promise of a more powerful description of syntax and suggested lines of investigation in areas of study other than grammar. The names of linguistics, of Chomsky and of transformational-generative grammar were brought to the notice of many who had had no idea that such a subject existed. The salutary results have been indicated, but there were some less desirable effects as well.

A strangely emotional attitude characterised many scholarly utterances, both for and against the new type of grammar, in the decade following 1957. Declarations typical of religious converts were made: 'I am a devout transformationalist' on the one hand, 'I am a staunch anti-Chomskyan' on the other. Such slogans are of minimal value in learned discussion.

Some non-linguists working in subjects invigorated by the new approach in grammar, appeared to believe that Chomsky had himself created linguistics and were apparently ignorant both of earlier approaches and of contemporary non-Chomskyan ones. It is difficult to feel that such writers had an informed view of the distinctive nature of the doctrine they so enthusiastically embraced and propagated.

It should be pointed out that as a descriptive technique this model of grammar is demonstrably inadequate. We have seen, for example, that one type of *and*-conjoining is not particularly amenable to handling within this framework. Secondly, while a sentence such as *The missionary is ready to eat* may be assigned two different structural descriptions (either $S_2 = $ NP Aux-*eat the missionary* or $S_2 = $ *The missionary* Aux-*eat* NP), *The missionary has been cooking for two hours* may not. Finally, it is not clear how we can give two different structural analyses to *The dean punched the bishop on the nose* and *The dean punched the bishop on the street-corner*. In terms of the listener's intuition, it seems that these are understood in different ways, the difference being associated with the relations between *bishop* and alternatively *nose* and *street-corner*; however, we know no method of handling this at the moment.

It is commonplace to talk of the Chomskyan 'revolution' and indeed the disciples of Chomsky are conscious of a great gulf between the past and themselves; to them structuralism represents a kind of Dark Ages. Yet no revolution is a holocaust and we must beware of imagining that linguistics began with Chomsky. His debt to the past is great. The idea of ordered rules, for example, dates from Pāṇini – publicised in the twentieth century by Bloomfield who in fact adopted a type of morphophonemic generative approach;[9] the idea of immediate constituents (on which the phrase-structure component relies) is due to Bloomfield, if not earlier; the notion of transformations derives, through Chomsky's teacher Zellig Harris, from mathematics.[10] (It is, of course, a mark of genius to reassemble familiar components in a new way.) Besides this, the concept of classes (of words, morphemes, etc.), the notions of morphemes and phonemes themselves and the battery of grammatical categories – all developed in the structuralist era – are conserved in the grammar of the *Syntactic structures* type.

Indeed the very idea of 'revolution' is suspect since by no means all linguists are working within the new paradigm. Many European and some American scholars refused to embrace transformational-generative grammar at all, others embraced it only to abandon it later. Certain of these scholars of both types defended their points of view in publications of varying degrees of weight.[11]

But in any case no study stands still and the *Syntactic structures* model did not long remain the only transformational-generative type of grammar. Chomsky himself suggested a major revision and then made smaller adjustments to *that*; other linguists brought out heterogeneous proposals for changes of greater or lesser radicalism to the different Chomskyan models. Some of these are described in Chapters 16 and 17. This of course had the effect of making nonsense of any credal declaration of the 'I am a transformationalist' type. Henceforth one would have to make clear what kind of transformationalism or what Chomskyan model one had embraced. This in turn created problems for the non-linguistic disciplines such as psychology, which were using Chomskyan grammar in their investigations. It was no longer sufficient to speak of 'the impact of transformationalism' on their field; the *type* had to be specified. Strictly speaking, each set of experiments or of speculations would have to be repeated whenever a new transformational model appeared. Life could become distinctly difficult.

That these later changes were made does not of course argue that the *Syntactic structures* model of grammar is 'wrong'. 'Right' and 'wrong' are not words which can be applied to linguistic theories; it is in the nature of things that as more data is examined, new problems are revealed and the theory is shown to be inadequate. A knowledge of *Syntactic structures* is essential to an understanding not only of the impact of transformational-generative grammar but also of the drift of subsequent developments, and indeed these individual later models are probably unintelligible without this knowledge. In fact we may go further. In Chapter 1 we stated that an earlier world-view may be retained with advantage in certain circumstances; many grammatical phenomena and relationships (e.g. those described in Chapters 11 and 12) may be more simply and lucidly handled in a *Syntactic structures* type of grammar than in a later model. In that sense, it has not been superseded.

FURTHER READING
Bach 1964; Chomsky 1957, 1968; Koutsoudas 1966; Lester 1970; Lyons 1970; Slobin 1971; Thomas 1965.

14. The Functions of Language

The 'inner core' of linguistics – *microlinguistics* as Trager has termed it[1] – is concerned with speech-sounds, grammar and meaning. So far we have said nothing about meaning; but it is necessary to do so before we continue our account of transformational-generative grammar, for its later forms attempt to include descriptions of meaning. Preliminary light on the formidable problems involved in the study of meaning, that is *semantics*, is shed by considering what purposes language serves. In the present chapter, therefore, we look at the functions of language before exploring approaches to semantics in Chapter 15.

It is necessary to warn against two misapprehensions common among literate people. It is often held that *the* function of language is 'to express thought and to communicate information' – to quote Dr Johnson, 'Language is the dress of thought'. This is obviously reinforced if one spends several hours a day sitting on one's bottom listening to lectures. Secondly, students of literature (especially in a foreign language that they may seldom hear spoken) may gain the impression that the 'real' use of language is to form the raw material of works of literary art.

If, however, we reflect on the use made of language, it is obvious that it fulfils many other tasks in addition to the communication of information. Indeed one may claim that the unadulterated use of language for transferring new information (with no other motive) is relatively rare in a community and is limited to teaching situations of various kinds, to news reports, and to gossip. A great deal of human language is used, for example, in greeting people; passing the time of day with them; buying bus-tickets, newspapers, food, and so on; asking questions; giving orders; in entertaining others; in religious services; in inciting or encouraging others, and so on.

The emphasis on language as a vehicle for thought comes from the historical preoccupation of philosophers with logical propositions, and their concentration on those sentence forms that could be analysed as expressing true or false propositions. Most of the sentences one can imagine being used for the purposes suggested above could not be adjudged either 'true' or 'false'.

The next point is that it is probably impossible to compile one single list of 'the functions of language'. The recognition of any such functions depends on the point of view of the analyst, and

171

since this is an area of investigation common to linguistics, philosophers, anthropologists and psychologists, it is not surprising that we find different inventories of the functions of language according to the writer's primary interest. We illustrate some of these. A very basic distinction is drawn by Lyons[2] between the *cognitive* and *social* functions of language-behaviour. The former refers to 'the transmission of propositional, or factual, information and discursive reasoning or "cogitation"; the second to the establishment and maintenance of social rapport'. (This latter is what has been termed by Malinowski *phatic communion*.) These functions are 'complementary rather than in contrast' and both must be accounted for in any unprejudiced description. It may be that in the past certain philosophers have neglected the social function while some anthropologists and social psychologists have neglected the cognitive.

A much earlier enumeration, made by A. Ingraham in 1903,[3] reveals perhaps the emphasis of a man of letters: to dissipate nervous energy (this applies to the release of sudden emotion of various kinds); to direct motion in others; to communicate ideas; as a means of expression; for the purposes of record; to set matter in motion (as in charms and incantations); as an instrument of thinking; to give delight merely as sound. And he adds a ninth: 'to provide an occupation for philologists'. Indeed this is by no means unimportant; not only do linguists spend a great deal of their time using language to describe language, but such 'language turned back on itself' as Firth said, or *metalanguage*, is a normal function in daily life, revealed in such utterances as *That's an odd way of putting it, 'Iris' is a lovely name for your little girl, Mrs Chew, That's an English accent you have, isn't it, Professor Sweet?* We notice that Ingraham omits any reference to the sheerly social, cohesive function of language.

A more modern, linguist's classification is that given by Abercrombie,[4] who describes language first as a means of social control which makes human society possible. The communication of thoughts is but a small part of this. Secondly, it acts as an 'index' to 'various things about the speaker, particularly his personality'; the *indexical features* give information about permanent or relatively permanent facts about the speaker (e.g. age and sex) and about temporary facts, both physical (e.g. that he has a cold) or emotional (e.g. that he is bored). Many of the latter affective indices are conditioned by the speaker's culture and are hence liable to misinterpretation by those of a different linguistic background. Thirdly, language acts to 'delimit social groupings, or classes, within a given community', either by accent or choice of words or also, one would assume, by grammatical features. (Information may be conveyed by

172

the second and third of these functions not only involuntarily but deliberately; the speaker may attempt to mislead his hearer about his age or sex or more usually his attitude or social grouping.) Fourthly, language brings men into relationship with the external world. 'Language mediates between man and his environment.' Fifthly, language is a material of artistic creation, and this includes not only written literary works but the poetic achievements of purely oral traditions.

Abercrombie illustrates the fourth function, that of mediation between man and his environment, by reference to differences in value between vocabulary items in different languages (see Figure 4 on p.37).[5] However, it may also be exemplified in a set of *semiotic functions* (admittedly incomplete) instanced by Lyons.[6] Firstly, in *deixis*, the attention of the hearer is drawn to an object by the speaker locating it in relation to himself, for example *Look here!*; the *deictic system* of a language includes personal pronouns, demonstratives, the definitive article and, by extending the frame of reference to include temporal relationships, to adverbs such as *now* and *then* and to tense systems. Secondly, *vocative signals* attract the attention of a particular person, e.g. *Look out!, John!* Thirdly, *nomination* is the assignment of a name; explicitly it occurs in *This is John* (combined with deixis). Finally Lyons recognises *desiderative signals* that 'indicate the desire . . . for some object' and *instrumental signals* that serve 'to bring about a particular state of affairs'. Quite obviously some of these semiotic functions will also be examples of social function. Furthermore a consideration of them, involving questions of the speaker's relationship to his environment and his hearer, of meaning and of the grammatical means by which they are conveyed, takes us into an interdisciplinary realm of interest to the semanticist, the grammarian and the philosopher.

A different, and pleasingly symmetrical kind of analysis is made by Roman Jakobson[7] who approaches the enumeration of language functions via a survey of the factors involved in any act of verbal communication. There are six of these: the (1) addresser sends a (2) message to the (3) addressee. To be operative the message requires a (4) context referred to (we might be inclined to expect a word such as 'referent' instead) a (5) code common to the addresser and the addressee; and finally a (6) contact, a physical channel and psychological connection between addresser and addressee. A message may be focused relatively more towards one or more of such factors rather than to the remainder. Such focusing determines the different functions of the message, as in the following examples.

Numerous messages are focused towards the context: this gives the referential, 'denotative', 'cognitive' function, typically used for

173

conveying information, for example *Nikos Skalkottas died in 1945.* Messages focused towards the addresser fulfil an *emotive* function, indicating the speaker's attitude towards what he is speaking about, for example *What an interesting book this is!* Such emotive function may be fulfilled by interjections or by the selection of appropriate intonation patterns. Orientation towards the addressee, the *conative* function, finds its expression in vocative and imperatival forms, for example *Come into the garden, Maude!*

These three functions, referential, emotive, and conative, may be held to refer respectively to three apexes: the third person ('spoken about'), the first person ('speaking') and the second person ('spoken to'). However, the other three factors in the speech situation may also be focused upon.

Focus on the contact serves to establish, prolong or discontinue communication, or to check whether the channel works, for example *Are you listening?* This is what Jakobson calls the *phatic function* (distorting Malinowski's term), for example *Goodbye!*, *Lovely weather, isn't it?*, and, in the case of much small talk, may exist only to keep the channel open. Focus on the code is the metalingual function (see above). This fulfils the important function of checking whether the addresser and addressee use the same code, for example *Do you know what I mean?*, *What precisely do you mean?* and is vital in any process of language-learning. Focus on the message is the *poetic* function of language. This covers not only poetry, but any situation in which the speaker is conscious of selecting one formulation rather than another and applies to puns, advertisements and slogans, as well as to verse: *Pick up a Penguin, I like Ike.*

We may illustrate the concern of one school of philosophy with the function of language by citing the view of J.L. Austin.[8] He distinguishes a class of *constative* utterances, often used to assert propositions and about which one may pose questions of truth and falsity. Opposed to this is a set of *performative* utterances, which do not report and are neither true or false, but they themselves, in their being uttered, enable the speaker to *do* rather than to say something: they may be termed *speech acts.*

Austin distinguishes five types of such performative utterances, and classifies them by the following 'more-or-less rebarbative names':

> *Verdictives* are 'typified by the giving of a verdict': *I should call him industrious.*
> *Exercitives* are decisions that something is to be so: *I order you to go, I nominate you my successor.*
> *Commissives* are promises or undertakings, committing the speaker to doing something, or announcing his intentions: *I promise to pay for the book.*

Behabitives 'are a very miscellaneous group, and have to do with attitudes and social behaviour'. 'Examples are apologising, congratulating, commending, condoling, cursing and challenging.'
Expositives make it plain how our utterances fit into the course of an argument or conversation: *I reply, I concede.*

This approach has proved useful to linguists and philosophers concerned with establishing the extent to which such *illocutionary* acts are overtly marked by grammatical means, and this again points to an overlap in the disciplines of linguistics and philosophy.

A comparison of the above lists of language-functions is instructive, for the differences arise from the preoccupations of the writers. It is not the case that one has identified a function that the others have overlooked: the theories lead to the facts. Thus we cannot add the above lists of functions together in the hope of arriving at a 'more exhaustive' list. This becomes even more apparent when we take into account the views of the psychologist W.P. Robinson[9] who includes among other functions: 'verbal behaviour as a means of avoiding other problems'; 'role relationships'; 'instruction'; and 'inquiry'.

It is clear that the use of language in situations is part of a communication channel that includes non-linguistic behaviour. Linguistic and non-linguistic may be inseparable from the point of view of the speaker and the hearer: cf. *Hand me over the* . . . (pointing) with the role of nudges, winks, facial expressions, tone of voice, and so on. Such deliberate non-linguistic communication may be called *paralinguistic.* Some information (about the speaker) may be conveyed unintentionally, such as whether a speaker is tired, angry, bored, and so on, either by the voice or by bodily movements and postures.

The conclusion is that an account of the functions of language depends on the viewpoint of the investigator; hence a linguist who attempts to consider this topic must widen his scope beyond the bounds of microlinguistics. For this reason the linguist, qua microlinguist, strictly speaking is not in a position to talk about the functions of language! Realisation of this perhaps rather saddening fact helps us to appreciate not only the vast problems involved in investigating meaning, but also the limitations necessarily accepted by every approach so far made to this study.

FURTHER READING
Abercrombie 1956; Austin 1962; Hinde 1972 (esp Lyon's paper, 49–87); Laver and Hutcheson 1972; Robinson 1972; Sebeok 1960 (Jakobson's paper 350–77).

15. Semantics: Theory and Problems

15.1 Scope of semantics. Human beings do not produce utterances for the sake of the phonetic, phonological and grammatical features discernible therein – unless they happen to be phoneticians and linguists going about their professional business; utterances are produced because they convey meaning. *Semantics* studies the nature of meaning and why particular utterances have the meanings they do.

15.2 Preconceptions of the educated. People who have received 'prescriptive' first-language teaching at school, who can consult a dictionary, and who may have learnt a second language, will already possess ideas about meaning; we may call these ideas *traditional semantics* since they are associated with traditional grammar. It is as well, therefore, to be aware of these notions and their limitations.

The basic unit of meaning is taken to be the word. So dictionaries are lists of words consulted when the meaning of an utterance is unclear. Yet demonstrably the meaning of an utterance is different from the sum total of the meanings of the individual words involved: compare *The secretary startled the burglar* and *The burglar startled the secretary*. Moreover, the choice of intonation tune, stress and tone of voice (at least in some languages) makes contribution to the meaning of spoken language. Clearly other factors besides individual word-meanings have to be considered in semantics.

Words are frequently held to 'name things', either directly or via a concept associated with the word in the mind of the speaker. As an example of this latter view the form of *chair* (i.e. the letters or noises) is said to be associated with the concept of chairs in general, and this concept is in turn associated with the example to which we apply the word *chair*. In this view the concept is the meaning of the word; the relationship between the word and the object to which it refers on any occasion is indirect, since it is mediated by the concept. This may be shown diagrammatically as the well-known semiotic triangle[1] of Figure 37. This idea, a variation of which is found in de Saussure's 'linguistic sign', dates back to the philosophy

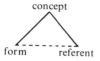

Figure 37

of Socrates and Plato. Inevitably it also leads to discussions about the nature of concepts.

The linguist *qua* linguist must not adopt the traditional view of words as naming things whether or not by means of concepts in the mind. For one thing, this would entail taking sides in disputes within philosophy (the existence of the nature of 'concepts' and 'minds'); for another, it raises further, troublesome questions, such as 'What sort of "things" are named by words like *honesty, defence, if, but, from, pursue, colourless?*'

But because words are held to name things, it may be thought that the meaning of some words may be stated by pointing at objects to which they refer: *ostensive definition*. This procedure (allegedly) can be used to answer the question of a foreigner, child or layman (e.g. *What is a carburettor?*) if a suitable object is visible. It is elaborated into a technique for second-language teaching (a component of the 'direct method') and, by replacing pointing by the drawing of pictures, is used in direct-method textbooks and in illustrated one-language and two-language dictionaries.

Yet it seems necessary that the enquirer must in some sense know the meaning of the word involved before he can understand an ostensive definition. It is not an uncommon experience to misunderstand an illustration in a direct-method book or in real life: for example, in an illustration does a label bearing the word *tyre* and an arrow refer to the 'tyre', the 'wheel' or 'rubber'? Often, to avoid this, verbal amplification is given, at which point the definition is no longer ostensive.

It is held that the meanings of words may be stated in other words, witness dictionaries. Yet this is conditional upon understanding the words forming the definitions. If we proceed to look up the meaning of each word used in a definition, and then continue to repeat this process, sooner or later we will encounter some word a second time: it is being used as part of an explanation of itself. This indicates an inherent circularity in the vocabulary; the problem arises of how to break into such a circle. This state of affairs tends to be overlooked in traditional semantics.

In fact, in explaining the meanings of words, speakers very often do not limit themselves to a restatement of the meaning in different words; they may use ostensive definition, they may use the word in an illustrative sentence, they may even use a foreign-language translation. Indeed it may prove inordinately difficult to state the meaning of a word in other words, especially that of the most common, such as *and*; in such cases an explanation may be given about how the word is used (e.g. 'to link two other words').

It may well be that the context in which a word is used is important, either because a word is limited to certain contexts (e.g. *piebald* used predominantly of *horses*) or because the context decides the meaning a word may have (e.g. *loud* applied to *noises* or *clothes*; cf. p.38). Larger dictionaries may indeed include information on contextual use, but in general traditional semantics underestimates the importance of context.

A common belief is that meaning of a word is clearly defined and that there is a 'correct' meaning. Dictionaries allegedly contain precise, correct meanings; a great deal of school-teaching of the mother tongue is devoted to teaching how to use words 'correctly'; and letters to British periodicals announce correspondents' displeasure with 'incorrect' usage of words. It is also commonly held that speakers must be in agreement about these meanings before they can understand each other. Both parts of this assumption may be shown to be false. Firstly, meanings of words change with time (e.g. *silly* once meant 'simple'). If such changes take place gradually, one must assume that the areas of meaning are not precisely delimited at any one moment. Secondly, it may easily be demonstrated that native speakers are not in agreement about the meanings of even the most common words, for example *big*, *white*; hence the meanings of these words *cannot* be precise. A useful illustration is to exhibit a thick, squat, cream-coloured volume and a long, broad, floppy off-white brochure and then to invite spectators to select the object they would bring in answer to *Bring the big, white book*; there is seldom complete unanimity.

Indeed the fact that speakers understand each other's utterances is no guarantee whatsoever that they are in agreement about the meanings of the words used; such agreement can never be proved. For example, in the experiment just described, if only one of the books is exhibited there is complete agreement about what to bring. It is only if misunderstanding occurs that one can make a statement, namely that the speakers are not agreed on the meaning of a word. Two-language dictionaries, and many language-learning materials, inevitably operate with the assumption that the words of one language may be translated into words of another language. In the case of tiny 'pocket' dictionaries, it would appear that there is a one-to-one correspondence between the words of two different

178

languages. However most learners of second languages realise that the situation is not nearly as simple.
Various classificatory terms are in common use. For example, different types of relationships are noted between the meaning of certain words. These are familiar to literate people, as are most of the descriptive labels.

Synonymy is the sameness of meaning of two words, e.g. *large, big.*
Homonyms are two different words (i.e. vocabulary-items) which are written identically and sound identical, e.g. *bear* (both beast and verb). *Homographs* are written identically but sound differently, e.g. *tear* /tiːr/ and *tear* /teːr/, in the writer's accent. *Homophones* sound identical but are written differently, e.g. *seam* and *seem.*
Multiple-meaning or *polysemy* characterises a word which has two (or more) related meanings, e.g. *mode* (= 'way'; 'fashion'; etc.) These are grouped together under one dictionary-entry, while homonyms appear under separate entries. However, there may be borderline cases.
One word may be allegedly opposite in meaning from another, the relationship being *antonymy*: thus *hot/cold*; *alive/dead*; *buy/sell* are all pairs of antonyms.

A further pair of terms (deriving from a distinction in logic) is *denotation* and *connotation*. Denotation is 'that to which the word actually refers', 'the primary meaning': for example, the denotation of *motor-car* is 'a dirigible, self-propelling assemblage of metal'. Connotation is 'the secondary meaning', 'the overtones': for example, the connotations of *motor-car* may include 'a means to enhance a deficient personality' or 'a device that causes an intolerable amount of noise, smell, and inconvenience'. In this usage of the words there will therefore be one denotation but an unlimited number of connotations for any one lexical item.
   Finally, it is realised that words may be used 'abnormally', and various kinds of such abnormal usage are conventionally recognised. For example *metaphor*: 'the use of a word in connection with an object to which it is not literally applicable' (e.g. *Sam is a pillar of the community*, cf. 3.1); *personification*: 'the application to an inanimate object of a word normally applied to a human being' (e.g. *the sighing of trees*); *metonymy*: 'the replacement of a normal word by the name of an object associated with its referent' (e.g. *the crown* for *the Queen*); *oxymoron*: 'the conjoining of contradictory terms' (e.g. *bitter sweet*). These and several others are found among

a heterogeneous list of traditional *figures of speech*, that is, stylistic devices, not all of which involve meaning.

15.3 Problems of semantics. The assumptions of traditional semantics are due also to the cogitations of philosophers who have always been occupied (*inter alia*) with problems of meaning – and until the seventeenth century the development of traditional grammar was intertwined with philosophy. However, linguists of the first half of the twentieth century (especially in the American tradition we have been considering) were unwilling to attempt the construction of a theory of semantics.

A structural linguist was concerned with the analysis of speech-sounds, phonemes, morphemes, words. Such isolates and the relationships they entered into could be described in terms of their behaviour within language, that is intralinguistically. But the study of meaning seemed to involve making reference outside language, that is to extralinguistic entities: it was considered by some that the linguist had no business to try to handle anything outside language. We have seen in the previous chapter, for example, that the linguist cannot deal with the functions of language without stepping out of microlinguistics and that other disciplines have a professional interest in that topic. For reasons of this sort, the study of meaning appeared to belong only to the activities of the philosopher, the psychologist, and the anthropologist, all of whom were attempting to grapple with meaning as it affected their own disciplines.

Secondly, the meaning of utterances appeared so complex that the construction of a theory seemed an impossible task. Thus Bloomfield (who admittedly interpreted *meaning* in a very particular way, see p.185) wrote: 'The statement of meaning is therefore the weak point in language-study, and will remain so until human knowledge advances very far beyond its present state'.[2] The nature of the complexity is indicated from now on. It seems that three major difficulties arise: (*a*) the question 'What *is* meaning?'; (*b*) the crucial importance of context to the meaning of utterances; (*c*) the fact that we can only talk about meaning *in language*.

The definition of *meaning* can be regarded as a basic question of semantics, that is the answer to 'What is *meaning*?' In the past this has been misunderstood as being a question that can be given a short informative answer like 'What is the county town of Lanarkshire?'; consequently direct answers have been given (e.g. 'Meaning is mental images'). Such answers proved insufficient, thus contributing to the pessimism of linguists.[3]

We adopt the view that *meaning* does not admit of a definition of this sort. The problems of definition have been touched on in

180

previous chapters: it may not be possible to give short definitions that convey very much information to the layman; moreover the physical sciences have elaborated very powerful theories concerning the nature of *light, matter, electricity,* and so on, without prior definitions of these words. We may therefore be emboldened to study meaning without a prior definition of *meaning.* So we continue to employ the word undefined. Every speaker of English knows (or thinks he knows) how to use it. Many theories of semantics have been advanced, each of which encompasses a different set of phenomena; it is therefore impossible to regard them as competing theories or mutually exclusive ones. Some are sketched below; these are all theories of linguists, not psychological and philosophical theories. It is by and large true to say that in linguistics advances were first in phonological theory and then in grammatical (though phonology has been continually reappraised). In the last few years increasing attention has been paid to semantic theory; however, recent work involves a knowledge of developments in generative grammar and also of recent developments in philosophy.

Human utterances are made in situations. It might seem that a semantic theory should encompass the meanings of utterances in situations, in which case it is tempting to regard the meaning of an utterance as being the function the utterance fulfils. The difficulties of this are formidable. Firstly, the situation is important, that is the persons involved and the surrounding circumstances. Consider the following fairly random examples:

(*a*) The utterance may be a favourite saying between the participants, e.g. *Read any good books lately?*, spoken merely to raise a smile.

(*b*) The utterance may be sarcastic, e.g. *Warm, isn't it?* in a freezing lecture room.

(*c*) The utterance may be a suggestion deliberately made to a contra-suggestible person to make him act in a particular way, e.g. *Don't bother to dry the dishes* in the hope that he *will.*

The function of utterances is apparently dependant on the concomitant circumstances as well as on the roles and the personalities of the speakers. If we required of a semantic theory that it could handle the function of utterances, then that would require that the theory should answer the question 'Why should utterance *x* fulfil the function *y* in situation *z*?'; this would entail the ability to analyse every conceivable situation in terms of what is relevant to the function of utterances. To construct a general theory with this ability seems to demand an omniscience not given to human beings.

Moreover, the problem arises of deciding how 'function' is to be understood. Is it the intention of the speaker or is it the reaction of the hearer? If it is the intention of the speaker, then the problem of eliciting intentions arises; if it is the reaction of the hearer, then misunderstanding on his part may lead to a situation in which the reaction is not the one intended. This would require us to say that the speaker had no control over the meaning of his utterance. And indeed it is often the case that an intended meaning is misunderstood. The great Italian dramatist Pirandello shows this situation at a tragic extreme:

> ... nelle parole ch'io dico metto il senso e il valore delle cose come sono dentro di me; mentre chi le ascolta, inevitabilmente le assume col senso e col valore che hanno per sé, del mondo com' egli l'ha dentro. Crediamo d'intenderci; non c'intendiamo mai! Guardi: la mia pietà, tutta la mia pietà per questa donna è stata assunta da lei come la piú feroce delle crueltà! [*I* put into the words I speak the meaning and the value of the things inside *me*, but whoever hears them interprets them with the meaning and the value they have for him, the meaning and value of *his* interior world. We imagine we understand each other; we never understand! Look: my compassion, all my compassion for this woman, she has interpreted as the most pitiless of cruelties!][4]

Thus the problems of semantics become also the concern of dramatists, for Pirandello's lead was followed by Ionesco, Albee, and Pinter among others. Non-comprehension seems to be a melancholy component of the society in which their characters live. But this is very far from saying that their utterances are meaningless.

Therefore, it is both too complicated and too arbitrary to regard the meaning of an utterance as being its function. It seems the linguist will have to confine himself to examining the meaning of the grammatical sentences that underlie utterances, paying no attention to the situation in which the utterance is spoken. For example, any utterance *Warm, isn't it?* is taken at its face value and the meaning of the grammatical sentence *Warm, isn't it?* is examined: we ignore the fact that it may be spoken jocularly or sarcastically or offensively. We are now examining something that is not natural human use of language; but this appears to be necessary.

Yet even if we restrict meaning to the meaning of sentences, we recognise various contributory factors. The grammar of the sentence contributes to its meaning as well as the individual meaning of the words: such grammatical meaning may be of various kinds (see below). In addition, certain strings of words may carry a meaning not deducible from the words in isolation or from the rules of grammar: *Ernest has kicked the bucket* has (normally) nothing to do with the individual meanings of *bucket* or *kick*.

The study of individual words may be undertaken from various viewpoints, for not all words carry the same kind of meaning. Some bear grammatical meanings (see 15.12), others lexical meanings, others a combination of both. Some words may be said to 'refer' to perceptible features of the world, such as *horse*, *green*; the nature of this 'reference' must be studied. Some words enter into relations with other words in the language, either paradigmatic (*hot* and *cold*) or syntagmatic (*duck* and *quack*); this relationship (either paradigmatic or syntagmatic) we may call *sense*. Meaning comprises both types of relationship: a full semantic theory will therefore have to include an account of both reference and sense. Moreover, two words may be reckoned to have the same reference, such as *stomach* and *tummy*, but they may have different overtones or connotations; this problem must also be handled.

Having indicated the formidable difficulties entailed in the construction of a coherent, consistent theory of semantics and having stated that there is at the moment no such theory, we sketch several approaches to the problem made by linguists during this century. We deal first with two general views about the meaning of utterances; both involve awareness of the importance of context.

15.4 Cultural background. The anthropologist Bronislaw Malinowski (1884–1942) became interested in the problems of meaning while studying the culture of the inhabitants of the Trobriand Islands (or Kiriwini Islands) off Papua; he discovered that word-for-word translations of many Trobriand expressions, poems or songs were meaningless if divorced from their cultural context. 'Culture' here does not refer to art galleries or string quartets but to 'the way of life' of a community, 'what people do and think'; it embraces occupations, religious and political organisation, ceremonies, customs, table manners, habitual ways of thinking, beliefs, education, morals, humour, etc.

To offer anything approaching a meaningful translation entailed explaining appropriate parts of the culture. For example, the type of text is important. Malinowski published what appeared to be a narrative of a journey,[5] this was in reality a 'boasting-song', such boasting being an important feature of their culture. Technical terms have to be explained, for example in the text he quotes (literally), 'front-wood' means 'leading canoe', and the import of phrases, for example (literally) 'we paddle in place' means 'we do not use sails', hence 'we are inshore', hence 'we are near our destination'. Clearly the understanding of a text requires a knowledge of the cultural context in which it is uttered.

Such an observation is true not only of 'exotic' languages but of any; the English word *run* as a technical term in cricket[6] is meaningless if translated literally into the language of a cricketless community; indeed all technical, sporting, religious or cultural terms are untranslatable if there are no exact cultural equivalents. Expressions such as *to shake hands* or *The University Ladies' Club will be arriving on their broom-sticks* convey nothing without a knowledge of the appropriate ritual or belief. The allusions of popular sayings or works of literary art are meaningless to the hearer unless a cultural background involving religion, literature, history and legend is available, cf. *Some village-Hampden* or *He met his Waterloo.*[7] Education may be seen to consist in part of the deliberate imparting of a cultural background that makes possible the comprehension of such texts.

In the same way, the nature of the text is important. Different types of utterance are made, each with a particular convention governing the comprehension of its meaning: we understand in different ways, for example the chants of cheer-leaders, a public reading of a poem, a news bulletin, a public proclamation, the singing of a patriotic song or the preaching of a sermon.

Words for abstract ideas important to a community may likewise be intelligible only with reference to that community, for example *salvation* and *enlightenment* in religious contexts. This is also true of moral and political terms, a point often misunderstood, especially if a too-ready identification of words in two different languages has been made. Hence when a new political or religious system is adopted by a community, the vocabulary will undergo change.

The conclusion, which seems incontrovertible, is that the cultural background of a community must be known before the sentences in the language of that community can be understood. Yet the recognition of the connection between culture and meaning does not help in the formulation of a general theory of meaning; all that can be done is to cite the relevant features of the culture on an *ad hoc* basis for particular sentences. We should note further that the idea of a homogeneous cultural community is too simplistic, at least when we are dealing with largish political units. All the inhabitants of England, for example, are in certain respects culturally different from those of other countries; but they may be grouped into increasingly smaller divisions: inhabitants of the North of England, of Yorkshire, of the West Riding of Yorkshire, of Leeds. But these regional differences are cross-cut by other cultural distinctions that may be shared by other groups outside the English-speaking community, distinctions of religion, education, occupation, politics, and so on. This complexity certainly affects the meanings of utterances (if only at the level of connotation). For example, *public school* means something different in England, Scotland and the U.S.A.; even the connotations of a proper name, such as *Chomsky, Churchill, John XXIII*, or *Nixon* will differ according to the cultural grouping of the hearers.

15.5 Behaviourism. Bloomfield advanced a view of the nature of meaning that became widely known and that still has adherents, the *behaviourist* view. Influenced by the psychologist J.B. Watson (indeed he carried Watson's views to extremes), Bloomfield adopted the behaviourist position that every human activity is the response to some stimulus; such activity included linguistic utterances. (Watson, and Bloomfield, rejected the necessity for entertaining notions, characteristic of a mentalist approach, such as *mind, will, concept, purpose, thought*; 'thinking is merely talking, but talking with concealed musculature'.[8] Bloomfield illustrated his behaviourist view of meaning in the stories of Jack and Jill.

Jill is walking; she sees an apple on a tree; she fetches the apple and eats it. This may be interpreted as a stimulus-response situation in which the stimulus is partly the light-waves reflected from the apple striking Jill's eye and partly the contraction of some of her muscles and the secretion of fluids in her stomach; the response is her getting the apple. The situation may be symbolised as:

$$S \rightarrow R$$

But if Jack is with her, then she makes a noise with her vocal tract, and Jack climbs the tree on her behalf, fetching the apple for her to eat. In this case, speech represents simultaneously a *substitute response* for Jill and a *substitute stimulus* for Jack. Thus:

$$S \rightarrow r-----s \rightarrow R$$

The practical importance of this utterance is that 'The gap between the bodies of the speaker and the hearer – the discontinuity of the two nervous systems – is bridged by the sound-waves'.[9] Therefore, for Bloomfield, the meaning of this (and any) utterance is 'the situation in which the speaker utters it and the response which it calls forth in the hearer'.[10]

And so to state the meaning of an utterance would be to identify the stimulus and the response. However, this is a staggeringly immense requirement, since he observes: 'We could foretell a person's actions (for instance, whether a certain stimulus will lead him to speak, and if so, the exact words he will utter), only if we knew the exact structure of his body at the moment, or, what would be the same thing, if we knew the exact make-up of his organism at some early stage – say at birth or before – and then we had a record of every change in that organism, including every stimulus that had ever affected the organism'.[11]

Such stimuli, moreover, include not only observable events exterior to the speaker, but internal bodily processes (e.g. glandular secretions, muscular contractions, soundless movements of the vocal organs), some of which are postulated, some even empirically *unknowable* – hence such a mechanistic view is, in this respect, no more 'objective' than a mentalist one. (It was necessary to postulate such bodily processes in order to account for the inconvenient fact of *displaced speech*, in which 'People very often utter a word like "apple" when no apple at all is present'. In the absence of an exterior stimulus, the speaker's body must provide the stimulus.)

Bloomfield recognised that words (his 'speech-forms') have meanings of some sort even when divorced from utterances, but was equally pessimistic here. 'We can define the meaning of a speech-form accurately when this meaning has to do with some matter of which we possess scientific knowledge . . . the ordinary meaning of the English word 'salt' is 'sodium chloride (NaCl)'. (This statement is itself of very debatable truth: is 'sodium chloride' really the *ordinary* meaning, and how do we know the meaning of *sodium* and *chloride* except through other words?) However, 'we have no precise way of defining words like "love" or "hate", which concern situations that have not been accurately classified – and these latter are in the great majority'.

For these reasons Bloomfield expressed his pessimistic obser- vation that the study of meaning would remain the weak point in language-study – which inhibited further examination of semantics by American structuralists. In his placing of the utterance within a situation, Bloomfield shows a certain resemblance to Malinowski's viewpoint; Malinowski, however, put his emphasis on the social role of utterances, while Bloomfield was concerned with the stimulus on the individual speaker. Fortunately Bloomfield's views on meaning are peripheral to the core of his linguistic work, which is not dependent on a behaviourist basis.

Behaviourist explanations of language may still be found, for example, in the works of B.F. Skinner, Professor of Psychology at Harvard University; his book *Verbal behaviour* appeared in 1957 and was a detailed attempt to account for the acquisition of language in the framework of a behaviourist learning theory. The review of this book by Chomsky has become a *locus classicus* in the mentalist-behaviourist debate re-invigorated by the advent of transformational-generative grammar (see 13.3).

15.6 Phatic communion. It is relevant to mention here a type of use of language called *phatic communion* by Malinowski ('actuated by the demon of terminological invention'). Phatic communion is language used only in order to be reassuring, 'to get over the strange and unpleasant tension which men feel when facing each other in silence'.[12]

Greetings fall into this category. The literal meanings may vary from language to language, e.g.

English	*How do you do?*;	
German	*Wie geht's?* /viˈgeːts/	(= 'How goes it?');
Gaelic	*Tha thu ann!* /ha uˈaʀ/	(= 'It's you!');
Hebrew	/ʃaːloːm/!	(= 'Peace!');
Amharic	/tˈena jistˈilliɲ/!	(= 'May He grant health on my behalf!');
	/indəmin addəru/?	(= 'How did you spend the night?');
Yakurr	/aplɔka o/?	(= 'Have you wakened up?');
	/ajə kɛ ma/?	(= 'Have you come?').

'After the first formula, there comes a flow of language, purposeless expressions of preference or aversion, accounts of irrelevant happenings, comments on what is perfectly obvious.' Or remarks on the weather. Phatic communion is a clear indication that language is not always used to convey information; here it fulfils a social function.

Since the use of phatic communion is only appropriate to a given type of situation in a particular language community (cf. *Mahlzeit!* /ˈmɑltsaɪt/ in German or *smakelijk eten* /ˈsmaklək ˈetə/ in Dutch at the beginning of meals, or *Malo fa'auli* in Samoan to a driver or boatman who has brought you to your destination), it might be held that there is an element of stimulus-response behaviour in this case. Nevertheless, the use of phatic communion is not *completely* determined by the situation, for an individual may not possess the 'predisposition to respond' and so remain silent. Such silence may itself carry a great deal of meaning, indicating the desire to be rude (which illustrates, if an illustration is necessary, that the non-linguistic behaviour of an individual – silences, gestures, facial expressions, etc. – is inseparable from his utterances from the point of view of the hearer-viewer).

Eskimo	English
/aput/	
/qana/	snow
/piqsirpoq/	
/qimuqsuq/	

Figure 38

15.7 Semantic field theory. We now consider approaches to the meanings of individual isolates of the sentence, in particular, to words. Undeniably, some words, though by no means all, enter into a relation of reference with features of the extralinguistic world; because of the philosophical problems entailed, we do not consider this further. We now examine something of the nature of the relations words may enter into with other words of the same language, that is sense-relationships; here we are concerned with so-called *semantic fields*.

This approach views certain sectors of a language's vocabulary as consisting of closely-knit fields, each being divided up in such a way that each element helps to delimit its neighbours and is in turn delimited by them. Thus the field corresponding to the English word *snow* is in Eskimo divided up by /aput/, /qana/, /piqsirpoq/ and /qimuqsuq/ (respectively 'snow on the ground', 'falling snow', 'drifting snow' and 'a snowdrift'). (There are in fact many more words in Eskimo that may translate *snow*.)[13] Such fields may be represented two-dimensionally as in Figure 38. The debt to Saussure's concept of 'value' (and his 'sheep-mutton' diagram) is obvious. But this type of phenomenon had also been pointed out in 1910 by Boas.

Attempts to find such semantic fields met with a certain amount of success, notably in the areas of colours and family-relationships. The spectrum of visible light being a continuum of wavelength-variation, there are no natural divisions whatsoever in the range of hues perceived by human beings. Since in addition luminosity (i.e. amount of light reflected) and saturation (degree of freedom from dilution with white) affect the colour perceived, it is not surprising that languages differ in the schemes by which their speakers classify colours.

Languages impose, as it were, different grids on the totality of colour-variation perceptible. Such differences may be expressed in terms of semantic fields. In Figure 39 hue is mapped on the

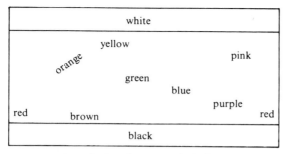

ENGLISH: eleven basic colour terms, including *grey*

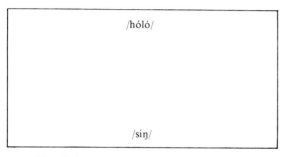

JALE (New Guinea Highlands): two basic colour terms

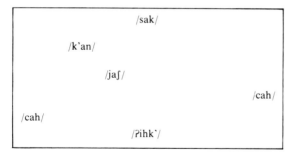

TZELTAL (Central America): five basic colour terms

Figure 39

horizontal axis, luminosity on the vertical; there being no place for
neutral hues, grey cannot appear, since it represents a mid-brightness
neutral hue between *white* and *black* (indeed in English *black* and
white ought to be on a different scale along with *grey* but are placed
where they are to facilitate comparison of languages).[14]

189

Indeed European languages also exhibit differences in colour-terms, for example Russian splits the area roughly covered by English *blue* into /'sinij/ and /gəlu'boj/ and Hungarian splits the area covered by *red* into *piros* /'pirof/ and *vörös* /'vørøf/. Terms for family relationships may show such inter-linguistic structural differences.

Thus the field of *grandmother* in English is split into those of *mormor* /'mɔrmɔr/ and *farmor* /'fɑrmɔr/ in Swedish; that of *grandson* into *sonarsonur* /'sonarsonər/ and *dóttursonur* /'douhtərsonər/ in Icelandic; that of *cousin* into *Vetter* /'fɛtər/ and *Kusine* /ku'zinə/ in German; those of *uncle* and *aunt* into *patruus, avunculus* and *amita, matertera* respectively in Latin; those of *brother* and *sister* by *batya* /'bɒcɒ/, *öcs* /øtʃ/ and *néne* /'neːne/, *hug* /hug/ respectively in Hungarian.

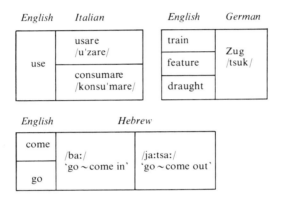

Figure 40

Similar types of semantic fields may be set up to deal with military ranks, academic hierarchies, aristocracies, and so on. Further semantic fields of fairly heterogeneous types can be set up, as in Figure 40. To these we may add the examples quoted in 6.2 of *wood* / *forest* /, *bois* / *forêt* /, *Holz* / *Wald* and of *know* / *can, connaître* / *savoir* / *pouvoir*.

Such examples show that the vocabularies of languages are non-isomorphic, that is that distinctions of meaning may have to be made in one language which are not made in another; moreover certain areas may be categorised in quite different ways in different languages. To this extent the value of a structural approach to semantics is justified. However it must be pointed out that by no means an entire vocabulary can be split into fields in this way. Surprisingly often an attempt to find a field composed of mutually-delimiting terms comes to nothing, even in those parts of a vocabulary where one might expect it. Is any field visible in *quick, fast, rapid, hurried*?

To the question of what constitutes a semantic field, that is what its co-ordinates are, one cannot give a satisfactory answer. Some fields may cohere together because they share some characteristic definable within one language, such as colours (using the terminology of physics), family-relationships (using words such as *male, parent, older*, etc.), shops (by enumerating goods sold or business transacted). But other fields, one has the impression, are set up mainly because they are connected with the translation of words in another language. Does an Italian feel any reason why *usare* and *consumare* should appear adjacently? Does an English-speaker see any reason for grouping *train, feature* and *draught*? While such fields underline the non-isomorphic nature of vocabularies, it should not be overlooked that the fields themselves may not be obvious in the sense that different fields may be postulated when a particular language is compared with others in turn. For this reason two-dimensional fields may present a very over-simplified picture of areas of the vocabulary. Thus *use* may be replaced with *employ* in the meaning of Italian *usare* (*I employed a new technique*) and with *need* in that of *consumare* (*This car needs a lot of oil*) but not vice-versa; yet *usare* cannot always be translated by *employ* and *consumare* very seldom by *need*.

We return to the question of the delimitation of semantic fields in 15.12.

15.8 Linguistic relativity. A semantic field may be divided in a way relevant to the culture of the language-community. Thus Roman Law treated paternal and maternal uncles differently; snow is important in the culture of the Eskimos, camels (for the varieties of which Arabic possesses hundreds of words) in that of the Bedouin Arabs; Victorian English contained many terms (*brougham, chariot, clarence, gig, governess cart, growler, hansom, landau, phaeton, victoria*, etc.) for various sorts of horse-drawn vehicles. And so on.

Such non-isomorphism of vocabulary strengthens the view that the world does not completely consist of naturally-classified entities, objects or features. Language operates as a device for classifying human experience and different languages may classify experience in different ways: such a view entails a belief in linguistic relativity, language being regarded metaphorically as a grid or prism, through which the world is viewed. This conception dates back to von Humboldt, if not further, and was obviously held by de Saussure.

191

In the twentieth century a development of similar ideas has become widely known as the Sapir-Whorf hypothesis.

Sapir was an anthropologist as well as a linguist and devoted attention to the relations between language and culture. It is clear that there are no connections between physical characteristics and language: round-headed people will not have a certain type of language, even at the phonetic level. It is also clear that there is no connection between culture and linguistic morphology: if a language is predominantly agglutinative, its speakers are not thereby revealed as warlike or interested in philosophy or technologically sophisticated. Nevertheless there *are* parallels between culture and language, as has been seen in the nature of vocabulary: this is scarcely surprising, since language does not exist apart from culture.

Sapir however went further. He suggested that language is like a predetermined road or groove which can be regarded as a symbolic system of reference (it is not of course *only* a referential system but that is one of its properties), so that to pass from 'one language to another is psychologically parallel to passing from one geometrical system of reference to another'. At times he seems to suggest that a language places difficulties in the way of those who would wish to look at the world differently: 'It is almost as though at some period in the past the unconscious mind of the race had made a hasty inventory of experience, committed itself to a premature classification that allowed of no revision and saddled the inheritors of its language with a science that they no longer quite believed in nor had the strength to overthrow'. Therefore 'the worlds in which different societies live are distinct worlds, not the same world with different labels attached.[15]

Benjamin Lee Whorf (1897–1941), by profession a chemical engineer, took up the study of American languages (in particular Aztec, Maya and Hopi) and became a pupil of Sapir. He wrote a large number of articles discussing the links between language, culture and thought, and is credited with a theory of the connection between them. Perhaps his clearest formulation is: 'Actually, thinking is most mysterious, and by far the greatest light upon it that we have is thrown by the study of language. This study shows that the forms of a person's thought are controlled by inexorable laws of pattern of which he is unconscious. These patterns are the unperceived intricate systematisations of his own language – shown readily enough by a candid comparison and contrast with other languages, especially those of a different linguistic family. His thinking itself is in a language – in English, in Sanskrit, in Chinese. And every language is a vast pattern-system, different from others, in which are culturally ordained the forms and categories by which

the personality not only communicates, but also analyses nature, notices or neglects types of relationship and phenomena, channels his reasoning, and builds the house of his consciousness.'[16]
It is not easy to condense his type of argument, but here are four examples:

(a) The English sentence *He invites people to a feast* splits into a subject and a predicate. The translation into Nootka /tɬ'imʃjaʔisitaʔitɬma/ consists of: (1) /tɬ'imʃ/, 'boiling'; (2) /ja/ 'result' = 'cooked'; (3) /ʔis/, 'eating' = 'eating cooked food'; (4) ·/ita/ 'those who do' = 'eaters of cooked food'; (5) /ʔitɬ/ 'going for'; (6) /ma/ '3rd person indicative'. Roughly 'Boil-ed-eat-ers-go-for-he-does'.[17]

(b) In English we have verbs and nouns; hence we tend to conceive of a world of things and actions. But in Hopi objects of short-term duration, e.g. 'lightning', 'meteor', 'puff of smoke', are verbs; while in Nootka there are no word-classes corresponding to nouns and verbs, only an inflecting word-class which is the equivalent of both, so that one may say 'it houses' (meaning 'house') or 'it burns' (meaning 'flame').[18]

(c) English has three words *insect*, *aeroplane* and *aviator*; Hopi has only one word for all three /masájtaka/, yet Hopi-speakers 'feel no difficulty about it'.[19]

(d) Most Indo-European languages are built on the same plan and thus offer the same analysis of the world (relatively); Whorf therefore lumps them together as SAE (Standard Average European). SAE carefully marks grammatical number and applies pluralisation to isolates of time, for example *ten days* (though these may never be perceived simultaneously as can e.g. *ten men*). Such cycles must in Hopi be expressed by an ordinal numeral, that is 'the tenth day', thus it does not mask the subjective 'becoming later' that is 'the essence of time'. Moreover SAE verbs have a 'three-tense system' that colours the thoughts of its speakers; Hopi verbs have no tenses but 'validity forms' denoting that the speaker reports the situation or that he expects it or that the situation is generally valid (corresponding respectively to our past *and* present, to our future, and to a timeless present (e.g. *We see with our eyes*). Hopi-speakers allegedly therefore view time as a relation of lateness; SAE-speakers view it as a quantity.

We have 'an objectified view of time, which puts before imagination something like a ribbon or scroll marked off into equal blank spaces, suggesting that each can be filled with an entry'. We therefore find in SAE culture '1. Records,

193

diaries, bookkeeping, accounting, mathematics stimulated by accounting. 2. Interest in exact sequence, dating, calendars, chronology, clocks, time wages, time graphs, time as used in physics. 3. Annals, histories, the historical attitude, interest in the past, archaeology, attitudes of introjection toward past periods, e.g. classicism, romanticism'.[20]

Whorf thus appears to suggest (*a*) that the world is differently experienced (i.e. perceived and conceived) in different linguistic communities; (*b*) that such differences are caused by the language; (*c*) that these differences then contribute to the nature of the culture of the speakers. It is difficult, however, to see to what extent he intends to take the causal connections as rigid: are we to assume that the language is in effect a strait-jacket from which it is impossible to free our thinking? Does it ultimately *predestine* our culture?

However, there seems to be no justification for such a strict interpretation. In the first place his evidence is almost totally from language. In many cases, the novelty is in the actual linguistic data he presents, but not in the types of difference he brings to our notice. Thus it was well known (and publicised by Bloomfield in 1933) that the number of word-classes in a language varied and that such word-classes did not correspond to pre-existent categories of reality. Similarly, it was common knowledge that the number of grammatical categories varied from language to language, as did the numbers of members in each; and it was well-known that these did not stand in a one-to-one relationship with 'units of meaning'.

The onus is therefore on Whorf to produce evidence of differences in the perception of the world by different language-communities correlating with differences in the grammatical structures. Is there any evidence, for example, to show within SAE that a French speaker *analyses* the situation he describes as *Il sort* /i sɔr/ differently from the English speaker who describes the same situation, using a directional particle and a progressive aspect, as *He is going out*?

The same objections hold about differences in semantic fields. An English speaker is not incapable of recognising differences in types of snow; it is clear that a language may make an unlimited number of descriptive distinctions (*falling snow, snow on the ground*, etc.). What is interesting is the grouping of entities under one-word labels. Is an Eskimo incapable of seeing a physical connection between his /aput/ and its possible later stages /qana/, /piqsirpoq/ and /qimuqsuq/? Does the English speaker see an identity between a *sleeper* and the *sleeper* in which he may be sleeping? It is instructive that speakers of languages with few colour-terms (e.g.

Hanunóo) may in fact describe colours more precisely as 'ash-coloured', 'turmeric-coloured', and so on.[21] Any experiments so far carried out on differences in perception by members of different language-communities have been inconclusive. In this respect the Sapir-Whorf hypothesis appears to be the answer to a non-existent problem.

In the same way, it is difficult to gather information on the conception of the world by speakers of different languages. What type of evidence *could* be produced? When Whorf talks of the 'metaphysics' of Hopi speakers, he cannot be referring to an explicit philosophical system; he appears to be referring to the linguistic structure – and so his argument is circular. Perhaps the most that can be said is that a language may predispose its speakers to think in certain ways. Thus certain philosophical fallacies may be due to the language of the philosopher. For example, the existence in SAE of a verb 'to be' has led to much speculation about the nature of 'being' and fallacies have arisen in the works of Plato, St Augustine, Kant and Hegel from the confusion of the functions of 'to be'. Such fallacies could not have arisen in, for example, Chinese into which 'to be' must be translated in one of at least six different ways. Nevertheless, the fallacies have been detected by SAE-speaking philosophers, thus proving that the language is not a strait-jacket to thought.[22]

Finally, there is no evidence that the type of evolved culture is due to the language. (Apropos the 'time-orientated' culture of SAE speakers, it should be recalled that not all SAE languages *have* a three-tense system: English and German have a two-tense system.) Apart from that one must query why it is that the Chinese, speakers of a tenseless language, kept historical records, and why some speakers of some SAE languages, such as Spanish and Gaelic, are much less obsessed with time than members of other SAE communities. Nevertheless in Whorf's writings there is much food for thought and research.

15.9 Structural semantics. We confine ourselves in the remainder of this chapter to approaches which deal with the types of meanings associated with the linguist's descriptive categories, such as word and sentence, recognised in utterances. We begin by considering words. A great contribution to semantics was made by the study of the sense-relations holding between individual lexical items in the elaboration of a theory of *structural semantics* by John Lyons.[23]

The notion of 'relation' is important. It is not the case that the 'meanings' of two words are established independently and then compared. On the contrary, the relationship is postulated as holding between the lexical items themselves. Such an approach has the advantage of not becoming entangled with problems of reference or the validity of 'fields'. We examine six such relationships. Lyons handles them in a framework that involves the notion of *implication*.

It is assumed that there are correspondences between affirmative and negative sentences in a language, each pair of correspondences being accounted for by the rules of the grammar (e.g. *The volcano is erupting* and *The volcano is not erupting*). We may then say that the negative sentence 'explicitly denies' whatever is 'explicitly asserted' by the affirmative sentence. One sentence S_1 is said to *imply* (= 'implicitly assert') another S_2 if it is not possible to assert explicitly S_1 and deny explicitly S_2, for example (S_1) *The volcano is in eruption* and *The volcano is erupting* (S_2). Similarly, one sentence S_1 *implicitly denies* another S_2 if it is agreed that the explicit assertion of S_1 makes impossible, without contradiction, the explicit assertion of S_2, for example *The volcano is dormant* and *The volcano is in eruption*.

(*a*) Let S_1 and S_2 be two sentences of identical deep syntactic structure and superficially identical except that where S_1 has lexical item *x*, S_2 has lexical item *y*: *That book was too dear* and *That book was too expensive*. If S_1 implies S_2, and S_2 implies S_1, i.e. S_1 and S_2 are equivalent, then *x* and *y* are synonyms. Such synonymy is context-dependent; we do not require that the words should be interchangeable in all contexts: clearly *dear* and *expensive* are not. Furthermore we do not take into account emotive features (i.e. connotations, associations, stylistic differences), but only the cognitive features (i.e. purely 'intellectual' meanings).

(*b*) Let S_1 and S_2 be two sentences of identical deep syntactic structure and superficially identical except that where S_1 has lexical item *x*, S_2 has lexical item *y*: *There is a tulip in that vase* and *There is a flower in that vase*. If S_1 implies S_2, but S_2 does not generally imply S_1, then *x* is a *hyponym* of *y*. Thus *tulip* is a hyponym of *flower*. Other words, such as *rose, daffodil, crocus*, are also hyponyms of *flower*, and may therefore be called *co-hyponyms* of each other. *Flower* may therefore be called the *superordinate* term. This relationship may be envisaged as in Figure 41. (Notice that this apparent field results from the relationships, not the other way round.) Hyponymy is 'transitive' in the sense that if the relation holds between *a* and *b* (*poodle* and *dog*), and between *b* and *c* (*dog* and *animal*), then it also holds between *a* and *c* (*poodle* and *animal*). Synonymy may be regarded as symmetrical hyponymy; it may be in fact that synonymy arises as a result of hyponymy.

Language-vocabularies do not operate as systematically as systems of scientific taxonomy (e.g. biological terms); there are gaps

flower				
tulip	rose	daffodil	crocus	iris

Figure 41

and asymmetries. It may be that there is no superordinate term where one might expect it: what is the superordinate term of *square* and *round*, or of *door* and *window*, or (in non-technical English) of *brother* and *sister*?

(*c*) Let S_1 and S_2 be two identical sentences of identical deep syntactic structure and superficially identical, except that where S_1 has lexical item *x*, S_2 has lexical item *y*, for example *Mr Volpe was flying a red kite* and *Mr Volpe was flying a green kite*. If S_1 implicitly denies S_2, namely if S_1 and S_2 are contradictory, then *x* and *y* are incompatible terms (e.g. *red* and *green*). The principle is that there must be some dimension of 'sameness' between the two terms; in this case the terms are co-hyponyms, even though there is no superordinate term for colour-words.

(*d*) Various kinds of 'oppositeness' are covered by the traditional term *antonymy*; we consider three of these now: *complementarity*, *antonymy* in Lyons's sense, and *converseness*.

Two-term sets of incompatible terms exist, such as *single* and *married*. A characteristic of such pairs is that (i) the denial of one implies the assertion of the other, *John isn't single* implies *John is married* and (ii) the assertion of one implies the denial of the other, *John is married* implies *John isn't single*. Such pairs are *complementary* terms.

(*e*) Comparison of adjectives may be regarded as a lexical device for grading according to some dimension or other. *Melanie is older than Callista* and *Daisy is older than Melanie* place these ladies in the order *Callista, Melanie* and *Daisy* on an age-scale. Such comparative sentences may compare two different things (*Ben is fatter than Stanley*) or the same thing in different 'states' (marked by tense, aspect or mood) (*Ned is running quicker than he ran yesterday, Ned is running quicker than he usually does, Ned is running quicker than he ought to run*), or they may compare two different things in two different 'states' (*Flavia is prettier than her mother was*).

Certain pairs (e.g. *bigger/smaller*) of comparative adjectives may be related in the following way: a sentence containing one of the pair applied to a noun phrase comparing it to a second noun phrase (*Glasgow is bigger than Dundee*) implies a sentence in which the second member of the pair is applied to the second noun phrase and compares it with the first noun phrase (*Dundee is smaller than*

Glasgow). Such pairs of adjectives are *antonyms* in Lyons's terminology (thus his term covers a narrower range than antonymy in traditional semantics). The above definition, though cumbersome, is not complete, in that it does not allow for comparison of 'states'. This could be remedied by introducing the words 'in one "state"' and 'in a second "state"' where appropriate. This covers such sentences as *Glasgow is bigger than Dundee used to be.* Often such antonyms are not used in the comparative degree, but in the positive: *This room is cold.* The explanation is that they are understood as being graded with reference to some relevant norm, viz. 'This room is colder than the relevant norm for rooms such as this'. The consequence is that the denial of one of a pair of antonyms does not imply the assertion of the other. Thus *This room is not cold* does not imply *This room is hot.* (Contrast complementary terms.)

Such antonyms have given rise to discussion. It is possible to assert *Melanie is older than Callista* and at the same time *Melanie is younger than Daisy.* When it was held that all adjectives denoted qualities, and further that *young* and *old* were opposite qualities, then the question arose why it was possible that adjectives of opposite meaning could be applied to the same noun (or why opposite qualities could be attributed to the same entity). We have now seen the explanation. For the same reason, a sentence such as *Glasgow is bigger than Dundee* cannot be satisfactorily analysed from the semantic point of view in terms of the embedded sentences *Glasgow is big* and *Dundee is big* (even though such a syntactic analysis may be possible).

The distinction between complementary terms and antonyms is not always drawn upon in everyday usage: thus *It's not a big table* may often imply *It's a small table.* But the speaker is conscious of the possible grading of antonyms and will draw upon it when necessary: *It's not a big table, but it's bigger than that one over there.*

(*f*) The third relation of 'oppositeness', that is *converseness*, is best illustrated by an example of e.g. *sell* and *buy*. Compare *Rodney sold a parrot to Sheila* and *Sheila bought a parrot from Rodney*; the first sentence both implies, and is implied by, the second; moreover the lexical substitution of *buy* for *sell* (or vice-versa) involves the permutation of two of the NPs (*Rodney* and *Sheila*) and changes in the selection of the preposition. Similar examples are *teach, learn*; *rent, hire*; *lend, borrow*. The precise nature of the permuting transformation is not the same in all cases of converseness, cf. *Roberta is Lew's wife* v. *Lew is Roberta's husband.* Therefore we cannot give a handy definition of the relation which fits all cases.

198

The beauty of Lyons's contribution is that a clear account is given of the relationships holding between certain members of the major word-classes in natural languages, these relationships being defined (assuming the original implications are agreed) without the necessity of attempting to establish the semantic content of each word separately. We are thus enabled to see that the vocabulary of a natural language in part at least exhibits a structure guaranteed by a general theory; Lyons's approach is therefore more rigorous than the ad hoc recognition of heterogeneous varieties of semantic field, a topic to which we return in 15.11.

15.10 Semantic components. The task of stating the semantic content of words is attempted by every dictionary-maker, as we have seen, in terms of other words; furthermore every dictionary entry is treated on an ad hoc basis. However, the attempt has been made to explore semantic content in terms of a hierarchical array of 'components', each of which may appear in more than one semantic specification.

For example, it is possible to arrange certain terms in a natural vocabulary into patterns, as in this well-known series:

man	woman	child
bull	cow	calf
cock	hen	chicken
drake	duck	duckling
stallion	mare	foal.

Our understanding of the meaning of these words allows us to say that the words in each vertical line have something in common which no other vertical line shares, and that the words in each horizontal line have something in common which no other horizontal line shares. All the words in the first column may therefore be designated 'adult-male', in the second as 'adult-female' and in the third as 'non-adult'. The three words in the first horizontal row are all 'human', in the second 'bovine', in the third 'galline', in the fourth 'anatine' and in the fifth 'equine'. Thus these fifteen words may be specified in terms of selections from eight semantic components, in a manner reminiscent of phonological distinctive features. So we may say that the meaning of the word '*man*' is the product of the components 'human' and 'adult-male'. It may be that some of these components may in turn be broken down into more basic components, as obviously 'adult-male' into 'adult' and 'male'. It is conceivable that we would describe all the words in a natural vocabulary in terms of such ultimate *semantic components*.

Such a view is not new; in fact it dates back to Plato's dialogue

The Sophist. However recently attempts have been made to apply this approach in the incorporation of a semantic section of a transformational grammar. We indicate something of this in 16.3. Suggested types of component also include those which appear in that of only one word and so distinguish it from others in the language, for example 'who has never married' of *bachelor*; and those which specify the type of word with which the word in question co-occurs, for example 'used only with an animate object' of *terrify*.

The advantages claimed are threefold. First, it can be held that there is a universal set of semantic components (deriving perhaps from the cognitive structure of the human mind); these components are then combined in different ways in different languages. Second, we may use the semantic components to judge whether a given combination of lexical items is acceptable or meaningless. Third, it may be possible to predict the meaning of a particular combination of lexical items by considering the semantic components of the items and of the deep-structure syntax.

Yet at present none of these claims appears to be justified. In the first place, there is no evidence to suggest that there *is* a universal set of semantic components. It is highly debatable whether it is possible to compile a closed list of components for even one language, such a closed list being necessary to guarantee description according to a general theory. Any piece of descriptive information seems capable of being a component, and the number of pieces of information is infinite. Furthermore components must be expressed in words, so unavoidably introducing the difficulty of circularity (see p.177) again – in what sense *could* the components be 'basic'? We cannot 'get outside language' to talk about meaning: this problem seems insuperable (see p.180).

The second claimed advantage would be the declaration of the semantic acceptability of a proposed combination of words if the restrictions imposed by the co-occurrence components were not violated. For example, *angry* would carry a marker stating that it must co-occur only with an animate noun, thus excluding **angry bookcase*. Unfortunately in real life the vast majority of questions of semantic compatibility present much greater problems than this. What kind of markers and relationships would have to be postulated to account for the incompatibility of **He took a suit-case out of the envelope*? Moreover, such incompatibility is adjudged on the basis of some 'normality' and in actual practice utterances often contain unexpected, bizarre and often allegedly incompatible combinations of words: e.g. *angry scene, That circle is square, Don't cut yourself on the marmalade, They combed the islands for signs of a shipwreck,*

Be jubilant, my feet, and so on. Poetic language is full of such combinations. To attempt to account for the 'poetical' nature of these combinations in terms of the violation of co-occurrence restrictions on an open set of components is no more scientific and probably less illuminating than the use of the traditional 'figures of speech' (personification, metaphor, metonymy, oxymoron, etc.) alluded to on p.179.

In the third place, it is not possible to predict the meaning of a sentence by considering the semantic components of the lexical items and the syntax, apart from anything else because not enough is known about the relevant deep-structure relationships. The example of the difference between *The Dean punched the bishop on the nose* and *The Dean punched the bishop on the street-corner* will suffice here; clearly the different understandings of the prepositional phrase are connected with the relationship between *bishop* and *nose*, and the lack of connection between *bishop* and *street-corner*. It does not seem possible to handle this deep-structure difference within a Chomskyan framework. (Perhaps a systematic account of such relationships however can be given in terms of a form of 'case-grammar', see 17.8.)

The adequacy of semantic components can also be criticised. At first sight, it appears that the analysis of *man* into 'male' plus 'adult' plus 'human' is adequate; yet it must be discussed whether these components are relevant to any use of the word. For one thing, the analysis comes from biology or physiology. For another, there is no guarantee that such components have any part to play in the correct use and understanding of a child, who may perhaps operate on quite different criteria (e.g. trousers v. a dress, a relatively deep voice, relatively shorter hair, presence of moustache, absence of perfume, and so on). Thirdly, connotational, emotive, stylistic, metaphorical meanings may on occasion be the sole reason for the use of a lexical item: *Be a man!*.[24]

15.11 Another look at semantic fields. Having explored something of structural semantics and semantic components, we return to the question raised earlier concerning the constitution of semantic fields. A claim made by proponents of componential analysis is that certain semantic properties and relationships may be defined in terms of semantic components, for example a set of lexical items whose meanings have certain features in common are held to constitute a semantic field. However the term 'semantic field' seems to be used to cover three different phenomena, of which only one can be defined in terms of a semantic component in common.

This type of field set up on the basis of translation equivalents does not seem to be relevant here: what component can *draught, train, feature* be said to have in common? Sets such as *bush, tree, shrub*; *father, mother, brother, sister* . . .; *red, orange, yellow* . . . might in fact appear to have a semantic component each in common. Yet certainly in the first case it is difficult to see what the component is, unless we turn to a botanical analysis. The truth appears to be that such fields are composed of co-hyponyms (even though a superordinate term may be absent, the co-hyponymy may be established by implicational rules). (There may of course be a more complex and refined statement possible, for example by considering transitivity of hyponymy in the case of colour and family-relationships, and by considering complementarity and converseness in the case of family-relationships.) It appears possible that so far from the components defining the field, semantic components may in fact be an attempt to restate relationships identified by implicational rules.

A third type of semantic field is sometimes discussed: a set such as *train, coach, locomotive, level-crossing, embankment* . . ., the semantic component proposed for such a set being 'concerning a railway'. Many technical vocabularies form such sets. But on examination it appears that such sets are examples of 'associative relations' in Saussure's sense with the attendant disadvantage that there appear to be no logical boundaries: if *embankment*, then why not *grass*, and if *grass* why not *daisy*, etc.? Any limits set appear to be quite arbitrary. Obviously, however, even though the boundaries are indeterminate or arbitrary, such sets *are* important in linguistic usage. Where no implicational relationships exist between the members of such sets (certain areas of technical vocabularies *will* be connected by implicational rules, such as instruments of an orchestra), there seems to be no reason to postulate a semantic component. Justification for recognising such fields may then be sought on the basis of co-occurrence in texts. The relationship between the items may therefore be a 'syntagmatic' type of sense-relationship, of somewhat greater complexity than, for example, *dog* and *bark*.

15.12 Grammatical meaning. A consideration of the meanings of individual words, however much still remains to be done in that domain, is not sufficient. Grammar makes a contribution to the meaning. A distinction has been made since scholastic times between what we might call lexical and grammatical meaning. For certain traditional grammarians only the 'major' parts of speech (nouns, verbs, adjectives and adverbs) had full meaning, since they were held to signify 'concepts' – this is 'lexical' meaning; the other 'minor' parts of speech contributed to the total meaning by imposing a certain organisation upon this raw material, that is 'grammatical meaning'. We extend this latter notion to include not only the eventual surface minor parts of speech but any grammatical form imposed in the generation of a sentence. A full semantic theory will therefore have to find a place for the types of meaning conveyed by such things as sentence modalities, relational functions, grammatical categories and the minor parts of speech. (The first verse of Lewis Carroll's *Jabberwocky* contains *only* grammatical meaning.)

The possibilities available under these four headings may be enumerated in any one natural language: hence we can say that the factors responsible for grammatical meaning form a closed set in a language.[25] By contrast the major parts of speech (or more accurately their underlying root morphemes) form an open set: not all members of a language-community will be acquainted with the same number, and any borrowings or neologisms will enter these classes. (Undeniably of course in a diachronic study we may find that a later stage of a language displays more or fewer members of a given grammatical category than an earlier.)

By 'sentence modalities' is meant the differences between declarative (*Leo built that hut*), interrogative (*Did Leo build that hut?*) and imperative (*Build a hut!*) sentences. This is an area of interest common to linguists and philosophers.

By 'relational functions' we mean such things as 'subject of', 'object of', 'possessor of' and 'modifier of'. These relationships are considerably more complex than may appear at first sight. For example, the role of the grammatical subject in English may be 'actor upon something else', 'causer of an action', 'instrument', 'actor alone', 'patient' or 'recipient' as respectively in the following:

(a) Blodwen picked up the hammer
(b) Blodwen shattered the pane of glass
(c) The hammer shattered the glass
(d) The pane of glass shattered
(e) Blodwen was arrested
(f) Blodwen was given a jail-sentence.

Similarly no one role is played either by the grammatical object or by a surface possessor (denoted here by *'s*) as may be seen in the following:

(g) Blodwen painted a picture
(h) Blodwen cleaned the picture
(i) Blodwen moved the picture
(j) Blodwen's picture was much admired.

In (g) *the picture* actually comes into being as a result of the verbal process, in (h) *the picture* undergoes a process, in (i) *the picture* is caused to do something, that is *move*, while (j) is triply ambiguous, the possible meanings being that *the picture* depicts, belongs to or was painted by Blodwen. The ambiguity present in such 'modifier relationships' as *Maria is a beautiful singer* has already been noted (see 12.13).

The meanings of the grammatical categories do not, as we pointed out in 9.10, stand in a one-to-one relationship with anything that can be called 'units of meaning'. But undeniably many of them make a contribution to the meanings of sentences, as we may see from the alternation of non-past and past or masculine and feminine in *Tony is President* v. *Tony was President* and in French *le poêle* /lə pwɑl/ 'pall' or 'stove' v. *la poêle* /la pwɑl/ 'frying pan'. The nature of these contributions must be investigated, as must the question of whether any such categories are genuinely semantically empty.

The meanings of the minor parts of speech must also be explored. The range of these meanings is extremely diverse. Some appear as the surface representatives of transformation that has taken place (e.g. *and, but*), hence with the meaning of the original instruction to apply that transformation; others may place the speaker or action in a relative temporal or spatial field (*now, there*); others appear as surface markers of relational functions, such as *with* in *Mr Hatt was killed with an axe* and *Mr Hatt was presented with a book*.

It is also necessary to examine whether any difference in meaning is carried by the application of certain optional transformations, such as those which account for the three sets of variants: (*a*) *A furious shop-keeper chased the burglar*, *The burglar was chased by a furious shop-keeper*; (*b*) *The Dean was sober on Wednesday*, *On Wednesday the Dean was sober*, *It was on Wednesday that the Dean was sober*; (*c*) *Harold smokes a pipe*, *Harold is a pipe-smoker*.[26]

The nature of these and similar grammatical meanings must be studied over the whole range of languages, and hypotheses advanced concerning the possibility or impossibility of recognising universally applicable categories. This will involve a consideration of the question whether or not there is any essential difference between the kind of meaning conveyed by lexical means and that conveyed by grammatical. At least in some cases, there would appear to be no difference, the choice between grammatical and lexical being imposed by the language: *I am writing* (progressive aspect, hence grammatical) and French *Je suis en train d'écrire* /ʒə sɥi ɑ̃ trɛ̃ dekrir/ (lexical).

We have already seen (in 8.12) that a rigid separation of the levels

204

of phonology and syntax appears not to be possible; we now see that it may be of benefit not to maintain a sharp distinction between syntax and semantics either. Much contemporary linguistic research is concerned simultaneously with problems of syntax and semantics and the nature of the relationship between them.

15.13 Semantic relations between utterances. One further area of research into meaning should be mentioned. This is the investigation of semantic relationships recognised by the analyst as holding between utterances or even as characterising one single utterance. They may be termed 'quasi-logical' in that while they are reminiscent of relationships within formal logic they are not part of or justified by that discipline. We have already encountered one such example in Lyons's implicational relationships. But whereas Lyons accepted the relationships between sentences and then went on to draw conclusions about the lexical items involved, the present type of investigation looks at the relationships between sentences themselves. Among these are:

1. *Synonymy* or *paraphrase*: *Suddenly the undertaker took out his false teeth* is a paraphrase of *Without warning the mortician removed his dentures*;
2. *Inconsistency*: *Millicent speaks fluent French* is inconsistent with *Millicent speaks only Icelandic*;
3. *Contradiction*: *Culpepper carefully lowered himself from the ground floor to the attic* contradicts itself;
4. *Tautology*: *Moriarty's moustache was on his upper lip* is tautologous;
5. *Entailment*: *Bubbles Sniggleworth has just flown to Vladivostok* entails *Bubbles Sniggleworth has just gone to Vladivostok*;
6. *Presupposition*: *Alfonso's servant has measles* presupposes *Alfonso has a servant*.

Linguists both within and outside the tradition of transformational-generative grammar are engaged in exploring the justification for these labels, the conditions that have to be recognised as necessary for their application and the consequences that result from them.

FURTHER READING
Bloomfield 1933, chs 2 and 9; Lyons 1966, 1977; Katz and Fodor 1963; Langendoen 1968, chs 1, 2 and 3; Leech 1974; Li 1976; Palmer 1976; Ullman 1964; Whorf 1956 (further readings in semantics will be suggested at the end of Chaper 17).

16. 'Chomskyan' Developments in Transformational-Generative Grammar

16.1 After *Syntactic Structures*. In 13.3 we indicated that proposals were made for alterations to the form of grammar introduced in *Syntactic structures*: indeed that first model of transformational-generative grammar might be regarded as obsolete by those who (we believe) mistake the nature of linguistic theories. The main changes suggested were that the sketchy morphophonemic component should be expanded and radically revised, that the scope of the grammar should be extended to include a semantic component, and that the form of the syntactic rules should be altered. Of course these proposals entailed further problems and in order to solve some of them yet further changes were suggested.

The argumentation for these proposals is highly technical and an adequate exposition of them far beyond our scope. However, we must not give the impression that *Syntactic structures* was the end of the story, and the following indications of later developments will help our reader tackle the original texts.

16.2 Generative phonology. The morphophonemic component of the *Syntactic structures* model simply converted single morphemes or combinations of morphemes into strings of phonemes (or alternatively of orthographic symbols). It is possible to imagine that this section of the grammar could be followed by a series of allophonic rules (of the type illustrated in 8.1) which would then give a segmental phonetic specification for every sentence produced by the grammar. While such a procedure would be successful up to a point, three kinds of weakness suggest themselves, all of them reminiscent of criticisms directed by prosodic phonologists at phonemic practice (cf. 8.11).

The first concerns the phonetic adequacy of the output. The allophonic variation would have to be formulated in terms of connected speech, not of individual words, and some method would have to be found to indicate phonemic replacements found at word-boundaries. Furthermore, relevant suprasegmental features would have to be specified by some means or other, in particular intonation, stress and rhythmic structure. Stress could perhaps be written in for every individual word, but we know that in connected speech not every word bears a stress, a fact that has consequences for vowel quality (see 8.6); apart from that, connected speech contains instances of what we called silent stress.

In the second place, it is noteworthy that certain morphemes show regular patterns of consonant-selection or vowel-selection in different environments. This is ignored in our suggested model. Thus the series of pairs *deride/derision, divide/division, elide/elision,* etc. exhibits both a consistent vocalic *alternation* and a consonantal one. In fact patterns of stress may also be found, e.g. in *telegraph/telegrapher/telegraphic, photograph/photographer/photographic,* etc. It would add to the power and generality of the morphophonemic component if such alternations could be shown to belong to patterns rather than simply be stated as though they were accidental properties of individual combinations of morphemes. This might be achieved by allowing rules to operate on those sequences of elements common to similar patterns of morphemes, or in the case of stress-placement on abstract word-structures (e.g. stated in terms of C and V). Indeed generative phonologies had already been written which took account of morpheme patterns in some such way, notably by Pāṇini (see 5.2), Bloomfield and Chomsky himself, to say nothing of the attempted derivations of morphs from concrete 'base forms' by means of the addition or subtraction of sounds.[1]

The third point concerns the suitability of phoneme theory (of any type) for the task in hand. We have already seen that the nasal in *ten* is in many accents alveolar while that in *tenth* is dental, an alternation that may be stated by a rule such as

/n/: [n̪] /θ, ð

Yet this specification does not state explicitly that there is an articulatory similarity (termed *similitude* by Daniel Jones)[2] between the fricative and the allophone of the nasal, that is that both are dental. That information allows us to posit a reason in terms of economy of articulatory effort for the selection of the particular nasal. It would be helpful if the phonetic specification could show such similarities explicitly, for then the grammar could be held to contain a greater degree of explanatory adequacy. This leads us to suppose that some preferable alternative to phonemic theory might be found.

Indeed Chomsky expressed strong objections to the bi-uniqueness principle attributed to what he called *taxonomic phonemics* (p.87, n.24). For example[3] some North American accents pronounce *rider* as [ˈɹaˑɪdɹ̩] and *writer* as [ˈɹaɪdɹ̩]. A type of strict distributional phonemics could phonemicise these only as strings of phonemes identical except that where *rider* contains /aˑ/ *writer* contains /a/ –

an absurdity according to Chomsky. Therefore he rejects any phonemic approach. (Of course if we allow overlapping of phonemes, i.e. both /t/: [d̥]/V ˑɹ and /d/: [d̥]/V ˑɹ, and are willing to accept grammatical criteria, then we can phonemicise as /ˈraɪdɹ̩/ and /ˈraɪtɹ̩/ respectively, /aɪ/ being a single phonemic unit, lengthened before a voiced plosive.)

Following *Syntactic structures*, forms of *generative phonology* were proposed which would provide a phonetic specification for every sentence produced by the grammar while avoiding the weaknesses outlined above; the most famous of these proposals are M. Halle's *The sound pattern of Russian* (1959) and Chomsky and Halle's *The sound pattern of English* (1968).

An outstanding change from the phonological models of post-Bloomfieldian structuralism was that the primitive phonological element was no longer the phoneme but the *distinctive feature*. The concept of distinctive features is associated with the Prague School (see 8.11) and one member of that circle, Roman Jakobson, has been particularly concerned with its development, both in Europe and in the U.S.A. Three points of importance came to be recognised.

Firstly, the distinctive features came to be explicitly regarded as binary choices and hence they could be listed as paired oppositions, for example 'vocality' v. 'consonantality' or 'nasality' v. 'orality'.[4] Such binary opposition could also be posited between the presence of a feature and its absence, for example 'vocality' and 'non-vocality' and (independently) 'consonantality' v. 'non-consonantality' – in this case, therefore, two independent choices instead of one and so four possible classifications rather than two (cf. the specifications of [a], [l], [p] and [h] below). The number of distinctive features felt necessary varies in the literature, as do their names: here is a representative selection:[5]

> *vocalic–nonvocalic*: vocalic sounds are produced with a periodic excitation and with an open oral cavity, that is one in which the most extreme degree of narrowing is a *constriction*, such as [a], [l], [r]; nonvocalic sounds are produced with an oral cavity narrowed at least to the degree of an *obstruction* or with an excitation that is not periodic, such as [p], [m], [θ], [h].
>
> *consonantal–nonconsonantal*: consonantal sounds are produced with an *occlusion* or *contact* in the central path through the oral cavity, such as [p], [m], [θ], [l]; nonconsonantal sounds are produced with lesser degrees of narrowing in the central path of the oral cavity, such as [a], [h].
>
> *grave–nongrave*: grave sounds are articulated with a primary narrowing located at the periphery of the oral cavity (i.e. at the

lips or in the velar or pharyngeal region), such as [p], [k]; nongrave sounds are articulated with a primary narrowing located in the central (i.e. dental-alveolar-palatal) region of the oral cavity, such as [θ], [t], [ʃ].

flat–nonflat: flat sounds are produced with a secondary narrowing at the periphery of the oral cavity, such as [u], [ɔ]; nonflat sounds are produced without such a narrowing, such as [i], [ɑ].

diffuse–nondiffuse: diffuse sounds are produced with a narrowing, which in degree equals or exceeds that of a *constriction* and is located in the front part of the vocal tract, such as [p], [θ], [t], [s], [i]; nondiffuse sounds are articulated with a narrowing which is either of a lesser degree or is located in the back part of the vocal tract, such as [ʃ], [tʃ], [k], [o]. The dividing line between *front* and *back* is further retracted for vowels than for other sounds; for the vowels, *front* includes almost the entire oral cavity, while for the other sounds, the dividing line between *front* and *back* runs between the alveolar and palatal regions.

compact–noncompact: compact sounds are produced with a 'forward flanged' (horn-shaped) oral cavity, such as [ɔ], [ɑ], [a], [tʃ], [ʃ], [k]; noncompact sounds are produced with a cavity that is not 'forward flanged' (gourd-shaped), such as [i] [e] [o] [p] [θ] [s]. This and the preceding opposition seem to have been originally one, namely 'compact' v. 'diffuse'. But compare the classifications of [i] and [o].

strident–nonstrident: this feature is restricted to consonantal sounds. Strident sounds are produced by directing the air stream at right angles across a sharp edged obstacle or parallel over a rough surface, thereby producing considerable noisiness, which is the major acoustical correlate of stridency, such as [f], [s], [ʃ]. Nonstrident sounds are produced with configurations in which one or several of the factors mentioned are missing, such as [θ], [p], [m].

voiced–voiceless: voiced sounds are produced by vibrating the vocal cords, such as [b], [m], [v]; voiceless sounds are produced without vocal vibration, such as [p], [f].

nasal–non-nasal: nasal sounds are produced by lowering the velum, thereby allowing air to pass through the nasal pharynx and nose, such as [m], [n]; non-nasal sounds are produced with a raised velum, which effectively shuts off the nasal pharynx and nose from the rest of the vocal tract, such as [b], [t].

continuant–interrupted: continuant sounds are produced with a vocal tract in which the passage from the glottis to the lips contains no narrowing in excess of an *occlusion*, such as [f], [v], [θ]; interrupted sounds are produced with a vocal tract in which the passage from the glottis to the lips is effectively closed by contact, such as [p], [m].

Other distinctive features suggested include *tense* v. *lax* (cf. 7.7), *syllabic* v. *nonsyllabic*, *stressed* v. *nonstressed*, and *checked* v. *unchecked* (checked sounds include ejectives, implosives and clicks).

Table 5

	p	f	d	n	s	g	i	u	ɔ	a
vocalic	−	−	−	−	−	−	+	+	+	+
consonantal	+	+	+	+	+	+	−	−	−	−
strident	−	+	−	−	+	−	−	−	−	−
compact			−				−	−	+	+
grave	+	+	−	−	−	+	−	+	+	+
continuant	−	+	−	−	+	−	+	+	+	+
nasal	−	−	−	+	−	−	−	−	−	−
tense			−							
diffuse	+	+	+	+	+	−	+	+	−	−
flat			−				−	+	+	−
voiced	−	−	+	+	−	+	+	+	+	+

As a result, specifications of speech-sounds may be displayed in columns as in Table 5,[7] (gaps are left where features are not relevant here or are implied by the presence of other features). This principle allows phonological elements also to be written as bundles of the appropriate distinctive features (cf. 8.11) and we can use it to specify phonological forms of morphemes in the lexicon of a transformational-generative grammar. For example, the entry specifying the essential underlying phonology of *dog* could be written[8] as in Table 6.

Secondly, these features were defined with reference not only to articulatory positions but also (or even predominantly) to acoustic properties of speech-sounds, as observed in spectrograms (see 7.7).[9] One result of this was that the sharp distinction between vowels and consonants made in articulatory phonetics disappeared so that the same inventory of features became applicable to both. Another was that the final phonetic specification of the output could be made in terms of the same features, and therefore the lists of essential phonological features specifying the lexicon-morphemes could be gradually converted into the actual surface-forms by adding or subtracting features according to ordered rules. For example, the plural morpheme in English could be listed (for 'regular' nouns) as

Table 6

$$
\begin{bmatrix}
-\text{vocalic} \\
+\text{consonantal} \\
-\text{strident} \\
-\text{compact} \\
-\text{grave} \\
-\text{continuant} \\
-\text{nasal} \\
-\text{tense} \\
+\text{diffuse} \\
-\text{flat} \\
+\text{voiced}
\end{bmatrix}
\quad
\begin{bmatrix}
+\text{vocalic} \\
-\text{consonantal} \\
\\
-\text{compact} \\
\\
\\
\\
+\text{tense} \\
\\
+\text{flat}
\end{bmatrix}
\quad
\begin{bmatrix}
-\text{vocalic} \\
+\text{consonantal} \\
-\text{strident} \\
+\text{compact} \\
+\text{grave} \\
-\text{continuant} \\
-\text{nasal} \\
-\text{tense} \\
-\text{diffuse} \\
-\text{flat} \\
+\text{voiced}
\end{bmatrix}
$$

the distinctive features which would yield an alveolar fricative ('consonantal, not compact, strident') but with no indication of voicing; voice or voicelessness would thereafter be automatically specified to agree with the voicing of the final consonant of the root morpheme (provided that this was not an alveolar or a palato-alveolar fricative). This voicing specification would look like:

$$
\begin{bmatrix}
+\text{consonantal} \\
-\text{compact} \\
+\text{strident}
\end{bmatrix}
\rightarrow [+\text{voice}] /
\begin{bmatrix}
+\text{consonantal} \\
+\text{voiced} \\
-\text{strident}
\end{bmatrix}
- \#
$$

According to the language, certain bundles will automatically receive features which, though not phonologically distinctive, are necessary to a phonetic specification of sounds. In English, nasals, for example, do not draw on a voice/voiceless opposition, hence they may be listed with no specification as to voicing; voice may be added automatically at a subsequent stage. In the same way, the previous specification of the vowel of *dog* would be expanded to include the features:

$$
\begin{bmatrix}
-\text{strident} \\
+\text{grave} \\
+\text{continuant} \\
-\text{nasal} \\
-\text{diffuse} \\
+\text{voiced}
\end{bmatrix}
$$

Rules that add features in these two ways characterise the form of a generative phonology. Thus no reference at all is made explicitly to phonemes, the derivation proceeding smoothly from an underlying abstract specification to a concrete phonetic description. Clearly the

211

term 'morphophonemic component' is no longer applicable and so the term *phonological component* replaces it.

Thirdly, it was hoped that the proposed list of distinctive features would be *universal*. This curious use of the word does not mean that every language draws on every opposition in the list, as one might suppose, but simply that (allegedly) there is a universal set of features of which the features in any particular language form a subset. 'No language contains all of these features.'[10] Not un-expectedly the list of distinctive features has grown in the history of generative phonology, but there is still no certainty that the last highest figure will not have to be exceeded in describing some hitherto unanalysed language; the assumption of certainty is one that cannot be made. It is simply not true to say that 'every new proposed feature is in a sense a proposed claim about all human languages'.[11]

One result of the desire to keep the list of universal features as short as possible is that the 'same' bundles of features would be used in different languages to specify sounds easily distinguishable by an articulatory phonetician, e.g. the respective exponents of [s] and [ʃ] in English and German. But it is difficult to see how the phonetic statement can be made as complete as possible without drawing on a much larger, perhaps infinitely large, set of descriptive labels.

Chomsky and Halle's *The sound pattern of English* applies a generative phonological framework to English. There is a great deal that is thought-provoking in this huge book but also much that has been criticised. In relation to its length, it devotes surprisingly little space to the subject-matter of the title: apart from an incursion into the history of an English sound-shift (see Chapter 18), much of the book is taken up with a discussion of the phonetic and phonological framework and with arguments for the best formulation and ordering of the rules. But two topics in English phonology in particular receive detailed attention: the placing of stress and the consonantal and vocalic alternations mentioned above.

One claim made is that the stressing of English words is astonishingly regular, hence stress is not written in as a feature of the lexicon entries, but may simply be added later on the basis of the phonological structure of the root morphemes. The conditions for marking the stressed syllable can be stated as a set of rules specifying the appropriate phonological structures and the position of the stress. When the stress has been allocated, its position may have to be changed if an affix of a certain type has been added to form some kind of derivation, as in *courage/courageous, graph/telegraph*. The rules for changing the position of stress themselves form a fairly

Table 7

(a)

[NP[A black]A[N[N board]N[N eraser]N]N]NP

1	1		First cycle
		1	
1	2		Second cycle
2	1	3	Third cycle

(b)

[N[N[A black]A[N board]N]N[N eraser]N]N

1	1		First cycle
		1	
1	2		Second cycle
1	3	2	Third cycle

(c)

[N[NP[A black]A[N board]N]NP[N eraser]N]N

1	1		First cycle
		1	
2	1		Second cycle
3	1	2	Third cycle

complex set. But if further affixes have been added the position of the stress may have to be changed yet again, as in the series *instrument/instrumental/instrumentality*. This further change of stress is effected by the same set of rules applied a second time, which accounts for the use of the term *transformational cycle*.

The transformational cycle may be applied several times over and strikingly it applies not only within words but within larger structures, as in the derivations of (a) *black board-eraser* ('board eraser that is black'), (b) *blackboard eraser* ('eraser for a black-board'), (c) *black board eraser* ('eraser of a black board') shown in Table 7.[12] The figures refer to alleged degrees of stress. Three stages are represented in the successive grouping of nouns and adjectives into their respective phrases; they are shown by the brackets, appropriately labelled by the syntactic rules, which are successively removed, beginning with the innermost. Each application of the

213

cycle increases the number of stress-gradations; since there is no theoretical limit to the number of applications of the cycle, this type of phonology is not limited to the four degrees of stress postulated by the neo-Bloomfieldians (see p.86). Furthermore, it is obvious from the labelled bracketing in terms of 'adjective', 'noun' and 'noun-phrase' that morphological and syntactic criteria must be taken into consideration; since in this way constituent structure is involved these rules governing stress-placement are transformational rather than simple rewrite rules. These transformational cyclical rules thus apply to the smaller constituents and then to increasingly larger ones until 'the maximal domain of phonological processes is reached'.[13] When the last application of the cycle has been made, certain sensitive unstressed vowels are 'reduced' to [ə].

The consonantal alternations are treated in a relatively simple way, features being added or changed in the abstract specifications so that final output pairs, such as *president/presidential, decide/decision*, are produced by the same set of rules. Vowels are more complicated. Clearly certain pairs are related, as in *divine/divinity, serene/serenity* and *profane/profanity*, but the postulation of underlying features and processes for these and similar pairs turns out to be quite lengthy.

As examples of the kinds of derivation proposed in *The sound pattern of English* (listed as segmental symbols rather than bundles of features) we have[14]

(a) *manager*
      mænVger
      mǽnVger   MAIN STRESS RULE (48a)
      mǽnVǰer   RULE (72)
      mǽnəǰər   VOWEL REDUCTION

(b) *managerial*
      mænVgeriæl
      mænVgériæl   MAIN STRESS RULE (48a)
      mænVǰériæl   RULE (72)
      mænVǰḗrīæl   TENSING RULE (80c, b)
      mænVǰéyrīyæl   DIPHTHONGISATION (78)
      mænVǰīyrīyæl   VOWEL SHIFT
      mænəǰıyrīyəl   VOWEL REDUCTION

In these derivations every cycle has been omitted except the last. The symbols of course are those of Chomsky and Halle, not of the IPA. The numbers refer to the sequence of examples in *The sound pattern of English*.

214

For detailed criticism the reader is referred elsewhere,[15] but we would point out that no previously unknown pairs of morphologically related words are presented; much of the justification of the book must therefore lie in the explanatory adequacy and generality of the postulated phonological rules. At least in some cases it is arguable that the sheer complexity of these rules testifies more to the ingenuity of the authors than to articulatory explanation; some cases seem quite artificial, for example the derivation of *spa* as[16]

> spæ
> spæw
> spæu
> spæʌ
> spaʌ
> spāʌ

Indeed W.S.-Y. Wang has pointed out that one rule is quite impossible to apply,[17] so that its explanatory adequacy is acutely suspect, to say the least.

The example of *spa* serves to remind us that the authors are concerned with one accent of English, namely a type of General American, and it is not at all clear whether the lexicon entries and rules are intended to apply to all accents of English. If they are, then no solution has been given to such problems as the specification of the vowels of *bad, bard, balm, bomb, caught* (see p.82), which group together in such different ways in various accents of the language. Clearly differences of this type present formidable obstacles to any attempt to derive all accents of English from the same underlying representations. Furthermore, the great complexity of Chomsky's proposed phonology seems in part to be due to the establishing of one single system to encompass words of every provenance, not only those of Germanic stock but Greek and Romance borrowings, as well as assorted importations such as *Conestoga, Monongahela, shillelagh, chianti, Ypsilanti* and *Winnipesaukee*. Exceptions to this system seem to receive somewhat cavalier treatment. This points to the utility of somehow recognising subsystems within the phonology of a language (cf. 8.12).[18] Finally it should be pointed out that not all grammatically and semantically related pairs or series of words can be handled by a phonological theory: for example, *go/went* or *tooth/dental*. All these considerations give food for thought about this particular form proposed for a generative phonology and about the place of generative phonology within a complete description of a language (see 16.4 onwards).

One of the main goals of generative phonology is not simply to describe relationships such as *manager/managerial* but to *explain* them as being in some way 'natural', so that a particular generative phonology will contain at least some measure of explanatory adequacy (see 16.2); many have held that this goal has been achieved, some have not. We cannot judge this here, for the question itself raises further issues. Cynically we might argue that any phonetic form can be related to any other we wish by means of complex rules, even *tooth/dental* for example, by drawing on conjectured historical development: at what stage does such a process become absurd, that is how do we assess explanatory adequacy? Is apparent complexity necessarily a good sign or a bad? Is careless or unworkable formulation of rules on the part of one phonologist sufficient reason for discarding the entire approach? Need a generative phonology employ distinctive features of the type suggested or indeed distinctive features at all? Clearly such discussion can become very wide. Nevertheless we must point out that generative phonology in the form described became extensively used, indeed *is* the dominant approach to phonology in some quarters.

16.3 A semantic component. One of the first steps in incorporating a semantic component into the framework of a generative grammar was taken by Jerrold Katz and Jerry Fodor in *The structure of a semantic theory* (1963).[19] They draw attention to the disagreement about the very nature of meaning, seen in the writings of semanticists; this they attribute to a failure to attack the basic question of the abstract form of a semantic theory. Such a characterisation would tell what phenomena the semantic theory was seeking to describe and explain, and what facts were relevant in semantic investigation. Katz and Fodor set out to supply what they require.

They point out that every speaker of a language can produce and can understand *any* sentence from the infinite set of sentences in his language although he only encounters a finite set in his lifetime. The speaker therefore must possess a set of rules which project the finite set to the infinite set; the formulation of these rules is the *projection problem*. Therefore what is asked for in a description of a language is a solution, according to Katz and Fodor, of this projection problem. Moreover since they talk of 'understanding' every sentence, a description of the meaning must be included.

Transformational grammars, they confidently assert, provide solutions for the grammatical aspect of any language (and 'grammatical' here includes syntax, phonology, phonemics and morphology); therefore to discover the goals of semantics we subtract the grammatical component from the solution to the projection problem, in other words 'Linguistic description minus grammar equals semantics'. 'Semantics takes over the explanation of the speaker's ability to produce and understand infinitely many new sentences at the point where grammar leaves off.' This marks one boundary of semantics. Another boundary is fixed in the recognition that a semantic theory cannot take account of the contribution of context to the understanding of utterances, whether context is understood to be the socio-physical circumstances of the utterances, or the surrounding linguistic context (for a reason similar to that advanced in 15.3 above). We therefore assume a context-free semantic interpretative ability shared by the speakers of a language-community, this ability to be reflected by the semantic theory.

Among the particular abilities of the speaker that the theory must reconstruct are the detection of non-syntactic ambiguities (as in *The bill is large*) and the use of semantic relations within an utterance to eliminate possible ambiguities (as in *The bill is large but need not be paid*). Another is the ability to recognise semantic anomalies, as in *He painted the walls with silent paint*. A third is the speaker's ability to paraphrase, for example to recognise the semantic relationship between *Two chairs are in the room* and *There are at least two things in the room and each is a chair*. None of these tasks can be carried out by the grammar.

Therefore a semantic theory encompasses phenomena not handled by grammar and not attributable to the particular socio-physical or linguistic contexts of utterances; within these boundaries it 'describes and explains the interpretative ability of speakers: by accounting for their performance in determining the number and content of the readings of a sentence; by detecting semantic anomalies; by deciding upon paraphrase relations between sentences; and by marking every other semantic property or relation that plays a role in this ability'.[20] After this clear account of the goals of a particular semantic theory, Katz and Fodor proceed to specify the components of their proposed form of solution to the problem. It should perhaps be pointed out that there is no *a priori* reason why a theory that sets out to achieve these goals should assume this form; the justification of the present model depends ultimately (as always) on its success, that is its external and its explanatory adequacy, and its superiority over other proposals.

Katz and Fodor's theory contains a *dictionary* giving the meanings of the morphemes in the language; this is necessary simply because morphemes *have* meanings and these cannot be accounted for in the syntactic component. But it is not sufficient, since even given the meanings of the morphemes (and each morpheme may well have more than one possible meaning) the syntactic component cannot

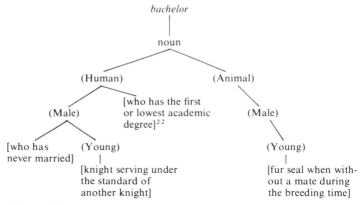

Figure 42

select the meanings appropriate in individual sentences, nor can it recognise anomalous combinations (e.g. *silent paint*) which are syntactically acceptable, nor can it recognise semantically equivalent sentences of different syntactic structure. Therefore a set of *projection rules* must also find a place in the theory to select the appropriate sense of each morpheme in a sentence; they will take account of the semantic relations between the individual morphemes in the sentence and of the interaction between meaning and syntax; the result will be to provide the correct semantic interpretation for every sentence in the language.

The dictionary entries contain in a systematic formal way the essential semantic information found in conventional dictionaries. Katz and Fodor require that the entries take the form of Figure 42.[21] Whether or not such a diagrammatic layout is literally envisaged for every morpheme is not clear, but the notion of a hierarchical 'branching' of meanings is important to the authors' reasoning. Such dictionary entries give various types of information, for example in the present case: firstly that there are four possible interpretations of the lexical item; secondly that the item is a member of the word-class Noun (indicated by a *grammatical marker*, here the ordinary word 'noun'); thirdly that certain meanings contain *semantic markers* (indicated by parentheses), such as (Human), shared with other meanings of this and of other lexical items – these are the semantic components described in 15.10, the systematic features of the semantic structure of the language; and fourthly that some meanings are characterised by features idiosyncratic to that meaning alone, the *distinguishers*, indicated by square brackets, such as [who has never married].

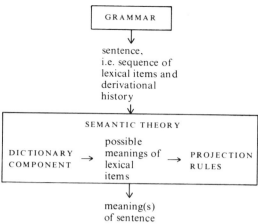

Figure 43

A further type of semantic information is necessary, an indication of the relation between features of certain combinations into which a lexical item may enter and the meaning which the item bears in those combinations. The authors' example is *honest*, which may carry the distinguisher [innocent of illicit sexual intercourse] only if it co-occurs with a noun containing both the semantic markers (Human) and (Female); this is notated later in the paper by angled brackets. Thus the branching in question, the 'path' in the dictionary entry, could be notated as *honest* → *Adjective* →(*Evaluative*) → (*Moral*) → [*innocent of illicit sexual intercourse*] ⟨(*Human*) and (*Female*)⟩.[23]

The semantic theory, consisting of the dictionary and the projection rules, is envisaged as being linked to the grammar in the following way: from the grammar each sentence produced, consisting of a sequence of lexical items and a derivational history, is fed into the semantic theory; from the dictionary each lexical item acquires its complete range of possible meanings; the projection rules then make a selection from the possible meanings of the individual lexical items in such a way that the appropriate meaning for the whole sentence is specified, as in Figure 43.[24]

The actual formulation of the projection rules need not concern us here; their effect is to scan the possible meanings of lexical items and delete those that are not permitted by the contextual restrictions contained in angled brackets, so *honest* cannot carry the distinguisher [innocent of illicit sexual intercourse] if it co-occurs with *man*, which lacks the necessary semantic marker (Female). This

219

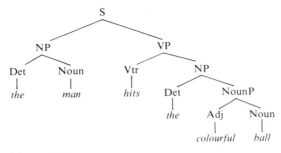

Figure 44

entails matching pairs of lexical items, the pairs to be matched being determined by the derivational history of the sentence, and producing the appropriate amalgamation of their semantic features; this meaning is then compared with that of another part of the sentence and a further amalgamation produced; the process is continued until the meaning of the entire sentence is established.

We may illustrate this with the sentence *The man hits the colourful ball*. Taken individually, various lexical items have more than one meaning; thus we may gloss *hits* as either 'collides with' or 'strikes with a blow or missile'; *colourful* as 'vivid in character' or 'bright with colours'; *'ball'* as 'dance-gathering' or 'globular object' or 'war-missile'. For example, the entry for 'colourful' would contain the paths:[25]

(1)   *Colourful* → Adjective → (Colour) [Abounding in contrast or variety of bright colours] ⟨(Physical Object) or (Social Activity)⟩

(2)   *Colourful* → Adjective → (Evaluative) → [Having distinctive character, vividness, or picturesqueness] ⟨(Aesthetic Object) or (Social Activity)⟩

But this ambiguity is reduced in our sentence where the meaning of 'dance-gathering' for *ball* is impossible, as is the meaning 'vivid in character' for *colourful*. It was in order to make it possible to mirror this knowledge on the part of the speaker that the contextual restrictions in angled-brackets were written in, thus the second path for *colourful* (the meaning 'vivid in character') cannot be chosen if the adjective modifies a noun containing the marker (Physical Object); similarly a restriction is written into both paths of the verb *hits* specifying that both meanings must have an object containing the marker (Physical Object).

The projection rules use the contextual restrictions in conjunction with the derivational history of the sentence in question, which we may represent here by a tree-diagram (although not all relevant grammatical information is capable of representation in this form), as in Figure 44. The rules then work from the bottom of this tree by amalgamating first of all the semantic elements of *the* and *man* on the one hand, and *colourful* and *ball* on the other; in this latter case only four 'amalgamated' meanings are possible, that is (*a*) 'dance-gathering bright with colours', (*b*) 'globular shape bright with colours', (*c*) 'war-missile bright with colours' and (*d*) 'dance-gathering vivid in character'. Strictly speaking these meanings should be expressed as markers and distinguishers, thus meaning (*d*) would be

> *Colourful + Ball* → Noun concrete → (Social Activity) →
> (Large) → (Assembly) → (Evaluative) → [[Having distinctive character, vividness or picturesqueness] [For the purposes of social dancing]].[26]

Further steps are to amalgamate the semantic elements of *the* and *colourful ball*, then those of *hits* and *the colourful ball* – in the course of which the possible meaning of *ball* as (Social Activity) is deleted – and finally those of *the man* and *hits the colourful ball*.

Of the individual lexical ambiguities possible, the only ones that remain in the sentence are the two interpretations of *hits* and the two (Physical Object) interpretations of *ball*; there are consequently four possible meanings for the sentence. These may be stated as different sequences of semantic markers and distinguishers; here is one example:

> *The + man + hits + the + colourful + ball* → Sentence → [Some contextually definite] → (Physical Object) → (Human) → (Adult) → (Male) → (Action) → (Instancy) → (Intensity) → [Strikes with a blow or missile] → [Some contextually definite] → (Physical Object) → (Colour) → [[Abounding in contrast or variety of bright colours] [Solid missile for projection by engine of war]].[27]

In this way, it is hoped, the semantic theory will specify the meanings of individual sentences and will be able to supply alternative readings in cases of ambiguous ones, whether the ambiguity is due to derivational history or to lexical ambiguity. Furthermore, the theory will be able to recognise semantic anomaly, as in for example **The man hits the aridity*, since it *cannot* assign a meaning, *aridity* lacking the necessary marker (Physical Object). It might even be possible to envisage a situation where the theory can recognise paraphrases in terms of the identity of the semantic components specifying the meanings of two different sentences.

221

It should be stressed that the semantic markers, it is claimed, are theoretical constructs in the same way as are atom, gene or noun phrase. 'A marker such as (*Human*) or (*Colour*) is, then, not an English word, but a construct represented by one.'[28] These purely semantic markers should not be confused with grammatical categories, the word *ship* may be treated as grammatically feminine in English, but it does not bear the semantic marker (Female). One other comment should be made about the theory in view of later developments: the theory operates on the output of the grammar and specifies the meaning of it – it may therefore be described as *interpretative*.

The import of the reservations expressed in 15.10 about componential analysis of this type may be seen more clearly: it is questionable whether the semantic markers *are* enumerable as units in a system, even for one language – and in the model here described the status of distinguishers within a system is mysterious; it is dubious on the one hand whether the syntactic information available is sufficient to allow semantic specification of sentences and on the other whether projection rules can be formulated to take account of the grammatical relationships we can describe.

16.4 Standard theory. By 1963 not only had Chomsky's *Syntactic structures* appeared but proposals had been made for the form of a phonological component in generative grammar and for the form of an interpretative semantic component. The time was now ripe to put together these syntactic, phonological and semantic components into one single model of a language; such a model would show the consistent relationships between the phonetic exponents of the sentences in a language and the semantic interpretations of these sentences. The first attempts towards presenting such a unified linguistic model were made in *An integrated theory of linguistic descriptions* (1964) by Jerrold Katz and P.M. Postal and in *Aspects of the theory of syntax* (1965) by Chomsky; the formulations proposed in these works were referred to by Chomsky[29] as the *standard theory*.

In the schemes sketched in 16.2 and 16.3 the output of the syntactic component is used as the input both to the phonological and to the semantic components. Katz and Postal are thus enabled to assemble these three in the following way, giving a picture of a 'linguistic description of a natural language'[30] as in Figure 45. The output of this descriptive device is the linking of the phonological representation of each individual sentence with its semantic interpretation (any ambiguity will be due only to word-ambiguity not cancelled out by the projection rules). Katz and Postal spend

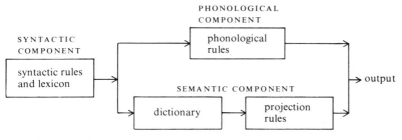

Figure 45

virtually no time on the phonological component, but it will be recalled that this operates on the final sequences of morphemes generated by the syntactic component. It appeared in 16.3 that the semantic component also operated on the final sequence of morphemes; however, we find that the exemplificatory sentences in Katz and Fodor are all fairly simple and indeed minimal attention was paid to the contribution of syntactic structure to semantic interpretation. The present 'integrated theory' involves a closer examination of the nature of this contribution, which in turn leads to a reappraisal of the form of the syntactic rules.

To allow the semantic component to operate on the final morpheme-sequence of a sentence which has undergone certain singular transformations presents problems. For example, in assigning meaning to *The contestants have almost all been chosen*, *John plays chess as well as Sidney* and *John does not go home*, the projection rules must know respectively what *almost all* modifies, what (if anything) to insert after *Sidney* and what semantic value (in fact nil) to give to *does*. These particular transformations – permutation, deletion and adjunction – do not add anything to the meanings and therefore it would be more convenient to allow the semantic component to operate not on the final sequences of morphemes but on the structural description of these sentences before they undergo any transformations; the above problems would not then arise.

Further, it is certain that all obligatory transformations, such as the above agreement-transformations and *do*-insertion, do not add anything to the meaning of sentences and therefore the semantic component could operate here also before the application of the transformations. Now if it were the case that all optional transformations, not just the two illustrated in the preceding paragraph, also contributed nothing to the meaning, then it would add to the simplicity of the grammar to allow the semantic component to operate on the structural descriptions of *all* sentences before any singular transformations were applied, namely on their underlying P-markers (i.e. on the tree-diagrams specified by the phrase-structure rules). It might be objected that some optional singular transformations, e.g. those which specify negatives and various forms of questions, make important contributions to meaning. However, a compelling paper, *Negation in English* by Edward S. Klima,[31] suggested that 'phenomena connected with negation could be described grammatically on the basis of a single negative element'; in a great many cases this element can be inserted as a sentence-marker *Neg* in the initial expansion of the symbol S. Thus *Jasper does not sing* is derived from *Neg + Jasper + sing*. (How exactly *Neg* may be rewritten subsequently and where it may appear cannot concern us here.) The point is that negation is no longer specified by an optional transformation. Similar reasoning may be applied, following Klima and Lees[32] to question transformations: a sentence-marker *Q* present in the initial expansion of S accounts for the ultimate form of *Does the bishop admire the actress?*; this marker plus a *WH*-element attached to the NP dominated by S (the 'subject') or the NP dominated by VP (the 'object') account respectively for *Who admires the actress?* and *Who does the bishop admire?*. This reasoning can be applied also the passive transformation which can be held to operate only where a marker *by Pass* is present in the VP. In all these cases the presence of a marker (which of course never reaches phonological form) ensures the later functioning of the transformation. The result is that these particular transformations are removed from the set of optional transformations in English. Further, since they may now be held to retain the meaning of the underlying structures they no longer present an obstacle to expressing the generalisation that singular transformations do not affect meaning. For generalised transformations it 'makes no sense' to ask whether or not they affect meaning. 'Here one can only ask how the meanings of the input structures are combined to yield a meaning for the output.'[33] Therefore, until evidence to the contrary is produced, the principle may be adopted that no transformations affect meaning, that 'transformations are meaning-preserving'. This principle, Katz and Postal state explicitly, 'is not a statement in the linguistic description of a language, nor is it a statement in linguistic theory, but rather it is a rule of thumb based on the general character of linguistic descriptions'.[34]

In the case of generalised transformations, somewhat the same arguments apply. It is necessary to find some means for combining the separate semantic interpretations of the set of underlying P-markers into a single semantic interpretation of the sentence as a whole. Katz and Postal consider embedding transformations first; these, it will be recalled (see 12.3) insert one string, the constituent, into another, the matrix. The authors claim that all matrix P-markers contain one or more *dummy elements* (i.e. morphemes which necessarily never occur in the final write-out), one type of which are *matrix-dummies*, symbolised by *md*; embedding transformations operate by replacing these matrix-dummies by the constituent P-marker. Thus the constituent string *the + lecturer + killed + the + linguist* is inserted into the matrix *the + lecturer + md + went + to + Vienna* to give ultimately the sentence *The lecturer who killed the linguist went to Vienna*. Of course these constituents may themselves contain matrix dummies (yielding sentences such as *The lecturer who killed the linguist with the dreadful wife went to Vienna* and so on in an infinite recursion).

The projection-rules that give a semantic interpretation to sentences thus derived are so contrived that they will be blocked when they encounter a matrix dummy; they can only proceed when the semantic interpretation of the constituent inserted at that point has been completed. Thus the projection rules can first of all give complete semantic interpretations only for P-markers that contain no matrix-dummy. In our above example, for instance, there must be no possibility that a 'complete' semantic interpretation of *the + lecturer + md + went + to + Vienna* is furnished before *the + lecturer + killed + the + linguist* has been semantically interpreted. This requires in turn that the projection rules must be able to know the order in which embeddings are carried out in order to distinguish semantically *I know that the boy who John likes hates Mary* from *The boy who I know that John likes hates Mary*;[35] these are derivable from the same three strings *I + know + that + md*, *the + md + boy + hate + Mary* and *John + like + the + boy*. (To produce the first sentence, the third string has been embedded in the second string and the result embedded in the first; to produce the second sentence the third string is embedded in the first string and the result embedded in the second.) Furthermore, the projection rules must be so constituted as to respond to the correct location of matrix-dummies in order to distinguish semantically *The man who is happy likes the man who is sad* from *The man who is sad likes the man who is happy*. Appropriate proposals were made in order to achieve these aims, and Katz and Postal assume that their treatment of embedding transformations can be extended 'without essential modifications'[36] to conjoining transformations.

One conclusion of this reasoning is that the diagram illustrating the 'linguistic description of a natural language' ought to be modified to show the output of the syntactic component to the phonological component emerging at a point different from that at which the output to the semantic component emerges, for while the former must necessarily pass through the transformational rules the latter must not.

In *Aspects of the theory of syntax* Chomsky devotes his first chapter to an account of the nature of generative grammars and their implications, discussing such topics as the justification of grammars, certain types of linguistic universals, and linguistic theory and language-learning. He introduces the terms *competence* (the speaker-hearer's knowledge of his language) and *performance* (the actual use of language in concrete situations); the distinction is reminiscent of 'langue' and 'parole' (see 6.2) but without de Saussure's emphasis on the social aspect of langue. 'A grammar of a language purports to be a description of the ideal speaker-hearer's intrinsic competence.'[37] This recalls Chomsky's statement in *Syntactic structures* that '. . . a grammar mirrors the behaviour of the speaker who . . . can produce or understand an indefinite number of new sentences'. The word 'behaviour' must not lead us astray: in describing 'competence' a grammar is not claiming to describe actual mental or neurological activities carried out in the production or comprehension of human language, 'a generative grammar is not a model for a speaker or hearer'.[38] There is enormous scope for discussion about this postulated ideal speaker-hearer, about the equally idealised 'completely homogeneous speech-community' and hence about the status of 'competence'. However, the bulk of the book is concerned with the form and the operation of the syntactic component, developing the model described above.

The syntactic component is now envisaged as consisting of a *base* and a *transformational component*. The base is that section that terminates in the output to the semantic component; it is partly similar to the phrase-structure rules of the previous model in that it consists of rewrite rules that apply to category symbols (e.g. NP, N, Det) and generally involve branching (e.g. S → NP + VP, which is now written S → NP⌢VP). A crucial difference is that whereas earlier models had simply rewritten category-symbols as lexicon-items (e.g. N → *horse, blunderbuss, kidney*) they are now rewritten as *complex symbols*, a complex symbol being an array of syntactic features that characterise classes of lexicon items, in the way that a class (*boy, girl, man . . .*) could be characterised by the array of features 'noun', 'count' and 'human' (see Chapter 9). Such syntactic features play an important part in Chomsky's reasoning.

The specification of these features cannot helpfully be made by means of a series of branching rules (of the type A → B + C) that result in a hierarchical tree, since it may be impossible to assign a

226

hierarchy to the features. For example, *John, Egypt, boy* and *book* are classifiable as both 'either Proper or Common' and 'either Human or Non-human'; but it makes little sense to rewrite 'Noun' into successive sub-classes, whether as (*a*) or as (*b*):

(*a*) (1) Noun → PropN, ComN
    (2) PropN → HumPN, NonhPN
    (3) ComN → HumCN, NonhCN
(*b*) (1) Noun → HumN, NonhumN
    (2) HumN → PropHN, ComHN
    (3) NonhumN → PropNhN, ComNhN

We simply cannot choose between these two; both exhibit the same drawback, a total inability to take account of a relationship which we have recognised, for example in the case of (*a*) that *boy* and *John* share the syntactic feature 'Human', and *book* and *Egypt* the feature 'Non-human'. This difficulty is due to the fact that the choices of 'Proper or Common' and 'Human or Non-human' do not stand in a hierarchy but involve cross-categorisation.[39] Quite obviously every relevant feature must therefore be stated explicitly so that such relationships may be recognised and the recognition put to use in the grammar.

One way of specifying these features is in the following notation; this has the effect of listing the sub-classes of a category (e.g. Noun) in terms of different combinations of syntactic features:[40]

(1) N → [+N, ± Common]
(2) [+Common] → [±Count]
(3) [+Count] → [±Animate]
(4) [−Common] → [±Animate]
(5) [+Animate] → [±Human]
(6) [−Count] → [±Abstract]

This allows us to define eight sub-classes of Noun, or (since we retain +N) more precisely eight classes of lexicon item in terms of lexical category (i.e. major word-class) and syntactic features, for example:

(*a*)
$$\begin{bmatrix} +N \\ +Common \\ +Count \\ +Animate \\ +Human \end{bmatrix}$$

(*b*)
$$\begin{bmatrix} +N \\ +Common \\ +Count \\ +Animate \\ -Human \end{bmatrix}$$

(*c*)
$$\begin{bmatrix} +N \\ -Common \\ +Animate \\ -Human \end{bmatrix}$$

(*d*)
$$\begin{bmatrix} +N \\ +Common \\ -Count \\ -Abstract \end{bmatrix}$$

These frameworks define classes containing the representative members respectively (*a*) *boy*, (*b*) *dog*, (*c*) *Fido*, and (*d*) *dirt*; the other possible choices specify classes containing respectively the items *book*, *virtue*, *John* and *Egypt*.

Rules of the above type, which Chomsky calls *subcategorisation rules*, are incorporated into the base component and apply after the phrase-structure branching rules; their effect is to produce arrays of features, as (*a*)–(*d*) in the previous paragraph, at certain points in the trees generated by the phrase-structure rules. Such rules are of course context-free and apply only to symbol N in Chomsky's exemplification. For example if we assume a set of phrase-structure rules (simpler than those actually used by Chomsky):

(1) $S \rightarrow NP\widehat{\ }VP$
(2) $VP \rightarrow V\widehat{\ }NP$
(3) $NP \rightarrow (Det) N$

and apply thereafter the subcategorisation rules illustrated, one possible write-out would be

$$\begin{bmatrix} +N \\ +Common \\ -Count \\ +Abstract \end{bmatrix} \widehat{\ }V\widehat{\ }Det\widehat{\ } \begin{bmatrix} +N \\ +Common \\ +Count \\ +Animate \\ +Human \end{bmatrix}$$

These complex symbols specify the respective sub-classes of nouns that alone can occupy their places in the string. If we then present the lexicon as an unordered set of entries such as

(*sincerity*), [+N, −Count, +Abstract, . . .])
(*boy*), [+N, +Det−, +Count, +Animate, +Human, . . .])

it will be possible to insert any member of the appropriate sub-class (but of no other) into the positions occupied by the respective complex symbols, provided that we supply a lexical rule which states that a lexicon entry may be substituted for a complex symbol if its syntactic features are not distinct from those of the complex symbol. The string may therefore be rewritten *sincerity*$\widehat{\ }$V Det *boy*, using the orthographic forms as a convenient shorthand.

This leaves the problem of how to specify any remaining complex symbols, such as that which will replace V. This is done by rewriting V as CS (i.e. a complex symbol which must of course include [+V]) and then by copying the syntactic features of the preceding N and of the following N into the complex symbol giving a contextual frame into which only a particular sub-class of verb may be inserted. Thus the above V will be rewritten as a complex symbol:

$$\begin{bmatrix} +\text{Noun} \\ +\text{Common} \\ -\text{Count} \\ +\text{Abstract} \end{bmatrix} - \begin{bmatrix} +\text{N} \\ +\text{Common} \\ +\text{Count} \\ +\text{Animate} \\ +\text{Human} \end{bmatrix}$$

The general rule which guarantees such copying is formulated by Chomsky as $[+V] \to CS/\alpha \widehat{} Aux - (Det \widehat{} \beta)$ where α is an N and β is an N. (In our account we have omitted consideration of Aux.) Thus if the lexicon contains an entry

(*frighten*, [+V, + −NP,
+[+Abstract]Aux − Det[+Animate], . . .])

then we may insert this item in the place of the remaining complex symbol and produce a string (rewriting 'Det') *sincerity frighten the boy*. Similar treatment may be applied to the symbol 'Adjective'. This particular type of rule, a *selectional rule* is context-sensitive, in contrast to the context-free subcategorisation of nouns.

Another kind of context-sensitive rule which Chomsky characterises is the *strict subcategorisation rule*, which 'subcategorises a lexical category in terms of the frame of category symbols in which it appears', for example:[41]

$$V \to CS/- \begin{cases} \text{NP} \\ \sharp \\ \text{Adjective} \\ \text{Predicate-Nominal} \\ \text{like} \widehat{} \text{Predicate Nominal} \\ \text{Prepositional-Phrase} \\ \textit{that-}\text{S}' \\ \text{NP (of} \widehat{} \text{Det} \widehat{} \text{N)S}' \\ \text{etc} \end{cases}$$

Chomsky draws on the distinction between 'selectional' and 'subcategorisation' to point a difference between two types of deviant sentence; those which break subcategorisation rules, such as *John found sad*, and those which break selectional rules, such as *Golf plays John*; while the latter may often be interpreted metaphorically, it is more difficult to assign a meaning to the former.

The result of the above rules is to produce a phrase-marker (P-marker) with lexical entries inserted into it; each of these consists of a specification of phonological features and of a complex symbol. The latter consists of syntactic features and also of semantic[42] features; it will be necessary to list every type of grammatical and semantic feature relevant to syntactic behaviour, thus *baby* will have to bear a marker 'Human' but will also carry a gender-marker, so that the pronoun *it* is correctly chosen. Chomsky does not deal in any detail with the various types of marker necessary. This output of the base is the *deep structure*, an idea which is already present in *Syntactic structures* in embryo. Every P-marker with lexical entries is then interpreted by the semantic projection rules to give its semantic reading.

Moving the dictionary from its previous place in the semantic component into the base seems to ensure that no semantically deviant sentences will be generated; the earlier models could generate such sentences but the semantic component would then be unable to assign an interpretation to them. Of course in the present model the projection rules still operate to give an interpretation of the meaning. A crucial feature here is the selection rules, and Chomsky discusses the possibility of assigning them to the semantic component; he does not do so, but points out that 'the interrelation of semantic and syntactic rules is by no means a settled issue',[43] which is interesting in view of later developments (see 17.1).

The deep structure is the input to the transformational rules, which carry out various operations to produce the *surface structure*; this in turn is the input to the phonological component (which we may regard as operating as sketched in 15.3). Whereas Katz and Postal had adopted as a methodological rule of thumb the notion that transformations do not affect meaning, Chomsky now regards this as an established fact: 'transformations cannot introduce meaning-bearing elements';[44] the principle allows him to use the output of the base as the input to the semantic component. (He was to change his mind in a couple of years' time.)

Another important development is that Chomsky adopts the position that there are now no longer generalised transformations; instead symbols S′ appear at points in the trees produced by the base; these will then be written out as further trees (in the manner of Katz and Postal's matrix-dummies *md*); hence embedded sentences actually appear as such in the deep structure. Chomsky also introduces a dummy symbol Δ to represent 'various unspecified elements that will be deleted by obligatory transformations'. In fact in *Aspects* Chomsky's focus of interest is not on the actual form of transformations and only the following example is adduced; however, it serves to illustrate the difference between strings produced by the base of standard theory grammar and those produced by the phrase-structure rules of the *Syntactic structures* model.

The man who persuaded John to be examined by a specialist was fired is derived from the three strings:

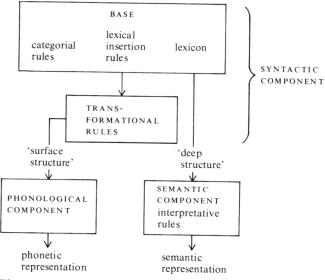

Figure 46

(1) Δ⌐Past⌐fire⌐the⌐S'⌐man⌐by⌐passive

(2) the⌐man⌐past⌐persuade⌐John⌐of⌐Δ⌐S'

(3) a⌐specialist⌐nom⌐examine⌐John⌐by⌐passive

First of all the passive transformation is applied to (3) and the result is embedded in (2) to give (in effect) *The man persuaded John of* Δ *John nom be examined by a specialist.* Two further transformations respectively delete the second appearance of *John* and replace Δ *nom* (this last itself a choice of Aux) by *to*, resulting in the phrase-marker for *The man persuaded John to be examined by a specialist.* This is then embedded into (1) and a relativising transformation applied, giving the phrase-marker for Δ *fired the man who persuaded John to be examined by a specialist by passive.* To this the passive transformation is applied and the original subject Δ is deleted. (We have of course represented the matrices of phonological features by orthographical symbols.) The result is a string of surface-structure items, which are then processed by the phonological rules to give the phonetic interpretation.

The complete model of 'standard theory' grammar thus appears as in Figure 46. (*Categorial rules* are the branching phrase-structure rules, i.e. the base rules apart from the context-free subcategorisation rules, the context-sensitive strict subcategorisation rules and the context-sensitive selectional rules; these last three may be termed the *lexical insertion* rules.)

In *Syntactic structures* the grammar is viewed as a device that can generate all the grammatical sentences of a language and no ungrammatical ones; this concept has now expanded to that of 'a device for pairing phonetically represented signals with semantic interpretations'.[45] The standard theory model has been constructed by putting together the three components previously described in this book and then making certain adjustments. But we have seen that both the phonological and the semantic components are subject to grave criticisms. The integrated theory must inherit these, and in addition it will exhibit new problems that have arisen as a result of the integration. It might indeed be contended that the descriptive apparatus is now so complex that it has ceased to provide clarification. It is not the case that any new relationships have been revealed; the justification for this present model must therefore reside in simpler or more powerful accounts of known phenomena – in this connection it is astonishing, and perhaps revealing, that in *Aspects of the theory of syntax* (or anywhere in the literature for that matter) there is not a single illustration of the pairing of the semantic interpretation of a sentence with its phonetic interpretation. One might pertinently pose the prior question of whether a system of rewrite rules (including transformational rules) – which proved an illuminating method of handling certain syntactic features in *Syntactic structures* – is the most suitable for handling semantic and phonological phenomena. It could be suggested that the same error is being committed as that which characterised the desire of some neo-Bloomfieldian structuralists that phonemes and morphemes should exhibit the same behaviour, namely the unjustifiable imposition of similarity of patterning. Be that as it may, problems of other sorts arose and the standard theory did not remain unchallenged for long, as we shall see.

16.5 Extended standard theory. Following the publication of *Aspects of the theory of syntax* in 1965, extensive attempts were made to apply standard theory to a variety of phenomena in actual language (in particular English); within a year so many difficulties had been revealed that alternative theories began to be proposed, although all of them in some measure merited the label 'transformational-generative'. In lectures and articles from 1966 onwards Chomsky himself drew attention to difficulties in the theory and proposed a modification; this revised version, the *extended standard theory*, is delineated and discussed most accessibly in his *Studies on semantics in generative grammar*, a collection published in 1972 of three articles which had already appeared separately. Our account confines itself to material from the second of these, 'Deep structure, surface structure, and semantic interpretation' (originally published in 1970); in the course of it Chomsky presents a succession of different types of sentences that pose difficulties of interpretation in terms of standard theory. His conclusion is that the deep structure alone does *not* (contrary to his previous position) contain sufficient information to lead to certain aspects of the required semantic representation.

He introduces first the concepts of *focus* and *presupposition*;[46] the focus of a sentence is the word or words either referring to the particular piece of information being requested or else conveying new information, for example the word *John* in *Is it John who writes poetry?* and *It isn't John who writes poetry*. The presupposition may be taken as the background information shared by the participants in the verbal exchange, thus in the two sentences quoted, the presupposition is that someone writes poetry (see also 15.13). (Contrast *Is it poetry that John writes?* where the focus is *poetry* and the presupposition is that John writes something.) Chomsky requires that the semantic representation must indicate in some way focus and presupposition.

In terms of the standard theory we would wish to obtain this information from the deep structure. In a sentence such as *It is John who writes poetry* we could postulate a deep structure such as [*the one who writes poetry*] *is John*, that is in terms of an embedded sentence (here shown in square brackets); the embedded sentence contains the presupposition and the predicate of the 'dominant proposition' is the focus. In this case, therefore, the required information is available in the deep structure.

However, this solution is not possible for all sentences. For example, we might wish to say that underlying *Is it in his study that John writes poetry?* is a deep structure, namely [*the place where John writes poetry*] *is in his study*, indicating focus and presupposition as previously. However, if we wish to extend such an analysis to *Does John write poetry in his study?* (assuming the same focus *study* and the presupposition that John writes poetry somewhere) then we would have to assume that the underlying deep structure is again something like [*the place where John writes poetry*] *is in his study*. This suggested deep structure is contrary to the assumptions of the standard theory that a phrase such as *in the study* is an adverbial modifier in a deep structure containing only one clause.

Even greater difficulties arise in that it may be impossible to supply a grammatical *cleft* sentence (of the *It is . . .* type exemplified in the previous paragraph) that can express the focus; thus if *shirt* is the focus of *Was he warned to look out for an ex-convict with a red shirt?* we can find no alternative form **Was it shirt that he was warned to look out for an ex-convict with a red?*. This would seem to suggest that the identification of the focus is not possible from the deep structure. Indeed, it may be demonstrable that the focus is not part of the deep structure, as in the case where *certain to win* is the focus of *Is John certain to win?* (eliciting a possible answer *No, John is likely not even to be nominated*); the deep structure of this sentence must be something like *Q+[John win] is certain*.

Furthermore, it is the phonological component that will assign stress and intonation; yet 'phrases that contain the intonation centre may be interpreted as focus of utterance' as in the above examples. (This is clearly seen in the non-Chomskyan example of *Was he warned to look out for an ex-convict with a red shirt?* where the unpredictable fall on the modifier indicates that the focus is not even within a given phrase but is a particular word.) It seems necessary, therefore, to propose that the focus is determined by the surface structure, that is in the phrase containing the 'intonation centre'. The result of this reasoning is that the semantic interpretative rules must have access to the surface structure (and indeed the output of the phonological component) in order to determine fully the semantic representation. The previous standard theory must therefore be modified to allow for this possibility. Figure 47 illustrates the new situation.

This argument is supported by reference to other phenomena that involve the effect of transformational rules; in these instances too the semantic component must have access to the surface structure (although not necessarily to the output from the phonological component). One such case is that of sentences that contain both a negative and a quantifier (i.e. a word such as *many, all, some, every*). It will be recalled that standard theory derives negatives from a negative element that appears in the first write-out of S. But the final surface position of *not* affects the meaning; for example, *Not many arrows hit the target* exhibits *sentence negation* while *Many arrows did not hit the target* exhibits *verb-phrase negation*. It will be observed that the relative order of negative *not* and quantifier *many* is different in these two sentences. However, the semantic paraphrase of *Not many arrows hit the target* is *The target was not hit by many arrows*, although the latter would be the syntactic passive transformation of *Many arrows did not hit the target*. But notice that the sequential order of negative and quantifier is the same in the two paraphrase-sentences.

This suggests that the relative order of negative and quantifier is of great importance; the principle may be stated that if the surface

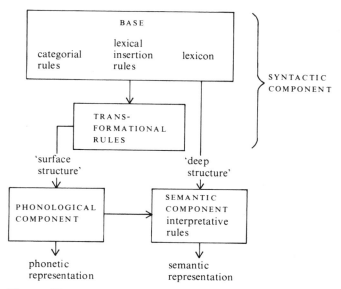

Figure 47

subject contains a quantifier, then sentence negation may be distinguished from verb-phrase negation by the position of the negative; but if the quantifier is part of a noun phrase that follows the verb, then the order of negation and quantifier is not variable, in which case sentence negation appears to be the only semantic interpretation possible. But precisely because the notion of 'surface subject' is involved Chomsky points out that this principle is inconsistent with standard theory. Here too the extended standard theory appears justified.

In the same way, differences of *topic* ('what one is talking about') and *comment* ('what is said about it') – a notion which we must distinguish from 'subject' and 'predicate' – affect our understanding of sentences as in *The sonata is easy to play on this violin* and *This violin is easy to play the sonata on*. Since these sentences would appear to share the same deep structure, this type of difference is yet another candidate for a principle of surface structure interpretation.

The same may be said, according to Chomsky, of the combination of certain modals and negatives: *John will go downtown* merely predicts, but *John won't go downtown* is ambiguous since it may also mean that he refuses to go downtown. Chomsky prefers to attribute this to an interpretation of surface rather than deep structure. A further example in support of extended standard theory is the role of stress in the reference of pronouns: whereas *John hit Bill and then George hit him* suggests that the recipient of both blows was Bill, *John hit Bill and then George hit him* suggests that the second blow fell on John. Intonation is probably involved in such examples as well as stress, but at any rate the clue to the meaning is given once more by the contribution of the phonological component. Again, the semantic interpretation of the perfect aspect may depend on some property of the surface structure: *Einstein has taught me physics* suggests that Einstein is still alive, but the passive transformation *I have been taught physics by Einstein* does not; the presupposition concerns the surface subject. Finally, the effects of changing an auxiliary or inserting *even* can be seen in the presuppositions conveyed by the sentences *John is tall for a Watusi, John would be tall for a Watusi, John is tall even for a Watusi* and *Even John is tall for a Watusi*; it is difficult to see how the deep structure can contain the appropriate information about whether John is or is not a Watusi, whether John is or is not tall, and whether Watusi are in general tall or not.

All the above examples indicate that the output of the base does not contain enough information for correct semantic interpretation, hence the semantic component must have access to the output of the transformational rules and of the phonological component. This therefore provides a counter-argument to the claim that transformations do not affect meaning; some apparently do, and in more subtle ways than had previously been thought of. It should be stressed that the modification does not affect the hypothesis that the grammatical relations specified in the deep structure are interpreted by the semantic component. The contribution of the transformational rules and the phonological component involve only such things as focus and presupposition, extent of negation, indication of topic, and pronoun reference. It is noteworthy in this connection that Chomsky uses considerably more examples of actual language than in *Aspects of the theory of syntax* and, more importantly, allows appeal to the speaker's knowledge of semantic facts in the construction of a grammar (which seems a departure from the position adopted in *Syntactic structures*). The types of semantic facts adduced include certain of the type of relations listed in 15.3. Recognition of these facets of meaning was to play an equally large part in the proposals of other linguists who suggested even greater modifications to standard theory.

FURTHER READING
See Chapter 17.

17. Generative Semantics and Case Grammar

17.1 Generative semantics. Extended standard theory was one answer to problems that seemed insoluble in terms of standard theory; another answer is found in *generative semantics*, the name applied to a body of proposals by George Lakoff, James D. McCawley, John R. Ross, Paul M. Postal and others. The beginning of this development may be seen in Lakoff's doctoral dissertation of 1965; since it had set out to be 'an exploration into Postal's conception of grammar', Postal also is associated with the origins of generative semantics. The dissertation appeared in that year as a laboratory progress report; although it was not formally published until 1970 under the title *Irregularity in syntax*, mimeographs of the original report had enjoyed wide circulation and exerted profound influence from 1965 onwards. Since that date many articles and papers have appeared; particularly important are anthologies of papers delivered by various scholars at two conferences in 1967 and 1969, published under the respective titles of *Universals in linguistic theory* (1968) and *Studies in linguistic semantics* (1971). In these three works we may trace a development from an acceptance of the general outlines of standard theory, although the various writers quarrelled with many details, to suggestions for a radical reformulation of transformational-generative grammar.

Generative semanticists are not in agreement on every particular, but they all hold that semantics plays a central role in syntax, a point of view totally unlike that of the 'standard' and 'extended standard' theories, where syntactic specification and semantic interpretation are strictly separated. Most work in generative semantics since 1967 has assumed the outlines of what Lakoff later[1] was to call the *basic theory*. This theory is not fixed but permits options. However, one essential feature is that an interpretative semantic component is not present, since the semantic representation is already present in the deep structure; indeed the semantic representation *is* the deep structure – to quote McCawley (1968), 'there is no a priori reason why a grammar could not . . . consist of, say, a "formation-rule component", which specifies the membership of a class of well-formed semantic representations, and a "transformational component", which consists of rules correlating semantic

Figure 48

representations with surface syntactic representations in much the same fashion in which Chomsky's "transformational component" correlates deep structures with surface syntactic representations'.[2] The general outline of a generative semantic theory is as in Figure 48. The principle of such a theory is a good deal simpler than that of extended standard theory and it retains the assumption that transformations do not affect meaning. The following examples of the insights and arguments advanced in support will illustrate the flavour of the reasoning.

In standard theory suitable environments are created into which are inserted appropriate lexical items consisting of phonological and semantic features. But in English there are 'gaps' in the patterns of available surface words: we may have *John is a transgressor*, *John's transgression . . ., John transgressed . . .*; but while *John is the aggressor*, and *John's aggression* exist, there is no **John aggressed. . . .* In standard theory sets such as *aggressor* and *aggression* would have to be treated differently from sets such as *transgressor* and *transgression* probably by being listed as independent nouns; but this would presumably make it impossible to show that *aggressor* is an agent noun. On the other hand, sets such as *transgressor* and *transgression* would be derivable from the lexical item *transgress* by transformations. This suggests that it would be an advantage to be able to specify the semantic features first, and to allow the insertion of lexical forms subsequently; thus there would be a surface form for the noun resulting from the agentive transformation of the underlying semantic features of **aggress*, but there would be no available form for a single verb containing these features. (Similar reasoning could presumably be applied to such pairs as *tooth* v. *dental* and *country* v. *rural*.) The conclusion is that at least some lexical insertions should follow transformational rules rather than precede them.

The recognition of certain other semantic and grammatical features gave weight to such reasoning. For example, sets of sentences such as *The sky came to be black*, *The sky became black*, *The sky got black* and *The sky blackened* are synonymous and we could postulate that the deep structures are identical up to the insertion of lexical items in standard theory. However, the surface structure of the fourth sentence differs remarkably from that of the

238

other three and this would have to be accounted for by transformations. Lakoff provides such a set of transformations[3] in which the 'came about' (or *inchoative*) element written out as surface verbs in the first three sentences is replaced by an *inchoative pro-verb* in the case of the fourth; this eventually combines with the phonological features of the lexical item *black* to yield a surface verb *blacken*. Naturally, the lexical items *came to be*, *became* and *got* must contain an inchoative marker to allow for correct interpretation by the semantic component.

Further sets of sentences turn out to be synonymous, such as *John hardened the metal* and *John brought it about that the metal hardened*. In much the same way as we argued for an inchoative element, we may here argue for a *causative* element in the interpretation of the surface verbs *hardened* and *brought it about*, and we may argue further for a derivation of the causative verb *hardened* by way of a causative transformation. It will be observed that this causative transformation operates on inchoative verbs: *John brought it about that the metal became hard*. Now from the semantic point of view we could regard *die* as the inchoative equivalent to *become dead* and *kill* the causative of this inchoative. However, in standard theory, while we could conceivably handle the relation of *hard*, *harden* (inchoative) and *harden* (causative) by transformational rules thanks to the phonological similarity, it would presumably be impossible to bring *die*, *dead* and *kill* into phonological relationship and hence impossible to derive them from the same underlying set of features. Consequently at least *dead* and *kill* would have to be listed as separate lexicon items and therefore as exceptions to transformational rules that specified other inchoative and causative relationships. If, however, we could delay the insertion of phonological features until after the relevant transformations had been applied, then *die* and *kill* could be treated by the same transformations as other inchoatives and causatives, with an overall gain in regularity.

A similar argument applies to other phonologically dissimilar words that are semantically related. For example, it may be maintained that in the pairs *see* v. *look* and *hear* v. *listen* the first word refers to a state and the second to an activity; we may designate them as *stative* and *non-stative* respectively. Formal recognition of this relationship also could be given by specifying the phonological features only after the appropriate transformational rules have been applied.

The consideration of various factors, in particular the restrictions that must be written into a transformational component, led Postal and Lakoff to the radical suggestion that in English adjectives and verbs constitute a single lexical category. They point out that many pairs of sentences, in which the one contains a verb and the other an adjective, are understood in the same way: *I desire that* and *I am desirous of that*; notice that the phonological forms of adjective and verb need not be similar: *I regret that* and *I am sorry about that*. Moreover, the selectional restrictions obeyed by adjectives and verbs are the same: *I know that, I am aware of that* but neither **The rock knows that* nor **The rock is aware of that*; such restrictions apply not only to subjects but also to objects and adverbials. Strikingly, both verbs and adjectives may be subcategorised as stative or non-stative and will obey the same restrictions imposed by this subcategorisation. For example, they claim that stative verbs will not occur with a true imperative, so that *Look at the picture* is possible, but not **Know that Bill went there*; adjectives exhibit the same behaviour, thus *Don't be noisy is possible* but not **Don't be tall*. In *Irregularity in syntax* Lakoff gives very convincingly nine arguments in favour of this point of view. Indeed the argument is taken further by Emmon Bach[4] who argues that nouns too come into this one lexical category; for example, there are stative and non-stative nouns, thus *Don't be a fool* but not **Don't be a mammal*.

One implication of this argument is that (because of phonologically dissimilar but semantically related verbs and adjectives) reinforcement is given yet again to the contention that phonological shapes should be assigned after the operation of at least some transformational rules; this hypothesis was explicitly enunciated by Bach in 1967.[5] The second implication is that if verbs and adjectives (and perhaps nouns too) are members of the same lexical category, then the categorial selection rules (i.e. those that indicate the general categories to which inserted lexical items must belong) must be reformulated, at least to the extent of removing the distinction between V and Adj. Consequently the surface distinction between adjectives and verbs (and perhaps nouns) may be held to be due to the operation of transformational rules and hence to be peculiar to individual languages.

This of course raises the question (to which no answer had previously been given) of what is implied in the choice of symbols such as N, V and Adj from *Syntactic structures* onwards to denote abstract elements to be subsequently rewritten. It is perfectly possible to regard them as symbols whose meaning is defined only in the subsequent rewriting, ultimately by the enumeration of a set of lexicon-items; in this view their similarity to the names 'noun', 'verb' and 'adjective' of traditional grammar is a mere mnemonic device and perfectly arbitrary shapes, such as numerals, could have been chosen instead. But an opposed viewpoint may be held, namely that there is some sort of notional basis independent of individual languages for a division between, for example, 'noun' and 'verb' and that consequently one might expect to find at least these fundamental categories represented in all languages.[6] This obviously important debate, which harks back to the Stoics and the Modistae, continues (and much clarification is given in Lyons 1977, Chapter 11).

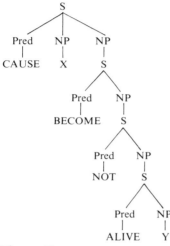

Figure 49

The previously-cited description by McCawley of the broad outline of generative semantics comes from a postscript to a paper delivered in 1967 and may be taken as one of the first statements of the generative semantic position. Thereafter more and more evidence was assembled to show that the deep structures were very much more abstract than had been thought and consisted only of semantic relations. The transformations themselves operated, at least to some extent, on *pre-lexical* elements, that is on semantic elements before the assignation of phonological shape or indeed the recognition of lexical-sized units. Thus the analysis of *kill* (which, as we have seen, would have to appear as some sort of irregularity in standard theory) could now explicitly show a derivation from underlying semantic elements that might also appear in other surface words *alive, dead* and *die*. This involves the postulating of abstract pro-verbs or predicates that assumed places in a hierarchical tree, as in Figure 49.[7] (It will be obvious that the order of verb,

241

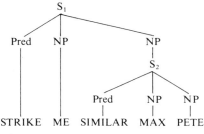

Figure 50

subject and object is different from that previously adopted; however, it was convincingly argued by McCawley in 1970 that this is the underlying order in English,[8] see also 17.2.) On this tree operates a predicate-raising transformation that raises the lowest predicate (here ALIVE) and attaches it to the main verb of the immediately higher main clause (here NOT) to produce a kind of compound verb (here NOT-ALIVE); this rule can be applied cyclically, giving in turn BECOME-NOT-ALIVE and CAUSE-BECOME-NOT-ALIVE. Thereafter this is assigned the lexical form 'kill' and the surface sequence of sentence items is imposed, thus giving eventually *X kills Y*.

In an important paper 'On the surface verb "remind"' (1970),[9] Postal applies this type of analysis to one meaning of *remind* and derives *Max reminds me of Pete* (in the sense 'Max struck me as resembling Pete') from the tree of Figure 50. The successive stages are (omitting the very important hierarchical trees):

(i) STRIKE ME SIMILAR MAX PETE
(ii) STRIKE ME MAX SIMILAR PETE
(iii) STRIKE SIMILAR ME MAX PETE
(iv) STRIKE SIMILAR MAX ME PETE
(v) MAX STRIKE SIMILAR ME PETE

Alternative transformations would in fact yield the semantically equivalent *Max struck me as resembling Pete*. (Of course it is impossible to derive in this way the superficially identical *Max reminded me of Pete* in the sense 'Max reminded me that Pete existed'.) It is important to remember that the above forms STRIKE and SIMILAR are not lexical items or even arrays of features equivalent in extent to semantic items but are semantic elements (which happen to occur also in the surface lexical items *strike* and *similar*). It will be seen that the semantic specification of *Max reminded me of Pete* is represented above by a tree and further that there is *no* verb *remind* in deep structure (such as would have to be

242

postulated in standard theory). Consequently, it cannot be assumed that 'the lexical items occurring in the surface structure of a sentence provide a minimal skeleton out of which its "deep structure" is formed'.[10]

Postal presents a vast array of evidence in support of the above derivation of *remind* and then goes on to give a clear statement of generative semantics and the differences between it and standard theory (which he calls *classical theory*). He sums up generative semantics in the following way. 'The deep structure of a sentence . . . *is* its semantic representation. The base component of the grammar must generate semantic representations directly. There are no projection rules. Semantic representations must be trees, rather than sets of markers. There must be transformations operating on "prelexical" structures.'[11]

Generative semantic theory therefore not only proposes a radical restructuring of transformational-generative grammar, but recognises a much wider array of semantic relations than is treated in Katz and Fodor's original theory; indeed it would seem that the recognition of some of these prompted Chomsky to propose his extended standard theory. In addition to the already mentioned features of presupposition, focus, topic, inchoative, causative and stative, generative grammarians took note of Austin's category of 'performative verbs' (see p.174) used in the performance of a 'speech-act' involving the speaker and his hearer, such as verbs of declaring, asking and ordering. It can be postulated that the 'highest' verb in the semantic representation of any sentence is such a verb;[12] they may indeed appear on the surface, as in *I hereby order you to open the door* and *I promise to give you ten dollars*, or may be deleted, as in *Open the door!*, *Where were you last night?* (deleting the verb of asking) and *Lyndon Johnson was an American* (deleting the verb of declaring). In this case, the subject of the highest verb will always be first person; from that fact it can be argued that the specification of person in deep structure is unnecessary (the subject of performative verbs will be first person, their indirect objects second person and anything else third person; it is of course not necessary that more than one should appear explicitly on the surface).[13]

The deep structure then turns out to be highly abstract and highly complex: for example, it can be held that there are eight pro-verbs in the semantic representation of *Floyd broke the glass*,[14] that is DECLARE (subject *I*), PAST, HAPPEN, ACTION (subject *Floyd*), CAUSATIVE, INCHOATIVE, BE, BREAK (subject *glass*); but this is not all. for according to Lakoff,[15] the semantic representation must also include the presuppositions, the topic and the focus.

We have said nothing about the contents of the *formation-rule component*, that is the rules that specify the semantic representations on which the transformational rules operate. At this point the linguist has to be *au fait* with symbolic (or algebraic) logic, for according to McCawley this component is capable of being represented in terms of symbolic logic with certain modifications.[16] In such a system there is of course no lexical subdivision into noun, verb and adjective; hence it may even be possible that these deep structure rules are the same for every language.[17] This is a startling thought, which runs quite counter to the implications of the Chomskyan standard theory.

17.2 Case grammar. Mention must be made of Charles J. Fillmore's paper 'The case for case' in *Universals in linguistic theory*; this outlines an approach that Fillmore called *case grammar*. It stands somewhat apart from the other proposals for the form of generative semantics, but it is important in publicising three topics that proved to be of significance: the order of elements in deep structure strings, the definition of 'subject' and 'object', and the recognition of different (essentially semantic) functional relations between deep structure elements. We examine first how these were handled in standard theory.

In both the *Syntactic structures* model and standard theory the first rules expand the initial symbol into a left-to-right sequence NP + VP with a further expansion of VP, yielding a possible string NP + Vtr + NP. This accords well with the favourite surface order in English sentences, 'subject-verb-object' or SVO. By altering the order of elements on the right-hand-side of these rules we could produce strings of the form VOS, SOV or OVS, which might indeed occur as the surface order in some languages.

However, there are languages whose favourite surface sentence order is VSO, for example Gaelic *Chunnaic an duine an cù* /ˈxuʀɪḳ ʌn ˈtɯnə ʌnˈkʰuː/ and Hebrew /ˈraːʔaː haːˈʔiːʃ ɛt haˈkɛlɛv/, both literally 'saw the man the dog'. It is impossible to produce this order in deep structure without either imposing an obligatory permutation transformation or else giving up the idea that the VP can be rewritten as Vtr and the object-NP (in either order). This suggests that there is no necessity for the order of the deep structure to be the same as that of the surface structure. Moreover, and more disturbingly, it raises the possibility that there may be no reason to postulate the existence of a deep structure VP at all – in other words the famous rewrite rule S → NP + VP may have to be abandoned (as indeed is the case in later generative semantic theory).

A definition of 'subject' and 'direct object' appears in *Aspects of the theory of syntax*[18] that is virtually the same as that given above in 11.2: the subject is the NP directly dominated by the node S and the direct object is the NP directly dominated by the node VP. The conclusion is that since this information is extracted directly from the phrase-markers nothing new is added by the use of the terms 'subject' and 'object'. This seems reasonable but of course it is still not clear how the projection rules can specify functional grammatical relationships, either in Katz and Fodor's *The man hit the colourful ball* or Chomsky's *Sincerity may frighten the boy*:[19] it is assumed that the left-to-right sequence is sufficient to show that the meaning is that the man hits the ball and not the other way round – this is unsatisfactory, for it requires us to read the semantic interpretation at least in part as though it were an English sentence. But in a semantic representation functional relations, that is who does what to whom, must be spelt out. Unfortunately it is by no means obvious what types of such relations must be recognised in semantic interpretation or how they may appear in surface structure.

It may be recalled that in natural languages 'case-systems' are found, recognised by both traditional and structuralist grammar (see p.xiv and 9.10); the number of items in these systems varies from language to language and it is seldom possible to recognise a unified meaning or function of individual cases in any language. Traditional grammarians and some modern ones have therefore written studies enumerating the functions of single cases in a given language, although it has often been assumed that the function of one particular case, the nominative – to mark the 'subject' of a sentence – is so transparent that it may be taken for granted. However, in standard theory case-endings are assigned automatically (by context-sensitive rules, see pp.140, 142) according either to their position in a deep-structure string or to the co-occurrence of specific types of lexical item; in themselves, therefore, certain of these case-endings are seen as having no function save that of noting an original geographical position (which may subsequently have been changed). Our previous example (see p.142) of *Miles necavit decanum* will serve again: the nominative and the accusative endings of *miles* and *decanum* respectively have been attached by generating the deep structure in a given order. In such a language the actual surface order is therefore irrelevant to recognition of 'subject' and 'object'. Certain other cases may indicate embedding transformations of various types, as the Latin *amor* (nom.) *Dei* (gen.), 'the love of God' derivable either from *Deus* (nom.) *amat* NP, 'God loves NP' or from NP *amat Deum* (acc.), 'NP loves God'. This example indicates a connection between case-endings and prepositions since a case-ending may be the translation equivalent of a preposition in another language (as above where the English *of* is the translation equivalent of the Latin genitive) or in the same language at a different historical stage, or indeed preposition or case-ending may be permissible alternatives. Other case usages yet may indicate some heterogeneous semantic relationships: Latin *Cave canem* (acc.) 'Beware of the dog' and *Cave cani* (dat.) 'Look after the dog'.

Yet the subject (and hence the nominative case) is by no means as clear-cut in its meaning as was assumed; in 15.12 six sentences were illustrated in which the subjects exhibited six different role-relationships, namely 'actor upon something else', 'causer of an action', 'actor alone', 'patient' or 'recipient'. Something of the same ambiguity was seen in the role of the object (typically an accusative) and of the relationship between the thing possessed and the possessor (in the genitive case).

Fillmore's solution towards a clear description of this confused situation is to make a sharp distinction between surface phenomena (such as case-endings, prepositions, choice of subject and object, and word-order) and a set of deep semantic-syntactic functional relations. It is hoped that this set of semantic syntactic relations will be very small and will perhaps be universal (here then is another early suggestion that at least part of deep structure relationships may not be peculiar to any one language). The grammar of individual languages will contain rules for specifying the possible surface forms these deep elements may assume. Rather confusingly *case* is reserved for the semantic-syntactic relationship and *case form* for the expression of this relation in surface structure.

Fillmore's provisional list of cases includes:[20]

> *Agentive* (A), the case of the typically animate perceived instigator of the action identified by the verb;
> *Instrumental* (I), the case of the inanimate force or object causally involved in the action or state identified by the verb;
> *Dative* (D), the case of the animate being affected by the state or action identified by the verb;
> *Factitive* (F), the case of the object or being resulting from the action or state identified by the verb, or understood as a part of the meaning of the verb;
> *Locative* (L), the case which identifies the location or spatial orientation of the state or action identified by the verb;
> *Objective* (O), the semantically most neutral case, the case of anything representable by a noun whose role in the action or state identified by the verb is identified by the semantic interpretation of the verb itself.

246

Examples of these are:

(1) *John* (A) *ran.*
(2) *John* (A) *opened the door* (O).
(3) *The door* (O) *was opened by John* (A).
(4) *The key* (I) *opened the door* (O).
(5) *John* (A) *used the key* (I) *to open the door* (O).
(6) *The door* (O) *opened.*
(7) *John* (D) *believed that he would win.*
(8) *We* (A) *persuaded John* (D) *that he would win.*
(9) *It was apparent to John* (D) *that he would win.*
(10) *John* (D) *is sad.*[21]
(11) *Chicago* (L) *is windy.*
(12) *It is windy in Chicago* (L).
(13) *John* (A) *painted the picture* (F).
(14) *John* (A) *murdered Bill* (D).

(Fillmore later suggests the additional Benefactive (B) and Time (T) cases, as presumably in *Reggipetto Vitello painted the portrait in 1650* (T) *for the Doge* (B).)

The basic structure of a sentence is now postulated to contain a *modality* constituent (M) specifying such things as negation, tense, mood and aspect, and a *proposition* (P), a tenseless set of relationships between a verb and a noun-phrase (or noun-phrases). All these components are viewed as being unordered, although clearly some sort of order must arbitrarily be imposed for the purposes of notation. The proposition itself consists of a verb and a set of one or more noun-phrases, each standing in a different relationship to the verb; the possible relationships are represented by the cases listed above. In fact the proposition may more simply be stated as a verb and a selection of case-categories, the noun-phrases being added subsequently. Absent from this scheme is any notion of a VP (hence there is no 'subject' and no 'direct object'). The rewrite rules will therefore be unlike those of the 'standard theory' base. We can represent the basic rule as

(1) $S \rightarrow M + P$

The expansion of P is in terms of a verb and at least one case category, no single category appearing twice. It may be written:

(2) $P \rightarrow V + C_1 + \cdots + C_n$

The result of applying these rules is to produce (unordered) sets of symbols such as $M + V + A$, $M + V + I + A$ etc. (values having been assigned to $C_1 \ldots C_n$). Each case-symbol may then be written out as a sequence of case-marker (symbolised by K) and an NP, except for one optional embedded S.

The nouns and verbs may thereafter be selected. The nouns are classified in terms of a label identifying the case-relations it may hold: for example, A and D relationships will involve only animate nouns, therefore only nouns bearing the feature [+animate] will be selected in these instances by means of a context-sensitive rule. The selection of verbs will depend on the array of cases in a particular sentence. For example, into the frame [___A] we may insert *run*, into [___A+I+O] *open*, into [___D] *sad*, into [___S+D+A] *persuade*, respectively as in the above sentences 1, 6, 2 and 8; into [___S] we could insert *interesting*, as in *It is interesting that Bill missed the symposium.*

Verbs may therefore be classified in terms of the case frame into which they may be inserted: thus *sad* will have a feature +[___D], *run* +[___A] and *persuade* +[___S+D+A]. Some verbs, such as *open*, may occur in various frameworks (see sentences 2–6 above), in which case the classification may show the optional features by parentheses: thus +[___O(I)(A)]. If one or either or both of two cases must be chosen (as with *kill* where either an animate Agentive or an inanimate Instrumental must be specified or both may be specified), then the device of linked parentheses can be employed to indicate this, thus +[___D(I()A)].

It seems that these lexical insertions will consist of phonological markers (though this is not made explicit) and semantic markers. In the case of verbs, the semantic markers only identify the activity having a result of a particular kind; notions of transitivity or intransitivity are omitted since the semantic representation will supply information about any personal agent involved, or any inanimate instrument, or person towards whom the action is directed, and so on, from the cases present. Semantic specifications are, in this way, simplified: *open* requires only one set of entries rather than two or three.

It is now feasible to show that certain of what Fillmore calls 'syntactically different words' are in fact semantically identical. This is the case with *like* and *please*; both may appear in a frame +[___O+D], but only *like* will allow the D to become the surface subject and only *please* will allow O to become the surface subject. (One assumes that because of their different phonological forms and their different choice of case for surface subject, Fillmore wishes to treat these as different lexical items which happen to have identical semantic markers. But the way is now open for treating them as the *same* deep lexical item and delaying the insertion of phonological forms until after the choice of subject has been made.)

Interestingly, Fillmore treats causatives and statives as being semantically identical and differing only in their possible case frames. In this way he can contrast *die* ($+[\_\_D]$) with *kill* ($+[\_\_D(I)A]$), and *hear* ($+[\_\_O+D]$) with *listen* ($+[\_\_O+A]$). The observation of the previous paragraph applies also to such cases.

The syntactic rules will now operate on the unordered sets to impose a final surface order (which in some languages may mean choosing a surface subject) and to indicate the surface form of the case-markers. This surface case form may be a preposition or an affix (including the case-endings of declensions in traditional grammar), or its presence may be reflected in a different word form (e.g. *I* v. *me*). There may indeed be a zero-exponent, in which case the word order may indicate the case relationship. Of course various types of transformations, such as the passive, may also be applied. Information about the transformational properties of individual lexical items will have to be attached when they are inserted so that the appropriate transformational operations may be carried out.

The following are the typical surface case forms in English:

A →	*by*:	*The door was opened by Henry.*
I →	$\left\{\begin{array}{l} with/\_\_A \\ by \end{array}\right\}$	*Harbottle knocked out Craigfender with a hefty blow.*
		Craigfender was knocked out by a hefty blow.
O →	∅:	*The Dean's wife drank all the gin.*
F →	∅:[22]	*Titania Nasegow carved the figurine.*
B →	'for':	*Patterson Blamp wrote the story for Miss Merrycork.*
D →	'to':	*Phoebe gave the python to Kenneth.*

L and T may be indicated by prepositions that themselves convey semantic information, thus *after the lynching, during the Blitz, under the radiator, between the sheets,* and so on; the choice of semantically empty prepositions is made by the individual noun associated with the case: *at Christmas, in January, on Friday, at* or *in the bank, in Anatolia, on* or *in the moon.*

The overriding subsequent rule in English is that the chosen surface subject loses its typical preposition, if it has one. The actual choice of surface subject in English seems to follow the principle 'If an A is present it becomes the subject; otherwise, if there is an I, *it* becomes the subject; otherwise the subject is the O'. (For example, *John opened the door with the key, The key opened the door, The door opened.*) It is however possible to have other choices

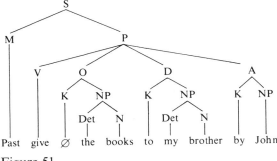

Figure 51

of subject. The tree in Figure 51 illustrates one deep structure which may appear in a variety of surface orders. The possible surface forms are:

(i) *John gave the books to my brother.*
(ii) *John gave my brother the books.*
(iii) *The books were given to my brother by John.*
(iv) *My brother was given the books by John.*

(Notice that in this case the 'non-normal' choice of subject has to be accompanied by a passive transformation.)

Certain verbal forms can 'absorb' the tense of the modality (as in the case of *gave*) but others (as in the case of *given*) require the insertion of *be* to carry the tense. This is typically the case with *hot* (which as a meteorological verb takes the frame +[___L]). A string, which we can represent as *Pres+hot+in+the+studio*, may appear finally either as *It is hot in the studio* or *The studio is hot*: in both cases *be* has been inserted. Moreover, if there is no surface subject, then one must be created in the form of the empty *it*.

Certain case frames may be filled by a blank verb, or zero, such as +[___O+L]. This also requires the insertion of *be* into M to carry the tense: thus *Pres+zero-verb+∅+many toys* (O) *+in+the+box* (L) finally to appear as *Many toys are in the box*, or (with the insertion of an empty *there*) *There are many toys in the box*. But there is another possibility. We may move the locative L to subject position, in which case it must leave behind a copy of itself (the noun being replaced by a pronominal form) and a different verb *have* must be inserted into M, to give *The box has many toys in it*. Thus the verbs *have* and *be* turn out to be semantically empty, functioning only as tense carriers (as was suggested in another context of these verbs in 9.10). A frequent case

250

of a zero verb occurs in English in the framework $+[\_\_O+D]$, which requires the choice of D as subject and the insertion of *have*: *I* (D) *have a book* (O).

Some languages do not require the insertion of *be*, especially if the tense is the present (see the Russian example in 9.12) and some languages do not require the choice of D as subject (Latin *mihi est liber*, literally 'to me is book') and others do not permit it (Gaelic *'Tha leabhar agam'* /ha 'l̯ɔʌr 'akəm/, literally 'is book at me'). Not unexpectedly, therefore, not only do *have*-less languages exist (such as Gaelic, Welsh and Hebrew) but comparisons of languages reveal divergencies in the number of *be*-like verbs and their uses. *Have* and *be* appear not to be deep structure verbs (unless perhaps a use of *be* = 'exist').

The process of creating a surface subject, resulting in the neutralisation of underlying case distinctions to a single form usually called the 'nominative', is termed *subjectivalisation*. Certain languages may be said to lack subjectivalisation, such as Basque. The sentences quoted in 9.10 illustrate the point: *Bettiri* (nominative) *ethorri da*, 'Peter has arrived' but *Joanesek* (ergative) *argitzen du Bettiri* (nominative), 'John is teaching Peter'. *Objectivalisation* may also occur, resulting in the neutralisation of case distinctions to a single form often called the 'accusative' where it is distinct from the subject forms.[23] Something of the sort may be seen in Fillmore's example of *John smeared paint on the wall* and *John smeared the wall with paint*; here it would be possible to postulate that *smear* is accepted into the frame $+[\_\_L+I]$ and that the transformational information is attached specifying that whichever NP was chosen as direct object must fall next to the verb and must lose its preposition.

A third process that obliterates deep case distinctions is that which forms nominals from sentences; it usually involves the 'genitive'. In this way *John's book* is derived from an NP consisting of *John* and an embedded S of the form $M+zero\text{-}verb+book$ (O) *to John* (D); by itself the embedded S would yield *John has a book*. Thus conversion to genitive may be seen to be a surface process; this point of view is strengthened when we consider the common Gaelic use of *an leabhar agam* ('the book at me') beside the possible *mo leabhar* (literally 'my book'). Fillmore states the rule for the form of such an NP as 'NP → N (S)', with of course the appropriate restrictions on the form of the embedded S.

Contrasted with this type of possession is another, which we may call *inalienable possession*. The difference is seen when we compare *my dog* and *my head*; it may be felt satisfactory, Fillmore claims, to derive the first from *I have a dog* but not the second from *I have a head*. In this case we can derive the second from an obligatory D complement, an *adnominal dative*, that is 'the head to me'. The suggested rule for this derivation is 'NP → N (D)'. This allows us to subcategorise nouns into those that require an adnominal D (nouns of inalienable possession) and those that reject it (nouns of *alienable possession*). Typically parts of the body and kinship terms fall into the category of inalienable possession.

The distinction may in fact be marked by the surface grammar; for example, in some types of Gaelic it is not possible to say **a'chas agam* /ʌ 'xas 'akəm/ 'the foot at me'; only *mo chas* /mɔ 'xas/ 'my foot'; compare also the French *Je me suis cassé le bras* /ʒəmsᵿikaselˈbra/ 'I have broken my arm' and *J'ai cassé ma montre* /ʒekasemaˈmɔ̃tr/ 'I have broken my watch'. The use in an older form of English of phrases like *Mary, wife to Henry* illustrates another recognition of this adnominal D. The Algonquian grammatical category of dependence (see 9.10) seems also to be a surface appearance of inalienable possession. Fillmore is careful to point out that examples of inalienable possession in languages always show some classifications contrary to reasonable expectation,[24] hence it must be treated as a syntactic category rather than a notional one.

Fillmore uses his theory to throw light on a variety of phenomena in natural languages and to suggest a framework for a typological classification of languages according to the processes employed in the derivation of the surface forms from the underlying case relationships. Indeed the paper is refreshing in view of the reluctance displayed elsewhere in the literature of generative grammar for providing examples in anything but English (though Fillmore must not be blamed for all the examples used in this present account).

Fillmore himself developed this approach (Fillmore 1970, 1971) subsequently, and others have also worked on case grammar. Reference should be made to a highly interesting though complex type of case grammar, claiming that cases are basically localistic (i.e. spatial or directional), developed by John Anderson.[25] But the paper described above not only provides a terminology for describing important fundamental similarities between languages but it makes clear to the layman unversed in symbolic logic the types of relationship that will have to be considered in deep structure. In particular it presents a cogent case for regarding the sets of symbols in deep structure sentences as being essentially unordered and for regarding 'subject' and 'direct object' as surface phenomena that need not necessarily be expected in every language. Fillmore concedes that his approach is based on semantic considerations but claims that if it is possible to discover a semantically justified universal syntactic theory by this method, then 'it is likely that the syntactic deep structure of the type that has been made familiar from the work of Chomsky and his students is going to go the way of the phoneme'. (From the present writer's point of view that is not equivalent to saying that it will become useless!)

17.3 Conclusion. We have briefly traced the expansion of the scope of grammar from being a device the object of which was to specify the set of syntactically acceptable sentences that form a language to becoming a device which, it was hoped, could match sound with meaning. Yet if we preserve the notion of scientific revolution, it may be possible to discern in transformational grammar the increase in problems and inconvenient observations that signal the inability of a theory to do what was expected of it, and thus may herald the end of a paradigm.

We have seen how the optimism of the standard theory has not been justified. It could be suggested that some American linguists indulge a fondness for having great 'insights' that later prove to be of limited application. Perhaps this is true to some extent, and one could question whether the standard theory was sufficiently tested before Chomsky embarked on the implications of it for such things as universal grammar and innate ideas. On the other hand it is equally possible to suggest, as we have done throughout this book, that it is in the nature of things that theories should be overtaken by events. One could claim to see in Chomsky's later proposals a case of the revolutionary-turned-reactionary fighting a rearguard action. In *Syntactic structures* Chomsky inveighed against 'ad hoc adjustment or loose formulation' – extended standard theory seems to smack of both. Yet here again we could equally well regard him as a visionary, for Ray Jackendoff has given more precise form to his suggested interpretative rules that are to operate on post-transformational strings.

Thus there are two broadly opposed camps, interpretative versus generative semanticists. Both sides employ arguments and technical mechanisms of great complexity (though this may be inevitable). Neither accepts any suggestion that they have returned to the viewpoint of the Stoics and the Modistae that we 'clothe our thoughts in words', for both Chomsky and Lakoff[26] reject any idea of 'directionality'; the object of their theories is the mapping of correspondences between meaning and sound, and whether this is achieved by the 'bifurcation' of one or the 'straight through' model of the other is immaterial. The mapping does not represent human behaviour, that is processes of thought, and neither type of semantic representation consists of 'thoughts'.

It is difficult to see how this debate will be resolved. Since there are few concrete experiments available to test linguistic theories of this type, linguists can enjoy the luxury of extended, even acrimonious, debate rather like theologians. The extended standard theory may seem artificial and contrived, yet the generative semanticists have not been able to answer all of Chomsky's extended standard theory proposals.[27] In fact both positions suffer from weaknesses, some of them shared. We have indicated more than once the formidable difficulty of semantic components, due to our inability to 'get outside' language in order to talk about it. The identification and justification of cases or functions is a similar issue: how many are there, how do we define them, and how do we distinguish *benefactive* from *dative*, for example? And it might be contended that phonological distinctive features are precisely a case in point of quite arbitrary inventions to deal with things that somehow or other must be distinguished. (Some linguists show a consequent anxiety to exhibit the 'naturalness' of their frameworks, lest they fall under this very reproach.) It may well turn out that each theory is for some purpose useful 'up to a point'. That it fails beyond that point may not mean that it should necessarily be discarded.

The contribution of generative-transformationalism has been immense, not only in the creation of excitement and enthusiasm in linguistics and beyond it, but also in the identification of linguistic patterns that will have to be taken into account in any theory of language. It is to be hoped that future descriptive and teaching grammars will treat such features as the expression of inchoatives and causatives, the indication of focus and topic, the effects of certain kinds of transformations, in their accounts of individual languages, even though not incorporated into a monolithic set of ordered rules. Apart from that, some proposals have been shown to be inadequate, and such negative conclusions are additions to our knowledge. Yet at the moment, in view of the vast number of publications appearing in connection with transformational-generative grammar, it is uncertain whether we are witnessing an enrichment or a disintegration. As this is being written, Chomsky is proposing a *revised extended standard theory*.[28] The question may never be settled. Linguists may find other topics more interesting and may simply go away and abandon the debate. In this connection we must point out that some linguists disliked the application of the concept of scientific revolutions to linguistic theory, and took particular exception to the claim that the appearance of *Syntactic structures* initiated such a revolution, on the justifiable grounds that they shared neither the methodological assumptions of the neo-Bloomfieldians nor those of the transformational-generative grammarians. There is, after all, more to language than grammaticality.

FURTHER READING
Phonology
Halle 1962, 1964; Hyman 1975; Jakobson, Fant and Halle 1951; Jakobson and Halle 1956; Postal 1968; Schane 1973.
Semantics
Katz and Fodor 1964.
Standard Theory
Burt 1971; Chomsky 1964, 1965; Jacobs and Rosenbaum 1968; Katz and Postal 1964.
Extended Standard Theory and Generative Semantics
Anderson and Kiparsky 1973; Bach and Harms 1968; Bever, Katz and Langendoen 1977; Chomsky 1972, 1975, 1976; Fillmore and Langendoen 1971; Huddleston 1976; Jacobs and Rosenbaum 1970; Jackendoff 1972; Lakoff 1970; Steinberg and Jakobovits 1971 (section on linguistics).
Critiques of Chomsky and Transformational-Generative Grammar
Chafe 1970; Derwing 1973; Hiorth 1974; Hockett 1968; Hudson 1976; Robinson 1975; Uhlenbeck 1972.

18. Human Language and Linguistics

18.1 Non-transformational approaches. In this last chapter we cannot bring our story to a pleasing conclusion and proudly finish with the words 'The End': this is a complete impossibility given human language and what we can discern as necessary for its description. Rather our intention is to draw the reader's attention to yet further areas of scholarship. For example, apart from the chapters on phonetics, phonology and semantics, our account of post-Saussurean linguistics has dealt exclusively with developments in the U.S.A., focusing on the fortunes of transformational-generative grammar. Yet although transformational-generative grammar has received the greatest publicity in recent years, especially in English-speaking countries, it does not possess a monopoly of the truth and, as we have seen, its future is uncertain. There has always been much of great value elsewhere. Other traditions exist, both in Europe and America, and competent linguists are familiar with their points of view and their arguments, for each possesses some unique insight into the nature of human language.

The beginner in linguistics must at least be told of the existence of non-transformational schools and given the firm instruction that if he wishes to become an informed scholar he must make their closer acquaintance. The student who knows only American structuralism and transformationalism will have a mental picture of one particular landscape of linguistics in which peaks of success and quagmires of uncertainty occupy well-defined positions. To read even one European survey of linguistics, such as those by Ivić, Lepschy or Leroy, provides a beneficial shock, for not only are new landscapes revealed, but we see our familiar terrain from a different, even apparently eccentric, angle and find its proportions and vistas altered. (Such a process is inevitable, for the beginner has to begin *somewhere*.) We remind readers (see p.42) that during the inter-war period linguistic endeavour was every bit as active in Europe as in America; the Second World War called a halt – in some cases temporary, in others alas more permanent – to virtually all European work in linguistic research. Much European pre-war and post-war linguistic investigation is of indisputable importance, as are certain American approaches which do not conform to the general outlines

256

already described. The present writer would be failing in his duty if he did not mention them.

One of the outstanding events in linguistics was the foundation of the Prague Linguistic Circle by Vilém Mathesius in 1926. This gifted group and their associates produced between 1929 and 1939 in a series of *Travaux du cercle linguistique de Prague* many papers of the highest significance. Prague linguists of this period had a tremendous breadth of interest, encompassing phonology, dia-chronic linguistics, language typology, the functions of language, the problems of semantics, morphology, stylistics, the meaning of grammatical categories, the teaching of languages, and the relation-ship between written and spoken language. Although the outbreak of the Second World War marked the end of one phase of the Prague School, by no means did it mark the end of the tradition. Happily publication of the retitled *Travaux linguistiques de Prague* was resumed in 1964; the tradition lives on.

The names of Rask, Verner and Jespersen suffice to indicate the outstanding contribution made by Danish scholars. This tradition was worthily maintained by Louis Hjelmslev (1899–1965) and H.J. Uldall (1908–57) (and it continues to flourish). Hjelmslev and Uldall in the late 1930s produced a new theory of language, *glossematics*, the aim of which was to establish a type of algebra for language; this would involve a systematic set of definitions which could be used to provide the description of any individual language.

One contributor to the *Travaux du cercle linguistique de Prague* was the French linguist André Martinet; he went on to develop a linguistic system explicitly based on the idea of 'function', a concept underlying Prague School linguistics generally. According to Martinet, the primary function of language is communication (though there are others of lesser importance). Increasing interest in and development of *functionalism* led later to the convention of the First International Colloquium of Functionalist Linguistics at Groningen in 1973.

The Englishman M.A.K. Halliday is responsible for a most interesting and original contribution to grammatical theory ex-pounded first in his *Categories of the theory of grammar* of 1961 as *scale-and-category* grammar; later this developed into *systemic* grammar, one aspect of which views languages as a series of interrelated systems and sets out to explore the various types of them. It may be that this approach will come to be revealed as of outstanding subtlety and significance.

In the U.S.A. acceptance of transformational-generative grammar was not universal. Some linguists had resisted the rigid requirements of post-Bloomfieldian structuralism and hence did not feel the necessity of embracing the new approach, for in a sense they had raised their criticisms first. One of these is K.L. Pike who had always stressed the necessity of a practical approach to the problem of language description and consequently rejected the doctrine of separation of levels, realising that a discovery does not proceed by mechanical steps but needs the intuition and 'analytical leaps' of the investigator. Pike initiated a *tagmemic* approach to grammatical description, a *tagmeme* being the correlation of a functional slot (e.g. 'subject') with the class of items (e.g. noun phrase) that fill the slot. A tagmemic grammar therefore consists, among other things, of a set of formulas listing possible constructions at the levels of sentence, clause, phrase and word. Many previously unanalysed languages have been described using this framework.

Another non-transformational approach was first proposed by the American Sidney M. Lamb in the 1960s. This views linguistic structure in terms of layers or strata; the outermost are those of meaning and of sound mediated by strata between them (since while a language relates sounds and meaning, the relationship is not one in which a sequence of elements of meaning corresponds to an identical sequence of sounds). This approach, *stratificational* grammar, takes account not only of substance but relationships: on each stratum is postulated a pattern of relationships specifying the permissible structural combinations of the elements of that stratum.

And there are other areas of importance which the experienced linguist must explore and assess, such as the categorial grammars of Ajdukiewicz and of Bar-Hillel, the dependency grammars of Tesnière and Hays, the theories of Shaumyan and other Soviet linguists, the very complex Montague grammar, significant developments of the Italian philosopher Croce's approach to language (shamefully neglected by English-speaking linguists) and Hudson's daughter-dependency grammar.

18.2 Diachronic linguistics. From Chapter 7 onwards we have dealt with synchronic phenomena in language. It is sometimes asserted that linguistics ought to be a purely synchronic study or indeed that it in fact *is*. This we would dispute emphatically. The great *loci classici* of twentieth-century linguistics, namely de Saussure's *Cours* and Bloomfield's *Language*, devote approximately half their length to diachronic phenomena, as does C.F. Hockett's very full *A course in modern linguistics* of 1958. Particularly in Europe twentieth-century linguists continued to tackle problems of historical linguistics. Antoine Meillet (1866–1936), Emile Benveniste and Jerzy Kuryłowicz pursued studies which were not iconoclastically different from the traditional tenor of nineteenth-century philology. Kuryłowicz in particular has applied creative imaginative scholarship brilliantly.

Nevertheless objections to the Neogrammarian point of view had been raised from the time it was formulated, for example by Hugo Schuchardt (1842–1927), the Romance philologist (to whom Schmidt seems to have been indebted for his wave-theory), and by Jules Gilliéron (1856–1926), the dialect geographer. Their legacy may be seen in the views of Matteo Bartoli (1873–1946) and Giuliano Bonfante who claimed very tellingly that individual languages were an abstraction, that there were no sharp historical breaks between stages of the same 'language' (e.g. Latin and Italian) and that postulated proto-languages on a family tree have no justification. This type of view reached an extreme form in the opinion of C.C. Uhlenbeck (1866–1951) that what was usually called 'genetic relationship' was in fact only the possession of many features in common based on ancient contact – in a sense the wheel had returned full-circle to the point at which Coeurdoux had written his letter from India (see p.18)!

Still, the attempted reconstruction of forms and the assumption of some sort of family-tree cannot, in the words of Mr W.C. Fields, 'be all bad'. Confirmation•of reconstructed forms has appeared on at least two occasions, namely in de Saussure's prediction about the existence of certain elements in Indo-European (subsequently found to exist in Hittite) and in Bloomfield's reconstruction of consonant-clusters in Proto-Algonquian (still attested in certain extant dialects). In spite of that modern research has turned from reconstruction to the observation of historical processes at work.

For example, Chomsky devotes a great deal of space to the statement of diachronic phenomena in rule-form. He states that adults are unable to modify their grammar except by the addition or elimination of a few rules; therefore when the language of adults undergoes a change, 'their grammar is modified only by the addition of the rule in question'.[1] However when children learn the language they construct for themselves a grammar which may be different from that of their parents, because it ranks higher in a measure of evaluation (presumably because it is 'simpler'). Therefore 'children and parents may have quite different grammars though speaking all but identical idiolects'. However, 'a rule that is added to the grammar may continue to function for many generations without causing changes in the lexical representations'. This allows Chomsky the possibility of incorporating information on the development of English phonology into a synchronic set of rules. Such ideas were further developed by Paul Kiparsky.[2]

A different type of approach examines the sociological factors which may condition sound shifts (or indeed any language-change). The idea had been advanced by Bartoli and Bonfante that prestige factors (not only military, political and economic but also literary, artistic and religious) played an important role in language-change. This was explored to some extent by J.L. Fischer[3] but it is the name of William Labov[4] which is associated with this type of investigation. Labov finds that there may be a social motivation for a sound-change, and one which is consciously applied. For example, the presence of post-vocalic /r/ among New York speakers of English is a prestige feature in that speakers who, he finds, do not normally use it are apt to introduce it if they wish to impress others; however there is a tendency to extend these situations of prestige so that the feature is thus introduced to new linguistic environments. Indeed in another study[5] Labov finds that for similar reasons certain 'old-fashioned' and obsolescent pronunciations have increased, so that a sound-change appears to be becoming reversed.

In several papers William S.-Y. Wang and others have examined the question of the nature and cause of sound-change;[6] they have produced evidence to show that at least in certain cases the Neo-grammarian hypothesis of sound-changes occurring gradually but irresistibly, and affecting all sensitive sounds unselectively, is untenable. As an alternative, Wang advances the notion of *lexical diffusion*; according to this, a sound-change may take place phonetically abruptly rather than gradually (i.e. there may be phonemic splitting rather than gradual allophonic differentiation). Moreover, and equally importantly, the change may at first affect only two or three words but thereafter spread to others over a period of time (perhaps hundreds of years). Wang's evidence is drawn from a number of languages. An English example concerns stress. Certain pairs of disyllabic nouns and verbs in present-day English are homographs, but the noun is stressed on the first syllable while the verb is stressed on the second, e.g. *import*: such pairs we may call *diatones*. Reference to English dictionaries from the sixteenth century to the present[7] shows that in 1570 the number of diatones was three (*outlaw, rebel, record*), in 1582 five, in 1660 24, in 1700 35, in 1800 70 and in 1934 150. There is therefore a steady increase in the rate of change. There appear to be 1,315 disyllabic noun-verb homographs, so that barely 11 % of the conceivable total has so far shifted: the sound-change has stretched over centuries and is presumably still going on. Quite obviously processes of lexical diffusion cannot be notated either in the familiar philological formula of the type 'p > f' or in the addition or the subtraction of a

260

transformational rule. The implications of this proposal are therefore profound.

It is perfectly possible that the next major focus of linguistic research could again be in diachronic phenomena: *how* sound-systems, grammars and meanings change and *why*. Advances in such fields of technology as computers and instrumental phonetics permit insights denied to nineteenth century philologists. Perhaps it is an omen that the First International Conference on Historical Linguistics was held in Edinburgh in 1973.

18.3 Animal 'language' and information theory. It is important to make the point that phonetics, phonology, grammar and semantics (whether synchronic or diachronic) by no means cover every topic of interest in the vast area of human language. Other fields of investigation, not strictly branches of linguistics, are concerned with other outstanding facets of our subject.

For example, is language really the prerogative of human beings? Animals behave in ways which may be interpreted as communicating and conveying information;[8] some recent books seem to put forward the view that there is *no* essential difference between animal behaviour and human behaviour[9] and it might be supposed that human language could be paralleled in the animal kingdom. In particular, three groups of animals have excited popular interest by their alleged power to communicate: bees, dolphins and monkeys.[10] However as far as we know there is nothing in the range of natural animal behaviour which remotely approaches the complexity of human language.[11]

Attempts have been made to teach a form of language to chimpanzees[12] but it is far too early to draw any conclusions and it is ill-advised to claim, as do two commentators[13] apropos one particular animal that 'this wonderful experiment seems to have established beyond doubt that a chimpanzee is capable of learning true language', unless 'true language' is taken to mean something vastly different from what we observe in human language. But clearly comparable experiments must continue in order to determine the nature and extent of the chimpanzees' communicative ability, whatever it may be.

We turn now to what may be called the 'efficiency' of language; this refers to features of individual languages considered as channels used for the transmission of 'information'. Our approach derives from the *information theory* (or *communication theory*) elaborated by Shannon and Weaver in 1948.[14] *Information* means technically the size of the possible choice among signals. For example, a light has a choice of two signals, 'on' and 'off'; a teleprinter keyboard has a larger number, viz. the number of symbols available plus a space. The selection of one signal of the teleprinter therefore holds more information than the selection of one signal of the light: as an illustration, the letter *h* is contained in one teleprinter-signal, but its flashed Morse code equivalent (four dots) requires seven light-signals (four 'ons' separated by three 'offs'). It may be that a signalling system places restrictions on the co-occurrence of symbols so that the amount of information in messages transmitted is less than it might be. Such limitations of choice are examples of *redundancy*. The recognition of redundancy is a striking application of information theory to language. For example, in English spelling, the letter *q* is always followed by *u*; hence *quick* contains less information than it could, for it cannot stand in contrast to, for example, **qaick* or **qjick*; and *q* is consequently used less often than *u*. This disparity applies also to other letters, to phonemes, to lexical items, even to phonemic opposition: /t/ and /d/ are used oftener and contrast oftener than /θ/ and /ð/[15] in English.

Natural languages exhibit a staggering amount of redundancy of many types. For example, the syntactic context may impose redundancy. Thus, in *Sevenhonk explained the principles —— potassium dating*, the slot may be filled only by a preposition, most expectedly *of*, though conceivably *in*, or by a participle, most expectedly *underlying*. If we know the precise length of the word required, then the choice is even more limited. Government and concord also exhibit redundancy. *From me* cannot stand in opposition to **from I*. *Leurs petits enfants sont méchants*, 'Their children are naughty', signals plurality five times (in the written form; in the spoken form, given the liaison, only two overt markers of plurality are heard /lœr pətiz ɑ̃fɑ̃ sɔ̃ meʃɑ̃/). Phonological structure imposes more redundancy, e.g. given a sequence /stCɪŋ/, only /r/ can be the C. Similarly, writing-conventions impose redundancy, e.g. the use of capital letters in English or in German. Individual phonemes in one system can show redundancy: English has no voiceless nasal series, though the distinctive features of voicelessness and nasality are necessary in a description of English consonants; hence it can be contended that English /m/, /n/, /ŋ/ show redundancy (because they always imply voice). Indeed any asymmetrical phonemic system involves redundancy (see 8.11).

In one sense, then, languages are highly inefficient communication channels; nevertheless such 'inefficient' redundancy fulfils a vitally important function: redundancy in communications signals counteracts 'noise'. 'Noise' in language may be the disappearance or distortion of part of the signal due to a loud noise, or a misprint, or a hole in the paper, or the interruption of a telephone circuit.

The loss of one letter of written English is not nearly as serious as the loss of a Chinese character; such is the effect of the greater redundancy of written English as compared to Chinese, or Post Office address codes, or telephone numbers. Indeed, entire words may be lost without misunderstanding. Thus telegrams with words 'missing', newspaper headlines, the use of initials (e.g. 'h & c') in classified advertisements, etc., are all intelligible. It is possible to talk in a noisy room and be understood, though not all one's words are audible; and we normally understand without difficulty on the telephone, though the fricatives /s/ and /f/ may be indistinguishable (hence the telephone alphabet, 'F for Freddy', 'S for Sugar'). Noise may also be imposed by the unfamiliarity of the topic of discourse, that is because there is no expectancy of occurrence (other than syntactic and phonological). Thus one has to listen harder to a lecture on an unknown topic than to a conversation about the weather.

At least one linguistic phenomenon may be explained in terms of redundancy: mutual communication between speakers of different dialects. Considering how accents of a language may differ, it is surprising that the speaker of an unfamiliar accent is ever intelligible. It is even more surprising when we think of differences of grammar and lexis, as in dialects. Such mutual comprehension would not be possible if languages were 'efficient' communications channels; it is only possible because utterances in language contain so much redundancy.

18.4 The application of linguistics. Linguistics is a study of human language, as anatomy is the study of the human body. However, in the same way that the findings of anatomy are 'applied', that is used by physicians, by artists and by those who construct chairs, so the findings of linguistic theory can be applied. 'The applied linguist is a consumer, or user, not a producer, of theories.'[16] Briefly we list some of those areas in which a linguistic theory has been applied with some success.

We consider first of all language-teaching. This area is so important, and so vast, that the term *applied linguistics* is often held to mean only language-teaching, including the teaching of a second language and of the mother tongue. In both, linguistic theory is relevant, although the theoretical linguist has no right to prescribe to the language teacher what aspects of linguistic theory are of importance in language-teaching: that is the decision of the language-teacher. In any case, the language-teacher will draw on other areas besides linguistics, such as theories of learning, classroom techniques, error analysis,[17] etc.; moreover he is inevitably

263

involved in decisions about *what* to teach, which may depend on the purpose or objective of the learner; and since no full linguistic description of any language has ever been made, the teacher must omit something from his exposition, for he can expound only what he can describe; nevertheless some people do learn second languages almost perfectly – in which case they must be learning what the teacher cannot expound.

In remedial language-teaching, in particular speech therapy, the therapist may find in linguistic theory a method to describe both the patient's imperfect speech and the goal of treatment, thus exposing particular, systemic faults and enabling him to draw up a course of treatment and programme of priorities. In the same way, the teaching of the deaf may use linguistic theory: for example, a knowledge of articulatory phonetics in encouraging speech, or of syntactic theory in analysing the difficulties of those who use sign-language.

Communications engineering may benefit from the application of linguistic theory in the design of experiments to assess the limits of tolerable loss of signal at different frequencies. (A great deal *is* lost in telephone circuits; the problem is: is it worth it, economically, to improve them?) The results may feed back into linguistic investigation, witness speech synthesisers[18] which help us to explore features of spoken natural languages; they also allow controlled variation in synthesised 'speech-sounds', a tool of great value in probing the perception of speech.

Linguistic theory contributes to the elaboration of theories of translation, with either the sole aim of enquiry, or the object of developing more efficient means of translation. Often there is interaction between the two, as in the development of translation theory by the Summer Institute of Linguistics, which exists to train those who wish to translate the Bible.[19] In connection with translation, we may mention machine translation. The links between this and communications engineering are obvious, in that electronic circuits and the notion of a code are involved, to say nothing of computer operations and memory banks. In the early 1960s, hopes were high that a capable method of machine-translating could be developed, to some extent because of a belief that languages were only codes, exemplified in Weaver's dictum 'When I look at an article in Russian, I say: "This is really written in English, but it has been coded in some strange symbols. I will now proceed to decode".' It is now apparent that language is more complicated than this, partly because of the recognition of the complexities of syntax and syntactic functions, partly because of the awareness of the essential context-sensitive nature of language. Therefore lower hopes of success in machine-translation were later entertained, although texts of a very restricted nature such as scientific papers may usefully be converted into intelligible forms which resemble other languages. Whether or not this merits the description 'translation' depends on standards of acceptability of target-language and of fidelity to the original texts; these standards are very much a matter of individual taste.

The devising of orthographies and the reform of spelling-systems may also use a linguistic theory. Those who give visible form to a hitherto unwritten language will have to devise a writing-system, having first analysed its phonology. It may however happen that an established writing-system is completely discarded and a new one substituted, a noteworthy example being Turkish which adopted the Roman script in place of the Arabic in 1928. An even greater change, though much less rigorously imposed, is Pinyin, the spelling of Chinese in Roman characters in the People's Republic of China. Or an existing spelling-system may simply be 'tidied up', i.e. made more 'simple' or 'rational'; this has happened to various languages, such as Danish, Dutch, German, Irish and Russian. Often these exercises use a phonemic analysis, but it may not always be possible or popular to devise a completely phonemic alphabet. For example, different accents may have to be accommodated, or there may be a desire that the written form should resemble some culturally dominant language, such as Spanish in the case of certain indigenous South American languages.

Various types of language planning may include the application of linguistic theory. Such planning may involve the 'purification' of a language (e.g. German from elements of Latin and French, Rumanian from Slavonic, French from English, Turkish and Persian from Arabic elements), the establishment of a 'national' dialect (e.g. Nynorsk in Norway), or the elevation of one language (from among quite different languages) to be the national one (e.g. Tagalog in the Philippines and Indonesian in Indonesia). (Some of these activities are due to political rather than linguistic factors.)

Literary studies of various kinds use the results of linguistic theorising. For example, the study of style, or *stylistics*, may use the descriptive frameworks of the phonetician, phonologist or grammarian; and the developing field of comparative literature, i.e. the study of literatures of different languages and cultures,[20] draws heavily on linguistics.

Forensic investigation has also benefited by techniques of linguistic description, e.g. in ascribing authorship (on the basis of style) to documents such as sections of disavowed statements. In the same way, one could imagine, not that a speaker might be positively identified, but that an individual could be excluded from further consideration, on the basis of dialect features in a tape-recording. A word of warning is necessary about so-called 'voice-prints': although these are admitted as evidence in certain states of the U.S.A. they are not by any means universally regarded as trustworthy.[21]

Finally we would point out that linguistics continues to exert an influence on, for example, behavioural psychology and psychiatry (in describing language behaviour), cognitive and developmental psychology (through the study of language acquisition), cognitive anthropology (in the study of kinship systems and folk taxonomies), computer science (in the study of computer languages), philosophy (in the study of 'natural logic' and formal languages), and education theory (in the study of language in the classroom and at home). And indeed there are fruitful areas of overlap, as we shall see.

18.5 Linguistics, related fields of study and the future. Disciplines which study human language directly or are in some way relevant to that study may be envisaged as multidimensional clusters of points connected by lines along which information flows in one direction or in both. Apart from linguistics, these include acoustics, aesthetics, anatomy, anthropology, communications research, computer science, education theory, electronics, literary criticism, mathematics, music, neurology, philosophy, physiology, psychiatry, psychology, semiotics, sociology, speech therapy, the visual arts and zoology. This array of different subjects, each with some relevance to human language, emphasises that the external world is not divided into discrete fields, each appropriately the object of a distinct study (any more than it is divided into classes of entities each appropriately expressed by a surface word-class in language). Once again the point of view creates the object. That human language is of interest to so many branches of study is an indication of the centrality of language to human activity. We examine now the interaction between some of these other disciplines and linguistics, and consider the nature of linguistics as a study.

We have seen an application of information theory to language; but other areas of mathematics have also been used, such as Boolean algebra, games theory, set theory, statistical calculus of probability and topology. This field may be termed *mathematical linguistics* and involves the use of mathematics as a metalanguage for human language. Yet we may also use natural language as a metalanguage for mathematics,[22] and this leads us to consider the status of mathematics as a language. It is possible to regard both mathematics and formal logic as artificial formalised languages constructed for particular purposes. One essential difference between natural language and mathematics is the extreme context-sensitive nature of the former and the context-free nature of the latter. Mathematicians and logicians may contend that language is too imprecise, vague and ambiguous for their uses, yet this very variability allows us to talk about an infinity of subjects and to be creative, not only poetically but scientifically. Mathematics and formal logic on the other hand deal with only a very few topics.

In the Western tradition the interests of philosopher and of grammarian have often overlapped. In previous chapters we have made reference to the Stoics, the Modistae, the rationalist philosophers of the seventeenth century and to the concern of philosophers with problems of meaning. In recent years this community of interest has deepened and philosophers as diverse as Ayer, Austin, Carnap, Frege, Korzybski, Popper, Quine, Searle, Strawson and Wittgenstein have explicitly dealt with philosophical problems posed by the fact of language; encouragingly, many philosophers are now aware of the work of linguists. However given the different starting-points of the linguist and the philosopher, each has his own approach to language and it must therefore not be supposed that an instant advance in language-theory could be made by adding together the work of a given linguist and a given philosopher.

Psychologists, as we have indicated, are becoming increasingly aware of the work of linguists and are adopting linguistic theories in their investigation of certain aspects of language; these include the perception of language, the acquisition of one's native language, second-language learning, bilingualism, language and the perception of the world, language and concepts, disorders of language and the relation of a grammar to postulated mental operations in actual linguistic performance. This vast and developing field is *psycho-linguistics* and linguists as well as psychologists are engaged in it.

Linguistics may be regarded as occupying a place in a more general theory of sign-systems of one sort or another (including language); such a subject was envisaged by de Saussure (although the idea dates back to the philosopher John Locke), and is known now as *semiotics*. It embraces not only language but also mathematics and formal logic, such things as traffic-signals and road-signs, gestures, rites, customs and clothes. Certainly insights of importance are gained into similarities in the systems according to which these various phenomena are used, yet it may be debated whether semiotic systems are not simply restricted and specialised artificial languages. If so, then semiotics presupposes linguistics. This viewpoint is strengthened when we observe that we can always use natural language as a metalanguage for non-linguistic semiotic systems but it is inconceivable that we could discuss language using, for example, the choice of signal afforded by traffic lights. Indeed we may paraphrase any of the above non-linguistic semiotic systems in terms of human language.

On the other hand, a comparison of natural language and the languages of the arts throws light on the natures of language on the one hand and of music and the visual arts on the other. In this case it is quite clear that the meaning of the languages of the arts cannot be paraphrased in ordinary language. Furthermore, it would appear that consideration of the languages of the arts requires some reference to aesthetics. We would also have to consider whether there is a 'language' of the literary arts in addition to, though contained in, the normal language which is its raw material.

Finally, we consider the interrelation of language and society, a field which merits the label *sociolinguistics*. Within this is studied the relationship between language and culture, the use of language in society (e.g. its role in rituals of all kinds, magic, religion, kinship organisations), language and social groups, and varieties of language.

The interdisciplinary areas may owe allegiance to two theories simultaneously, e.g. in psycholinguistics, a linguistic and a psychological. If there are competing theories in any one discipline, as in linguistics, then the difficulty is all the greater; furthermore, if the theory adopted is then superseded by another, a reappraisal must take place (as happened in psycholinguistics following the appearance of Chomsky's *Aspects of the theory of syntax*). The solution to the problem of being at the mercy of other people's theories is to construct your own, therefore it is perfectly possible that a theory of psycholinguistics could come into being which would delimit the scope of the subject; this would be independent of the theories of linguistics and psychology. Having established its theories and its procedures, it would then be in a position to consider its relationship to other disciplines.

The history of linguistics shows such a development. At the time of the First Congress of Linguists in 1928 the autonomy of linguistics was insisted upon; this allowed linguists time to become aware of their tasks and to develop theories and techniques without interference. Now that linguists have done this to some extent, we are able to consider the relationship between linguistics and other disciplines. At the same time it is perfectly clear that at the moment there is no single approach to linguistics which one could unreservedly describe as preferable to all others and it is impossible to predict any future developments. The writer of a linguistics textbook has therefore the task of expounding that which is most widely familiar and that which he believes important – and the two may not coincide.

Some of the problems inherent in describing human language have been illustrated. Language is not only a device for conveying information, it has other roles. And a description readily falls into sets of oppositions: body activity or mental activity, the idiolect or 'the language', the individual or the community, the concrete or the abstract, the synchronic or the historical; hence the differing tasks of the instrumental phonetician, the describer of 'a language', the psycholinguist, the sociolinguist, and so on. Such 'division of labour' is apparent from the very beginning in the difference between Dionysius Thrax and Pāṇini. For all linguists have carefully chosen a particular segment of the available data, and have forged a technique for the purpose – Pāṇini, Dionysius Thrax, de Saussure, Bloomfield, Chomsky. Every description is a fiction, and so too are the dichotomies: language itself is not divided. For example the notion of 'system' is suspect: Mathesius, Sapir, Daniel Jones were all aware of the 'oscillation' in a given 'état de langue'; and this oscillation, the present writer believes, illustrates the artificiality of the synchronic/diachronic opposition: in the synchronic *is* the diachronic.[23] Indeed the notion of one homogeneous language spoken in a homogeneous speech-community, while no doubt encouraged by the existence of individual language-names, is false and is not borne out by everyday experience (or by sociolinguistic studies).

We have pointed out that some linguists seem emotionally committed to their theories, in part because few experiments can be devised to choose between them. But this commitment may also be due to the obscurity of much that has been written, for many linguistic publications show a disgraceful lack of clarity. And this may prove no drawback to their influence! As J.K. Galbraith[24] has remarked, obscurity may help to win converts: if a reader has *struggled* to understand, he feels a commitment to the conclusions ('After so much pain light') and if the text is ambiguous, the reader may have found what *he* wants in it.

It has been the concern of this book to grind an axe, namely that theories determine areas of study and that theories are never final. Such is the present speed of developments in theory that new points of view are presented in scholarly papers rather than in full-length books; indeed these papers are sometimes out of date by the time they reach print, private discussions having taken place by means of preprints and conferences. For these reasons we have emphasised the historical development of linguistics; it would be ludicrous to claim that the most recently published proposals contain the greatest known wisdom or utility. It may be that a future linguistics will be as unlike anything we know as a set of rewrite rules is unlike the grammar in Dr Johnson's *Dictionary*. But whatever form a future linguistic takes, it will never reach a final stage of alleged omniscience about language. The words of Xenophanes, translated by Karl Popper,[25] make the point:

> The gods did not reveal, from the beginning,
> All things to us, but in the course of time
> Through seeking we may learn and know things better.

> But as for certain truth, no man has known it,
> Nor shall he know it, neither of the gods
> Nor yet of all the things of which I speak.
> For even if by chance he were to utter
> The final truth, he would himself not know it!
> For all is but a woven web of guesses.

FURTHER READING
Non-Transformational Approaches
Berry 1975, 1977; Cook 1969; Hjelmslev 1963; Ivić 1965; Lepschy 1970; Leroy 1967; Lockwood 1972; Makkai and Lockwood 1973; Martinet 1962, 1964; Mohrmann et al. 1963a, 1963b; Muir 1972; Mulder 1968; Vachek 1966a, 1966b.
Diachronic Linguistics
Anderson 1973; Chen and Wang 1975, 255–81; Lehmann and Malkiel 1968; Lehman 1973; Samuels 1972; Stern 1931; Wang 1976, 61–72.
Wider Aspects
Aitchison 1976; Barry et al. 1965; Barthes 1967; Caton 1963; Chao 1968; Cherry 1957; Cooper 1972; Corder 1973; Greene 1972; Garvin and Spolsky 1966; Greenberg 1957; Guiraud 1975; Hacking 1975; Hinde 1972; Hockett 1967; Householder 1971; Hymes 1964; Jakobovits and Miron 1967; Jakobson 1973; Katz 1972; Kavanagh and Cutting 1975; Kess 1976; Kilmister 1967; Laver and Hutcheson 1972; Linden 1976; Minnis 1971; Ortiz and Zierer 1968; Perren and Trim 1971; Revzin 1966; Robey 1973; Robinson 1972; Rosenberg and Travis 1971; Saporta 1961; Sebeok 1960; Slobin 1971; Smith 1966; Trudgill 1974; Wilks 1972.

Notes and References

Chapter 1

1. The problem of adequate definition appears again at various points in this book, notably Chapters 10 and 18.
2. The reasons for the recognition of a new period are touched on in Chapter 10. As far as linguistic 'non-conformists' are concerned, there is no space to mention them in our account.
3. 'Das Höchste wäre, zu begreifen, daß alles Faktische schon Theorie ist' (Goethe *Wilhelm Meisters Wanderjahre*, 1829, repr. Zurich 1949, 327); 'on dirait que c'est le point de vue qui crée l'objet' (Saussure 1916, 23); 'all observation involves interpretation in the light of our theoretical knowledge' (Popper 1963, 4th ed. 1972, 23).
4. My debt to Karl Popper and Thomas Kuhn in terms of intellectual excitement is huge. I have drawn on their writings to give me a useful framework, but I make no claim to have represented their views. In an introductory textbook it would be inappropriate to discuss the status of linguistics as a 'science' or whether the linguistic points of views described constitute 'theories' strictly speaking. (See Gellner 1977; Kuhn 1961; Lakatos and Musgrave 1970; Popper 1963.)

Chapter 2

1. Firth 1937 in repr. 1964, 4.
2. Cassirer 1946, 48 and 45.
3. e.g. in Judaism, Christianity and Islam.
4. Cassirer 1946, 48; Ogden and Richards 1923, ch. 1.
5. The original consonants were YHWH, written down without vowels. These four letters were read out as /ʔədoːnaːj/ *Adonai* ('The Lord'). When vowel signs were subsequently added to the Biblical text. YHWH received those of *Adonai*, giving *YəHoːWaːH*, though of course *Adonai* continued to be its spoken realisation. A later Bible-translator missed the whole point.

Chapter 3

1. The first trio of explanations may be described as onomatopoeic; but comparison of so-called onomatopes reveals that while they may be of striking phonological structure (see Chapter 8) they convey nothing of their meaning to the uninitiated – who e.g. would *guess* that *bow-wow* represents a dog but *boo-hoo* weeping?
2. This particular example is due to the Roman Honoratus Maurus (4th century A.D.).
3. Plato trans. Jowett, repr. 1970, 130.
4. See the view of Diocles the Magnesian in Diogenes Laertius 1925, II, 158.
5. Diogenes Laertius 1925, II, 110–263.
6. This might be more helpfully translated into English as 'parts of a sentence' (see pp.xiv–xvii).
7. One example of mistranslation: the Greek means 'the object case' or 'the case caused', from /aitiaː/ 'a cause'; the Latin translator (Varro) fastened on another meaning of /aitiaː/ 'an accusation'.

271

8. e.g. Battaglia and Pernicone 1954; Podadera 26th ed., Madrid 1952.
9. Thomas of Erfurt in Bursill-Hall 1971, 134–321.
10. See Chapter 4.
11. Humphreys 1945, 10 and 17.
12. Weseen, 3rd ed., repr. 1946, 37.
13. Smith, 2nd ed., repr. 1967, ix.
14. See the correspondence columns of *The Scotsman*, 23 and 24 October, 1973.

Chapter 4

1. Partly reprinted in Ellis 1871, III, 804–16.
2. Herodotus, *The histories*, Book 2, 4.
3. Webb 1669.
4. Becanus 1569.
5. Scaliger 1610.
6. Reportedly by one André Kempe or Andreas Kemke; see Max Müller 1862, 131, n.; and Waterman 1963, 13.
7. Süssmilch 1766.
8. Rousseau 1755.
9. Essentially the view of Herder in his prize-winning essay; he later rejected it in favour of divine revelation.
10. Part of the theory elaborated in Condillac 1746 and 1798 (posthumous).
11. Heyse 1856; adopted for a short time by Max Müller, see Müller 1862, 391–2.
12. Noiré 1877 and 1917.
13. Sweet 1900, 35 and 37; Paget 1930; Jóhannesson 1949. See further Sayce 1880, II, 300; Andrus de Laguna 1927; Wilson 1937.
14. Jespersen 1922, 440; it also forms part of 'Speculations on the origin of speech and its communicative function', from Langer 1962.
15. 'Der Mensch ist nur Mensch durch Sprache; um aber die Sprache zu erfinden, müßte er schon Mensch sein', W. von Humboldt, *Über das vergleichende Sprachstudium in Beziehung auf die verschiedenen Epochen der Sprachentwicklung* (1820), in Humboldt 1843, III, 252.

Chapter 5

1. Guichard 1606.
2. In 'The Third Anniversary Discourse, on the Hindus' in Jones 1799, 19–34, see 26.
3. Monboddo in 1773 (Burnett 1773, I, 412–22) had thought it possible, though not probable, that 'Teutonic', Persian, Greek and Latin 'must all be dialects of the same parent language'. Unfortunately he also attempts to show that Latin and Hebrew are related.
4. Schlegel 1808, repr. 1975, 137.
5. Schleicher 1869, 28; Schleicher 1866, 137.
6. e.g. the Germanic branch is traditionally divided into three sub-branches; yet each individually shares certain features with only either the one or the other of the remaining two: Sayce in Wright 2nd ed. 1954, 375–7; Prokosch 1939, 30; Priebsch and Collinson 1948, 39. For a similar non-Indo-European situation see Hetzron 1972, 119–24.
7. Bloomfield 1933, 321–45; Sturtevant 1947, 34.
8. Bloomfield 1933, 316 (adapted).
9. 'Passive in $-r$' is an oversimplification; related but non-passive forms in $-r$ occur in Phrygian (known from inscriptions) and in Indo-Iranian; Kuryłowicz 1964, ch. 3.
10. For the origin of the name see Jankowsky 1972, 125 n.2.
11. Later developments in Germanic account for the 'wrong' medial consonants in German and for their identity in English.
12. Conway 1887.

13. Brugmann and Delbrück, 1897, I, 67.
14. There is no descendant of Classical Latin futures. The perils of reconstruction may be illustrated by comparing languages derived from English and attempting to reconstruct a 'parent'. See Todd 1974; Lockwood 1972, 118–21 and 136–7.
15. e.g. Wright 1907, repr. 1962, I, 23.
16. e.g. Priebsch and Collinson 1948, 16–17 and 26–31.
17. Some accounts allege a 'change' of Middle High German −*c* > Modern German −*g*, e.g. *tac* 'day' v. *Tag* ; but both are /tak/ ; cf. Super 234.
18. Sweet 1877, v.
19. See Chapter 6.
20. Meillet 1925.

Chapter 6

1. We retain *langue* /lãg/ and *parole* /parɔl/ as technical terms in English.
2. Saussure 1962, 175.
3. Asterisks mark impossible forms.
4. Saussure 1962, 20.
5. See Chapter 9.
6. Boas and Powell repr. 1966, 70.
7. This was not the first survey of North American Indian languages to appear. Among its predecessors were Powell 1891 and C.C. Uhlenbeck 1908.
8. A linguistic counterpart is surely the intellectual climate in the 1770s and 1780s, cf. p.20, n.3.
9. Bloomfield 1933, 3; but see also Bloomfield 1926, which uses the postulational method but does not define 'science'.
10. Robins 1964, 7–8, cf. Hjelmslev 1953, 11.
11. Chomsky 1957, 55–6.
12. Martinet 1960, trans. 1964, 26.

Chapter 7

1. Allen 1953.
2. Koerner 1973, 37–42.
3. But contrast Hjelmslev's view of the place of phonetics, Hjelmslev 1953.
4. We have simply avoided the problems involved in segmentation; see Menzerath and Lacerda 1933.
5. An accent spoken by certain Englishmen, see p.78.
6. Kingdom 1964; Ladefoged 1967, Part 2; McClure 1972.
7. Pike 1943, 143–5.
8. Muratori 1949; Ladefoged 1964 and 1971, 52; Chao 1968, 25; L.A. Iles, personal communication; Catford 1968.
9. Henderson 1971, 62–4; Ladefoged 1971, 62–3.
10. But see Ladefoged 1975, 208; and Mitchell 1969.
11. Ladefoged 1975, 203; Henderson 1971, 50–3.
12. Ladefoged 1971, 34.
13. Honikman 1964.
14. Ladefoged 1975, 219–23; Ladefoged 1967; Stetson 1951; Gimson 1962, 50–2.
15. Gimson 1962, 55; Stetson 1951; Ladefoged 1967 and 1975, 222.
16. Abercrombie 1964a, 1964b and 1971.
17. Scott 1940; Abercrombie 1964b.
18. Abercrombie 1967, 104.
19. Kratochvil 1968, 37; Urhobo data from John Kelly.
20. MacMahon, Simpson and Mason 1976; MacMahon and Simpson (forthcoming).
21. Anthony and Farquharson 1975; Williams, Farquharson and Anthony 1975.
22. Fromkin and Ladefoged 1966; Abbs and Watkin 1976.

273

23. Anthony 1954; Abercrombie 1957; Ladefoged 1957; Hardcastle 1972.
24. Fant 1968; Warren 1976.
25. Ladefoged 1975, 159–91; Potter, Kopp and Green 1947; Fant 1968.

Chapter 8

1. Term *allophone* invented by B.L. Whorf, see Jones 1967, 265, n.51.
2. It might be contended that phonetics also deals with form since it assumes equivalence between different speech-sounds; strictly speaking therefore we have a hierarchy of form.
3. Again the assumption of equivalence between speech-sounds; hence strictly speaking an allophone is not pronounceable, but only individual occurrences of it.
4. Gleason 1955, 61.
5. Jones 1967, 253.
6. Sapir in Mandelbaum 1963, 47. But we cannot assume that native speakers are oblivious to allophonic differences: many Germans (non-phoneticians) are aware of their *ach-Laut* [x] and *ich-Laut* [ç].
7. Allen 1974, 9.
8. Baudouin de Courtenay in Stankiewicz 1972, 149.
9. Jones 1967, 154.
10. Trubetzkoy 1969, 248.
11. Not every French-speaker will pronounce these sentences in this way.
12. Witness the scholars who talk on BBC London's Radio Three and on the programmes of the Open University (Milton Keynes, England).
13. Jones 1937.
14. e.g. see *Der Spiegel* (Hamburg) issue of 1 August 1977, 97.
15. Gimson 1962, 82.
16. Halliday 1966; O'Connor and Arnold 1973.
17. e.g. Bloomfield 1933, 131–5.
18. Whorf 1956, 223.
19. Based on tables by David Abercrombie, see Abercrombie 1979.
20. O'Connor 1973, Chapters 5 and 6.
21. Jones 1967, 30; Gimson 1962; MacCarthy 1944; Bloomfield 1933; Henderson 1971, 76; Trager and Smith 1951.
22. Trager and Smith 1951 may be taken as typical.
23. Trager and Smith 1951, 50–2.
24. This is termed *bi-uniqueness* in Chomsky 1964, 80. but cf. Joos 1942; We have used the principle in our exposition of phonemic theory, but problems may arise if one admits grammatical criteria, see Chapter 16. See further Chao 1934 and Bloch 1941.
25. Bloomfield 1933, 79, had already referred to phonemes as 'bundles' of 'distinctive features' but he apparently understood these in purely articulatory terms.
26. Phonetically final /z/ may be whispered, but that does not affect the argument. This is an instance of Trubetzkoy's 'vierter Fall', Trubetzkoy 1939, 74.
27. But see Henderson 1948.
28. Lyons 1962.
29. Firth 1948 in Firth 1957, 122; Ullendorff 1955, 158, n.3.

Chapter 9

1. Harris 1942, Harris 1946, Hockett 1947, Bloch 1947, Nida 1948 and Hockett 1954: all in Joos 1957.
2. Bloomfield 1933, 217 apropos French adjectives; a similar change could be made for Samoan passives, cf. Marsack 1962, 70.
3. Honey 1956 in Householder 1972, 279. ([ɡ] is a creaky-voiced unrounded open back vowel.)

4. Bloomfield 1933, 241.
5. See e.g. Thalbitzer in Boas 1911, quoted in Hill 1958, 438.
6. Wendt 1961, 321.
7. An expansion of Bloomfield's *minimum free form*, cf. Bloomfield 1926 in Joos 1957, 27; see Lyons 1968, 201ff.
8. Sapir 1921, 34.
9. Lyons 1968, 197.
10. Robins 1964, 224–5.
11. e.g. Fries 1957, 87–141; Honey 1956 in Householder 1972.
12. Fries 1957, 110; Honey 1956 in Householder 1972, 286; Hockett 1958, 224.
13. Hockett 1958, 225.
14. An exception is the *cognate accusative* tolerable with certain verbs: *He slept the sleep of the just*. A further difficulty is the noun in *He walked two miles*; is *walk* then a transitive verb?
15. For the completely opposite point of view, see Palmer 1971, 189.
16. Hockett 1958, 223.
17. Kwee 1965, 8.
18. Exceptions are found in Portuguese and in written mediaeval Venetian and in reflexive verbs in French, German and other languages.
19. A.W. Ward, see Grattan and Gurrey 1925, 211.
20. Carlo Cassola, *Il taglio del bosco*, Verona 1970, 179.
21. Bloomfield 1926 in Joos 1957, 28.
22. Bloomfield 1933, 172.
23. Wells 1947 in Joos 1957, 186ff; Gleason 1961, 128ff.
24. Various ways of displaying these relationships are found; we use that of Robins 1964.
25. e.g. Hill 1958.

Chapter 10

1. Bloch and Trager 1942, 79.
2. Lyons 1968, 135–7, discusses the various uses of *formal*.
3. Harris 1951, 3.
4. Harris 1951, 6.
5. e.g. Fries 1952; Hill 1957.
6. e.g. Moulton 1962; see Gage 1961.
7. Bloomfield 1933, 161; Harris 1951, 156; Hockett 1958, 123.
8. Hill 1958, 468.
9. Hill 1958, 90.
10. Hill 1958, 120.
11. Harris 1951, 12; Gleason 1961, 196; Hall 1964, 130.
12. Kuhn 1970.
13. Masterman in Lakatos and Musgrave 1970; Matthews 1974, 216; Hiorth 1974, 163; Botha 1975.

Chapter 11

1. For a discussion of the advantages of context-sensitive grammars, see Lyons 1968, 235–47.
2. Chomsky 1965, 69; but see Chapter 17 and Fillmore 1967 in Bach and Harms 1968, 33ff.
3. The sacrilege of adapting Chomsky's rules is not serious; in Chomsky 1957, 39, he deliberately formulates the rule that appears here as (10) in a different way so that he can argue for the present form of (10) and for (13). His treatment of verbal number applies only to the present tense, but it must clearly also apply to the past since he introduces *be*; hence the present (11) and (14), which in turn necessitate the present (18).
   Chomsky does not explain the provenance of NP_{an} and NP_{in} in (17), nor

do I. Attempts to incorporate syntactic features such as 'animate' and 'inanimate' satisfactorily into a grammar revealed difficulties, a solution to which was proposed by Chomsky some years later (see pp.226–9).

Chapter 12

1. Charles Dickens, *American notes*, repr. Oxford University Press 1957, 173.
2. See Lyons 1977, ii, 423.

Chapter 13

1. Chomsky 1957, 5.
2. *The Listener*, 29 July 1971, 141–5.
3. Chomsky 1967, 2–11.
4. Greene 1972, 107–38.
5. Slobin 1971, 41–66.
6. But this view has been challenged, see Chapter 18.
7. See the account of Bloomfield's view of meaning in Chapter 15.
8. Salmon 1969.
9. Bloomfield 1939; Chomsky's own M.A. thesis *Morphophonemics of modern Hebrew* (1951) contains a series of 42 ordered rules.
10. Harris 1957; Harris 1962.
11. Derwing 1973; Uhlenbeck 1973; Hiorth 1974; Robinson 1975; Hudson 1977.

Chapter 14

1. Trager 1949; cf. Lyons 1965, 14.
2. Lyons 1972, 73.
3. In his *Swain School Lectures*, quoted in Ogden and Richards 1923.
4. Abercrombie 1948, repr. In Abercrombie 1956.
5. i.e. the semantic fields and non-mystical culture-bound linguistic relativity expounded in Chapter 15.
6. Lyons 1972, 73–5.
7. Jakobson 1960, 350–77.
8. Austin 1962, paperback ed. 1971, 150.
9. Robinson 1972, *passim*.

Chapter 15

1. Ogden and Richards 1923, ch. 1; their terms are *symbol, thought* and *referent*.
2. Bloomfield 1933, 140.
3. A list of proferred definitions is given in Ogden and Richards 1923.
4. Luigi Pirandello *Sei personaggi in cerca d'autore*, 1921, ed. Silvio d'Amico 1958, Milan.
5. Malinowski 1923.
6. An interminable ball-game described by Mr Groucho Marx as 'an excellent cure for insomnia'.
7. See Thomas Gray *Elegy written in a country churchyard* and any history book concerning the Corsican Napoleone Buonaparte in 1815.
8. Bloomfield 1933, 28 and 142–3.
9. Bloomfield 1933, 26.
10. Bloomfield 1933, 139.
11. Bloomfield 1933, 33.
12. Malinowski 1923.
13. Boas 1911; Duncan Pryde *Nunaga: ten years of Eskimo life*, London 1972, 30–5, gives six other words for further types of snow and indicates that there are many more – this book also gives the lie to the legend prevalent among linguists that Eskimo, though diffused over a wide area, is dialectally remarkably homogeneous: such is apparently not the case.
14. Figure adapted from Berlin and Kay 1969, 22, 24, 31.
15. Sapir 1924 in Mandelbaum 1963, 153; Sapir 1921, 100; Sapir 1929 in Mandelbaum 1963, 162.

16. Whorf 1942 in Carroll 1956, 252.
17. Whorf 1941a in Carroll 1956, 243 (with altered transcription).
18. Whorf 1940 in Carroll 1956, 215.
19. Whorf 1940 in Carroll 1956, 216.
20. Whorf 1941b in Carroll 1956, 138–9 and 153.
21. Conklin 1955 in Hymes 1964, 191.
22. Graham in Verhaar 1967.
23. Lyons 1968, 443–70; Lyons 1977, 270 ff.
24. The writer once overheard a woman say of her pet 'That dog is a little monkey!'; she seemed unaware of the incongruity.
25. Lyons 1968, 435.
26. This is the area of topic, focus and presupposition, developed as functional sentence perspective by the Prague School (18.1) and found also in Chomsky (16.5) and Halliday (p.257). See ch. 16, n.46.

Chapter 16
1. Bloomfield 1939; Chomsky 1951; see 9.3; Hockett 1954.
2. Jones 1960, 217, 219–21.
3. Chomsky 1964; this problem had already been raised in Joos 1942, see Halle 1962.
4. Jakobson 1939.
5. Halle 1962 in Fodor and Katz 1964, 326–7.
6. Jakobson and Halle 1956, 42; Schane 1968, 21; Schane 1973, 26. See also Ladefoged 1971.
7. Based on Halle 1962 and Halle 1964, in Fodor and Katz 1964.
8. Halle 1964, in Fodor and Katz 1964, 339.
9. Pulgram 1959; Fant in Malmberg 1968, 173–7; Jakobson and Halle 1956, 31–49; Jakobson and Halle in Malmberg 1968, 411–49.
10. Jakobson, Fant and Halle 1951, 40.
11. Grinder and Elgin 1973, 193.
12. Chomsky and Halle 1968, 21.
13. Chomsky 1968, 37. This domain is 'in simple cases, the sentence itself'; presumably the 'simple cases' are of sentences not phonological domains. See 16.3 and 17.1 for other types of rule applied cyclically.
14. Chomsky and Halle 1968, 53.
15. e.g. Derwing 1973, especially chs 4, 5 and 6.
16. Chomsky and Halle 1968, 215.
17. Wang 1968. The rules in question is (33) on 243 of Chomsky and Halle 1968.
18. Schane 1968 recognises the necessity of postulating subsystems ('learned' v. 'unlearned') in French.
19. Katz and Fodor in Fodor and Katz 1964.
20. ibid. 486.
21. ibid. 500.
22. In Katz and Fodor's diagram these are parentheses, presumably a misprint; in their preceding Figure 4 they appear as the expected square brackets.
23. ibid. 501.
24. ibid. 504 (adapted).
25. ibid. 507.
26. ibid. 508.
27. ibid. 513.
28. ibid. 517.
29. Chomsky 1972, 66.
30. Katz and Postal 1964, 161.
31. Klima in Fodor and Katz 1964, 246–323.
32. Lees 1960.

33. Katz and Postal 1964, 30–1.
34. ibid. 157.
35. ibid. 54–5. The second sentence, containing *who . . . that* is not possible in the present writer's English, where the *that* must be deleted.
36. ibid. 47.
37. Chomsky 1965 4.
38. ibid. 9.
39. ibid. 79.
40. ibid. 82.
41. ibid. 94.
42. ibid. 164.
43. ibid. 159.
44. ibid 132.
45. Chomsky 1964, 9.
46. Interest in this type of distinction (*functional sentence perspective*) has been a feature of Prague School linguists, at least since Mathesius 1924 and Mathesius 1939. Developments have been made in the past two decades by a group of younger members, in particular Jan Firbas, and their work has found many followers in the Soviet Union (e.g. Raspopov) and Germany (e.g. Boost). Western scholars have recently given attention to this important area of investigation, e.g. Halliday 1967a, 1967b, 1968 and 1970.

Chapter 17
1. Lakoff in Steinberg and Jakobovits 1971, 236.
2. McCawley in Bach and Harms 1968, 165.
3. Lakoff 1970, 32–40.
4. Bach in Bach and Harms 1968, 117.
5. ibid. 117–21.
6. Lyons 1966.
7. Postal in Fillmore and Langendoen 1971, 233.
8. McCawley 1970.
9. Postal in Fillmore and Langendoen 1971, 236.
10. ibid. 246.
11. ibid. 249.
12. McCawley in Bach and Harms 1968, 155–61.
13. ibid. 158, developed from an idea in Thorne 1966.
14. Bach and Harms 1968, viii.
15. Lakoff in Steinberg and Jakobovits 1971, 234.
16. McCawley in Steinberg and Jakobovits 219 and 222 ff.
17. Bach in Bach and Harms 1968, 114.
18. Chomsky 1965, 71–2.
19. ibid. 106–9.
20. Fillmore in Bach and Harms 1968, 24–5. He revised it in Fillmore 1970.
21. Note particularly the definition and examples of dative. Note also that Fillmore adopts the view that verbs and adjectives represent the same deep structure element.
22. Presumably also *to* and *into*, e.g. *His delight changed to disappointment* and *Some years ago the Chaplain turned the Dean into a pumpkin.*
23. It might be argued that Spanish lacks objectivalisation in view of the regular *Veo la casa* (O) 'I see the house' but *Veo a María* (D) 'I see Mary'; *a* is the typical D marker in Spanish.
    It would seem that every underlying case in English (including T e.g. *Monday was very stormy*) except B can function as surface subject; **The Emperor was built the palace* seems not possible.
24. This is seen in the Italian adnominal D *mia madre* 'my mother' versus the

alienable *la mia cantina* 'my cellar'; however, *la loro madre* 'their mother' and
la mia nonna 'my grandmother' are the regular forms when *loro* or *nonna* are
involved.

25. Anderson 1971.
26. Chomsky 1972 70; Lakoff in Steinberg and Jakobovits 1971, 237.
27. Chomsky in Jacobs and Rosenbaum 1970, reprinted in Chomsky 1972, 11–61.
28. Chomsky 1975. All semantic interpretation now occurs at surface level.

Chapter 18

1. Chomsky 1968, 251.
2. Kiparsky 1968.
3. Fischer 1958.
4. Labov 1966.
5. Labov 1963.
6. Wang 1969, 9–25; Chen and Wang 1975, 255–81.
7. Sherman 1973, 46–82.
8. Altmann 1967; Barry 1965, 32–47; von Frisch 1967; Gardner and Gardner
   1969; Hayes and Hayes 1952; Norris 1966; Premack 1970.
9. e.g. Morris 1967; Morris 1969; Tiger and Fox 1972.
10. von Frisch 1967.
11. Hockett 1958, 574–85.
12. Linden 1957.
13. Russell and Russell 1971, repr. 1973, 185.
14. Shannon and Weaver 1949.
15. (This was known to printers and journalists long before information theory, see
    E.A. Poe's stories *The gold-bug* and *X-ing a paragrab*.) Chao 1968, 170–3; cf.
    Classe 1957.
16. Corder 1973, 10.
17. Error analysis must of course be based on an adequate linguistic theory, though
    it goes beyond it.
18. Fant in Malmberg 1968, 173–277.
19. Nida and Taber 1969.
20. Steiner 1975.
21. Ladefoged 1975, 187–9; Hollien 1974.
22. Halmos 1968.
23. Simpson 'Oscillation and language-change' (forthcoming).
24. *The Listener*, 24 February 1977, 236.
25. Popper 1963, 4th ed. 1972, 152–3.

Bibliography

ABBS, James H. and WATKIN, Kenneth L. (1976) 'Instrumentation for the study of speech physiology' in Lass.

ABERCROMBIE, David
  (1948) 'Linguistics and the teacher' repr. in Abercrombie 1956.
  (1956) *Problems and principles in language study*, London.
  (1957) 'Direct palatography' *Zeitschrift für Phonetik* 10, 21–5.
  (1964a) 'A phonetician's view of verse structure' *Linguistics* 6, 5–13, repr. in Abercrombie 1965.
  (1964b) 'Syllable quantity and enclitics in English' in Abercrombie et al., repr. in Abercrombie 1965.
  (1965) *Studies in phonetics and linguistics*, London.
  (1967) *Elements of general phonetics*, Edinburgh.
  (1971) 'Some functions of silent stress' in Aitken et al.
  (1979) 'The English we speak in Scotland' in Aitken and Macarthur.

ABERCROMBIE, et al., eds (1964) *In honour of Daniel Jones*, London.

AELIUS DONATUS (1926) *Ars Minor of Donatus: for one thousand years the leading textbook of grammar*, trans. W.J. Chase, Madison.

AITCHISON, Jean (1976) *The articulate mammal*, London.

AITKEN, A.J. et al., eds (1971) *Edinburgh studies in English and Scots*, London.

AITKEN, A. J. and MACARTHUR, Tom, eds (1979) *The languages of Scotland*, Edinburgh.

ALLEN, J.P.B. and van BUREN, P. eds (1971) *Chomsky: selected readings*, London.

ALLEN, W.S.
  (1953) *Phonetics in Ancient India*, London.
  (1974) *Vox graeca* (2nd ed.) Cambridge.

ALTMANN, S.A., ed. (1967) *Social communication among primates*, Chicago.

ANDERSON, James M. (1973) *Structural aspects of language change*, London.

ANDERSON, John M. (1971) *The grammar of case: towards a localistic theory*, Cambridge.

ANDERSON, S.R. and KIPARSKY, P., eds (1973) *A festschrift for Morris Halle*, New York.

ANDRUS de LAGUNA, Grace (1927) *Speech: its function and development*, repr. Bloomington 1963.

ANTHONY, J. (1954) 'New method for investigating tongue positions of consonants' *Science Technologists' Bulletin*, Oct–Nov., 2–5..

ANTHONY, J. and FARQUHARSON, I.M. (1975) 'Clinical research in speech pathology' *Journal of laryngology and otology*, LXXXIX, 12.

280

Bibliography

ARENS, Hans (1969) *Sprachwissenschaft: der Gang ihrer Entwicklung von der Antike bis zur Gegenwart*, (2nd ed.) Munich.

ARLOTTO, Anthony (1972) *Introduction to historical linguistics*, New York.

ARNAULD, A. and LANCELOT, C. (1660) *Grammaire générale et raisonnée*, repr. Paris 1969, with intro. by Michel Foucault.

AUSTIN, J.L. (1962) *How to do things with words*, London, repr. 1971.

BACH, Emmon
(1964) *An introduction to transformational grammars*, New York.
(1968) 'Nouns and noun phrases' in Bach and Harms.

BACH, E. and HARMS, R.T. (1968) *Universals in linguistic theory*, New York.

BACON, Roger (1902) *The Greek grammar of Roger Bacon and a fragment of his Hebrew Grammar*, ed. Edmond Nolan and S.A. Hirsch, Cambridge.

BARRY, Gerald et al., eds (1965) *Communication and language*, London.

BARTHES, Roland (1967) *Elements of semiology*, trans. A. Lavers and C. Smith, London.

BATTAGLIA, S. and PERNICONE, V. (1954) *Grammatica italiana*, Turin.

BAUDOUIN DE COURTENAY, Jan (1895) 'An attempt at a theory of phonetic alternations', German original, trans. in Stankiewicz 1972.

BAZELL, C. E. (1952) 'The correspondence fallacy in structural linguistics' *Studies by members of the English Department, Istanbul University* 3, 1–41, repr. in ed. Hamp 1966, 271–98.

BAZELL, C.E. et al., eds (1966) *In memory of J.R. Firth*, London.

BECANUS, J. Goropius (1569) *Origines Antwerpianae*, Antwerp.

BERLIN, B. and KAY, P. (1969) *Basic colour terms: their universality and evolution*, California.

BERRY, Margaret (1975) *An introduction to systemic linguistics*, vol. 1, *Structures and systems*, vol. 2 (1977) *Levels and links*, London.

BEVER, T.G., KATZ, J.J. and LANGENDOEN, D.T., eds (1977) *An integrated theory of linguistic ability*, Hassocks, England.

BLOCH, Bernard
(1941) 'Phonemic overlapping' repr. in Joos 1957.
(1947) 'English verb inflection' *Language* 23, 399–418, repr. in Joos 1957.

BLOCH, Bernard and TRAGER, George L. (1942) *Outline of linguistic analysis*, Baltimore.

BLOOMFIELD, Leonard
(1926) 'A set of postulates for the science of language' *Language* 2, 153–64, repr. in Joos 1957.
(1933) *Language*, Chicago; London 1935, repr. 1970.
(1939) 'Menomini morphophonemics' *Travaux du cercle linguistique de Prague* 8, 105–15, repr. in V. Makkai 1972.

BOAS, Franz, ed. (1911) *Handbook of American Indian Languages*, Bulletin 40, Part 1, Bureau of American Ethnology, Washington. Intro. by Boas repr. in Boas and Powell 1966.

BOAS, Franz and POWELL, J.W. (1966) Introduction to *Handbook of American Indian languages* and *Indian linguistic families of America north of Mexico*, repr. Lincoln, Nebraska.

281

BOLINGER, Dwight, ed. (1972) *Intonation*, London.

BONFANTE, G. (1947) 'The neolinguistic position' *Language* 23, IV, 344–75.

BOPP, Franz (1856) *A comparative grammar of the Sanskrit, Zend, Greek, Latin, Lithuanian, Gothic, German and Sclavonic languages*, trans. E.B. Eastwick (2nd ed.), London.

BOTHA, R.P. (1973) (with the collaboration of W.K. Winckler) *The justification of linguistic hypotheses: a study of nondemonstrative inference in transformational grammar*, The Hague.

BREND, Ruth M., ed. (1974) *Advances in tagmemics*, Amsterdam.

BRONSTEIN, A.J. (1960) *The pronunciation of American English*, New York.

BRUGMANN, K. and DELBRÜCK, B. (1897) *Grundriß der vergleichenden Grammatik der indogermanischen Sprachen* (2nd ed.) Strasburg, vol. I.

BULLOKAR, William (1586) *Bref grammar for English*, London, repr. Berlin 1906 in Max Plessow *Geschichte der Fabeldichtung in England bis zu J. Gay*.

BURNETT, James, Lord Monboddo (1773) *Origin and progress of language*, 6 vols. Edinburgh 1773–6.

BURT, M.K. (1971) *From deep to surface structure: an introduction to transformational syntax*, New York.

BYNON, Theodora (1977) *Historical linguistics*, Cambridge.

CARROLL, John B., ed. (1956) *Language, thought and reality: selected writings of Benjamin Lee Whorf*, Cambridge, Mass.

CASSIRER, Ernst (1946) *Language and myth*, trans. S.K. Langer, New York, republished 1953.

CATFORD, J.C.
(1964) 'Phonation types: the classification of some laryngeal components of speech production' in Abercrombie et al.
(1968) 'The articulatory possibilities of man' in Malmberg.
(1977) *Fundamental problems in phonetics*, Edinburgh.

CATON, Charles E. (1963) *Philosophy and ordinary language*, Urbana.

CHAO, Yuen Ren
(1934) 'The non-uniqueness of phonemic solutions of phonetic systems' *Bulletin of the institute of history and philology, Academia Sinica*, IV, 4, 363–97, repr. in Joos.
(1968) *Language and symbolic systems*, Cambridge.

CHAPPELL, V.C., ed. (1964) *Ordinary language*, New Jersey.

CHEN, Matthew Y. and WANG, W.S.-Y. (1975) 'Sound change: actuation and implementation' in *Language* 51, 255–81.

CHERRY, Colin (1957) *On human communication*, repr. New York 1963.

CHOMSKY, Noam
(1951) 'Morphophonemics of modern Hebrew', M.A. thesis (unpubl.).
(1957) *Syntactic structures*, The Hague.
(1964) *Current issues in linguistic theory*, The Hague.
(1965) *Aspects of the theory of syntax*, Cambridge, Mass.
(1967) 'Recent contributions to the theory of innate ideas' *Synthese* 17c, 2–11, repr. in ed. Hudson 1970.
(1968) *Language and mind*, New York.
(1972) *Studies on semantics in generative grammar*, The Hague.

Bibliography

(1975) 'Questions of form and interpretation' *Linguistic analysis* I, 75–109.

(1976) *Reflections on language*, London.

CHOMSKY, Noam and HALLE, Morris (1968) *The sound pattern of English*, New York.

CLASSE, André (1957) 'Phonetics of the silbo Gomero' *Archivum linguisticum* 9, 44–61.

COBBETT, William (1819) *Grammar of the English language*, London, repr. with additions 1826.

CONDILLAC, Étienne Bonnot de
(1746) *Essai sur l'origine des connoissances humaines*, Paris.
(1798) *La langue des calculs*, repr. Paris 1803.

CONKLIN, H.C. (1955) 'Hanunóo color categories' *Southwestern Journal of Anthropology*, 11, 339–44, repr. in Hymes 1964.

CONWAY, R. Seymour (1887) *Verner's law in Italy*, London.

COOK, Walter A. (1969) *Introduction to tagmemic analysis*, London.

COOPER, David E. (1972) *Philosophy and ordinary language*, London.

CORDER, S. Pit (1973) *Introducing applied linguistics*, London.

CRYSTAL, David
(1969) *Prosodic systems and intonation in English*, Cambridge.
(1971) *Linguistics*, London.

CULLER, Jonathan (1976) *Saussure*, London.

DANTE ALIGHIERI (1890) *De vulgari eloquentia*, trans. A.F.G. Howell, London.

DERWING, B.L. (1973) *Transformational grammar as a theory of language acquisition*, Cambridge.

DINNEEN, Francis P. (1967) *An introduction to general linguistics*, New York.

DIOGENES LAERTIUS (1925) *Lives of eminent philosophers*, trans. R.D. Hicks, 2 vols., repr. 1970.

DIONYSIUS THRAX (1883) *Dionysii Thracis ars grammatica qualem vetustissima exhibent*, ed. G. Uhlig, Leipzig.

DURKHEIM, Emile (1895) *Règles de la méthode sociologique*, Paris.

ELLIS, A.J. (1871) *On early English pronunciation*, Part III, London.

FANT, Gunnar (1968) 'Analysis and synthesis of speech processes' in Malmberg.

FILLMORE, C.J.
(1963) 'The position of embedding transformations in a grammar' *Word* 19, 208–31.
(1968) 'The case for case' in Bach and Harms.
(1970) 'Types of lexical information' repr. in Steinberg and Jakobovits 1971.

FILLMORE, Charles J. and LANGENDOEN, Terence T. eds (1971) *Studies in linguistic semantics*, New York.

FIRBAS, Jan
(1962) 'Notes on the function of the sentence in the act of communication' *Sborník prací filosofické fakulty brněnské university*, A10, 133–48.

283

Bibliography

(1964a) 'From comparative word-order studies' *Brno studies in English* 4, 111–28.

(1964b) 'On defining the theme in functional sentence analysis' *Travaux linguistiques de Prague* I, 267–80.

(1965) 'A note on transition proper in function sentence analysis' *Philologica Pragensia* 8, 170–6.

(1966) 'Non-thematic subjects in contemporary English' *Travaux linguistiques de Prague* 2, 239–56.

(1967) 'It was yesterday that . . .' *Sborník prací filosofické fakulty brněnské university*, A15, 141–6.

FIRTH, J.R.

(1935) 'The use and distribution of certain English sounds' *English Studies*, XVII, 1, repr. in Firth 1957.

(1937) *The tongues of men*, London, repr. 1964.

(1957) *Papers in linguistics 1934–1951*, London.

FISCHER, J.L. (1958) 'Social influence on the choice of a linguistic variant' *Word* 14, 47–56.

FISCHER-JØRGENSEN, Eli (1975) *Trends in phonological theory*, Copenhagen.

FODOR, J.A. and KATZ, J.J., eds (1964) *The structure of language: readings in the philosophy of language*, Englewood Cliffs, N.J.

FRIES, C.C. (1957) *The structure of English: an introduction to the construction of English sentences*, London.

FRISCH, Karl von (1967) *The dance and orientation of bees*, trans. L.E. Chadwick, London.

FROMKIN, V.A. and LADEFOGED, P. (1966) 'Electromyography in speech research' *Phonetica* 15, 219–42.

FUDGE, Erik C., ed. (1973) *Phonology*, London.

GARDNER, R.A. and GARDNER, B.T. (1969) 'Teaching sign language to a chimpanzee' *Science* 165, 664–72.

GARVIN, Paul L. and SPOLSKY, Bernard (1966) *Computation in linguistics: a case book*, Bloomington.

GELLNER, Ernest (1974) *Legitimation of belief*, London.

GESENIUS, Wilhelm (1833) *Lexicon manuale Hebraicum et Chaldaicum in veteris testamenti libros*, Leipzig.

GIMSON, A.C. (1962) *An introduction to the pronunciation of English*, London, 2nd ed. 1970.

GLEASON, Henry Allan

(1955a) *Workbook in descriptive linguistics*, New York, repr. 1964.

(1955b) *An introduction to descriptive linguistics*, New York, 2nd ed. 1961.

GRAHAM, A.C. (1967) '"Being" in Classical Chinese' in Verhaar.

GRATTAN, J.N.G. and GURREY, P. (1925) *Our living language: a new guide to English grammar*, London.

GREENBERG, Joseph H. (1957) *Essays in linguistics*, Chicago.

GREENE, Judith (1972) *Psycholinguistics: Chomsky and psychology*, London.

GRIMM, Jakob (1822) *Deutsche Grammatik*, I (2nd ed.), II–IV, Göttingen 1822–37.

GRINDER, J.T. and ELGIN, S.H. (1973) *Guide to transformational grammar*, New York.

GUICHARD, Étienne (1606) *L'harmonie étymologique des langues hébräique, chaldäique, syriaque, grèque, latine, françoise, italienne, espagnole, allemande, flamende, angloise*, Paris.

GUIRAUD, Pierre (1975) *Semiology*, trans. G. Cross, London.

GUSSENHOVEN, C. and BROEDERS, A. (1976) *The pronunciation of English*, Groningen.

HACKING, Ian (1975) *Why does language matter to philosophy?*, Cambridge.

HALL, R.A. (1964) *Introductory linguistics*, Philadelphia.

HALLE, Morris
(1962) 'Phonology in generative grammar' *Word* 18, 54–72, repr. in Fodor and Katz 1964.
(1964) 'On the bases of phonology' in Fodor and Katz.

HALLIDAY, M.A.K.
(1961) 'Categories of the theory of grammar' *Word* 17, no. 3, 241–92, repr. Indianapolis (n.d.).
(1963) 'Intonation systems in English', repr. in McIntosh and Halliday.
(1966) 'Some notes on "deep" grammar' *Journal of linguistics* 2, 57–67.
(1967a) 'Notes on transitivity and theme in English', Part I, *Journal of linguistics* 3, 37–81.
(1967b) 'Notes on transitivity and theme in English', Part II, *Journal of linguistics* 3, 199–244.
(1968) 'Notes on transitivity and theme in English', Part III, *Journal of linguistics* 4, 179–215.
(1970) 'Language structure and language function' in Lyons.
(1973) *Explorations in the functions of language*, London.

HALMOS, P.R. (1968) 'Mathematics as a creative art' *American scientist* 56, 4, 375–89.

HAMP, Eric P. (1966) *A glossary of American technical linguistic usage 1925–1950*, Utrecht.

HARDCASTLE, W.J.
(1970) 'Electropalatography in speech research' *Occasional Papers*, University of Essex Language Centre 9, 54–64.
(1972) 'The use of electropalatography in phonetic research' *Phonetica* 25, 197–215.
(1976) *Physiology of speech production*, London.

HARRIS, Zellig S.
(1942) 'Morpheme alternants in linguistic analysis' *Language* 18, 169–80, repr. in Joos 1957.
(1946) 'From morpheme to utterance' *Language* 22, 161–83, repr. in Joos 1957.
(1951) *Methods in structural linguistics*, Chicago; retitled *Structural linguistics*, 6th impression 1963.
(1957) 'Co-occurrence and transformation in linguistic structure' *Language* 33, 283–340.
(1962) *String analysis of sentence structure*, The Hague.

285

HAUGEN, Einar (1951) 'Directions in modern linguistics' *Language* 27, 211–22, repr. in Joos 1957.

HAYAKAWA, S.J. (1965) *Language in thought and action*, 2nd ed., London.

HAYES, K.G. and HAYES, C. (1952) 'Imitation in a home-raised chimpanzee' *Journal of comparative physiology and psychology* 45, 450–9.

HENDERSON, E.J.A. (1949) 'Prosodies in Siamese: a study in synthesis' *Asia major* (New series) I, 189–215, repr. in Palmer 1970, and Jones and Laver 1973.

HENDERSON, E.J.A., ed. (1971) *The indispensable foundation: a selection from the writings of Henry Sweet*, London.

HERDER, Johann Gottfried (1772) *Abhandlung über den Ursprung der Sprache*, repr. in *Herder's Sämmtliche Werke* V, Berlin 1891.

HERODOTUS (1954) *The histories*, trans. Aubrey de Selincourt, London.

HETZRON, Robert (1972) *Ethiopic Semitic: studies in classification*, Manchester.

HEYSE, Karl (1856) *System der Sprachwissenschaft*, ed. H. Steinthal, Berlin.

HILL, Archibald A. (1958) *Introduction to linguistic structures: from sound to sentence in English*, New York.

HINDE, R.A., ed. (1972) *Non-verbal communication*, Cambridge.

HIORTH, F. (1974) *Noam Chomsky, linguistics and philosophy*, Oslo.

HJEMSLEV, Louis
(1936) 'Essai d'une théorie des morphèmes' in *Proceedings of the IVth international congress of linguistics 1936*, Copenhagen 1938.
(1953) *Prolegomena to a theory of language*, trans. Francis J. Whitfield, Madison, Wisconsin, revised 1961.

HOCKETT, Charles F.
(1942) 'A system of descriptive phonology' *Language* 18, 3–21, repr. in Joos 1957.
(1947) 'Problems of morphemic analysis' *Language* 23, 212–26, repr. in Joos 1957.
(1954) 'Two models of grammatical description *Word* 10, 210–31, repr. in Joos 1957.
(1958) *A course in modern linguistics*, New York.
(1967) *Language, mathematics and linguistics*, The Hague.
(1968) *The state of the art*, The Hague.

HOLLIEN, Harry (1974) 'Peculiar case of "voiceprints"' *Journal of Acoustical Society of America* 56, no. 1, 210–13.

HONEY, P.J. (1956) 'Word classes in Vietnamese' in *Bulletin of the School of Oriental and African Studies* 18, 534–44, repr. in Householder 1972.

HONIKMAN, Beatrice (1964) 'Articulatory settings' in Abercrombie et al.

HOUSEHOLDER, Fred W. (1971) *Linguistic speculations*, Cambridge.

HOUSEHOLDER, Fred W., ed. (1972) *Syntactic theory 1: structuralist*, London.

HUDSON, Liam (1970) *The ecology of human intelligence*, London.

HUDSON, R.A. (1977) *Arguments for a non-transformational grammar*, Chicago.

HUMBOLDT, Wilhelm von (1841–52) *Gesammelte Werke*, I–VII, Berlin.

286

Bibliography

HUMPHREYS, G.S. (1945) *Teach yourself English grammar*, London, repr. 1967.

HYMES, D., ed. (1964) *Language in culture and society: a reader in linguistics and anthropology*, New York.

ISAČENKO, A.V. (1948) 'On the conative function of language' Russian original in *Recueil linguistique de Bratislava* I, 45–57, trans. in Vachek 1966b.

IVIČ, Milka (1963) *Trends in linguistics*, Serbo-Croatian original, trans. Muriel Heppell, The Hague 1965.

JACKENDOFF, Ray (1972) *Semantic interpretation in a generative grammar*, Cambridge, Mass.

JACOBS, R.A. and ROSENBAUM, P.S. (1968) *English transformational grammar*, London

JACOBS, R.A. and ROSENBAUM, P.S., eds (1970) *Readings in English transformational grammar*, Waltham, Mass.

JAKOBOVITS, Leon A. and MIRON, Murray S., eds (1967) *Readings in the psychology of language*, Englewood Cliffs.

JAKOBSON, Roman

(1931) 'Prinzipien der historischen Phonologie' *Travaux du cercle linguistique de Prague* 4, 247–67, repr. (in French) as an appendix to Cantineau's translation of Trubetzkoy 1939 and repr. in Jakobson 1962, I, 202–20.

(1939) 'Observations sur le classement phonologique des consonnes' in *Proceedings of the third international congress of phonetic sciences*, Ghent, repr. in Jakobson 1962, I, 272–9.

(1960) 'Linguistics and poetics' in Sebeok.

(1962) *Selected works*, The Hague.

(1973) *Main trends in the science of language*, London.

JAKOBSON, Roman, FANT, C.G.M. and HALLE, Morris (1951) *Preliminaries to speech analysis*, Cambridge, Mass., repr. 1969.

JAKOBSON, Roman and HALLE, Morris

(1956) *Fundamentals of language*, The Hague, 2nd ed. 1971.

(1968) 'Phonology in relation to phonetics' in Malmberg.

JANKOWSKY, Kurt R. (1972) *The neogrammarians*, The Hague.

JESPERSEN, Otto (1922) *Language, its nature, development and origin*, London, repr. 1949.

JÓHANNESSON, Alexander (1949) *Origin of language*, Reykjavík.

JOHNSON, Samuel (1975) *Dictionary of the English language . . . to which are prefixed, a history of the language, and an English grammar*, London.

JONES, Daniel

(1937) 'On received pronunciation', Supplement to *Le Maître phonétique*, April–June.

(1960) *An outline of English phonetics*, 9th ed., Cambridge.

(1967) *The phoneme*, 3rd ed., London.

(1967) *English pronouncing dictionary*, 13th ed., London.

JONES, W.E. and LAVER, J. eds (1973) *Phonetics in linguistics: a book of readings*, London.

Bibliography

JONES, Sir William
(1786) 'The third anniversary discourse, on the Hindus, delivered 2nd of February 1786' in Jones 1799, I, 19–34.
(1799) *The works of Sir William Jones*, 6 vols., London.

JONSON, Ben (1640) *The English grammar*, in *The workes of Benjamin Jonson*, London.

JOOS, Martin (1942) 'A phonological dilemma in Canadian English' *Language* 18, 141–4.

JOOS, Martin, ed. (1957) *Readings in linguistics*, Washington, repr. as *Readings in linguistics I*, Chicago 1966.

KATZ, Jerrold J. (1972) *Linguistic philosophy: the underlying reality of language and its philosophical import*, London.

KATZ, J.J. and FODOR, J.A. (1963) 'The structure of a semantic theory' *Language* 39, 170–210, repr. in Fodor and Katz 1964 and in Rosenberg and Travis 1971.

KATZ, J.J. and POSTAL, P.M. (1964) *An integrated theory of linguistic descriptions*, Cambridge, Mass.

KAVANAGH, James F. and CUTTING, James E., eds (1975) *The role of speech in language*, Cambridge, Mass.

KENYON, J.S. (1946) *American pronunciation* (9th ed.) Ann Arbor.

KESS, Joseph F. (1976) *Psycholinguistics: introductory perspectives*, New York.

KILMISTER, C.W. (1967) *Language, logic and mathematics*, London.

KING, Robert D. (1969) *Historical linguistics and generative grammar*, Englewood Cliffs, N.J.

KINGDON, Roger (1964) 'The representation of vowels' in Abercrombie et al.

KIPARSKY, Paul (1968) 'Linguistic universals and linguistic change' in Bach and Harms.

KLIMA, E.S. (1964) 'Negation in English' in Fodor and Katz.

KOERNER, E.F.K. (1973) *Ferdinand de Saussure: origin and development of his linguistic thought in western studies of language*, Braunschweig.

KOUTSOUDAS, A. (1966) *Writing transformational grammars: an introduction*, New York.

KRATOCHVIL, Paul (1968) *The Chinese language today*, London.

KUHN, Thomas (1970) *The structure of scientific revolutions*, (2nd ed.) Chicago.

KURYŁOWICZ, Jerzy (1964) *The inflectional categories of Indo-European*, Heidelberg.

KWEE, John B. (1965) *Teach yourself Indonesian*, London.

LABOV, William
(1963) 'The social motivation for a sound change' *Language* 19, 273–309.
(1966) *The social stratification of English in New York City*, Washington.

LADEFOGED, Peter
(1957) 'Use of palatography' *Journal of speech and hearing disorders*, 22, no.5.
(1964) *A phonetic study of West African languages*, Cambridge.
(1967) *Three areas of experimental phonetics*, London.

288

(1971) *Preliminaries to linguistic phonetics*, Chicago.

(1975) *A course in phonetics*, New York.

LAKATOS, I. and MUSGRAVE, A. eds (1970) *Criticism and the growth of knowledge*, Cambridge.

LAKOFF, George

(1970) *Irregularity in syntax*, New York

(1971) 'On generative semantics' in Steinberg and Jakobovits.

LAMB, Sidney M. (1962) *Outline of stratificational grammar*, rev. ed. Washington 1966.

LANGENDOEN, D.T. (1968) *The London school of linguistics: a study of the linguistic theories of B. Malinowski and J.R. Firth*, Cambridge, Mass.

LANGER, Susanne (1962) *Philosophical sketches*, Baltimore.

LASS, Norman J., ed. (1976) *Contemporary issues in experimental phonetics*, New York.

LAVER, John and HUTCHESON, Sandy, eds (1972) *Communication in face to face interaction*, London.

LEECH, Geoffrey (1974) *Semantics*, London.

LEES, R.B. (1960) *The grammar of English nominalisations*, Bloomington.

LEHMANN, W.P.

(1967) *A reader in nineteenth-century historical Indo-European linguistics*, Indiana.

(1973) *Historical linguistics: an introduction*, 2nd ed., New York.

LEHMANN, W.P. and MALKIEL, Yakov, eds (1968) *Directions for historical linguistics*, Austin.

LEPSCHY, Giulio C. (1970) *A survey of structural linguistics*, London.

LEROY, Maurice (1967) *The main trends in modern linguistics*, trans. Glanville Price, Oxford.

LESTER, M., ed. (1970) *Readings in applied transformational grammar*, New York.

LINDEN, Eugene (1974) *Apes, men and language*, New York.

LLORACH, Emilio Alarcos (1951) *Gramática estructural según la escuela de Copenhague y con especial atención a la lengua española*, repr. Madrid 1969.

LOCKWOOD, David G. (1972) *Introduction to stratificational linguistics*, New York.

LOCKWOOD, W.B. (1972) *A panorama of Indo-European languages*, London.

LOWTH, Robert (1762) *A short introduction to English grammar*, London, repr. 1787.

LYONS, John

(1962) 'Phonemic and non-phonemic phonology: some typological reflections' *International journal of American linguistics*, 28, no.2, 127–33, repr. in Jones and Laver 1973.

(1965) 'The scientific study of language' University of Edinburgh Inaugural Lecture, no.24.

(1966a) 'Firth's theory of "meaning"' in Bazell.

(1966b) 'Towards a "notional" theory of the "parts of speech"' *Journal of Linguistics* 2, 209–36.

(1968) *Introduction to theoretical linguistics*, Cambridge.

Bibliography

(1970) *Chomsky*, London.
(1972) 'Human language' in Hinde.
(1977) *Semantics* (2 vols.), Cambridge.
LYONS, John, ed. (1970) *New horizons in linguistics*, London.
MACCARTHY, P.A.D. (1944) *English pronunciation*, Cambridge.
McCAWLEY, J.D.
   (1968) 'The role of semantics in a grammar' in Bach and Harms.
   (1970) 'English as a VSO language' *Language* 46, 286–99.
   (1971) 'Where do noun phrases come from?' in Steinberg and Jakobovits.
McCLURE, J.D. (1972) 'A suggested revision for the cardinal vowel system' *Journal of the International Phonetic Association* 2, no.1.
McINTOSH, Angus and HALLIDAY, M.A.K. (1966) *Patterns of language: papers in general, descriptive and applied linguistics*, London.
MACMAHON, M.K.C. and SIMPSON, J.M.Y.
   (forthcoming, a) *The blue film of Arthur*, Glasgow.
   (forthcoming, b) *More blue film of Arthur*, Glasgow.
   (forthcoming, c) *Preliminary conclusions from examining X-ray video-tapes of English language articulations*, Glasgow.
MACMAHON, M.K.C., SIMPSON, J.M.Y. and MASON, W.R. (1976) *The inside story of Arthur*, videotape, Glasgow. (Ref. no. IVC/9/76/8A)
MAKKAI, Adam and LOCKWOOD, David G. (1973) *Readings in stratificational linguistics*, Alabama.
MAKKAI, Valerie Becker, ed. (1972) *Phonological theory: evolution and current practice*, New York.
MALINOWSKI, Bronislaw (1923) 'The problem of meaning in primitive languages', Supplement to Ogden and Richards.
MALMBERG, Bertil (1963) *Phonetics*, New York.
MALMBERG, Bertil, ed. (1968) *Manual of phonetics*, Amsterdam.
MANDELBAUM, D.G., ed. (1963) *Selected writings of Edward Sapir*, Berkeley.
MARSACK, C.C. (1962) *Teach yourself Samoan*, London.
MARTINET, André
   (1949) *Phonology as functional phonetics*, Oxford, repr. 1955.
   (1960) *Eléments de linguistique générale*, trans. E. Palmer as *Elements of general linguistics*, London 1964.
   (1962) *A functional view of language*, Oxford.
MASTERMAN, Margaret (1970) 'The nature of a paradigm' in Lakatos and Musgrave.
MATHESIUS, Vilém
   (1911) 'On the potentiality of the phenomena of language', repr. in Vachek 1966b.
   (1924) 'Několik poznámek o funkci podmětu v moderní angličtině' ['Some notes on the function of the subject in modern English'] in *Časopis pro moderní filologii* 10, 244–88.
   (1928) 'On linguistic characterology, with illustrations from modern English' in Vachek 1966b.
   (1939) 'Verstärkung und Emphase' in Vachek 1966b.

MATSUMURA, Yoshihiro and SIMPSON, J.M.Y., eds (forthcoming) *Varieties of English*, Edinburgh.

MATTHEWS, Peter H. (1974) *Morphology: an introduction to the theory of word structure*, Cambridge.

MEILLET, Antoine (1925) *La méthode comparative en linguistique*, Oslo.

MENZERATH, P. and LACERDA, A. de (1933) *Koartikulation, Steuerung und Lautabgrenzung*, Berlin and Bonn.

MICHAEL, Ian (1970) *English grammatical categories and the tradition to 1800*, Cambridge.

MINNIS, Noel, ed. (1971) *Linguistics at large*, London, paperback 1973.

MITCHELL, T.F. (1969) Review of Abercrombie 1967 *Journal of linguistics* 5, 153–64.

MOHRMANN, C. et al., eds
(1963a) *Trends in European and American linguistics 1930–1960*, Utrecht 1963.
(1963b) *Trends in modern linguistics*, Utrecht.

MORRIS, Desmond
(1967) *The naked ape*, London.
(1969) *The human zoo*, London.

MUIR, James (1972) *A modern approach to English grammar*, London.

MULDER, J.W.F. (1968) *Set and relations in phonology: an axiomatic approach to the description of speech*, Oxford.

MULDER, J.W.F. and HERVEY, S.G.J. (1973) 'Postulates for axiomatic functionalism', presented in Groningen 1973 (mimeographed).

MULDER, J.W.F. and HURREN, H.A. (1968) 'The English vowel phonemes from a functional point of view and a statement of their distribution' *La linguistique*, I, 43–60.

MÜLLER, Max (1862) *Lectures on the science of language*, 3rd ed., London.

MURATORI, C. (1949) 'A linguistic curiosity in Equatoria Province' *Sudan notes and records*, XXX, Part 1, Khartoum.

MURRAY, (1814) *English grammar*, 25th ed., York.

NIDA, Eugene A. (1948) 'The identification of morphemes' *Language* 24, 414–41 in Joos 1957.

NIDA, Eugene and TABER, Charles R. (1969) *The theory and practice of translation*, Leiden.

NOIRÉ, Ludwig (1877) *Der Ursprung der Sprache*, Mainz.

NORRIS, K.S., ed. (1966) *Whales, dolphins and porpoises*, Berkeley.

O'CONNOR, J.D. (1973) *Phonetics*, London.

O'CONNOR, J.D. and ARNOLD, G.F. (1973) *Intonation of colloquial English*, 2nd ed., London.

OGDEN, C.K. and RICHARDS, I.A. (1923) *The meaning of meaning*, London.

ORTIZ, Alejandro and ZIERER, Ernesto (1968) *Set theory and linguistics*, The Hague.

PAGET, Richard (1930) *Human Speech*, London. repr. 1963.

PALMER, F.R.
(1971) *Grammar*, London.
(1976) *Semantics*, Cambridge.

291

Bibliography

PALMER, F.R., ed. (1970) *Prosodic analysis*, London.
PALSGRAVE, J. (1530) *L'esclarcissement de la langue françoyse*, London, repr. Paris 1852.
PEDERSEN, Holger (1931) *The discovery of language: linguistic science in the 19th century*, Harvard, repr. Indiana 1959.
PERREN, G.E. and TRIM, J.L.M., eds (1971) *Applications of linguistics, selected papers of the Second International Conference of Applied Linguistics, Cambridge 1969*, Cambridge.
PIKE, K.L.
    (1954) *Language in relation to a unified theory of the structure of human behaviour*, Glendale, Calif. 1954–1960, 2nd ed. The Hague.
    (1961) *Phonetics*, Ann Arbor, repr.
PITTENGER, R.E., HOCKETT, C.F. and DANEBY, J.J. (1960) *The first five minutes: a sample of microscopic interview analysis*, New York.
PLATO (1970) *Cratylus*, trans. Benjamin Jowett, ed. R.M. Hare and D.A. Russell, republished in *The dialogues of Plato*, vol.3, London.
PODADERA, L.M. (1952) *Análisis gramatical de la lengua española*, 26th ed., Madrid.
POPPER, Karl (1972) *Conjectures and refutations*, London 1963, 4th ed.
POSTAL, Paul M.
    (1968) *Aspects of phonological theory*, New York.
    (1971) 'On the surface verb "remind"' in Fillmore and Langendoen.
POTTER, R.K., KOPP, G.A. and GREEN, H.C. (1947) *Visible Speech*, New York.
POWELL, J.W. (1891) *Indian linguistic families of America north of Mexico*, Washington 1891, repr. with Boas 1911 in Boas and Powell 1966.
PREMACK, D. (1970) 'The education of Sarah' *Psychology today* 4, 55–8.
PRIEBSCH, R. and COLLINSON, W.E. (1948) *The German language*, 3rd ed., London.
PRISCIANUS, (1819) *Institutiones rerum grammaticarum* in *Prisciani Opera*, ed. A. Krehl, Leipzig 1819–20.
PROKOSCH, E. (1939) *A comparative Germanic grammar*, Philadelphia.
PULGRAM, Ernst (1959) *Introduction to the spectrography of speech*, The Hague.
RASK, Rasmus (1818) *Undersøgelse om det gamle Nordiske eller Islandske Sprogs Oprindelse*, repr. in L. Hjelmslev *Rasmus Rask's Udvalgte Afhandlinger*, Copenhagen 1932–1937.
REMMIUS PALAEMON, Quintus (1857) *Ars grammatica* in vol.5, ed. H. Keil *Grammatici latini ex recensione Henrici Keilii*, Leipzig.
REUCHLIN, J. (1506) *De rudimentis Hebraicis*, Pforzheim.
REVZIN, I.I. (1966) *Models of language*, trans. N.F.C. Owen and A.S.C. Ross, London.
ROBEY, David, ed. (1973) *Structuralism: an introduction*, Oxford.
ROBINS, R.H.
    (1964) *General linguistics: an introductory survey*, 2nd ed., London 1971.
    (1967) *A short history of linguistics*, London.
ROBINSON, I. (1975) *The new grammarians' funeral: a critique of Noam Chomsky's linguistics*, Cambridge.

ROBINSON, W.P. (1972) *Language and social behaviour*, London.

ROSENBERG, J.F. and TRAVIS, C., eds (1971) *Readings in the philosophy of language*, Englewood Cliffs, N.J.

ROUSSEAU, Jean-Jacques (1755) *Discours sur l'origine et les fondements de l'inégalité parmi les hommes*, trans. as *A discourse upon the origin and foundation of the inequality among mankind*, London 1761.

RUSSELL, Clair and RUSSELL, W.M.S. (1971) 'Language and animal signals' in Minnis 1971.

SALMON, Vivien (1969) Review of Chomsky 1967 *Journal of linguistics* 5, 165–87.

SAMUELS, M.L. (1972) *Linguistic evolution with special reference to English*, Cambridge.

SAPIR, Edward
(1921) *Language: an introduction to the study of speech*, New York.
(1924) 'The grammarian and his language' repr. in Mandelbaum 1963.
(1929) 'The status of linguistics as a science' repr. in Mandelbaum 1963.
(1933) 'The psychological reality of phonemes' (French original) trans. in Mandelbaum 1963.

SAPORTA, Sol. ed. (1961) *Psycholinguistics: a book of readings*, New York.

SAUSSURE, F. de (1916) *Cours de linguistique générale*, Paris, 5th ed. 1962, trans. Wade Baskin as *Course in general linguistics*, New York 1959.

SAYCE, A.H. (1880) *Introduction to the science of language*, 2 vols. London.

SCALIGER, J.J. (1610) *Diatriba de Europaeorum linguis* in *Opuscula varia antehac non edita*, Paris.

SCHANE, Sanford A.
(1968) *French phonology and morphology*, Cambridge, Mass.
(1973) *Generative phonology*, Englewood Cliffs, N.J.

SCHLEGEL, Friedrich von (1808) *Über die Sprache und Weisheit der Indier*, Heidelberg, repr. in *Kritische Ausgabe*, Munich 1975, 8.1, 105–433.

SCHLEICHER, August
(1866) *Compendium der vergleichenden Grammatik der indogermanischen Sprachen*, Weimar.
(1869) *Die deutsche Sprache*, Stuttgart.

SCOTT, N.C. (1940) 'Distinctive rhythm' *Le maître phonétique*, 6.

SEBEOK, T.A., ed.
(1960) *Style in language*, New York.
(1966) *Portraits of linguists*, vols. I and II, Bloomington.

SHANNON, Claude E. and WEAVER, Warren (1949) *The mathematical theory of communication*, Urbana.

SHERMAN, D. (1973) 'Noun-verb stress alternation: an example of the lexical diffusion of sound-change in English', POLA Reports, 2nd series, 17, 46–82.

SIMPSON, J.M.Y.
(1967) 'The main features of the Scots pronunciation of English' (mimeographed), Edinburgh.
(forthcoming a) 'Oscillation and language change', Glasgow.
(forthcoming b) *The sounds and spelling of Gaelic*, Glasgow.

SLOBIN, D.I. (1971) *Psycholinguistics*, Glenview, Illinois.

SMITH, Alfred G., ed. (1966) *Communication and culture*, New York.

SMITH, F.K. (1967) *Teach yourself Latin*, 2nd ed., repr.

SPANG-HANSSEN, Henning (1963) 'Glossematics' in Mohrmann et al. 1963a.

STANKIEWICZ, E., ed. and trans. (1972) *A Baudouin de Courtenay anthology*, Indiana.

STEINBERG, D.D. and JAKOBOVITS, L.A., eds (1971) *Semantics: an interdisciplinary reader in philosophy, linguistics and psychology*, Cambridge.

STEINER, George (1975) *After Babel: aspects of language and translation*, London.

STERN, Gustaf (1931) *Meaning and change of meaning*, Göteborg.

STETSON, R.H. (1951) *Motor Phonetics*, 2nd ed., Amsterdam.

STURTEVANT, Edgar (1947) *An introduction to linguistic science*, New Haven.

SUPER, Charles W. (1893) *A history of the German language*, Columbus, Ohio.

SÜSSMILCH, J.P. (1766) *Versuch eines Beweises, daß die erste Sprache ihren Ursprung nicht vom Menschen, sondern allein vom Schöpfer erhalten habe*, Berlin.

SWEET, Henry
> (1877) *A handbook of phonetics*, London.
> (1900) *The history of language*, London.
> (1906) *A primer of phonetics*, 3rd ed., Oxford.
> (1910) *The sounds of English: an introduction to phonetics*, 2nd ed., Oxford.
> (1913) *Collected papers of Henry Sweet* arranged by H.C. Wyld, Oxford.
> (1971) See Henderson.

TERNES, Elmar (1973) *The phonemic analysis of Scottish Gaelic*, Hamburg.

THALBITZER, William (1911) 'Eskimo' in Boas.

THOMAS, O. (1965) *Transformational grammar and the teacher of English*, New York.

THOMAS OF ERFURT (1971) *Grammatica speculativa*, ed. and trans. G.L. Bursill-Hall, London.

THORNE, James P. (1966) 'English imperatives' *Journal of linguistics* 2, 69–78.

TIGER, Lionel and FOX, Robin (1972) *The imperial animal*, London.

TODD, Loreto (1974) *Pidgens and Creoles*, London.

TOGEBY, Knud (1951) *La structure immanente de la langue française* (*Travaux du cercle linguistique de Copenhague* v), Copenhagen.

TRAGER, G.L. (1949) *The field of linguistics* (SIL Occasional Papers 1), Norman (Okla.)

TRAGER, George L. and SMITH, Henry Lee (1951) *An outline of English structure*, Washington.

TRNKA, B. (1966) 'Vilém Mathesius' in Sebeok, vol.2.

TRUBETZKOY, N.S. (1939) *Grundzüge der Phonologie*, repr. Göttingen 1971, trans. C.A.B. Baltaxe as *Principles of phonology*, Berkeley 1969.

TRUDGILL, Peter (1974) *Sociolinguistics: an introduction*, London.

UHLENBECK, C.C. (1908) 'Die einheimischen Sprachen Nord-Amerikas bis zum Rio Grande' in *Anthropos* 1908 and 1910.

UHLENBECK, E.M. (1972) *Critical comments on transformational-generative grammar 1962–1972*, The Hague.

ULDALL, H.-J. (1957) *Outline of Glossematics I: a study in the methodology of the humanities with special reference to linguistics* (*Travaux du cercle linguistique de Copenhague* x, 1), Copenhagen.

ULLENDORFF, Edward (1955) *The Semitic languages of Ethiopia: a comparative phonology*, London.

ULLMAN, Stephen (1964) *Semantics: an introduction to the science of meaning*, Oxford.

VACHEK, Joseph (1966a) *The linguistic school of Prague*, Bloomington.

VACHEK, Josef, ed. (1966b) *A Prague school reader in linguistics*, Bloomington, 2nd printing.

VAIHINGER, H. (1924) *The philosophy of 'as if'*, London.

VARRO, Marcus Terentius (1938) *On the Latin language*, with trans. R.G. Kent, London.

VERHAAR, J.W.M., ed. (1967) *The verb 'be' and its synonyms* (*Foundations of language*, Supplementary series, vol.I), Dordrecht.

WALLIS, John (1971) *Grammatica linguae Anglicanae*, trans. and ed. as *John Wallis's Grammar of the English language* by J.A. Kemp, London.

WANG, W.S.-Y.
(1968) 'Vowel features, paired variables, and the English vowel shift', *Language* 44, 695–708.
(1969) 'Competing changes as a cause of residue' *Language* 45, 9–25.
(1974) *Phonetics*, Englewood Cliffs, N.J.
(1976) 'Language change' *Annals of the New York Academy of Sciences* 280, 61–72.

WARREN, Donald W. (1976) 'Aerodynamics of speech production' in Lass.

WATERHOUSE, Viola G. (1974) *The history and development of tagmemics*, The Hague.

WATERMAN, John T. (1963) *Perspectives in linguistics*, Chicago.

WEBB, John (1669) *An historical essay endeavouring a probability that the language of the empire of China is the primitive language*, London.

WEINREICH, U., LABOV, W. and HERZOG, M.I. (1968) 'Empirical foundations for a theory of language change' in Lehmann and Malkiel.

WELLS, Rulon S. (1947) 'Immediate constituents' *Language* 23, 81–117, repr. in Joos.

WENDT, Heinz F. (1961) *Sprachen*, Frankfurt am Main.

WESEEN, M.W. (1946) *Words confused and misused*, London, 3rd ed., repr.

WHATMOUGH, Joshua (1956) *Language: a modern synthesis*, London.

WHORF, B.L.
(1940a) 'Science and linguistics' in Carroll, 1956.
(1940b) 'Linguistics as an exact science' in Carroll 1956.
(1941a) 'Languages and logic', repr. in Carroll 1956.

295

(1941b) 'The relation of habitual thought and behavior to language' in Carroll 1956.

(1942) 'Language, mind and reality', repr. in Carroll 1956.

WILKS, Yorick A. (1972) *Grammar, meaning and the machine analysis of language*, London.

WILLIAMS, G.T., FARQUHARSON, I.M. and ANTHONY, J. (1975) 'Fibre-optic laryngoscopy in the assessment of laryngeal disorders' *Journal of laryngology and otology*, LXXXIX, 3.

WILSON, R.A. (1937) *The miraculous birth of language*, London.

WRIGHT, Joseph

(1907) *Historical German grammar*, vol.I, London, repr. 1962.

(1910) *Grammar of the Gothic language*, London, 2nd ed. with Supplement by O.L. Sayce 1954.

Index

Index

237, 244-53; -marker, 248; -morpheme, 142; -relation, 248; -system, 110, 245
Cassola, Carlo, 275n20
Catalan, 23
Caucasian languages, 23
causative, 110, 239, 243, 249, 254
Celtic, 20, 23, 24, 27, 28, 33, 102
Chad languages, 23, 59
Chao, Yuen-Ren, 73
Chatino, 61
checked sound, 210
cheeks, 62
Cheremis, 23
children: syntactic development of, 167, 168; acquisition of language by, 16, 259
Chinese, xiii, 13, 15, 20, 24, 25, 44, 61, 64, 74, 77, 98, 105, 108, 109, 110, 192, 195, 263
Chomsky, Noam, 130, 131, 146, 147, 163, 164, 165, 166, 168, 169, 170, 186, 201, 207, 208, 212, 214, 215, 226, 228, 229, 230, 243, 245, 253, 254, 259, 268, 269, 277n26
Christian Church, 13
cine-photography, 64
Circassian, 23
circularity, 124, 177
class-cleavage, 106, 107
classical theory, 243
classification, 32, 68, 119, 163
classifiers, 109
classroom techniques, 263
clause, xiv, 118, 164, 233, 242
subordinate, 117, 151
click, 54, 55, 210
closeness, 88
Cobbett, William, 11
code, 173, 174
Coeurdoux, G.L., 18, 19, 259
cognate forms, 21, 27
cognitive features, 196
co-hyponym, 196, 197, 202
colloquial, 120, 146
colloquials, 77
colour, 188, 189, 190, 191, 202
command, 111
comment, 235
commissives, 174
common, 227ff
communication, 41, 93, 171, 173, 175, 261, 262, 264, 266
community, 184, 185, 187, 269
compact, 209, 210, 211
comparative: literature, 265; philology, 19, 20, 31, 32, 33, 35, 36, 129, 259, 260, 261
competence, 226

complement, xiv, 110, 158
complementarity, complementary terms, 197, 198, 202
complete closure, 51, 52, 53, 54
complex symbol, 226, 228, 229
component, adjectival, 159
computer, 127, 166, 261, 264, 266
concept, 36, 176, 177, 185, 202, 267
concord, 112, 113, 114, 119, 139, 140, 262
concrete, 68, 93, 96, 98, 123, 124, 133, 134, 147, 269
conditioning, allophonic, 69
Congregatio sacra de propaganda fide, 13
conjugation, xiv, xv, 7, 141
conjunction, xiv, 7, 8, 111, 114, 122
'connective', 148
connotation, 110, 179, 183, 185, 196, 201
consonant(s), 43, 44, 51, 54, 58, 59, 60, 61, 66, 70, 74, 75, 77, 80, 81, 82, 84, 85, 86, 88, 89, 90, 91, 92, 101, 207, 210, 211, 262
consonantal, 208, 210, 211
constituent (v. matrix), 225
constituent, 117, 125
-analysis, 117; discontinuous, 117, 121, 138; immediate (=IC), 116, 119, 121, 131, 140, 149; morphemic, 101; relations, 121; types, 118; structure, 133, 141, 214; ultimate, 116
constriction, 209
construction, 116, 117, 119, 121
contact, 173, 174
context, 115, 125, 134, 166, 173, 178, 180, 217, 262
cultural, 184; -free, 228, 229, 231, 267; phonetic, 69, 70; -sensitive, 69, 70, 134, 138, 139, 229, 264, 267, 275n1; syntactic, 262

contextual restrictions, 220
continuant, 209, 210, 211
continuous, 111
contoids, 59
contradiction, 205
conventionalist, 6, 36, 129
converseness, 197, 198, 202
co-occurrence, 104, 107, 109, 112, 125, 126, 139, 151, 202, 262
co-ordinative, 116, 117, 121
Coptic, 13, 23
copula, 113, 150ff
copying into CS, 228, 229
Cornish, 23
corpus, 119, 120, 124, 126, 127, 128, 163, 164
-approach, 119

Index

300

Index

Index

Old: Armenian, 27; Church Slavonic, 13; English, 26, 32; French, 31; Frisian, 26; High German, 26, 32; Norse, 26; Persian, 28; Saxon, 26
onomatope, onomatopoeic, 271n1
openness, 88
'operator', 121, 151
'oppositeness', 197, 198
oral, 208
  cavity, 47, 55, 209; closure, 62; sounds, 49, 61
organs of speech, 47, 51, 65
orthography, 22, 58, 94, 133, 134, 147, 206, 231, 262, 265
Oscan, 23
oscillation, 269
oscilloscope, 66
Osthoff, Hermann, 30
Ostyak, 23
output, 147, 148, 149, 150, 160, 163, 165, 166, 210, 222, 224, 230, 234, 236
oxymoron, 179, 201

Pahlavi, 23
palatal, 52, 53, 56, 60, 61, 209
palatalisation, palatalised, 60, 90
palatality, 88, 91
palate, 50, 52, 60, 65
palato-alveolar, 60
palatography, dynamic, 65
Palsgrave, J., 14
Pāṇini, 19, 97, 169, 207, 269
paradigm (Kuhn's), 129, 130, 253
paradigmatic, 39, 75, 103, 104
paralinguistic, 175
paraphrase, 205, 217, 218, 221, 234, 239
Paris, Linguistic Society of, 16
parole, 36, 44, 128, 226, 273n1
participle, xv, 8, 262
particle, 40, 104, 105, 107, 134ff, 194
parts of speech, 7, 8, 9, 40, 105, 202, 203, 204
Pashto, 23
passive, xv, xvii, 7, 111, 146, 249, 274n2
  in '-r', 28, 30, 33, 272n9; -reflexive, 112
Passy, Paul, 46
past, 111, 124, 204
  definite, 44; tenses with prefixed 'e-', 28, 30
pattern, patterning, 7, 45, 93, 232
paucal, 108
Paul, St, 3
perfect, xvi, 75, 111, 236
  used as past, 28, 30
perfective, 111

permutation, 135, 136, 138, 142, 151, 166, 198
Persian, xi, xii, 20, 23, 71, 109, 265
person, xiv, xv, xvi, 8, 108, 113, 124
  first, xv, 91, 111, 174, 243; fourth (=obviative), 112; second, xvi, 109, 111, 139, 174, 243
personification, 179, 201
Peter, St, 3
pharyngal, 52, 56, 67
pharyngalisation, pharyngalised, 61, 63
pharynx, 49, 50, 52, 54, 61, 65
phatic communion, 172, 187
philology, comparative see 'comparative philology'
philosopher, philosophy, 6, 7, 10, 41, 66, 166, 168, 171, 172, 173, 174, 175, 176, 177, 180, 181, 195, 266, 267
phonation, 48, 63, 65
phonematic unit, 90, 91
phoneme, 68, 69, 87, 88, 96, 97, 119, 120, 123, 132, 164, 169, 180, 206, 211, 232, 253, 262
  alternative interpretations of, 83, 84, 85; changes of, 80; compound primary, 85; juncture, 86, 90; 'marginal', 71, 79; mutually conditioning, 71; overlapping of, 208; primary, 85; realisation of, 81; replacement of, 81; restricted to segments, 74; secondary, 85; segmental, 75, 89; selection of, 76, 83; sequences of, 75, 84, 94, 124; specification of, 70, 71
phonème, 73
phonemic: alphabet, 72, 265; analysis, 68, 73, 74, 85, 86, 89, 265; approach, 92, 208; grouping, 72, 82; intuitions, 73; opposition, 88, 89; practice, 206; system, 74, 75, 79, 85, 87, 88, 89, 121, 262; theory, 92, 207
phonemicist, phonemics, 68, 85, 86, 207, 216
phonetic: classification, 68; environment, 87; feature, 91; misrepresentation, 85, 89; representation (=interpretation), 231, 232, 235; similarity, 83, 84, 86; specification, 80
phonetician, phonetics, 33, 36, 40, 45, 46-67, 68, 176, 256, 261, 265
  articulatory, 46, 64; instrumental (=experimental), 46, 64-6, 261, 269; scope of, 46, 68
phonological, 119, 120, 127, 263
  analysis, 74, 85, 92; approach, 92; basic elements, 88; characteristics, 91; component, 212, 222,

Index

symbol, 276n1
  allophonic, 68, 101, 247, 252, 262, 264; complex, 228, 229; 'float', xi, xii, 58; for archiphoneme, 89; in t. -g. grammar, 132, 133, 134, 135, 137, 138, 139, 140, 141, 165; IPA, x-xiii, 47, 214; phonemic, 68, 80, 84, 86, 101; prelexicon, 135; segmental, 214; syllable-boundary, 71; word-boundary, 70; written, 33, 94
symbolic logic, 244, 252
synchronic, 33, 36, 44, 258, 259, 261, 269
synonym, synonymy, 179, 196, 205
syntactic, 103, 106, 107, 119, 121, 131, 141, 158, 159, 161, 167, 214, 217, 223, 230, 237, 238, 252, 263, 264
  component, 222, 223, 226, 231, 235; context, 262
syntagmatic, 38, 39, 75, 90, 103, 104, 202
syntax, xvi, 8, 86, 93, 103, 121, 122, 141, 163, 168, 200, 201, 205, 216, 218, 237, 264
synthetic, 98, 141
Syriac, 23
system, 36, 37, 44, 128, 269
  deictic, 173; in language, 257; morphological, 121; of aspect, xvi; of descriptive categories, 124, 222; of grammar, 77; of tense, xvi, 40, 173, 193; phonemic, 69, 71, 72, 74, 75, 78, 79, 85, 88, 121, 262; phonological, 89; plosive and nasal, 87, 88; vocabulary, 77; vowel, 81, 82, 87, 88; word-class, 121

Tagalog, 26, 265
tagmeme, tagmemic, 258
Tai, 26
Taiwanese, 24
Tamil, 25
tap, 52, 53, 61, 67
tape-recording, 266
'ta-ra-ra-boom-de-ay' theory, 16
'ta-ta' theory, 16
tautology, 205
teeth, 50, 52, 59
Telegu, 25
tense (in grammar), xiv, xvi, 8, 40, 108, 110, 111, 113, 124, 131, 133, 144, 151, 247, 250, 251
  carrier, 250; marker, 151; -morpheme, 144
tense (in phonetics), 67, 210, 211
Tesnière, Lucien, 258
Thai, 26, 58

312

theory, 1, 2, 42, 43, 44, 121, 129, 175, 206, 226, 263, 264, 267, 269, 271n4
  education, 266; games, 266; grammatical, 168, 181; inbuilt, of language, 167; linguistic, of language, 131, 163, 164, 167, 170, 253, 254; of learning, 263; powerful, 2; semantic, 180, 181, 183, 184, 199, 200, 203, 216, 217, 219, 221; set, 266; syntactic, 264
Thomas of Erfurt, 9
Thorne, J.P., 164, 278n13
thought, 185, 253, 276n1; see also 'language' and 'thought'
Tibetan, 13, 25
Tibeto-Burman languages, 25
Tigre, 23
Tigrinya, 23
time (case), 247ff, 278n23
Tiv, 62
Tocharian languages, 23, 29
Tojolabal, 54
Tolomei, Claudio, 18
tone, 70, 74, 85, 90
  -group, 74; -languages, 64, 74, 75, 85, 101; -patterns, 75, 76, 101
toneme, 74
Tongan, 25, 26, 110
tongue, 50, 52, 53, 54, 55, 56, 57, 60, 61, 62, 65, 67
topic, 235, 236, 243, 254, 277n26
Totonac, 72
trachaea, 47
tradition, 3, 19, 46, 85
Trager, George L., 73, 74, 171
transcription, 47, 58, 84, 91, 101
  phonemic, 74; phonetic, 119; reading, 91; word-spaces in, 74
transformation, 169, 204, 239, 241, 242, 249, 254
  adjectivalising, 159; adjunction, 139, 140, 223; and meaning, 224, 230, 236, 238; causative, 239; conjoining, 147, 225; deletion, 139, 223; double-based, 147; embedding, 147, 150-62, 163, 225, 231, 245; generalised, 147-62, 224, 230; obligatory, 135, 136, 146, 223, 230, 244; optional, 135, 136, 139, 142, 146, 151, 167, 204, 223, 224; passive, 143, 155, 156, 157, 158, 231, 236, 250; permutation, 136, 138, 142, 151, 198, 223, 244; predicate-raising, 242; question, 224; restrictive relativising, 152, 154, 231; single-based (= singulary), 147, 149, 223, 224; Tq, 143; Tw, 151, 157